Psalms

A memoir

Hirsch Grunstein

In memory of

my parents
Benzion and Henia Grunstein

our rescuers
Gaston and Adrienne Van Damme
Alice Van Damme and Maurice De Viaene
Emile and Léontine Van Damme
Joseph and Josephine Van Poecke
René Govaerts

For my children Eva, Ethan and Judah

For my grandson Ezékiel

ACKNOWLEDGMENTS

I am indebted to professor William Black, whose writing class I had the good fortune to attend, for taking interest in my work — his extensive comments and critique helped shape this memoir.

I am grateful to my friend Siegfried Spira for steering me away from a lesser pursuit to devote myself to this enterprise.

I thank Naomi Schub and Sally Arteseros for their editing.

I also want to thank my dear friend, Alice Pless, for her counsel and support; and Judy Kepes for her help in the cover design.

We came to the question: How is it with the women and children? I decided to find a clear solution here as well. I did not consider myself justified to exterminate the men - that is, to kill them or have them killed - and allow the avengers of our sons and grandsons in the form of their children to grow up. The difficult decision had to be taken to make this people disappear from the earth.

From a speech by Heinrich Himmler to a gathering of German Reichsleiter and Gauleiter at Posen on October 6, 1943

CONTENTS

FOREWORD

Of the more than 60,000 Jews residing in Belgium (population eight million) at the outbreak of World War II, over 55,000 remained in occupied Belgium. Of them, more than 25,000 were deported to Auschwitz. The remaining Jewish population — less the few who made it to Switzerland and other havens — found refuge among the population, and in Catholic and lay institutions.

This is a memoir spanning the four years of German occupation: of events I lived through or witnessed; of life in hiding; of intense and memorable conversations — some, seared in memory.

I also resorted at times to fictionalized conversations (inspired by actual interchanges) as a means to convey more vividly certain events, race laws and decrees, people's reactions and emotions, the mood and atmosphere around the young teenager I was at the time.

For accuracy about certain events, works by the following authors were consulted:

Ephraim Schmidt, *Geschiedenis van de Joden in Antwerpen;*

Lieven Saerens, *Vreemdelingen in een Wereldstad;*

Maxime Steinberg, *L'étoile et le fusil* (four volumes), *Un pays occupé et ses juifs;*

Serge Klarsfeld, Maxime Steinberg, *Mémorial de la Déportation des Juifs de Belgique.*

CHAPTER 1 — TO FRANCE AND BACK

Friday, May 10, 1940

The Germans invaded at dawn.

My parents stood, ashen-faced, by the radio: in the span of a brief announcement, their world — the Yiddish-speaking immigrant community, peaceful Antwerp, hospitable Belgium — had dropped away. In its place, the fear of bombs and plunder; the specter of race laws and despoliation that had befallen the German Jews. A tense silence filled our small dining room.

My father was the first to weather the shock: "We've got to pack."

"Whereto?" my mother asked wanly.

"I'll find out in town," my father said. We had no telephone.

"Are the Germans coming?" my brother asked.

"Yes," my mother answered.

Though he was only six, he understood. He had picked up enough in months past from the pervasive talk about Hitler and the refugees from Germany.

"Where are we going?"

"We'll know as soon as papa is back, my little lamb."

To France. I knew. "What food are we going to take along?" I asked. A trek to the unknown called for provisions, a staple feature in travel stories.

"Don't talk nonsense," my mother snapped. "Loading up on food," she mumbled dismissively. "We'll be in big trouble if we can't buy it."

Silly question. I should have known better. Deep down, I was looking forward to the newness, the adventure: I was twelve and the sun was shining.

My mother got busy laying out on her bed and on the dining table the items to be packed. Within minutes, our apartment turned into a staging area. Soon to be abandoned.

I stepped out on the balcony. The bright morning sun was warming up our side of the street. There was an eerie stillness, unlike the normal silence before the matinal sounds of hooves on the cool cobblestones, of children on their way to school. The modest, three-story row houses looked impenetrable, the luminous sky, more distant and serene. Day-to-day normalcy had slid in the past. A strange, unmoored present filled its space.

We left home that afternoon. My parents carried, each, a suitcase, my brother and I, our backpacks.

Antwerp was astir with crowds of harried people lugging valises, a good many with children in tow, on their way to board a train, to catch a bus.

"Look how scared even Flemings are of the German," my mother remarked, visibly moved. "Leaving home and belongings behind. Uprooting themselves. As if they too might be persecuted."

"They were under occupation not so long ago," my father said. "They must know."

The Belgians "knew" indeed: they remembered the atrocities the Germans had committed during the first World War: the burning of villages in reprisal for acts of sabotage, the execution of hostages, the mustard gas attacks on their soldiers, the hunger, the deportation to Germany of half a million men to replace German laborers serving in the military. Within days two million people of a population of eight million would flee west to the Coast, and south to France.

The country's entire Jewish population of roughly sixty thousand, mainly immigrants from Eastern Europe, joined the exodus, except for about eight thousand men age seventeen and up, refugees from Austria and Germany who were arrested by the Belgian authorities: the outbreak of hostilities had turned them into enemy aliens. They were evacuated to internment camps in the south of France, where they ended up in the hands of the Vichy French, who turned them over to the Germans.

We got off the bus in La Panne, a small town by the French border, on the North Sea. On the westernmost tip of Belgium, it lay outside the invasion route to France, beyond the IJzer river where the Germans were stopped in World War I.

We stood in our topcoats — my father wore a homburg, my mother a hat — by the valises and the knapsacks, and waited, as agreed upon in Antwerp, for uncle Avrum to pick us up. He, aunt Esther, their two boys, Harry and Manny, and an orphaned cousin, the oldest, also named Harry, had left before us.

The two Harrys, sturdy boys, showed up, bareheaded and tie-less, in their jackets — cheerful and relaxed, like vacationers. Uncle Avrum had found an apartment. Carrying my parents' suitcases, they took us to a street of bourgeois houses, some with stone or wrought iron balconies and bay windows: La Panne's main street, on the route going north, parallel to the shoreline. It was swarming with refugees, overdressed men and women with a searching or anxious look in their eyes, some holding children by the hand, trying to find shelter, or a food store. Not a hint, in the din of crawling, honking, exhaust-spewing cars, of the dunes, the beach and the surf one short block away. Not a whiff of the bracing sea air.

We climbed three flights of creaking wooden stairs. Aunt Esther opened the door.

"*Oy gevalt*," my father exclaimed. "I left my bathing trunks in Antwerp."

Aunt Esther burst out laughing. "We'll go to the casino instead," she reparteed. "Win big."

It was my father's turn to laugh. Uncle Avrum grinned briefly. My mother was in no mood for humor. My cousin Manny, age ten, was sizing up the newcomers. Harry, his sixteen-year old brother, and the other Harry, nineteen, had the confident stance of young men aware of their strength and looking forward to the challenges ahead. My brother Salomon, six, gravitated to Manny. I was taking in the scene of bittersweet hilarity.

✡ ✡ ✡

And we waited… for the French and the British to defeat the Germans.

The two Harrys formed a singing jazz band in the living room (where the five of us slept) and butchered *South of the Border*, *Alexander's Ragtime Band*, and *Where is the Tiger?* as they drummed on a piece of furniture. They also wrestled. My brother Salomon and my youngest cousin, Manny, would pass the time on our fourth-floor balcony and spit on the passers-by. They scored once, on a big, round, naked head that turned crimson with rage. I was the boy in the middle, ignored by the older set and uninvolved with the younger one.

The parents kept to the kitchen where they discussed at length the bits of news and the rumors — like reading tea leaves — that my father and my uncle gleaned on their errands. The Dutch had surrendered after five days following the terror bombing of Rotterdam. The Belgians were fighting a desperate holding action. Should we wait for the Allied reinforcements? Or should we try for Dunkirk from where boats were said to be taking refugees to England?

A few more days went by. Antwerp fell. Then Brussels. Finally, the savior we had been waiting for: a French military convoy appeared, to the ecstatic cries of "Vive la France!" and "Victoire!" It was heading north to the Belgian front. I was about to take my turn on the balcony when my aunt Esther rushed past me into the living room:

"To the slaughter!" she blurted out, horrified, as if she were seeing the carnage. "How they are leading these children to the slaughter!"

My mother followed her, grim-faced.

I moved to the railing: lorry after covered lorry was rolling by. Some soldiers pushed their heads — no helmets — and shoulders out the back, through the slit in the tarpaulin. They smiled and waved — a few with cap in hand — at the people jamming the sidewalks, crowding onto the balconies, squeezing into windows. They were young; recent conscripts, no doubt. The loose collars of their uniforms made some of them look like young boys. I watched, with dampened joy, until the last lorry rolled out of sight.

✧ ✧ ✧

We left La Panne with our sights set on Dunkirk. A cart — a two-wheeler with inflated rubber tires — held our luggage. But the French border guards were letting mainly Belgian nationals across: the "foreign element," they sneered, harbored German spies. The "Poles" were turned back with a contemptuous motion of the hand. Both sets of parents held Polish passports.

We waited in a meadow, with hundreds of other families. Yiddish was the dominant language. The men were milling about, gathering the latest rumors about the German advance and the Allied moves, about the opening of the border; trying to find anything that rolled, even a wheelbarrow, to move their families' belongings; or idling about, smoking nervously. The women stayed put, watching warily over their children and feeding them. Most families had brought only scant provisions. People shared or exchanged food. We waited, weary, under a clear sky, in balmy spring weather.

Rumors spread that the border would be opened "Soon," then, "This afternoon," then, "Tomorrow morning." Indeed, some people with foreign passports had been seen crossing over to France. Many trekked back to La Panne. A woman near us broke down sobbing. Her husband consoled her gently:

"Now, cry no more," I heard him say in Polish.

"I can't stop it," she said. "My heart is crying."

"My heart is crying," my mother repeated softly.

Night fell. An eerie, hushed quiet descended on the meadow. Ghostly faces, reflecting the light of the stars, moved slowly in the dark. Anguish glimmered in the eyes. Once, the peace was disturbed by the drone of planes circling overhead. "German planes..." The word spread. Women's voices rang out, imploring:

"Extinguish your cigarettes... Men, please, extinguish your cigarettes." Red dots would move above ground and flare up like fireflies.

"Don't worry. They can't see us from up there," some man would shout.

"They can... They can."

"They can't. Besides, we are cupping them with our hands. Don't worry."

"It shines bright when you draw on it... For God's sake! Extinguish your ciga..."

"Keep quiet! They'll sooner hear your yammer than see a cigarette."

Morning broke. The French relented. A wave of energy coursed through the crowd, causing a crush at the border post. Valises got in the way. Children cried. The French officials checked identification papers, confiscated some passports, on impulse, it seemed — my father had to leave his behind. We got across.

✡ ✡ ✡

The only bus we could clamber on took us inland, to St-Omer, away from Dunkirk but only a short stretch of road from

Calais further down the coast. Boats were leaving from Calais for England, we were told.

We repaired to a café. Sitting by the large picture window I saw silvery birds moving stealthily in the sky. Suddenly they dropped tiny black eggs. I knew right away what they were, yet kept looking. They hardly grew as they were coming down faster and faster and spreading out. Riveting. Moments later the window rattled: a brief, violent tremor. Nobody had moved.

Onward to Calais, on foot, amidst other clusters of refugees, after fruitless attempts at hiring a taxicab. We kept discarding more and more of our belongings, including my brother's backpack with the silver candelabrum — my grandmother's wedding gift — that my mother tossed in the ditch by the road. It was hurting his back.

We trudged on, unaware that we were heading toward the Germans advancing east from the French coast: they had gotten there first.

"A tank!" came an anguished, muffled cry.

We froze: a black cross, with four bold white borders, on drab, gun-metal gray — a cross, yet not a cross. We knew from the first instant that it was not an Allied tank. There it was, down the dirt road, out of nowhere.

"A German tank," someone ventured.

"Impossible!" was the emphatic retort.

"Then what is it?"

"Dutch!"

The tank turned slowly, moving like a tortoise, rolled down the shaded dirt road and disappeared. A fugitive tank, I reasoned. Fled all the way from Holland... Hard to believe. Still, a comforting thought.

We went to a nearby school and waited with other refugees in an empty classroom, in silence, relieved to have found shelter and a place to sit down. Grim, drawn faces around. I picked up an illustrated, large-print schoolbook. Joan of Arc heard voices, I read. How benighted. Did the French really believe that? Was that France? Flat, sun-soaked countryside shrouded in stillness; tall weeds along the road; low, dark-red, old brick structures with hardly a straight line. France had beckoned like the promised land. How drab, compared to the Belgian countryside, the colorful patchwork of cultivated fields and tree-lined pastures, the nice, well-built houses.

We picked ourselves up and moved on, wearily. Calais had become a mirage.

Then, that same afternoon — we had joined other refugees in the big country kitchen of a hospitable French farmer — we saw through the window approaching German soldiers. Those of us who were sitting stood up. Silence fell. I glanced at my parents: my father slipped his wallet containing cash on top of an armoire behind him. His face was impassive. My mother had her worried look. Afraid, all along, of being robbed of money and valuables, they had entrusted me with my mother's jewelry. I was carrying it in a little pouch hanging from my neck down in my underpants: soldiers on the prowl were not likely to search children, the thinking went. A child I was in the eyes of strangers and small for my age. But my parents treated me like a son who could be entrusted with confidences, even missions; I was dependable and did as I was told without grumbling.

The door opened wide. I saw grass and foliage through the doorway before the first soldier in *Feldgrau* appeared, rifle at the ready, and entered the room. A second followed. Were they looking for enemy soldiers, stragglers who would wander about, some with a finger on the trigger? They found men, women and children in their coats and hats, standing amidst their baggage: mute, with pinched lips, or wide-eyed, unprepared, waiting tensely for what might come next. I stood, transfixed. The soldiers turned around and left. My father retrieved his wallet.

The silence lasted a minute or so until a man moved to close the door. People began talking within their own groups. Ours was the largest, fourteen in all: a young widow with her little girl, Hélène, and a couple with a boy my age, the Fleischers, had attached themselves to us. My brother, at six, was the youngest. We had to find a place to spend the night and to wait out, in the days to come, the developments on the battlefield. Surely, the Allies would counterattack.

The farmer entered the kitchen. The Germans were moving fast, he informed us. We had to expect more such visits given the proximity of his farm to the main road. The men in our group approached him. He told them of a farmer with lots of space — a big house and barns. "Down this dirt road, on the right," my father repeated as we walked out the door.

✡ ✡ ✡

The farmer put us up, for cash: the women and children on mattresses in the large kitchen; the men, including my two older cousins, in the barn. He would also sell us food; and he gave us sacks which the two Harrys, standing with bared torso and wielding pitchforks with great élan, took turns stuffing with fresh straw for the men's bedding. The kitchen would become ours, an exclusive haunt, except for the twenty minutes or so a day the farmer's wife needed to do some cooking for her husband and herself.

A shock awaited us in the barn: a wounded English soldier was lying on his back in the straw. A large, dark stain had spread across the right leg of his pants. A tightly knotted cloth around the middle of the thigh had stemmed the loss of blood. The villagers must have picked him up by the road or in a field and brought him to the nearest farm. The Englishman was staring up, expressionless, almost stony-faced. My father shook his head:

"What utter misery," he mumbled. "*Nebbekh*" ("the pity of it").

No one thought of approaching the wounded soldier. No one could speak a word of English.

I was still in the barn with the men when a German motorcyclist and an officer seated in the sidecar rode onto the farmyard. Our farmer took them to the barn. The officer took a quick look at the soldier's bloody leg, bent over to have a brief, low-voiced exchange with him, and left with his sidekick. The Englishman looked more alive; his eyes were moving, noticing people and things. Two German soldiers returned before dusk, took the Englishman out on a stretcher and drove off in a command car.

We settled in for the wait. Days passed.

The men, all three of them diamantaires, talked about the world of diamonds and, in bitter tones, about the situation.

"It's lost," lamented Mr. Fleischer, a German Jew. "France is disintegrating. No direction, no army, no government. What a catastrophe. *Kolossal.*"

"This France is just another Poland," my uncle chimed in.

"*Ganz genau*" ("Precisely"), Mr. Fleischer agreed. "*Eine Polnische Wirtschaft haben die*" ("Polish order they have"). Meaning, chaos. A coined phrase in German. The German Jews used *Polnische* and *Jüdische* interchangeably, the latter with the *Ostjuden,* the East European Jews, in mind.

My father, ever the optimist, held his peace. He had no ammunition against the doomsayers. Only faith.

The women kept busy cooking, and running mini-washes in oversized cooking pots in the farmyard. The men, the two big boys mainly, would do the heavy lifting.

The younger set were bored and restless. Fleischer, the boy my age, had a sour mien most of the time. He played the violin, his parents informed us in a reverent undertone. This made him seem even more distant, as none of us boys of the clan played an instrument. Fleischer and I never talked to each other.

We kept mainly to the large inner farmyard or the kitchen. We had become an attraction of sorts. Village boys and girls in ill-assorted, shabby clothes and coarse shoes, with bony knees, would stop at the gate for a look at the foreigners, and giggle, some baring bad teeth. They would still giggle amongst themselves as they moved on. I took a few short walks on the dirt road running by the farm. The rare villager I crossed moved slowly in scuffed work shoes or clogs, wearing shapeless, frayed clothes. Slack worker caps would shade closed, weather-beaten, lined faces.

One afternoon, villagers ambled into the farmyard in a steady trickle. They were in good cheer, smiling and making friendly chitchat. They clearly had come — more were still arriving — for some event. Their quiet demeanor on our farmer's property seemed to show respect for his standing and wealth, an impression reinforced by their confining themselves to the far side of the large rectangular yard, in front of the barn, by the entrance. As the gathering grew into a cozy mass of about two dozen people, the mood turned festive. And we learned what was to take place — the slaughtering of a pig.

The animal appeared, herded and prodded to one side of the yard by several men who were moving jerkily around it. The men and the boys amongst us were lined up along the opposite side, by the kitchen, the choicest spot for watching the spectacle. The women in our party remained inside. The animation among the villagers rose. Sensing danger, the pig tried to get away, but was restrained by means of ropes tied around its hind legs. Silence fell when the butcher was about to make his move. Suddenly he thrust a pointed rod into the animal's throat, then pulled it. The pig shrieked, releasing a jet of dark blood. With its snout pointing heavenward, it emitted long, rending shrieks for what seemed a long time, blood gushing from the wound. The villagers were talking, laughing, pointing, jesting. The pauses between shrieks lengthened, the shrillness abated: the pig was groaning. It flinched a few times, struggling to remain standing. The blood was flowing thin; the basin containing it was removed. The animal flinched one last time and fell on its side. Moments later it lay down its head, tried to raise it, forelegs flailing. Down again. The forelegs stopped moving. The blood stopped trickling out. A spasm. And, suddenly, just a gray-pink mass with a dark hole in the throat and two sticks jutting out. A creature no more. The butcher was already cutting off the head. He cut up the animal, sorted the innards, washing them, dexterously, intently, without a wasted movement.

Our farmer, who owned a radio, dropped by every day with the news. The war was going badly: the Belgian army had surrendered. The Germans were advancing on all fronts. There was talk, but no sign, of an Allied counteroffensive. The farmer was the tallest man in the kitchen where he would stand, planted, like someone who could not conceive of uprooting himself and leaving his homestead behind. He would recount in a calm voice the day's events to the band of refugees who lived from one news fix to the next.

The nice weather held up: blue, cloudless skies day after day; or just a few little white puffs, up high, floating past. Once I accompanied my father and my uncle on a walk in the pasture by the farm and listened as they cursed France's ineffectual government, its shoddy army, and denigrated the backward French, their primitive way of life, their eating habits — "Wine in the soup. Imagine." "And slurping the bottom of it straight from the plate." My father would marvel at the sky, inhale hungrily the fragrant air, point to some yellow or blue flowers whose name none of us knew, in any language. They would stop to bask in the sun, or admire the horses. Pointing to a powerful-looking animal:

"Do you think this horse could pull by itself all the diamonds in the world?" my father asked.

Uncle Avrum laughed: "I don't know. Maybe not. But I would be satisfied with what it can pull. What a strange thought," he continued, "a horse pulling a load of diamonds instead of manure."

There was not a hint of war about, except for the foreignness of the men in their dark suits and no ties, the Yiddish sounds rising in the tremulous air, the long silences under the serene, foreign sky.

The much-awaited Allied counteroffensive failed to materialize. The French declared Paris an open city. The British retreated to their island. The news was disheartening day after day. We found ourselves mired in a forlorn French village inside ever-expanding conquered territory. When the farmer told us that the refugees were streaming back, going home seemed, suddenly, the only way out of our predicament. Our parents packed light. Our little band left early the next morning.

✡ ✡ ✡

The multitudes of homebound people clogging the roads and vying for transportation grew as we moved further north and into Belgium. Ordered by a jubilant Führer to ease their plight and facilitate their return, the German military directed the human flow cheerfully and courteously — they even put captured trucks at the disposal of refugees, to be returned to the German authorities in the large cities. Some officers gave refugees a lift in their command cars. They would pass a column of weary returnees by nudging them aside, patiently. Soldiers would wave at gawking children.

We were trudging along when a German convoy returning from the front moved up slowly and stopped. A soldier leaned out of his troop carrier and surveyed the column of refugees. Addressing my father who happened to be nearest to him,

"Do you speak German?" he asked, using the formal "*Sie.*"

"Yes."

"Why did all these people leave their homes?"

"We were afraid of you."

"*Aber wir tun ja garnichts*" ("But we do no harm"), the soldier said. The convoy resumed its slow advance.

"They do no harm," my father echoed, an incredulous smirk on his face. "They should burn like a candle."

More than fifty years later a friend told me that during the return trek from France in the spring of 1940 his family got a lift in a German command car. In the course of a polite conversation, his mother, a woman with blond hair and blue eyes, told the officer sitting in the front passenger seat:

"You will now be able to return to civilian life."

"I will not take off this uniform," he replied, "until the last Jew is wiped off the face of the earth!"

CHAPTER 2 — ANTWERP - I

My father raised the window shade in the dining room, setting off a welcoming burst of sparkles from the crystal bowl on the shining, lightly-dusted glass-topped table: we were back, in the familiar light and space, among the familiar objects and furnishings.

My mother got busy in the kitchen. My father set out on a round of errands as if on a voyage of discovery. He came back with a bounty, bread from the baker further down the street; fruit and vegetables from the grocer around the corner. Neither had fled.

"Avrumaleh stayed at home, with the family," my father reported. Avrumaleh (a diminutive for Avrum), was my father's older brother, a short, very devout man.

"He put his trust in God," my mother remarked, shaking her head.

"The Hirschmans are home," my father continued. Relations of ours, they were the only other Jewish family on our street.

"I meant to tell you to check on them. How did they fare?"

"They also got stuck in some hole in France. What else?"

"Who else is around?"

"A number of Jews have returned, he told me. More are trickling back. But the *shtetl* seems abandoned."

"Not a sound from above or below," my mother remarked. "Our neighbors would have noticed our presence by now, had they returned from the flight."

We were indeed alone in the small, three-story house.

My father left again. He got some eggs, butter, and cheese. On his way back he ran into a Flemish neighbor from across the street. The two men stopped to exchange a few words, for the first time since we had moved into our apartment a year earlier. The neighbor had stayed home.

"I can understand," my mother said. "With six daughters. To venture out on the road with such a large brood. Wasn't he afraid to stay?"

"He didn't expect Antwerp to be fought over. His oldest daughters are back at work."

"Quite normal. Nobody will bother them. They are sitting, secure, on their soil. How enviable."

"But he is worried about what's to come if the war lasts. There was hunger during the last war. Men in large numbers were taken to Germany, he told me, and pressed into forced labor. 'We got rid of them only some twenty years ago,' he said with contained anger. 'And here they are again.' "

"All I wish is to fare no worse than the Flemish," my mother said.

"From your mouth to God's ears."

Most refugees were back. But only half of the Jewish residents had returned. Many of them were waiting it out in France's Unoccupied Zone, the country's south stretching from the western Pyrénées to the Swiss border, with Vichy as its capital. A great many of them flocked to Nice, a cosmopolitan city with a resident American consul. Some refugees had managed to cross the Channel in small boats. Others had escaped to Spain and Portugal. To spy a Jew on the street was a treat for us, to run into a friend or an acquaintance, a joy. "Who else is around?" was the question on everyone's lips.

The city had the Sunday morning look without the relaxed atmosphere. Traffic was light. Schools were closed. Some stores, mainly specialty and luxury shops, remained shuttered. The port, the continent's busiest, was idled. Antwerp's diamond industry, the mainstay of the Jewish community, was laid still. The general mood was a tense wait-and-see. There was triumphant anticipation among the fringe groups who, for years, had championed the New Order of the Third Reich. The day was near, they gloated, when all the peoples of Europe would rally around Germany and the foreign dross would be removed forever. The press and radio turned pro-German.

We settled into a tenuous normalcy, keeping close to home, aware, every waking moment, of the Germans' presence. They would march in lockstep, in their military caps, unarmed, and sing at the top of their voices, *"Wir fahren gegen England"* ("We are off against England"). They seemed unstoppable.

The future loomed, dark, in my parents' minds — what would it hold for the Jews? For Jews of modest wealth, like us? The ground had shifted, as in an earthquake, and they were waiting for the aftershock.

✿ ✿ ✿

"*Zuh tee'n goornish*" ("They do no harm"), people would remark with amazement and relief. "They are treating us no worse than the Flemish." The blackout, the rationing of food, applied to all alike. We had freedom of movement.

The diamond trade resumed, tentatively at first, but unhindered, though hobbled by the severance of the London connection — the source of the rough goods — and the flight of the big firms to the south of France and across the Channel. The precious stones were in demand, the industrial kind in particular. Word spread among the refugees, especially the diamantaires still wandering in the Unoccupied Zone. They came back in ever growing numbers, some at the urging of relatives in Antwerp. The Germans provided special busses for their return. It all fostered the impression that they would defer to the civilized West in their attitude toward the Jews.

That summer of 1940 was the first we did not spend with our relatives amidst the pinewoods of Heide or by the wide beaches of silky sand in Ostend or Blankenberghe. I knew boredom: no school, nor friends. Like me, they kept close to home. Some had not returned from the south of France. The city park — we lived nearby, on the Jacob Jordaensstraat — offered relief. I would often bring my roller skates, or play ball or marble games with the boys. We would congregate at the park's wide Loosplaats entrance, a corner frequented mostly by Jews.

The most accomplished skaters were two girls: Dora Muehlstein and Rachel Akkerman. They cut graceful figures in their short tutu-like skirts — the strong, well-formed legs of the former, the long, lissome legs of the latter showing to great advantage. They would gather speed, pirouette and skate backwards in long strides, effortlessly. I felt clumsy skating in their space. I had a crush on Rachel Akkerman, the older and prettier of the two. I could never figure out how to approach or impress her, not even how to draw her attention. When she was around I would refuse to sit down next to my mother on her occasional visits to the park and eat, like a good boy, the snack that she brought for me and my brother.

I was much better at playing ball, and especially nimble at marble games. Once, when my father and I were walking through the park on our way home after Shabbat morning services, I spotted a group of boys absorbed in a game. I asked my father for permission to join them. He used the time to sit down on an empty park bench, at a distance from the hustle and the noise, and take in the sun.

"I won a lot," I told him on the way back, and jingled the winnings inside my pocket.

"With how many did you start?" he asked me.

"With two, the minimum," I said. "I borrowed them," I hastened to add, to reassure him that I had not taken marbles to *shul*; (a bit sacrilegious, by our code). "I returned them as soon as I won my own." Not an entirely kosher deal, on a Sabbath, not to mention the carrying of marbles home. But then, I was not *that* strict in my religious observance.

My father grinned. I felt proud.

The summer drew to an end. In September my brother started second grade at the Hebrew day school Tachkemoni. Founded in 1920, that institution was both a public school — it had a Flemish and a French section, with its State-appointed Flemish principal and staff — and a private Hebrew school with a Jewish staff. My brother was enrolled in the French section where I had been a pupil for the previous six years.

I passed the entrance exam to the *Koninklijk Atheneum Antwerpen*, the Royal [Flemish] High School for boys. Despite the simplicity of the test, gaining admission to that prestigious institution felt like a rite of passage. It was housed in an imposing, dark-gray, temple-like building that dominated Anneessens Square, north of Antwerp's fashionable artery, the De Keyserlei, in a part of town where I had never ventured. Tachkemoni, a modest, crowded, three-story structure squeezed between the small row houses of narrow, winding Lange Leemstraat, had receded into a vanished past.

I was assigned, like most Tachkemoni boys, to the special, first-year transition, or D- class for freshmen whose mother tongue was not Flemish. (Depending upon our grades, we would be

moving up, for our second year, to the A-, B- or C-class.) Among
the Tachkemoni alumni were four classmates of mine: Zalcman,
a bespectacled, brooding chap; shy, guileless Mayersdorf, a recent refugee from Germany with a hopeless German accent and
a sunny smile that disarmed his teasers; savvy, fearless Strassberg;
and Menda Zangen, one of the few classmates I called by his first
name. We lived close by. I had been to his house, to his birthday parties. We were now spending more time in each other's
company than ever before. We would walk back from school together, across the De Keyserlei, along Quellinstraat with its fine
shops, down the city park's outer roadway along staid Quentin
Matsijslei, circle the flower parterre surrounding the Statue of
Ambiorix on Loosplaats, onto Jacob Jordaensstraat where I lived,
and part where my street and his, the Antoon Van Dijckstraat,
intersected.

A new world opened up — I was moving for the first time
amongst non-Jews. Few were the Gentiles I had known until then:
the neighborhood merchants; the barber in the Jewish quarter;
Dr Baten, the pediatrician who kept reassuring my mother that
I was in good health — "thin and on the small side is not sickly";
and the State-appointed teachers in charge of the public curriculum at Tachkemoni — they had been distant and condescending, and quick to mete out severe punishments, from beatings to
suspension of the free Thursday afternoons. (One of them had
come to class, once, in his Blackshirt uniform and boots.) Our
Jewish teachers were the ones we had felt free to argue with and
dared annoy, though they would just as readily resort to the thin,
square wooden ruler as their Flemish counterparts. The principal — an intimidating figure with big, ice-blue eyes — would
stand at quitting time at the gate and inspect us as we filed out,
two abreast, in silence. His long, brown, square-cut beard and
flowing mustache did not soften the severity of his mien. (He
turned out to be an adherent of the New Order.)

Our high school principal, though just as stern and unsmil-
ing a disciplinarian, was not harsh or condescending; he was said
to have a Jewish son-in-law. Our professors, Gentiles all, treated
their students with respect, Jew and non-Jew alike — equal praise
for equal work, impartial scorn for sloth. They were more accessible than the Flemish teachers at Tachkemoni. We had a clas-
sicist for Latin; for Flemish, a linguist in Germanic languages; a

real mathematician; a known geographer who had published an authoritative world atlas.

Menda and I made friends with Roald Bingen, a French-speaking youth and a devout Catholic. He sometimes used cards with the images of saints as book markers. Even Jennart, a member of the Rexist (pro-Nazi) youth, an athlete, the tallest by a head, was friendly. He was annoyed at the vocal pro-English few in our class: Flemings should know better where their future lies, he confided to me, under his breath. He sat behind me. Some of our professors also showed their pro-English leanings, however subtly, with as little as a throwaway English word. Jennart was amused by Menda, who knew everything in the book but could not run or jump (Menda was exempt even from the calisthenics portion of the gymnastics hour which entailed also buck vaulting and exercising on the gym ladder). "It's racial," Jennart decreed.

"There are Jewish boxers, you know," I retorted. I had in mind Max Baer, the Jewish heavyweight from America.

"The exception that confirms the rule," he snapped.

My horizon widened: there was, out there, a world of learning as different from ours as Latin was from Hebrew and math from Talmud; a view of history as different from ours as the founding of Rome by Romulus was from God's covenant with Abraham, a history without the tragic ring, the moral drumbeat of the Bible, without our singular burden and failings. The Romans and the Greeks, the idolatrous barbarians in Jewish history class, turned into the civilizers of the ancient world. A new learning, and as much of a challenge as ours, a universal patrimony, mine, like language and music. I wanted to soak it all in, to get to the essence of it — a vague "it," a hidden "essence," the something that gave me pause when I came across the quotation from Pascal: "*Dans les champs de l'observation, le hasard ne favorise que les esprits préparés*" ("In the fields of observation, chance favors only the prepared minds"). It stuck in my memory. To be prepared. For the morning when I would wake up a man.

I threw myself into my studies. To keep abreast of the class despite our absences — Jewish students were excused from school on Saturdays and Jewish holidays — Menda and I would, after Shabbat morning services, wait at noon for school to let out, and get the course notes and the homework assignments from Christian friends. On many a Saturday our teachers, considerate of their Jewish students, would just review the week's material and put off tackling a weighty new topic until Monday.

Once, seeing me working on my Latin, my mother recited "amo, amas, amat," then, "rosa, rosa, rosae," reminiscing, wistfully. She had attended the public high school for girls in her Polish hometown Kolbuszowa — none of her five sisters had — after some impassioned pleading with her mother: that was before the first world war, when public high school was not the proper place for a Jewish girl. My father teased her about it:

"O là làà... *Gymnasium*," — "high school" in German — he would say in a tone of mock admiration.

"You are jealous."

"Why didn't you finish?" he once asked.

She laughed. "You know very well."

"But *I* don't," I said.

She had gone to a Saturday night event at her high school, my mother recounted at the supper table. An acquaintance passing by the brightly-lit window recognized her. "She was dancing!" he came running to tell her mother. "With a young officer!" My grandmother was mortified. "*Schluss*" ("finished"), she decreed.

"Now don't you tell anyone that you didn't finish second grade," she got back at my father.

"You didn't go to school!?" my brother asked, lurching towards my father.

"No..."

"How come?" I broke in.

"The teacher, a Pole, insulted me. An antisemitic slur. I refused to go back to the classroom."

"But didn't you have to? The authorities...?"

"Back then — the year was... 1907 — they were not that strict."

"And your mother?" — He had lost his father when he was three — "Didn't she..."

"Mother accepted it. She got me a tutor for Polish and German. And I continued *kheder* [one-room bible and prayer school for boys]."

He also picked up modern Hebrew as a young man, a rich Flemish, and a flawed French.

———

In October two young Jewish couples moved into the two empty apartments: the Rosenzweigs on the top floor, the Janowskis on the ground floor. The High Holidays were upon us, then the festival of Sukkoth. The leaves turned, the days were getting short. The trees stood bare. I was looking forward to each coming day.

✡ ✡ ✡

Late October, 1940, five months into the Occupation:

A German decree prohibits the slaughter of warm-blooded animals without prior sedation. It bans, in effect, Jewish ritual practice: no more kosher meat. The word "Jew" had not been mentioned.

"So they are getting busy with us," my mother said in a low, almost lifeless voice.

My father, who had brought the news home, kept silent.

"We'll buy at the Flemish butcher across the street," my mother declared. "The children's health comes first."

"Of course."

"Feeling for the suffering of cattle," she muttered.

"They also listen to Bach," my father dropped.

My mother prepared the meat the kosher way, salting it, to drain the blood.

The Flemish butcher gained a number of Jewish customers. My father would mention the friendliness of the butcher and his wife, a couple past middle age; "They ask about the children."

I didn't give the matter a second thought, absorbed, as I was, by my new life centered around school and friends.

Just days later. My father walked in and turned around to close the door, in a lingering, out-of-the-ordinary stance. Usually, he would close the door behind him while looking toward the kitchen to meet my mother's gaze. He took off his topcoat and hung it in the armoire in the bedroom. My mother stepped into the dining room.

"They are getting busy with us in earnest," he said.

"What now?" my mother asked.

"We have to register in a separate register for Jews. By November 30th. Every Jew over fifteen."

"So. They want us squarely in their sight," my mother said. "To what end?"

"The devil knows," my father answered. "Certainly not to hand out honey cake." And, after a moment's pause, "This is only the beginning of the story. There are more decrees. A whole list."

My mother stiffened.

"Lawyers can no longer practice. And journalists. Jews are barred from teaching in non-Jewish institutions."

"Like in Germany..."

"Jews must be dismissed from public office," my father continued. "By year's end."

He paused.

"All Jewish enterprises must register and declare their assets."

"So theeere", my mother said in a tone of gloom. "They are going after the wealth. Of course."

"The public establishments — restaurants, cafés and hotels — must display the sign 'Jewish Enterprise' in German, Flemish and French."

"Diamantaires?" my mother asked.

"Nothing specific to the diamond business."

"That will come."

My parents were standing, downcast, by the dining room table.

"What do they say in town?" my mother asked.

My father had a nervous chuckle: "That it could have been worse," he said, anticipating my mother's reaction.

"Our Jews," my mother said with a mixture of scorn and derision. " 'Could have been worse.' "

"Yes, worse. How many Jewish lawyers are there in Antwerp, the argument went. Four? Five? How many more in all of Belgium? And how many functionaries? And professors? Or journalists? Some even expressed relief that the Germans had stopped there."

"Relief?"

"Yes, relief. The Germans, the reasoning went, are just trying to stamp out the nefarious Jewish influence over Aryans. Their old bugaboo."

"Jews have a reassuring explanation for everything," my mother sighed. *"Halleveye"* ("It should only be so"). And after a short pause, "Where does one register?"

"At City Hall."

"So the Flemish city employees will do the registering?"

"Yes," my father said. "A ready work force."

They moved to the kitchen where my brother and I were finishing our dinner.

I left for afternoon classes.

That evening not a word was spoken during supper. My mother had served. My father had cut the bread, sliced the tomatoes, removed the red peel off the thin slices of the Gouda cheese. Last had come the coffee — my brother's, *café au lait*; mine, the same but darker; my parents', black, in tall glasses, topped with the thick skin skimmed off the boiled milk. My mother had finished chewing the residue of the sugar cube through which she had sipped her coffee. She broke the silence.

"I don't like that registering, that accurate accounting they want of us, the declaring of assets. Won't they set their sights on the diamond world next? That's where the wealth is."

"Keeping the diamond business going seems to be in their interest. Diamantaires are still returning from the south of France. To make a living."

"Some, most likely, have no choice: how long can a family with children live on the road? Only the very rich can wait it out in Nice."

"And those who chose to come back when they had the means to stay..."

"Are irresponsible fools," my mother interjected. "Choosing to live under the German to enjoy the comforts of home, or to earn more money..."

"Would you have wanted to stay there, had we outrun the Germans?"

"Esther and Avrum would have stayed. We would have stuck together."

"You mean Avrum would have supported us had we run out of money."

"No. I mean that I would have borrowed from him."

"With the intention of paying back."

"After the war. Help, yes. Charity, no."

"And had we been in Nice by ourselves? Say Avrum got a visa to... anywhere, and off they sail on an American or some other neutral country's ship. What then?"

"I know what you are getting at, but I'll answer you anyway: to live free with the dread of running out of money is the lesser evil. Here we do indeed have some control over expenses. But not over what we own. They can take it away any time."

"Then shouldn't we pack and run?"

"I expected you to ask that question."

"It is not a trick question. Would you consider it?" my father asked.

"I don't have the courage. To entrust ourselves to a smuggler... To run borders and risk falling into their hands. Like turning ourselves in... And the fear of running out of money in a foreign land — that alone takes away whatever resolve I might have mustered." She sighed. Then:

"Could *you* bring yourself...? Avrum is preparing to—"

"I am not Avrum," my father snapped. "Avrum dares look the devil in the eye. And you are not Esther. Avrum decides and Esther follows. I can move only with your firm and wholehearted backing. And I would."

There was silence before my mother murmured, "Let's see what happens." She seemed lost in thought. My father's features were drawn. My brother and I kept quiet.

The following day, at supper, my parents' conversation drifted back to the decrees.

"Just out of curiosity," my mother said, "how will they know that someone did not register?"

My father raised his eyebrows: "They won't verify? All they have to do is look up the city register, or better even, the files of the Foreigners' Police — we are almost all foreigners — and our Jewish names will jump out at them, with address, nationality, birthplace, profession, what have you. Even the religion, come to think of it. It was mentioned on our Polish papers which we submitted to the police." In the peace treaty of 1919 the Jews of Poland — almost ten percent of the population — had been granted the status of a recognized and protected minority. German and Austrian Jews had the J for *Jude* stamped on their passports.

"I understand," my mother said. "I didn't mean to suggest..." she trailed off. "God protect. To defy them..."

"It would be jail, a fine, and the confiscation of property."

"Is that what it says?"

"Yes. They don't play around. Even the *guerr* [convert to Judaism] must register. Even a former *guerr* who has reverted to Christianity."

"What's the idea?"

"Go, figure. I am not about to ask them for an explanation."

"So who is a Jew?"

"A Jew, they have ruled, is someone with three Jewish grand-parents, or someone who adheres or has adhered to the Jewish faith. A *guerr*, it seems, gets to shoulder our bundle of *tsooris* [woes] and may even bequeath them to his grandchildren."

"Strange," my mother said with a touch of whimsy, "if a goyishe grandfather converts to Judaism and becomes the third Jewish grandparent, would that make the grandchildren into Jews?"

"A talmudic question," my father said with an appreciative grin.

"Where does it say all of that?"

"In their *Verordnungsblatt*" ("Decree bulletin").

"In German?"

"In German, Flemish, and French. From what I heard, they call it '*Verordnung gegen die Juden.*' "

"*Against* the Jews... That blunt... And the registering by the city employees is in there as well?"

"Yes. They are to register those of us who request it."

"What? Those who *request* it? We are *asking* for a *favor?* Unbelievable."

"I too was taken aback. But that apparently is the language: brutal vis-à-vis the Jews, quite circumspect with the Flemish."

"Why that delicateness?"

"I don't know. Our experts were debating that very question. Someone mentioned the Belgian constitution. I left in the middle."

"Our Jewish experts," my mother mumbled. "The Belgian constitution. As if the Germans give a hoot about the Belgian constitution."

They fell quiet.

"*Ah velt*" ("Some world we live in"), my mother muttered.

My father went to City Hall, as did almost everyone else, stood in line, produced his and my mother's identity cards, and registered the two of them. He returned, grim-faced. The talk was low-key, he reported. Some men tried to make light of it. Most were silent.

Uncle Avrum did not register.

The Belgian constitution had, indeed, been a factor in the unfolding of events: it barred racial and religious discrimination. The Germans had wanted the Belgian State to promulgate the *Measures against the Jews* in its official publications of ministerial orders, and enforce them. The country's administrators refused, citing their oath to uphold the law of the land.

The Germans relented, to retain the Belgians' goodwill in administering the country — the occupation regime, short on administrative and police personnel, was one of oversight only. They issued the Jew-decrees in their *Verordnungsblatt*, implicating the Belgian state and local authorities in their execution.

The country's officials went along:

The few Jewish functionaries and public school teachers were put on paid leave of absence. Again, the constitution was upheld. The university professors fared in a similar way. (The insignificant number of Jews affected by the "cleansing" of the public sector reflected the small size of the Jewish population holding Belgian citizenship — about 3,200.)

As for the mandated registration, the Interior Ministry instructed the town and city halls to register only the Jews who presented themselves: Passive execution of the decree where "the victim spontaneously puts his head on the block" — the metaphor used in a legal opinion — did not violate the law. And it enjoined the municipalities to hand the registration records over to the German Authorities.

The race laws did not cause a ripple among the population.

In Antwerp, City Hall posted bills, signed by the mayor, with the scheduled registration dates. (More than one thousand Jews did not register.) And it printed the "Jewish Enterprise" signs in large, bold letters, charging the Jewish establishments one franc apiece.

The Germans got the cooperation they needed.

The shock the measures caused among the Jews was short-lived. The Jew-registration, soon forgotten, had appeared as a threat only in its flouting.

———————

There would be another census in the summer of 1941. It mandated individual entries for the children fifteen and under as well. The country's municipal employees also stamped JOOD-JUIF in bold, red, 1.5-cm tall characters on the ID cards that the registrants, as all residents of Belgium age fifteen and older, citizens as well as foreigners, were required by law to carry at all times.

A year later, in the summer of 1942, the consolidated Jew-registers served as the index file for issuing the *tsetl* (slip), as the dreaded summons was dubbed. It ordered the recipient to report at the Dossin barracks in Mechelen, the town midway between Antwerp and Brussels from where the Jews of Belgium were deported. It also allowed for capturing people in their homes, and for emptying out the homes whose contents were shipped to Germany in freight trains with signs saying, "From our friends in Belgium."

The index file was found after the German debacle and hasty retreat in the summer of 1944. It contained 56,186 individual index cards.

Our day-to-day life did not change. I left the divining of the Germans' intentions to my parents and to our political pundits — most of them were irrepressible optimists.

"The Germans are done in," my father quoted one of them.

"How so?" my mother asked.

"For them, it's either a blitzkrieg victory, or defeat," my father explained. "And they muffed it in the air over England."

"Do they lose heart if it takes them a little longer?"

"No," my father said, laughing. "The reasoning is as follows: You need lots of oil and rubber to wage war. Germany has neither. Her supplies are bound to run out. As long as the English keep fighting, the Germans are losing."

I was impressed by the ability of our strategists to analyze the situation, and, for that matter, to interpret a speech, to read between the lines. War was interesting.

"And how long will their losing last?"

"Can't be very long, they say, given the destructiveness of modern warfare. But how long, really, only one God knows."

"And what do the pessimists have to say?"

"The Germans may no longer invade England, but they'll bring her to her knees by devastating her towns and cities, as they did to Coventry, and by decimating her merchant marine."

"Well?"

"Nonsense. England is standing firm. No one has ever brought her to her knees. 'You can't defeat the Bank of England,' the saying goes."

"*How clever.* Meanwhile the Germans have gotten busy with us. Miracles are what we need."

"We'll manage, with God's help."

✪ ✪ ✪

"Rav Brod is packing his bags," my father dropped.

He had returned, a bit melancholy, from the small gathering where the Rav had announced his decision. That evening he sat, pensive, at the supper table. My mother opined:

"He is afraid, like everyone else. He wants out. Why not, if he has the means, and the connections?"

"*That* he has," my father replied. "The help of his *hasidim* (followers) at this end. And, most probably, American papers in Nice. The Antwerpians in New York, it seems, are waiting for him. Still, a strong leader. It's a shock."

A respected scholar, Rav Brod had succeeded chief rabbi Amiel, one of the founders of Tachkemoni, at Congregation *Shomrei Hadas* (the Guardians of the Faith). We belonged to the *Makhzeekei Hadas* (the Keepers of the Faith). The *makhers* (officials) of the two congregations had forever been feuding, so much so that each had patronized its own kosher butcher, trusted, alone, to uphold the laws of ritual purity. The two synagogues, Antwerp's largest, were a few hundred meters from each other, on Oostenstraat.

The Rav paid a visit, once, to our synagogue. It caused a stir. A short man with a gruff voice, he moved briskly. His was a strong presence.

He made it to New York.

Our rabbi, Rav Rottenberg, stayed with his flock. He could have traveled on a Swiss passport to join his daughter in Switzerland. Instead, he was to perish with most of his children and grandchildren.

✡ ✡ ✡

Diamantaires, Jews and Gentiles alike, must declare their diamond holdings with the *Diamantkontrolle* office, the occupier ordered.

Diamantaires registered a token amount, if any, to gain legitimacy. Trading, almost all in undeclared goods, continued at the diamond bourse, spurred by the need for cash, or the necessity to eke out a living, or the search for bargains: With demand weak and prices low — diamonds fetched higher prices in the French Unoccupied Zone and beyond — the precious, easy-to-carry goods were a good investment for people planning an escape. Hardship or greed drove some to smuggling.

The traders still gathered at the diamond bourse and other trading floors. Their anxiety waned as weeks, then months, went by without the anticipated surprise inspections. The Germans made house raids, though, and incarcerated a number of diamantaires after confiscating their "illicit" goods. They acted on tips by one named Bach, a diminutive Jew with a napoleonic complex. Bach was said to have harbored a long-simmering grudge against Jewish diamantaires. He had an entrée to the Gestapo and would strut on the Jewish street, all puffed up with his fame and power.

"A young Jew should shoot him dead," I once muttered.

My mother turned to me in disbelief, alarmed:

"Where did you learn to talk this way?" she said tersely. And, after a pause: "We Jews don't do that."

I knew not to repeat such thoughts.

Eventually, Bach disappeared, to Breendonck, the Belgian World War I fortress the Germans had turned into a concentration camp and equipped with a torture chamber. He had walked into the office of the German police chief to ask that some Jewish acquaintances of his, inmates at Breendonck, be set free.

My father had stopped almost all activity well before the latest decree. But he continued to frequent the diamond bourse to be with his cronies, to gauge the mood of the *shtetl*, hear the latest news, find out what people were doing. With no money coming in, my parents dipped into the nest egg my mother, the thrifty one, had built over the years — she had always run her household on a budget, held the line at moderate-rent apartments, eschewed luxuries such as a fur coat, despite my father's entreaties. Jewelry, yes: It doubled up as an investment. The most valued possession, to her, was a padded bank account: it meant financial security, the holy grail of her material striving. "It calms the nerves."

December 1940 brought sudden cheer: The British forces in Egypt, in a lightning thrust out of their defensive positions, had overrun Sidi Barrani (we relished the sound of the name), a spot by the Mediterranean inside Egypt near the Libyan border. They took 14,000 prisoners and captured the plentiful supplies the Italians had laid in and the airstrip they had built in preparation for their next advance into Egypt. They rushed on across the border, rolling up the fortified positions guarding the approaches to Libya and taking another 25,000 prisoners. At long last... The English had gone on the offensive and scored big; in just three days of swift moves they had eliminated the Italian threat to Egypt.

The news in the days to come was even more exhilarating: From Sidi Barrani the British surged along the coast to Sollum. Then to Bardia. The port city of Tobruk surrendered. Then came the spectacular dash from Tobruk across the desert to the coastal township of Beda Fomm, cutting off the Cyrenaican bulge. The Italians, massed in the port city of Benghazi where they intended to halt the British, began streaming south on the coastal road, hoping to break out of the trap, only to hit the roadblocks at Beda Fomm. The BBC, Britain's trusted voice, reported that in the two months since their initial thrust on Sidi Barrani, the British, losing fewer than 500 men, had taken 130,000 prisoners, with huge quantities of matériel and supplies. Italy's Libyan army had ceased to exist. We were elated.

The victory in North Africa heralded a reversal of fortune. The beginning of the end, we dared to hope. Our faith in England soared.

I had followed the dazzling blitz with mounting excitement, on the radio, in the newspapers, on the map. I became a war buff. And now, I expected in my enthusiasm, onward to Tripoli; bag Tripolitania. It was stretching west, ripe for the plucking. Deny the Axis a foothold in North Africa. This should happen in less time even than it took to overrun Cyrenaica. A drive-through, I predicted.

I waited.

All remained quiet until a newly arrived German general named Rommel, assuming command of the German units dispatched to bail out the Italians, repeated the British feat in reverse, taking thousands of prisoners and tons of supplies. We were stunned: Were they truly invincible? (Little did we know that the battle-hardened units of the North African campaign had been sent to Greece, on Churchill's orders, in response to that country's appeal for help; German troops had been massing at its border. Only one eviscerated division, augmented with troops untrained in desert warfare, had been left in the towns along the Cyrenaikan coast, in a static, defensive stance, Italian style.)

The Germans gloated, breaking into the regular radio broadcasts with triumphant *Sondermeldungen*, special announcements, preceded and followed by martial music.

✲ ✲ ✲

I, too, noticed my father's burdened stance, his pale mask of silence when he came in the door. My mother joined him in the dining room. Her eyes searched his. It took a moment before he came out with the news: "An expulsion order. Not for us," he hastened to add.

"For whom?"

"The 'white cards'" (short for "temporary residents" — mostly refugees, bearers of white identification cards).

"Where to?"

"It doesn't say."

"Oy..." It took a while before my mother asked,

"When are they supposed to leave?"

"This *Shabbas*. The Flemish police is serving them with the order."

"Out of the country?"

"The order says to bring along food for three days."

"That's a bad sign."

"The spouse and children can join the head of household who got an evacuation order. That's about all I heard."

Another pause.

"Won't the German get busy next with the 'yellow cards'?" my mother asked. My parents carried the yellow identification cards of the permanent foreign residents.

"...Apparently not."

My mother looked away, anguished.

"Esther will soon be leaving," she said, wistfully. Uncle Avrum was planning his family's escape to Nice ever since our return from France.

My father remained silent. He took off his topcoat. They both came to the kitchen where my brother and I were eating lunch. My mother finished serving us and began serving my father.

"December," she mumbled. "The cold. The misery."

My brother and I finished our meal and left for school.

The first train left Antwerp on December 21 under German military escort with more than two hundred people on board including children. When word came from the deportees, relief swept through the community: "Limburg! A stone's throw away. We'll be able to send them packages." Letters arrived. The relocation story unfolded.

The convoy had stopped in Hasselt, the capital of Limburg, a Flemish province bordering Holland. Germans in uniform, Belgian gendarmes and functionaries had been waiting at the station. There the deportees were told their destinations: various townships in the province. Ordered to do so by their governor, the local authorities performed all the administrative and police tasks for the *Feldkommandantur*, from registering and housing the new arrivals to keeping tabs on their whereabouts.

Eight more trains left in less than two months. The Antwerp police had provided the lists. At the Germans' behest, the governor of the Province of Antwerp forwarded the expulsion orders to the municipalities; the mayors signed them, bearing the municipal seals, and the police delivered them. The police department arranged for a Red Cross presence on the trains; only the gravely ill were exempted. Antwerp policemen accompanied the expellees to the train station on the appointed day — they did not use force on the Jews who refused to go along. They escorted all nine convoys. They tracked down dodgers and kept them locked up in a military warehouse until their deportation.

Over 3,000 Jews, including more than 600 children under fifteen, ended up in Limburg. Almost as many would-be recipients had either vanished without a trace or were not at home when the police came knocking. My classmate Mayersdorf, a recent refugee from Germany, went with his widowed mother. Our teachers stopped taking down his absence after a couple of days. They asked no questions: it was not unusual for a Jewish student to drop out without explanation.

The news from Limburg was reassuring: aside from having to report daily to the municipal administrations, the evacuees were free to move around in their assigned localities. The local authorities had provided shelter in barracks, in unoccupied buildings and requisitioned houses. Most of the locals were hospitable — some met the arrivals from Antwerp with compassion and generosity — despite the food shortages and other hardships of that first, harsh winter under the Occupation. Aid poured in from Jewish organizations and the Belgian Red Cross. A number of young men had offered to work in the coal mines but were barred by the *Feldkommandantur* in Hasselt from seeking gainful employment. The evacuees drew welfare benefits from the Belgian State. "That is Belgium," the old-timers crowed.

In January 1941, only weeks after the first convoy had left for Limburg, a smuggler took Uncle Avrum, Aunt Esther and my cousins Harry and Manny across the border to France. (My other cousin Harry remained in Antwerp. He was living with the family of a close friend ever since his mother, Aunt Khantshe, died — he was seventeen at the time. He had lost his father as a young child.)

My mother felt isolated. She had been surrounded in Antwerp by a brother — an old-timer who had sponsored my father's membership in the Diamond Bourse — and two sisters. The three sisters would see each other almost daily, at the home of Aunt Khantshe, the oldest. Khantshe had taken care of my mother who was three years old when her father died — my grandmother was too busy providing for a large brood. Aunt Khantshe died of cancer before the war. That day my mother, overcome with grief, walked past me without noticing me. Her brother Itshe had outrun the Germans and landed with his family in New York. Now, Esther was gone.

Avrum instructed his smuggler, a trustworthy pro, to contact my parents upon his return to Antwerp. This led to hand-wringing asides: the journey to Nice was dangerous — families that had been intercepted were never heard of again. "Avrum *had* to get away," my mother confided to me, intimating that he had personal reasons to avoid the Germans' attention. What could they be, I wondered, aside from the open secret that he had slipped out of Frankfurt with more of his fortune than the few marks would-be émigrés were allowed to take out of Germany? "And he is wealthy," my mother added. He had prospered in Antwerp, as he had in Frankfurt. "On the road, money is like water," she continued. "We would not hold out, even if we made it to Nice." That winter, without the slightest inkling as to how the Germans would address their Jewish problem, my parents' overriding concern was to stretch their savings until the liberation. I sensed my mother's anguish. Yet I could not conceive of a day without food or shelter. I did not want for anything. I had a good time in school and with friends. A twelve-year old boy's untrammeled life.

Decades after the war my cousins told me that they were taken to the French border in two light pickup trucks. The first, with Avrum and his older son under the tarpaulin, got across. The second was stopped. Esther kept her cool: she engaged the German soldier in conversation, played a bit of the coquette. He let them go. In Paris they took the train to the Unoccupied Zone, equipped with a German-issued *laissez-passer* which Avrum had secured for a huge sum in American dollars through an acquaintance who knew a high German officer's French mistress. They made it to Nice.

In March, less than three months after the first convoy left the city, the Limburg Jews were allowed to trickle back to Antwerp — women and children first: they had become a physical and financial burden on Limburg and the State in a time of scarcity. One day Mayersdorf was back in class. He looked healthy. No one asked him any questions, except Menda, a close friend of his; they were similar types: quick studies and reserved, self-effacing almost. Mayersdorf answered the professor's math questions as if he had not missed a class.

Of the men, many were barred from returning to Antwerp and moved to Brussels. Some of them had their families join them. A few hundred young men were sent to a labor camp in Limburg. The last were set free in January 1942, one year after leaving home.

My parents and their circle of acquaintances looked at the homecoming of the "Limburgers" as a victory of sorts.

But this "victory" was illusory: the Limburg operation was a rogue undertaking of the Antwerp *Feldkommandantur*. Berlin's strategy would be to concentrate us in urban centers, not to disperse us in the provinces. Indeed, later that year, in August of 1941, the Germans decreed that Jews could no longer take up residence outside the cities of Brussels, Antwerp, Liège, and Charleroi. Yet the Limburg episode reinforced the impression that, in the West, German harassment and persecution, however capricious and harsh, would be bearable.

We got on with our lives. My mother baked delicious cakes for the Sabbath that lasted us into the week. My father bought a wine-making kit: the Sabbath wines, including the Hungarian Tokay, were no longer available.

✧ ✧ ✧

That first winter after the invasion saw a record snowfall that covered the city with a thick blanket that crackled under one's feet. The sight of nature's white, aloof splendor could be soothing, even uplifting, taking people's minds off the daily grind, the food rationing, the shortages of clothing, of paper, the blackout, wartime's tedium. The streets were alive with plodding pedestrians, smiling as they extended right-of-way courtesies to each other in the narrow, trench-like passages of trampled snow. We trudged to school, playful and boisterous. The bright, cold weather, unusual for Belgium, prompted my father to take his fur-lined coat from Poland out of mothballs for a jaunt in the bracing air. He described, with a glint of nostalgia in his big gray-green eyes, scenes of the Polish winter, the vast expanses of snow, and one particularly intoxicating horse-and-sleigh ride in the dead of night through the forest to neighboring Rzeszow, to rouse a doctor and bring him to his mother-in-law who complained of chest pains. "Indigestion, it turned out," my father recounted with a mischievous laughter. "The doctor was annoyed."

Our park turned into a pristine landscape of shades of white, from the cold, grainy dull of the shady spots to the silvery glitter of the sunlit expanses. The snow erased all lines and edges and buried the benches under elongated cocoons. Outcroppings lost their contours, like children hiding under a thick duvet. Charcoal tree trunks stood out, bold sentinels coiffed extravagantly in glistening white with streaks of black.

Crowds descended on the park during the weekend. The atmosphere was festive. The people gave themselves over to the moment, to the pleasure of moving around, of playing in the snow. Amateur sculptors converged on the central meadow and fashioned elaborate snow figures, from animals in various poses to snowmen, using bits of coal for eyes, and other props such as hats and scarves and straw brooms. The finished sculptures as well as the works in progress attracted a steady procession of viewers.

I threw myself into a line of boys sliding on their heels and their behinds down an incline and ending up in a heap at the bottom, to rush back up and come down with undiminished exultation. I broke away from the boisterous band when it got too crowded, to watch the revelers on the ice. Skaters whirled around in the large area of the frozen lake that the city had cleared of snow, by the boathouse. The swift and the graceful moved in wide concentric circles. Novices kept to the center or stayed on the outside; they made clumsy runs in all directions, stopping now and then to take a breather or for an excited chat. People fell. Scarves fluttered. Bonnets flew off. Puffs of condensed breath dotted the air. A new game took hold on the fringes of the snow-plowed area of the lake: sliding over the ice on one's soles and heels. Men would blaze a foot-wide "slide path," by running a short distance, gathering momentum, then swinging their bodies ninety degrees to the left as they rammed the edge of their right foot into the coarse, snow-encrusted surface. That sudden thrust scraped a length of about four inches of hard, thin snow off the ice. Each repeat run bared another few inches of black ice. A slide path was born.

Now the participants ran, then slid into the ever receding thin snow cover. The path stopped where the most forceful sliders came to a natural halt; it could reach forty, even fifty yards. A return path parallel to the original one made for a swift, giddy return. People in long lines would run up to the slide paths, plant their feet on the ice, toes pointing sideways, and slide forth in high-wire poses, some steady as dancers, others flailing for balance, or squatting, rotating on their own axes, falling and sliding forth on their bottoms or rolling out of the way. I joined the revelers; I made countless runs, trying to reach top speed. Pileups added to the merriment. Squeals and laughter filled the air. Now and then adults, bent over, would guide forth wary, or jubilant, children. Sometimes, a swifter, stronger slider would catch up with the preceding one and the two would move on in tandem, or fall together, laughing. I, too, got an occasional assist from the back, or joined up with someone in front of me; it heightened my sense of camaraderie. Not for one instant was I conscious of being a Jew among non-Jews. Fired up, I started my own slide path. Other boys joined in. We ran and slid, hot and gleeful, shouting and laughing.

With dusk approaching — sky and snow had blended into a dull whiteness — people began trickling out. I left for home, contented.

✷ ✷ ✷

My parents stood by the dining room table, exchanging anguished glances. I had overheard snatches from their brief, low-voiced aside:

"The Germans?" my mother had asked.

"No. Flemings."

"Were people hurt?"

"Not that I heard."

I wanted to know.

"They set the Oosten and the Van den Nestlei *shuls* on fire," my father told me.

My parents stood for a while longer, looking at each other. My mother broke away toward the kitchen, head low and grim-faced.

That Easter Monday, April 14, 1941, (a holiday), Flemish pro-Nazi militants and a flock of enthusiastic hangers-on had streamed through the Jewish quarter huddled around the Central Station, smashing the windows of Jewish shops before converging on Antwerp's two main synagogues on quiet, residential Oostenstraat. They used Torah scrolls, sacred books and prayer shawls as kindling to set the two sanctuaries ablaze. They also gutted and torched Rav Rottenberg's house, adjacent to the Oosten *shul*. The Rav escaped with his family. It all happened fast. The two unarmed Flemish policemen at the scene, caught unawares, were powerless to stop the arson. The bicycle-mounted gendarmes arrived too late. The firemen were delayed.

The mob had been fired up by a viewing of the German movie *Der ewige Jude* (The Eternal Jew), which compares the world migration of Jews out of Mesopotamia to the global spread of rats from their original habitat in Central Asia. It shows swarms of rodents — the Jews in society — alighting from a sewer in a frightening infestation. A scene in which the Führer "prophesies," in a 1939 speech, that a war would bring about "the annihilation of the Jewish race in Europe" put the audience into a trance. What to my parents had seemed inconceivable in the civilized West had just taken place: a pogrom, unhindered.

Yet the Flemish Kristallnacht had taken the German military brass by surprise. They soon realized that the "spontaneous show of the Antwerpians' wrath" touted by the antisemitic press had been planned: uniformed photographers of the German propaganda service who snapped pictures of the synagogue burnings had staked out choice spots in anticipation of the arsonists' arrival, and the Gestapo with its own Jewish agenda was implicated in the attack. In tackling the Jewish question, the Military Occupation Authority used the lesser evil approach — a concession now and then to the already wary, constitution-centered, indispensable Belgian Executive. They were not going to let the Gestapo or the SS and their hotheaded Flemish acolytes dictate the conduct and pace of their *Judenpolitik*. Members of the German occupation force and security services were ordered to keep away from civil unrest.

The news of the raid on the Jewish quarter and the sack of the synagogues receded in my mind like the distant rumble of a dying storm. We had switched a good while back to the Moriah *shul* in the Terliststraat near the park, much closer to home. That's where I would be celebrating my bar mitzvah six weeks later, at the beginning of June; I was preparing for it. Our *shul* in the Oostenstraat had stopped being a part of my life: facing the other side of a rampart-like structure that supported the railroad tracks, it lay beyond the narrow perimeter I moved in. And the Jewish quarter, also on the other side of the tracks, the place where the kosher food and the religious articles came from, where the school-age children spoke mostly Flemish, not French, as their second language, seemed even more remote to me. I had been there only once, before the war, with Strassberg, a Tachkemoni classmate. Our association had been fortuitous, and a fleeting one, for Strassberg was not one of us good Jewish boys who took school seriously. He was good at sports, and got average grades without putting in any effort. He alone dared question a teacher's edict to his face. In fourth grade a Flemish teacher had read in class (I was absent that day) a story about crimes committed by a repellingly portrayed Jew. Parents complained. Officials of the Ministry of Education came to Tachkemoni to investigate the matter. A number of my classmates were asked to write individual accounts of what they had heard. They handed in their reports, after which Strassberg overheard boys in the courtyard compare notes — no one in the group, it turned out, had mentioned the Jewishness of the villain. "Bunch of imbeciles!" he lashed out at them. The teacher, he lectured them, would now deny that he read the offending stuff and claim that the complaint's purpose was to stir trouble for him. In fifth grade, Mr. Govaerts, our Flemish teacher, would not tolerate the slightest infraction to the rule of silence. The first time Strassberg was caught talking under his breath to his bench mate, Mr. Govaerts told him to keep his mouth shut, warning, "Who won't listen will be made to feel" — a Flemish saying. The second time, Mr. Govaerts snapped, "Strassberg!" and summoned him with a motion of the head to step outside. Holding a thin, square wooden ruler in his right hand, he ushered Strassberg out the door. The two disappeared into the hallway. The door closed. And with his head wedged, face down, between Govaerts' knees, Strassberg took blow after blow with the thin ruler on his buttocks. It seemed to take a long time. Not a sound was heard from the hallway. We waited with bated breath, awed. Strassberg was the first to reenter the classroom. Short — my height — he walked with his usual gait, head high, with a hard look in his black eyes, his thick, black hair undisturbed. Mr. Govaerts, a hulk of a man, followed, red in the face, a thin strand of loosened reddish hair hanging over his high forehead. The third time, punishing Strassberg took on the motions of a ritual.

My foray into the Jewish quarter resulted from a chance school-yard encounter with Strassberg that led to a tentative exchange; I asked him on the spur of the moment to come by my home on the following Saturday afternoon. He nodded. My mother was there when he showed up. I had told her that we would be quiet so as not to disturb her and my father's *Shabbas* afternoon nap, but she wanted to see the friend I had never mentioned. When Strassberg stepped into our small living-dining room, he looked at my mother, just looked at her. I could see the dismay on her face: no manners! ("Greet" [the shopkeepers], she would whisper to me upon entering a store and, "Bid them goodbye," when I would fail to do either, berating me afterwards: "How often must I remind you? You stand there like a clay *golem*.")

"We are going for a walk," I said. I wanted to get out. Staying in the apartment would no longer have been fun.

"Be back soon," my mother said. "We'll be going to the park."

"Do you always have to go with your parents?" Strassberg asked when we reached the bottom of the stairs.

"No."

"Like this afternoon."

"Well... I *want* to."

He looked sideways at me, grinning, with a twinkle in his eye.

"I don't think your mother likes me," he said when we got onto the sidewalk. True enough, I knew it — "Ill-bred," she would later say of Strassberg. "Not a friend for you." But his frankness took me aback: that was the kind of truth I would have kept mum about, to avoid embarrassing the other person.

"No, not at all," I protested. "What makes you say that?"

"She didn't say hello to me."

"We are supposed to say it first."

"Why?"

"I... I... It's a rule, I think."

"Oh. Rules."

"Where do you live?" I asked.

"There," he pointed with his hand, "there, on the other side." On the other side of the wide, fortress-like rampart of bricks and

stone that cut through the city from the Central Station south-
wards to Berchem Station and supported the railroad tracks
joining Antwerp to Mechelen and Brussels. There, in the Jewish
quarter.

"Oh..."

"You want to go there?" he asked.

"Yes."

We lived at the time on Simonsstraat, a street along the railroad rampart. The nearest, tunnel-like opening to the "other
side" was just paces away, on the corner of the Lange Kievitstraat,
a cross-street that ran from the park, under the railroad tracks,
deep into the Jewish quarter. Traipsing behind Strassberg on a
sliver of sidewalk, I stepped, for the first time, into the penumbra
of the narrow tunnel, the gate to what felt like a walled city. We
emerged into the open and walked abreast on the shady side
of the narrow, cobblestone street. On the opposite side the little old two- and three-story houses, pressed against each other,
were soaking up the sun. The reflected sunlight would flare up
in window after blinding window, moving apace with us. Closed
shops; some shuttered. Shallow inner courtyards. Few people
were ambling by. Quiet reigned. A world away from mine — I felt
it keenly.

We kept walking in silence. Pointing to a lean man about
twenty paces in front of us, Strassberg remarked:

"This is the older brother of Toby" — a classmate.

"One can see the resemblance," I said, to acknowledge his
remark and say something.

He burst out laughing: "How can you see a resemblance? All
you see is his arse."

"You can tell," I held out.

It was the first time I saw him laughing, and so wholeheart-
edly. I had never seen him crack a smile in school, even when the
whole class was amused. We walked some more, exchanging few
remarks.

"I'll be heading home," I said after a while.

He walked me back a stretch. We parted.

The invaded Jewish quarter, huddled around Central Station,
had remained to me a remote place. I did not associate it with the
peaceful, otherworldly street I had seen in Strassberg's company.

I could never have imagined the raucous shouts of visceral hatred, the crashing sound of falling glass, the jagged holes in
smashed-in windows, the pillage, the mess. Just broken windows
in unnamed streets was all I could think of, a vicious prank that
antisemites perpetrated on Jews. Over there. It did not come up
in conversations with my friends; nor had the synagogue fires. We
had not been directly involved; and we felt protected. My parents
had talked about it fleetingly, in undertones. "The shards... The
looting," my mother had muttered. "The fright... The sorrow." I
knew of the pogrom that had raged in their *shtetl*, in Poland. But
that was in a bygone era, in a faraway, backward place.

A second incursion into the Jewish quarter, three days later,
foundered in the face of a vigorous presence of Flemish police
and gendarmes — the Germans had kept their distance. That
put an end to militant-led mob attacks against Jews and their
property. "This is Belgium, not Poland," it was said with relief;
with pride, almost. Only the Germans had to be feared.

The Occupation Authority decreed a general 10:00 PM curfew, citing the disturbances "provoked by the Jews" and the need
to prevent them in the future. They lifted it after two days; and
slapped us with a 7:00 PM to 7:00 AM curfew — four months before imposing one on all of the country's Jews.

✡ ✡ ✡

The curfew, more than any other restriction up to then, set
us apart from the Gentiles. Daylight would still linger at nine
o'clock, and the days were getting longer. Late street-corner conversations would end abruptly. People would hurry to the safety
of their homes, as if chased by invisible pursuers. Children picked
up the tension preceding curfew time — they would notice their
mothers glimpsing at the clock, repeatedly, waiting for a dad or
an older brother or sister. One day, a four-year-old girl, Tamara,
the daughter of acquaintances, spotted a flight of birds speeding
across the sky as she and her mother were hurrying home minutes before the curfew.

"Look, Mommy," she exclaimed, pointing up. "Jewish birds.
They are hurrying back to their nests."

By seven — curfew time — we had pulled back behind closed
doors, cut off from relatives and friends. One evening, I stepped
out on the balcony around supper time: the street, deserted,

looked forbidding. I wondered about the domestic tableaux behind the opaque windows in the stone façades, families staying
indoors because they chose to. And I saw the chasm, as wide as
the street, between us: we, a handful of Jews in their midst, came
from elsewhere. Ours was a different creed. A separate destiny.
Even without Germans. I retreated from the balcony and closed
the glass doors.

Harry, my twenty-year old cousin who had fled with us to
France, had to come earlier for supper to be back in his lodgings
on time. He would habitually show up late and leave too close to
curfew time, getting my parents all worked up about his safety
and ours.

"We don't want to have to worry whether you made it back
safely," they would berate him.

"No need to worry. I'll be fine," my cousin would brush them
off.

The tension was building until one day my father could not
contain himself:

"We don't want to be a party to your being out beyond curfew time!" he burst out. "And I don't want the Germans to know
where you are coming from if, God forbid, they stop you."

"I wouldn't tell them."

"I don't *want* you to have to answer them one way or the other!"
My father's voice was rising. "You are to leave from here in plenty
of time to make it home before the curfew!"

"For all uncle knows, I may not even be going home. What
difference..."

"That's *your* choice. It's *your* life. But *not from here* at or past
curfew time!" My father was livid. "Listen carefully: don't bother
showing up *one* minute past six! We won't answer the door!
And you are not to leave from here *one* minute past quarter to
seven!"

Harry stopped coming. My mother was distraught — her late
sister Khantshe's son! One day he showed up, to say goodbye: he
was leaving for the French Unoccupied Zone. We were happy to
see him. My mother could not hide her anguish. When his letter
arrived, from Nice, she was jubilant: "Finally, out of danger, with
magnaten on both sides: Esther and Avrum on Khantshe's side
and the Leschkowitzes on Kracher's [his late father's] side." Both
sets of aunts and uncles had made it to Nice.

A *magnat*, in my mother's lexicon, was someone who did not have to worry about income or expenses no matter how long the economic *Krisis* lasted.

We got used to living under the curfew. It hardly inconvenienced us, we told ourselves, as most days we were all home by six o'clock. My mother would prepare supper. My father helped out or did some reading. I would do my homework on the dining-room table. My brother would read a comic book, or mosey around. We then gathered for a leisurely meal around the kitchen table. At the approach of dusk my father and I would face east and recite the afternoon and evening prayers. My brother would go to bed first, grumbling about my staying up. I would read or finish my homework or listen to my parents' conversations, about who was leaving town, who had been caught, about the goings-on in Antwerp's "*shtetl*." We would listen to some music on the radio. And to the news: Rommel was poised at the Egyptian border. The BBC confirmed it. The war was dragging on.

In the morning the street looked inviting again. I would be on my way to school where I was a student like everyone else.

✿ ✿ ✿

Stunning news broke in May, 1941. Rudolf Hess, Hitler's deputy, had landed in Scotland near the estate of an old acquaintance, the BBC announced in a short communiqué. The German radio, equally brief, ascribed Hess's solo flight to a mental disorder.

The event generated as much excitement in the *shtetl* as the victory at Sidi Barrani. The absence of commentary on the BBC, the ready concession by the Germans, as if the vault of the second-in-command of the Third Reich to Britain were a non-event, only fueled speculation that something big was afoot.

"A turning point," my father quoted one of our pundits. "Could be more significant than a trumpeted military victory."

"How so?" my mother asked.

"It was either prearranged, or Hess knows that the war is lost and jumped ship, as some say. It could be the beginning of the end."

"The beginning of the end," my mother repeated, shaking her head. "I have heard that before. How nice. Have they run out of oil and rubber?"

My father chuckled. I, too, smiled.

"No," he said. "Our strategists solved that problem a long time ago. Oil they can get from the Romanian wells. And from coal, apparently. Rubber they can make synthetically."

"So, what's there to be optimistic about?" my mother asked. "They just conquered Greece and Yugoslavia. They are advancing on Suez. Maybe Hess has, indeed, gone mad."

"Highly doubtful," my father retorted. "But regardless, with all their conquests they are like the card player who can't quit with his winnings. In the end they'll lose everything and much more. The only thing that will remain is suffering."

"Not a rosy scenario," my mother muttered.

"Try to see things a bit more optimistically," my father pleaded. "The mood is upbeat. There is even talk in town of people putting off their escape plans. *Something* must be cooking."

"Maybe you are right," my mother conceded. "Let's hope." And, after a short pause, "Imagine, the havoc that criminal has wreaked."

She made her way to the kitchen.

Less than two weeks after Hess's bolt across the Channel, the Germans announced triumphantly the landing of their troops on Crete — a massive airborne drop, the BBC reported. No one harbored illusions about the outcome of a lightning assault which inflicted heavy losses on the defenders, sustained hardly any itself and managed to secure two airports. Meanwhile Rommel was advancing on Egypt, eyeing Suez, and German U-boats were tearing into the transatlantic convoys that kept Britain afloat while her cities were savaged from the air. The euphoria attending the Hess episode thinned out and vanished like a wisp of smoke.

Then, one day in late May, the *Bismarck*, the pride of the modern German navy, sank the battle cruiser *Hood*, the symbol of Britain's supremacy on the high seas. We heard the news on the Flemish radio. The broadcast of light music had stopped suddenly. There was a moment of disconcerting silence before a male voice bellowed, *SONDERMELDUNG!* (special announcement!) *SONDERMELDUNG!* Minutes of German martial music followed. My brother and I had traipsed behind my parents into the dining room. The wait was enervating. Finally, we heard the exulting announcement of their naval victory "somewhere in the Atlantic." The communiqué in full-throated, guttural, hard-edged German — how different, it struck me, from the soft-spoken German of the Jewish refugees — was followed by more martial music. My parents looked dumbstruck.

"Are they ruling on the sea as well?" my father wondered aloud. "Do they have better ships?"

I kept quiet. My faith in England's invincibility seemed paltry in the face of that gloomy setback.

That evening, the BBC gave details: The *Hood* went down in the North Atlantic, between Iceland and Greenland. My heart jumped: "Between Iceland and Greenland" was way out west! "With all 1500 men on board," the communiqué went on. Just minutes into the naval engagement. A direct hit in the munitions hold. "Between Iceland and Greenland..."

To my parents, the somber announcement sounded more dreadful even than the gloating *Sondermeldung.*

"In just minutes," my father muttered.

"The fate of the *Bismarck* is sealed," I said.

My father raised his eyebrows, incredulous, yet curious. And I explained that England lay between the site of the sinking and the ports of Northern Europe in German hands, that the English navy and air force were bound to intercept the *Bismarck*, that failing to do so would be an even greater humiliation and defeat. The next day he repeated my prediction to his cronies, quoting me and invoking my knowledge of geography, an important subject even in the lower grades of elementary school, yet foreign to the East European Jews of my parents' generation: to them, whether savvy business men, students of German philosophy or Talmud scholars, reading maps was an arcane art. Three days later the Germans announced the valiant end of the glorious *Bismarck* at the hands of a perfidious enemy who had used overwhelming sea and air power. I was quite flattered when my father told me, his eyes shining with pride, how impressed his friends were with me. "They may even ask for your opinion, now that you are a recognized strategist," he said half-jokingly. My reputation was made. It didn't go to my head, though, as quite often a little bit of knowledge would in later years; I soon forgot about it. I didn't even mention it to my friends: to us boys growing up in Antwerp, map-reading, like bike-riding (another skill quite alien to the bourgeois immigrants of my father's generation) was nothing to brag about.

✡ ✡ ✡

I was getting ready, during that month of May, for my bar mitzvah. Mr. Groebel, my third-grade Tachkemoni teacher, was preparing me, as he had done for my friend Menda a few months earlier. A lean man with a gaunt face, he was meticulous to a fault, yet gentle. He never laughed, or even smiled. Menda and I, his two favorite pupils, had shared a front-row bench in his class. One of the games we played while Groebel had his back turned was trying to push one another off the bench. Once I caught Menda off-guard and catapulted him out. He landed with a thud on the floor. I was taken aback by the effect of my attack. Groebel was stunned: Menda Zangen! His star pupil. Menda picked himself up, sat down, and took a tongue-lashing, head bent, face red, lips pinched — I also kept my mouth shut. Suddenly Groebel looked at me — the whole class must have been grinning in my direction — and realized that no one chooses to crash-land like an otter. He motioned me into the corner, by the blackboard. Wrong corner: I turned around and faced the class when Groebel did, and smiled and made faces. A few boys returned my smile. Groebel caught me in the act. He looked at me, more disappointed than angry. I waited, showing contrition. He took his time, then slowly motioned me back to my seat. I behaved: I would sometimes push the envelope, but knew not to pierce it.

I celebrated my bar mitzvah a few days after the sinking of the *Bismarck*. The *shul* was packed for the festival of Shavuoth. Relatives and friends were there. The solemnity of the cantor's chanted call to the bar mitzvah boy, "*Yah-ah-MOD*" ("STAND YE"), which he repeated in his stentorian voice, moving up the scale, brought the *shul* to a hushed silence. Draped in my new *tallith* (prayer shawl) I walked up the aisle to the podium in the center of the sanctuary and ascended to the Torah. On cue, I intoned the introductory *Barkhu* (Bless the Lord.) The pitch was right, my voice, strong; I enjoyed its sound in the silence around me. The congregation's full-throated response, "Blessed be the Lord who is blessed for all eternity," washed over me like a bracing ocean wave. I was launched. Mr. Groebel had prepared me thoroughly. I cantillated the passages from the Torah and the prophets, in the same clear, sure voice, feeling in command — I even paused once, like the Torah reader would, and waited for the rising rumble of conversations to subside, then coasted joyously through the concluding blessings. I had passed the initiation rite into manhood.

In the afternoon about ten friends my age and my brother gathered around our dining table which had been extended for the occasion. I gave the regulation speech, one of the bar mitzvah boy's first grown-up acts. I had insisted on writing it without Mr. Groebel's help, in Hebrew. It was short and uninspired: mainly quotations, no substance. It had nothing of the *d'var torah*, the learned disquisition on a biblical or talmudic theme that marked some bar mitzvah speeches. But my friends and brother, even those among the guests who, like Menda, or Mayersdorf, that other class whiz, might have enjoyed an intellectual intermission, were glad to resume the savoring of the delicious cake my mother had baked, the hot chocolate, and the fruit.

I would henceforth put on *tefillin* (phylacteries) in the morning and fast on Yom Kippur, like a man, and be eligible for an *aliyah* (ascending to the Torah) during services. And I would be responsible for my sins. But sinning was not something I was much concerned about. True, I was not so very punctilious with my daily prayers, and I would hurry them along. But peccadilloes were not sins. Sinners, in my book, belonged in the broader category of "the others," along with contrabandists, drunks and the like. One was born into sin, or sank into it through some kind of infernal process. Or by seduction, like the men of Israel in the plains of Moab, taken down by the Moabite women.

The *tefillin* ritual made a difference, though: standing, sometimes with my father, in full morning prayer regalia — the prayer shawl around my shoulders, the black leather strap of the arm phylactery spiraling around my left forearm, and the black head phylactery strapped to my forehead — made me feel inducted in the confraternity of Jewish men.

✵ ✵ ✵

May 31, 1941:

The economic decree of October past is broadened:

All Jewish businesses (over and above the public establishments mentioned in the October decree) must display the sign "Jewish Enterprise" in the three languages.

Jewish-owned buildings must be declared.

Jewish-owned securities and bank funds must be deposited in designated currency banks. The title holder is allowed to withdraw a monthly amount for living expenses based on the number of mouths to feed.

Jews must be removed from the company boards on which they serve.

Moreover, the German authorities are empowered to appoint administrators to Jewish-owned enterprises, stop their activities, and transfer them to other parties.

"Getting ready to take it all away," was how my mother responded to the news. "Dispossess everyone." And after a pause: "They want us to perish."

"They'll perish first," my father retorted. Lowering his voice, "Enterprise owners, people with bank accounts have long since salted away all they could, I'm sure."

"I'm not worried about them," my mother concurred. "They'll manage. But all these struggling little shops."

"You think they'll be taking over a widow's little sewing shop?"

"You are making fun. If I understand what it says, they can order them to fold," my mother replied. "Some door-to-door collections for the poor we will have then," she continued with a sigh. "Where will they stop?" meaning, surely, Will they widen the net to include us? So far, we were not affected.

Nothing happened.

The decree's last clause orders Jews to turn in their radios by July 1.

My father turned in ours. Like most if not all Jews, he would have done so even in the absence of tax records (the sets were registered for the collection of the radio tax) out of fear of the random search, the rifling; the dread of standing assembled in a room and being glowered at by a Gestapo agent; the terror of the punishment.

My mother put a vase in the empty spot. My parents missed the German language broadcasts on the proscribed BBC — I had huddled with them on occasion; they had listened eagerly to its trusted reporting on the war's progress, its commentaries and morale boosts. A speech by Churchill would infuse new hope, a spell of tranquillity. It would show on their faces.

We also missed the music, the sweet-sounding aria, the light Mozart, the popular song. My mother went about her housework in silent busyness. We even missed the German broadcasts. We knew how to interpret their "strategic retreats," how to gauge their *Sondermeldungen*, the truly triumphant ones, repeated at frequent intervals, like the surrender, to Rommel, of Benghazi with its entire British garrison and tons of equipment and the *Sondermeldung* for its own sake, to give the impression of initiative and mastery in an otherwise lackluster stretch of war, like the sinking of a hundred thousand tons of Allied merchant shipping: "They are scraping the bottom of the barrel. They must be in trouble," my father had concluded.

The news, now, traveled by word of mouth. We also gleaned it from the collaborationist newspapers. We had become adept at reading between the lines. News was the prism through which we tried to glimpse our fate. My father would bring it home, along with the commentaries, arguments and bons mots of our strategists and political pundits.

"Jews. Fooling themselves," my mother once interjected. "Things will be all right just because they say so."

She paid closer attention to the pessimists, though still clinging, at times, to her glowing impressions of the Germany she had glimpsed in Frankfurt, before Hitler, during her visit with Aunt Esther.

"The people of Goethe and Schiller" — a worn phrase usually dripping with sarcasm, she once mused in the presence of a German Jew, as if hoping for a reaffirmation of her old sympathies.

"No more, Frau Grünstein," he said gently. "Today it is the people of Goebbels and Streicher. Alas. Hitler is dead-serious, and they believe his every word. I know them, Frau Grünstein. They will do anything he says."

"You mean his ravings about the end of the Jews in Europe?"

"Yes. They'll stop at nothing."

German Jews. They had always taken Hitler and the Germans at their word. The East European Jews had made fun of them for taking everything at face value, without a grain of salt, like the Germans, so gullible, couldn't even laugh at themselves. *Yekkes*, they, and other Jews with a similar mindset, were called. To many of those refugees Belgium had been a way station, no safer than

Poland before the German invasion, or Denmark and Norway. "Envious is what they are, of our undisturbed, comfortable life," had been the head-shaking reaction to the doomsayers. "They want us, also, to pull up stakes."

Envious, perhaps, they had appeared then, and gullible; believing in Germany's superior power. *"Bei uns in Deutschland"* ("Back home in Germany"), they would still say with pride, the dismissed intellectual and the dispossessed factory owner; the plumber who fixed the drain in our kitchen sink: he showed off his kit of gleaming, sophisticated, neatly arrayed German tools lying on their sides. "They don't have such tools anywhere, even in America. I'll make a fortune there. A Jewish Hitler in Palestine, that's what we need." They had moved on, most of those who had the means or the connections, and spread all over the globe, wherever they could find asylum.

My parents believed those German Jews now, but they still wanted to put their hope on the prestige and the civilizing power of the West to stay the barbarian's hand.

✢ ✢ ✢

One day in June an official-looking letter bearing German insignia arrived in the mail, addressed to me, *den Herrn Henri Grunstein*. I was to appear at the *Kommandantur* on the Belgiëlei the following Saturday at nine in the morning and bring the letter with me.

"I'll take him," my mother said to my father after getting over her consternation. "I don't want you in there." A softer tableau, that of a mother and child.

"I'll go by myself," I said.

"Don't talk nonsense. To walk in there like an abandoned child... Not to mention the suspicion it would arouse. Smart idea."

It was a short walk, that balmy Saturday, to the *Kommandantur*, a stately house near Boduognat Square. I wore my short-pants suit, a white shirt and tie. My mother wore a well-tailored but simple dress. She handed the letter to a *Feldgendarme*. He looked at it, glanced at his watch, said, *"folgen Sie mich"* ("follow me"), knocked on a door, waited for an answer, walked in, came out without the letter, let us in and closed the door behind us.

An officer sat at a desk, absorbed in some papers. When he finally looked up he asked my mother:

"*Ist das*" — he looked at the letter — "*Herr Henri Grünstein?*"

"*Jawohl. Das ist mein Sohn*" ("Yes. This is my son"), my mother answered. She spoke a fluent German.

"Please, sit down," he said, using "*Sie*," the formal plural. He motioned at a chair.

"I am sorry to have importuned you. But I must ask your son a few questions," he said as if it were a duty he could not shirk.

"*Bitte sehr*" ("As you please").

"How old are you, young man?" he asked me, using the familiar "du."

"Thirteen," I answered in Flemish.

"*Dreizehn. Ja*," he confirmed. "And to which school are you going?"

"*Het Koninklijk Atheneum.*"

"Atheneum?"

"*Gymnasium*" ("High school"), my mother clarified.

"*Ach so. Sehr schön.* You must be a very good student. Are you?"

"Well..." I was groping for an appropriately modest answer when my mother interjected:

"He does his best. *Er ist ein braver Junge*" ("He is a good boy").

"Tell me, who is Simon Bronner?"

"A friend, a school friend." From Tachkemoni. His family fled Germany in the thirties. Settled in Antwerp. Outran the invading Germans. Made it to America.

"He wrote you a letter."

"Oh..."

It was not his first. Why wasn't it delivered — censored, of course — like all other mail from abroad?

"Unfortunately, I cannot give it to you." He paused briefly. "It contains stamps."

"Oh."

Just like Bronner, I thought. Says and does. He would send me American stamps, he had written; I should send him European war stamps. Great, I had answered. Bronner was a sharp stamp trader. Good in math and Talmud. Impetuous at times: he had a chipped front tooth from a fall, or a fight. We had played ping pong. He and his older brothers had a special room just for ping pong. At age twelve Bronner already had his father's gruff voice.

"Stamps," the officer explained, "are used by spies to transmit secret messages. As a rule we hold such mail for three months. I must follow the rules. We figure that after three months the information is useless and we release the mail. Then you can come and pick up your stamps. Do you understand?"

"Yes." It sounded like the end of the interview.

"Tell you what," the officer said with a wave of the hand, "I'll let you see them."

Addressing my mother: "That's all I can do," he said.

"I fully understand. Why even... It isn't really..."

"*Doch, doch*" ("Yes, yes"), he insisted.

He pulled a fat envelope from a drawer. He emptied it on his desk. The stamps fell in a heap. He spread them out a bit. "Come closer," he enjoined me. I stepped up to his desk and leaned over slightly.

I saw a bunch of ordinary, postmarked stamps, with duplicates, even triplicates among them, and defective stamps, one with a corner torn off. I recognized my friend Bronner: quick, decisive, not one to agonize about a stamp and examining it for defects. He must have bought one of those glassine envelopes that are stuffed indiscriminately with stamps of whatever variety. Dismay gave way, almost instantly, to unease: did spies use duplicates and triplicates and all sorts of defects to convey secrets? I looked up at the officer to signal that I was through. I didn't want to have anything to do with that embarrassing and compromising heap.

"Now, that looks like an interesting one," he said as he pushed a stamp toward me.

I gave it a glance. I felt that I was watched, that I had been watched all along. He moved another one toward me, but I had already straightened myself up.

"Don't you want to look some more?" he asked engagingly.

"No, thank you."

"Your friend also wrote you a letter. Would you like to read it?"

"...Yes."

I could not have cared less. Once more, I felt ill at ease. I was aware of the widespread use of code in letter-writing. "We are staying indoors much of the time, because of the inclement weather," my mother's sister Surtshe had written from Kolbuszowa shortly after the German invasion in the summer of 1939. She would also refer to the Germans as "our good friends," or "our visitors," depending on the context. Menda and I would trade clever lines: his parents got mail from Poland and Holland. But "No" would have been an awkward, even unnatural response. And the officer was too obliging. I glanced at the first, note-size page only, recognizing Bronner's undisciplined handwriting, then put the letter down on the desk.

Turning to my mother: "Did you ever live in Germany?" the officer asked.

"No."

"Wherefrom do you speak such a good German?"

"From school."

"*Schön. Sehr schön.* Well, I have no other questions. You can go now. *Guten Tag.*"

"*Danke sehr. Guten Tag.*"

"*Goeden dag.*"

We left. Only after crossing the wide Belgiëlei with its tree-lined roadway flanked by tramway tracks did my mother break the silence:

"Whose idea was it?"

"Bronner's."

"It figures. They are sitting there, secure and worry-free." After a short pause — trying to glimpse their secure and worry-free life? — she continued, "We have to watch our every move. They'll use every pretext to oppress us."

My father was waiting at home, anxious.

"Nu?" he asked, his big gray-green eyes shining, his bushy eyebrows raised almost halfway up his large forehead.

"Don't ask. Bronner, that friend of his, sent him an envelope full of stamps from America."

"Yes?"

"Spies use stamps to communicate."

"So what happened?"

My mother recounted in a few sentences what had transpired at the *Kommandantur.* "And he wanted to know where my fluent German came from."

"What did you tell him?"

"From school. And that was that."

"Altogether quite civilized for a German," my father remarked.

"Yes, quite civilized. He even offered me a chair," my mother said mordantly. "They should meet a tortured death. You stand there as if you don't exist until he deigns to look up from his desk," she continued with contempt. "When I think of my visit with Esther in Frankfurt, how courteous, how helpful they could be."

"Why not? You were one pretty young woman."

"*Ja, das war einmal*" ("that was then"), my mother said wistfully.

"*Das ist noch immer*" ("it still is"), my father retorted.

"I meant their courteousness," my mother said.

They laughed. A private little joke, I sensed.

"Is our spy supposed to return in three months to pick up his stamps?" my father asked.

"No. Our spy *may* pick them up after three months. They can keep them."

"Were you afraid?" my father asked me.

"No."

"Nice stamps?"

"Lousy."

"Did you send him any?"

"No."

I was going to send him choice, carefully inspected German-issued stamps from the *Generalgouvernment* in Poland, among others. I was getting them off the envelopes that Aunt Surtshe sent us. I didn't mention it, feeling rather foolish now.

"Good you didn't."

That was the end of my correspondence with Simon Bronner.

My father and I went on to *shul*. His lateness elicited unspoken inquiries — raised eyebrows with the slight uptick of the chin. The brief explanation earned me broad smiles and warm, congratulatory handshakes. They made me feel important. I walked over to greet Uncle Avrum, my father's brother. He knew about the German summons. He put his arm around my shoulders:

"Tell me," he said, "were you on time at the *Kommandantur*?"

"Yes. Of course."

"You see? You can be on time. Why are you always late for *shul?*"

I did not answer. I was not going to give up my Saturday sleep-ins.

"The Most High," my uncle continued, "is more important than the German."

I felt chastened. I returned to my seat.

✳ ✳ ✳

Aunt Surtshe wrote from Kolbuszowa. My father was standing by the dining room table, reading aloud; he often would, with letters of moment — mail from Poland was opened with the dread of bad tidings. My mother would listen intently, taking in the thrust of the missive before reading it for herself: sharing the fresh news at a slight remove dampened the eventual shock.

My maternal grandmother had died, Aunt Surtshe informed us. At the age of seventy-one. Heart problems. The letter arrived after the thirty-day mourning period, sparing my mother the hardship of sitting *shiva.*

"In her own home," she whispered. "At least that much."

"She died in time," my father later said to me.

I understood.

June 22, 1941: The Germans invade Russia, opening an immense front.

So there. The age-old lust for *Lebensraum* and the vast resources in the east, the lure of winning where Napoleon had lost, the raw desire to crush that other tyrant. And nothing to stop them: sitting pretty from the Arctic Circle to the Spanish border and astride the Mediterranean where the British lost Greece, Crete and Cyrenaika with a heavy toll in men and matériel, in ships and planes. Britain, though undefeated, was not a threat. Our strategists tapped their foreheads: To have missed that one, when it should have been obvious from the start! We were exulting: To have Russia on our side was as sweet, almost, as having America join the fray. Finally, the war they deserved; they would bleed to death. "As long as they don't take us down with them." Thus spoke a lone pessimist.

But joy turned into anguish. Within weeks the Germans had knifed their way into the Russian heartland, advancing on Moscow and Leningrad and across the Ukraine, taking hundreds of thousands of prisoners. The puppet press splashed across the front pages the exuberant and detailed German communiqués, with maps of the war theaters and gushing commentaries. The BBC news, which traveled through the grapevine, would confirm the German triumphs. Was Russia going the way of France?

Weeks stretched into months. The Russians were holding up. Then came the first snow, falling heavy. It caught the Germans in the field, short of Moscow. Hope surged.

Aunt Surtshe wrote from Kolbuszowa around the time the Germans invaded Russia.

"We moved into a small, overcrowded space," my father read.

"Oy," my mother groaned. "Driven from their home. A ghetto. A real ghetto." She looked stricken. "Surrounded with Poles."

"For clothes we can get food."

"Out with it right away!" my mother said fiercely. "Pack and send. Let's keep only what we need."

My father dispatched regularly a sackful of neatly folded clothes. He liked packing and worked methodically at it.

"That should keep them going for a good while," he would say, contented yet subdued, after readying a shipment.

"The clothes keep us alive," Surtshe wrote.

"To keep them alive, if only I can keep them alive," my mother said, pursing her lips. "Having to rely on the kindheartedness of the Poles," she murmured, her voice trailing off in a sigh. In her eyes, the same distant, anguished look she had upon returning, before the war, from a visit to her older sister Khantshe whom she revered and who was sick with cancer. "Oy, bitter, bitter."

Close in age and the youngest of seven siblings, the two sisters had been inseparable. They had kept up a correspondence ever since my parents left Poland in 1930. They had survived the pogrom of 1919 together.

My mother once recounted with bitterness how one dark night during the pogrom — she was nineteen — she and Surtshe eluded rampaging peasants by running across the fields to the house of a Polish acquaintance, a *mieszczan*, she added in Polish, a townsman, to set him apart from the peasants. The pursuers banged on the door: they wanted the Jewesses. The son in the family, a Polish nationalist, urged his father to turn the Jewesses out. "The *mieszczan* and his wife kept us all night until we could return safely home," she said in a calm, almost reverential tone.

Kolbuszowa bore the brunt of a pogrom pandemic that started in Rzeszow and spread to four other towns — partitioned Poland had just been reunited into an independent state and the peasantry was celebrating. Nine Jews were killed in my parents' hometown. Women and girls were raped.

My father had also been able to outrun his knife-wielding pursuers. For a long time afterwards he felt a lingering pain in his back which no doctor could alleviate or explain, until a German "*Nervenartzt*" ("neurologist"), probing into his life, concluded that it was all in his head. The pain stopped.

"The pogrom lasted three days," my mother continued." A special police unit stopped it. They executed two of the *pogromniks* in front of the courthouse, when the looting of Jewish property had spilled over to the post office. I went to watch the executions." Bringing her hand to her chest, "It quickened my heart," my mother said with a glee undimmed by the intervening decades.

✡ ✡ ✡

The first year of high school ended. I could now pin a second star on my black velvet *Koninklijk Atheneum* cap. We got our grades. Menda came in first, Roald Bingen, second. Their grades hovered shades below 100/100, way ahead of the rest of us. (More than any other Christian classmate, Bingen had helped Menda and me keep up with the class despite our absences on Saturdays and the Jewish holidays.)

My ranking was a respectable third, though I put in more work than Menda. I had to drill Latin words into memory; he knew them after one reading. Once, as our class stood in line at our assigned post in the courtyard, I found out that he had overlooked the vocabulary we would be tested on first thing that morning. I fed it to him under my breath as we walked two abreast, up the stairs and down the hallway; I was reprimanded twice for breaking the rule of silence. Menda's was the perfect score. I messed up two out of ten Latin word formations.

We were let out — free for two months. I soon realized that mine was not freedom: I found myself with nothing to do. My mother would send us out to the park, my brother and me, to get some fresh air. But I had outgrown last summer's marble games and roller-skating. My friends from high school did not frequent the park. It did not cross my mind to venture into the "wilder," more solitary areas, the vast "non-Jewish" park, certainly not with my brother in tow.

My father would take us on Sunday morning walks. He had taken me, before I had to spend my Sunday mornings in Hebrew class, on walks to the flea market, or the harbor, by the *Steen* castle where the *Flandria* tour boats were moored. The memory of those delightful ambles never surfaced during our circum-scribed strolls in the occupied city.

Sometimes Mother took us along on her errands, but I found that just as confining, and often preferred to stay at home. Swimming in the nearby pool on the Nerviersstraat — a mod-ern, gleaming facility — was out of the question: a frivolous exer-cise in these troubled times, downright reckless, in my mother's eyes, given the risk of physical injury inherent in all sports. The family was to hunker down: hard times might be closing in on us. It dawned on me, one day, that she had stopped singing the Yiddish, German, and Polish love songs and light-hearted ditties I still remembered from my childhood.

My brother and I were left to our own devices. We had no common games or common interests: he was almost six years my junior. I had never been much of a big brother to him, aside from having to watch over him in the park, or at home, in the absence of our parents. And he resented me in that role. He had ceased looking up to his older brother the day I played a cruel trick on him. It happened before the war; I was eleven, he was six. I would take him to the Sunday afternoon movies at the Cinéac on the De Keyserlei to see American cartoons, or Tarzan, or Stan Laurel and Oliver Hardy. Often Manny and another cousin, Charles, a son of Aunt Khantshe, both only two years younger than I, would pick us up — we lived clos-est to the Cinéac. Sometimes Rachel, Charles' sister (my age), would be of the party. (With so many of us running interfer-ence we managed, on occasion, to have my brother slip through without paying.)

One Sunday, I didn't want him to tag along. I wanted unhampered fun with the big boys. As the three of us were getting ready to leave, my brother grabbed hold of me, crying, and would not let go. My mother looked at me, wondering at first, then imploring, Why don't you? hoping that I would take him along without being ordered to do so. She didn't want to foist him on me. "Tell you what," I told my brother, "let's play instead a game of hide and seek. You hide first." His face lit up. He ran to the rear of the apartment. We slipped away. I heard his scream as we ran down the steps.

Decades later the memory surfaced: the scene by the front door was etched in my mind. I would hear my brother's scream and feel a surge of guilt and shame.

The weekdays stretched, boring and aimless, from breakfast to supper. I had long since read all the books I possessed, of Jules Verne, Karl May, Fenimore Cooper, Jack London, Robert Stevenson, Dostoyevsky, the mystery novels. And we were not buying new books; it never occurred to me. Visiting a bookstore, or even picking up a five-franc, low-quality-paper pocket book at the stationer's were peacetime treats. We patronized food stores only, and the Jewish shoemaker. The public library did not come to mind either; I had never visited it. (Out of bounds now, anyway: quite a ways outside our tight perimeter.) Books, before the war, were bought, or borrowed, from friends, or from the Hebrew class library at Tachkemoni — I had slogged through *Robinson Crusoe* in non-vocalized Hebrew in fourth grade. "You'll like this one," Silberstein, our teacher, had said to me during library hour one Friday morning. It was a mesmerizing read. Robinson Crusoe was my first hero.

I began to browse through my parents' books, an eclectic collection in four languages: like many Jews from West Galicia, the part of Poland under Austrian rule until the end of World War I, my parents were fluent in Polish and German. My father, an autodidact, had mastered Hebrew as well. Yiddish was the mother tongue.

I passed over the sacred texts and related works of rabbinical commentaries my father had brought from Poland. I looked more closely at the books bearing his "ex libris" imprint followed by "Kolbuszowa": Zionist writings in Hebrew and German — Achad

Ha'am, Herzl, Hess; the Hebrew poets of the national renais-
sance; works of world literature in non-vocalized Hebrew such as
Anna Karenina, and Knut Hamsun's *Hunger*; Yiddish authors; fat
yearbooks of the scholarly Hebrew periodical *Ha-t'kufah*; and a
number of other books and publications.

There were Polish books, mother's: she was in love with the
tongue of Adam Mickiewicz, from her days in high school before
World War I. She raised me in Polish, until kindergarten brought
about a shift in languages: I took to French — I spoke it in class.
My mother dropped Polish — she took her French lessons a bit
more seriously. And Yiddish became the sole language spoken at
home. I forgot Polish, over time, but remembered enough words
and verb structures to understand what my parents wanted to
hide from me, mainly the unflattering goings-on in town and in
the family: an illicit affair, a divorce, the dissolute behavior of a
relative, or a rumor of dishonesty attaching to a diamantaire. (A
blemished reputation was quite damning in a trade where dealers, Jew and non-Jew alike, sealed a transaction with a handshake
and the words *mazel 'n brookhe* (good luck and blessing), a business
practice as binding as an oath or a signed contract.) My mother
kept up her Polish with some of her acquaintances. But German
had become my parents' primary reading language: works by
Thomas Mann, Franz Kafka, Max Brod, Heinrich Graetz, and
others, almost all acquired in Antwerp, lined the shelves. My father loved books. And he loved to buy books.

"When will you read all of this?" my mother had asked about
some of his purchases.

"I'll get around to them. This set just came out. It's a must."

Or, "That fat work of reference belongs in a professor's library. How often will you reach for it?"

"It matters not how often," my father had replied.

"It just takes up space. And it costs money."

My mother loved the thrill of a good story. She favored the
novels of the German-Jewish writers Lion Feuchtwanger, Jacob
Wassermann, Franz Werfel. Yet, ever since the outbreak of war,
she had not opened a book: "Nerves," she would plead. She kept
busy, mending socks, sewing buttons, knitting. She would pause,
at times, with the familiar searching look in her brown eyes —
they seemed to darken. My father would settle down with a book,
or with the Torah portion of the week after his *Shabbas* nap.

I spotted Stefan Zweig's "Selected Novellas." They had shortness and my mother's rave review to recommend them. I opened the black-linen-covered book with golden lettering. I had never read German before. I picked a passage at random: the language was more difficult than I had been used to hearing, with a much richer vocabulary, longer sentences with numerous clauses and sub-clauses. I had followed without straining my parents' conversations with German Jews — they revolved mainly around Hitler, finding a safe haven, and the *Bei-uns-in-Deutschland* reminiscences reflecting, at times, unfavorably on Belgium ("jealousy and uprootedness speaking," my mother would remark). I had understood the German radio broadcasts, their propaganda and their war communiqués. I had even spoken a simple German with my cousins from Frankfurt.

I decided to tackle Stefan Zweig starting with the first novella, *Running Amok.* What I managed to understand with the help of Flemish and Yiddish — languages kindred to German — and from the context carried me through the narrative without the help of a dictionary.

Little by little the pace picked up: the retakes took less time, they were less frequent. The story emerged, flowing ever more freely, of a competent physician running, mindless, hurtling, with open eyes, into an abyss of his own making. It could only happen out there, I mused, in the colonies, in Asia. Even the word "amok" was from over there.

A couple of weeks later I finished the second novella, "Letter from an Unknown Woman," the long confession of a woman's lifelong, obsessive, secret love for a man, ever since, as a twelve-year old girl, she had caught sight of him. He had moved into the apartment across the hall from hers, a writer, young and handsome, with his valet, and with stacks of leather-bound books. He knew her only one night. She bore his child. It died at age seven. Afflicted with the same disease that felled her child, she wrote him that fifty-page letter, agitated, yet so eloquent; in one long night. "I shall no longer be alive when you read these lines." He seemed to recall, vaguely, a little girl across the hall, a candlelight dinner, a night of amorous abandon. He tried, in vain, to summon a face: a faded memory, like a distant, disquieting music.

Each story left me perplexed: I had been afforded a glimpse into the vagaries of the heart. A mystery, to me. So unlike the people in our circle. Or even outside it.

Those reading spells broke up the day and lightened somewhat the weight of time.

I also taught myself how to read Yiddish. It is written phonetically using Hebrew characters, but it circumvents the absence of vocalization in Hebrew with a few simple conventions that do away with the guesswork. The lack of reading practice slowed my pace to a crawl: I had to decipher the long words. I could read German faster. My speed increased gradually as I read on, but perusing a Yiddish text remained laborious. I was pleased with having overcome another challenge and left it at that.

When reading fatigue set in, I was at a loss for what to do.

Once I walked the length of the park, and, stepping for the first time since the outbreak of war outside our tight, self-imposed perimeter, I took stately Maria-Theresialei where it converged with the Quellinstraat. The shade of the overarching foliage gave the short avenue the feel of an exclusive enclave. I had entered another world.

A couple of minutes later I alighted on wide, tree-lined Frankrijklei. I had plied that avenue on occasional Saturday or Sunday afternoons before the war. I used to stare at the solid burgher houses, at the ornate stone buildings, at the stately mansions: the Antwerp of the landlords, handed down the generations. Jews like us rented. Our only possessions were the family silver, the photographs, and the sacred books my father had brought from Poland. I had wondered then, Who were the people behind those tall curtained-off windows?

I stepped up on the avenue, glancing avidly at the imposing structures. They looked as I remembered them — familiar and inscrutable. Yet something had changed: they no longer seemed the impregnable castles from before the war. Didn't the Germans requisition sumptuous abodes for their officers and police? I imagined the wealthy owners moving stealthily behind the draped windows, between the fabric-covered walls hung with old masterworks... vulnerable, yes, was how I pictured them, more so than the common people of modest means, the workers who kept things running and drew nobody's attention. The Germans might dispossess the rich, just so, at random, because they could.

That was what black-booted conquerors in command cars did. Us they robbed because we were Jews. A big difference. With one thin, common strand. I felt less estranged from them.

At the end of Frankrijklei I turned left onto Maria Henriëttalei, reentered the park at one end of the southern roadway and walked its entire length to our haunt at the Loosplaats. The tour had left a sobering impression.

The days were at their longest. Night would start its slow descent at ten o'clock. The long hours of slowly graying light felt at times like an unnerving wait for darkness to fall, for a new day to dawn. We missed, on balmy evenings, the short after-dinner stroll to the park, the occasional encounter with acquaintances. The vacations by the North Sea and amidst the fragrant pinewoods of Heide were of a lost world; they did not come to mind.

Weekends brought relief, with our Sabbath, and theirs. The candle lighting ritual at home on Friday evenings had become more intense. After reciting silently the blessing over the candles, my mother, head bent, hands cupping eyes and cheeks, would whisper in Yiddish — we could hear the sibilant sounds. She would emerge looking serene, or worried, saying, "I prayed my heart out, for us all," and get busy. My father and I would recite the afternoon and evening prayers. At seven or thereabouts we would gather for dinner: white tablecloth, the good silver; *kiddush* (the sanctification of the Sabbath over wine); *zmeerus* (the hymns) — my father would sit back, relaxed, and modulate in his pleasant voice the joyous Eastern European melodies, in the Ashkenazic pronunciation. I accompanied him. The hymn before grace, the *sheer hama'alot* (the song of ascents, Psalm 126), we sang, with my brother joining in, in the Sephardic taught at Tachkemoni. My mother would sit in silence during the devotional singing — a man's thing.

The long evening ushered in "a day that is all good" — nothing happened, nothing would happen on Shabbat, a day when life's tumultuous onrush subsided. The soaring chant of the *hazan*, on the morrow, the chatter during the Torah reading, the smiles, the handshakes, the comfort of being surrounded by one's own people suffused the morning with cheer. By my parents' afternoon nap and the stillness in the house I knew that the world, our world, was at rest. Shabbat colored every mood, even boredom — I did not feel the urge to drive it away. Shabbat surrounded us on the street, like an aura. Its atmosphere pervaded my uncle Avrum's dining room. He would stand profiled, a short man with a long, untrimmed beard, in the large window, and study a tractate of the Talmud spread open on top of a credenza. I would face my cousin Shloimeh across the dining table, trying to concentrate on some fine talmudic argument — he had offered to tutor me on Shabbat afternoons, to keep up the study practice begun at Tachkemoni. Aunt Rakhtshe and Shloimeh's younger sister Rookhel — she was eighteen, he was twenty six — would read. Tractates and books got slammed shut the moment my parents walked in with my brother: time for the parents to schmooze, for tea with cake, for my cousins to engage my brother, the benjamin, in teasing banter that he kept going with his quick-witted, irreverent repartees.

Shabbat also reigned at Menda's: on an overcast afternoon we would sit around in the semi-darkness (lights could not be turned on) talking, telling stories. His mother would lead us in song. Even the long evening past curfew-time felt lighter: Shabbat was not over until nightfall. And there was another, different Sabbath day to hold back the coming week.

I liked Sundays. The shops were closed. The churchgoers in their Sunday attire brought color and decorum to the streets and to the expanse of sidewalk in front of the church on Loosplaats, where they gathered in friendly clusters after Mass, just as we had done after synagogue services before the war. The cafés were alive with the ring of voices and the perpetual swirl of tobacco smoke. There was a lightness in the air, a sense of respite. For us, the mundane was reasserting itself, but without rushing in: errands only — the bakery and the grocery nearby opened for a couple of hours in the morning; light chores around the house; a casual visit with Menda. My father would take my brother out for a walk.

Curfew time on Sunday marked the passing of the two Sabbaths. Soon the week would be upon us, the bustle in the streets, the stretches of boredom at home. On Monday, I would be looking forward to the next weekend and longing for high school.

✻ ✻ ✻

One day the bell rang: it was my cousin Harry.

My parents looked at him, dumbstruck: "People would give anything to be safe, in Nice. And you come back!? What got into your head? Why didn't you stick with the Grosses and the Leschkovitzes?"

"They left Nice."

"Without you..."

"They had visas. They left me parting-money. Quite generous."

"Money."

Within weeks Harry announced that he was returning to France, on a smuggling mission. My parents were unable to talk him out of it, nor could the friends he had been living with since the death of his mother, my Aunt Khantshe.

Shortly after his departure a fat envelope arrived. It was taped over with the censor's brown strip. Harry had written from a prison in France a long letter in Flemish expressing regrets for what he had done, apologies for the trouble he had caused, for having identified my parents to his interrogators. It struck me as a long, last farewell.

My mother was heartbroken — "If Khantshe knew, she would return to her grave," she muttered — and terrified: would the Germans want to know more about the uncle? There was no place to go.

As the days went by, my father regained some color and appetite.

We never heard from Harry again. He was twenty. He was deported to Auschwitz from the assembly camp of Drancy, near Paris.

✻ ✻ ✻

The Germans had blocked the diamond exchange's two entrances. The word "razzia" ("raid") had buzzed through the great trading hall like the whir of an arrow. The dealers who carried undeclared goods, my father among them (he had sought to raise cash), threw their small, silk-paper-wrapped packets of diamonds in the trash cans, or stuck them with glue paper to the underside of the tables. The Germans knew where to look. They retrieved the loot, even from the spittoons, searched the dealers and led away a couple of them caught with undeclared merchandise.

"Only money damage," my mother said, trying to calm my father who was visibly shaken. "Thank God for that."

His drawn, pale mien did not leave him for the rest of the day. He spoke little for several days. "It's eating him," my mother told me. "The fear, the humiliation as much as the loss." A visceral fear of their raw, unbridled power had drained the blood from his face. "I worry about him," my mother confided to me.

"The bourse must be empty," my mother once wondered at the dinner table.

"There are many fewer people, I am told," my father said. "They still meet there. To arrange deals. The transactions take place elsewhere."

"How cumbersome. What if it's no deal? They go back, this one for another buyer, that one for another source?"

"Some, apparently, are still taking risks. Or else they turn to *our* buyers" — a mini-consortium of four diamantaires who were buying up diamonds privately for high-ranking German officers.

"The sellers are pretty much at their mercy, aren't they?"

"It's a made-to-order buyer's market."

"Working for the Germans," my mother said with bitterness. "Getting rich on the backs of others. What some will do for money."

"Getting rich, and feeling secure."

"You mean, they can count on German protection?"

"Most probably. As long as they don't pull a fast one."

Le carré d'as (the four aces), that group was called: they liked playing a foursome of cards, Jews living in the same apartment building as one of them knew to tell. How did they get in cahoots with the Germans, I wondered. Who approached whom? How? Since when did Germans pay for what they wanted? What exactly went on between the Germans and the four Jews? Why four? Was there so much business to transact? A group of mystery men they were to me, except for the one I had met, the father of a schoolmate, a short, pudgy man.

I did not ask any of the questions that were popping up in my mind. Keeping silent was a way of signaling that I would not "carry out of the room" what was being discussed in the privacy of the home. I also knew that some of my questions would strike my parents as naïve, foolish even. To them it was a clear case of people who had jumped at the opportunity to deal with German officers bargain-hunting for diamonds on the sly — goods seized in raids ended up in the coffers of the Reich or in the pocket of a Gestapo agent. I also learned, after the war, how the collusion had started: one member of the quartet, a refugee from Germany, had run into an acquaintance in German uniform. The encounter led to a business relationship. More officers got included. There was enough demand to occupy four diamantaires.

A year later, in the summer of '42, when thousands got their "work" orders and the sweeping roundups would turn Antwerp into a teeming hunting ground, the officers secured the safe passage of the foursome and their families to Switzerland.

✲ ✲ ✲

Life hardly changed. Early on in the Occupation my father had taken over most of the shopping and other errands. It often meant standing in line by the bakery or the butcher shop. Food stores might be sold out before the end of the Jew-curfew at seven in the morning. The baker would set aside a loaf for us, the butcher, an order of meat. We bought much food on the black market, from the shopkeepers, from the milkman. There was no shortage of fruit and vegetables. In the pre-curfew days my father would join the queue by the bakery as early as five in the morning, before dawn. I would spell him off at six, for half an hour, on my days off from school. That would give him time to wash up and shave. He would then return and I would go back to sleep.

My father also devoted much time to the Tachkemoni school. He had joined the committee that kept the Jewish studies alive by raising money in the community and hiring Hebrew teachers. He and other volunteers had replaced some of the committee members who had fled or had resigned. It was a collegial group of men who liked to meet and work together. And to trade news.

My mother was absorbed in the running of her household, its rules and rhythm unchanged by the Occupation and its decrees: regular, balanced meals with snacks of fruit in between. Always a neat, bright tablecloth — a white one on Shabbat — covering the kitchen table. She baked delicious cakes for the Sabbath. A maid came on wash and heavy cleaning days. My mother did the ironing. She would put away the neatly pressed shirts, underwear and socks, and take out, twice a week, a change of clothing for my brother and me, preventing us from upsetting her ordered stacks in the armoire. Everything had its place. She brooked no clutter.

Her life outside the house was limited to errands and to meeting one or another acquaintance, or conversing at length with Madame Zangen, my friend Menda's mother, on their way back from the neighborhood grocer.

Our pundits were mostly upbeat, as always: the Germans were embroiled on three fronts now, the Russian, the Atlantic, and the Mediterranean. Russia would deal the final blow.

"But how long will that game last?" my mother wondered aloud.

"You always come back to that same question," my father replied. "We *will* slog through."

That summer of 1941 I sensed more keenly than during the busy school year how fixated my parents were on the here and now, on getting by. Lying low, like birds in an exposed nest. I noticed more readily my father's thin-lipped silences, my mother's distant, pensive or worried stares. She could tell from the expression on his face, from his demeanor, the moment he walked in the door, if there was a new decree, or sad news, or if he had simply crossed Germans on the sidewalk. Just two soldiers walking abreast projected the power of the German Reich:

"They should get an apoplexy," he grumbled one day. "The heart beats like a robber's."

"Can't you cross over to the other side?"

"Not on the Quentin Matsijslei," my father retorted. The park was on the other side.

"One should give them a wide berth," my mother said with a sigh while looking away, trying to suggest, not instruct.

"One can also exaggerate and invite sporting abuse," my father said testily. "When there will be a decree ordering Jews to get off the sidewalk, I will get off the sidewalk." And, after a pause: "They are pretty restrained, one must admit. It's just the sight of them, the fright. It's a relief to see one of them strutting with a Flemish whore. At least you know what's on his mind."

And I would overhear more low-voiced exchanges between my parents about Nice or Switzerland. They would stand side by side in the dining room, or in the kitchen, my father looking pained, my mother, cupping her face or wringing her hands, debating whether to go or not to go, usually after another family in our circle had taken the leap.

"I'm leaving the decision to you," I heard her say once. "I'll go along with whatever you..."

There was silence.

One day, they disappeared into the bedroom. Had it come down to specifics? Smuggler? Finances? Logistics? False papers? A long adventurous journey, white mountains, green valleys, lakes. The vacation land of the rich. A bit scary, but exciting.

We stayed.

I couldn't wait for classes to start.

✡ ✡ ✡

A late August, 1941 decree confines the Jews of Belgium to four cities: Antwerp, Brussels, Liège, and Charleroi. It also imposes on them a curfew: they are to remain in their domiciles listed in the Jew-registers between 8:00 PM and 7:00 AM, except in Antwerp where the seven-to-seven curfew decreed four months earlier in the wake of the Easter Monday pogrom remains in effect.

Aunt Esther wrote from New York — West 93rd street; a newsy letter, with Rosh Hashanah wishes for a happy New Year. They had arrived after a long stay in Cuba, via Spain and Portugal.

✡ ✡ ✡

My brother started third grade at Tachkemoni. I started my second year of high school in the A-class for top students, with Menda and Roald Bingen. Zalcman ended up in the B-class; Strassberg, in the C-class. Menda and Roald got competition from the star of the first-year A-class, intense yet reserved Janneke Peeters. The three whizzes would routinely pen the Latin homework assignment during the following period and hand it to the needy among us, making sure to exclude anyone of the pro-German chaps; that bunch got an assist from Fransen, another pro-German leaning student. The recipients of this manna were savvy enough to make some minor changes or slip an error or two into the copies they handed in.

I was rubbing elbows with my classmates again, walking home with friends. We waded into geometry, a new discipline. We wrestled with the denser texts in the *De Viris Illustribus Urbis Romae*; the anthology's editor even included some simplified chapters of Livius. We tackled the intricacies of French grammar; studied the history of Europe, the geography of the world; made forays into Flemish and French literature. Even the weekly Jewish religion hour with rabbi Sapira was sometimes interesting. (Belgian law required public high schools to provide an hour a week of instruction in each student's religion. Those who opted out of the religion hour were to take "Morals," a course in ethics with occasional digressions — depending on the professor's inclinations — into political science, even philosophy.) Once, rabbi Sapira talked animatedly about the universal character of our religion. As proof he quoted from a High Holidays prayer, the *Nessaneh toikef*: "All mankind passes before Thee like a flock of sheep."

"*All* mankind," he emphasized. "To be counted. On Judgment Day." He paused for effect.

I found it strange that he had plucked a verse from a prayer rather than quoting the prophets or mentioning Jonah's mission to the heathen of Nineveh. But then, I found the rabbi to be rather strange, a thin man with a yellowish, creased face, like an old apple, a soft voice and a hard edge. So God was looking after everybody. That was fine with me.

Only later did I start wondering: The God of Abraham, Isaac and Jacob. The God of Israel. The God who chose the land He promised us as His dwelling place. Hadn't He pegged us for preferential treatment?

"Is our religion a universal one?" I asked Menda on the way home.

He stood still, looked up, frowning, let out a long "Uh" trailing off in a sigh: "No. We can't claim that," he said. "Ours is a national religion."

There was a short, unpleasant episode: the school had instituted a daily, mid-morning milk break to boost the diet of its students in a time of food shortages. We would file, a few classes at a time, into the service area in the basement where long tables were lined with white bowls of boiled milk — it was still luke-warm. I would hold my breath to cut out the smell while ingurgitating the nauseating beverage.

Strictly-observant Jews abstained: the white, enameled bowls were not kosher since they also served to hold non-kosher food. Rabbi Sapira informed us that he had requested that the Jewish students get distinctive bowls to be kept separate from the regular, white ones. I was annoyed: religiosity gone haywire, I felt; setting us apart. Our principal, Dr Adhémar de Smet, announced the two-bowl régime, with a few words about dietary purity laws and with an enjoinder — strongly worded, strict disciplinarian that he was — to be respectful of other peoples' religious customs, for they embodied spiritual values that all religions share. It was heartwarming, especially under German occupation, to hear someone learned and in authority treat us and our religion with respect. But where, for the uninitiated, was the spiritual in a separation of bowls? Our friend Bingen, a devout Catholic, might be open to an explanation. "But how many," I pondered, "will think that their white bowls, to us, are unclean because Gentiles are using them?"

The following day there was, in the service area, a separate table set with a few yellow bowls. I was embarrassed by that self-imposed separateness. I kept my place at my class's table.

"Shouldn't you be sitting over there?" a gentile classmate asked with a bemused smile.

He must think that we are strange, I felt, and stand-offish.

I felt guilty for shunning fellow Jews. Menda was among them. I did not touch the white bowl, not without trepidation.

To my relief, the program lasted less than two weeks: it was deemed cumbersome and disruptive.

The Moriah *shul* was packed on Rosh Hashanah — the second under the Occupation, the first under the persecutions. Less-observant, even non-observant Jews had come to hear the sounding of the *shofar*, the ram's horn.

The *hazan* was leading us through the holiday liturgy. It was studded with many *piyyutim*, devotional, often arcane, poems that were read or chanted responsively. I enjoyed some, even tried to remember a catchy or gripping stanza, but gave up on the difficult ones, despite knowing many or all of the words. Tachkemoni had not prepared us for the depth and intricacy of the High Holidays liturgy.

The worshippers had settled into their cozy shul-going ways, diluting some of their devotions with low-key chatter. Yet when the congregation rose for the *Aveenu Malkaynu* (our Father, our King) High Holidays prayer, a collective fervor gripped the assembled; the long litany of supplications gushed forth like a torrent:

"Our Father, our King, we have sinned before Thee.
. . . .
"Our Father, our King, renew for us a good year.
"Our Father, our King, abolish all evil decrees against us.
"Our Father, our King, annul the plans of our enemies.
. . . .
"Our Father, our King, rid us of every oppressor and adversary.
. . . .
"Our Father, our King, remove pestilence, sword, famine, captivity, destruction, iniquity and persecution from the people of Thy covenant.
. . . .
"Our Father, our King, have compassion on us, on our children and our infants.
. . . .
"Our Father, our King, act for the sake of those who were slaughtered for proclaiming Thy Oneness.
. . . .
"Our Father, our King, do it for Thy sake if not for ours.

Deep-seated anguish had risen to the surface and spent itself. The last supplication was sung with abandon by cantor and congregation:

"Our Father, our King, be gracious to us and answer us, though we have no merits; deal charitably with us and save us."

The Torah reading that followed was drowned, as usual, by the rising rumble of conversations; among the women as well, in the glass-paneled galleries. The *gabbai* (beadle) had to pound on the lectern to quash the ever-resurging noise.

Silence fell when the *hazan* made his way to the podium for the sounding of the ram's horn. Of medium height, broad-faced with big, velvety-black eyes and high, reddish cheekbones, he had a pitch-black Herzl-like beard showing fleshy red lips, and long earlocks curling down in thick spirals. His *tallith* covered his head and came down over his broad shoulders. He looked intense and powerful.

He intoned the opening words of the prefatory prayer, and a rolling thunder of male voices broke over my head. After the introductory blessings, silence fell once more. The *hazan* stood in the *shofar*-blowing stance, holding the tip of the ram's horn between index and middle fingers of the left hand, by his lips, and the widening body of the horn, twisting sideways and up, in his right hand. The *gabbai*, leaning over the lectern, uttered in an undertone the first prompt, and a note soared, strong, pure, demanding. The *gabbai* kept calling forth, and the *hazan* kept sending aloft the ancient sounds, the single blasts, the broken threesomes, the staccato sequences, wresting them without a sputter from the exacting instrument. They were to ascend and plead before the Throne for the pardon of our sins. Rosh Hashanah. Judgment Day.

The *hazan* then led the return of the two Torah scrolls to the ark. He chanted the reader's *Kaddish* and the *Musaf* service started with the silent recitation of the long *Ameedah* prayer. Soon we would reach that other gripping moment in the Rosh Hashanah service, the prayer known by its Hebrew opening words, *Oo-nessaneh toikef* (let us therefore proclaim forcefully).

The men stand shoulder to shoulder. The small children sit in the pews, sucking on candy or pulling at the fringes of their fathers' prayer shawls, or stand in their fathers' seats and look around. The bigger boys are squeezed between their elders. My brother is standing to my father's left. I am standing to my father's right, with one foot in the aisle. From my forward spot I have a clear view of the *hazan*. I can see his face in profile. He stands at his lectern, facing the open ark. His *tallith* covers his head and shoulders and flows down his back like a tent. He is flanked by two little boys, his sons.

He intones on a high note the introductory verse to the *Nessaneh toikef* and a deep rumble erupts and fills the *shul*, "Let us therefore proclaim forcefully the holiness of the day, for this day is awe-inspiring...." Silence returns with the end of the prayer's first section. The *hazan* repeats it in a modulated, vibrant chant. His two boys, their earlocks dangling at the edge of the lectern, chime in resolutely, a choir of two. Now and then, the *hazan* drapes his sons with his large, black-sleeved arms, cupping a little shoulder with each hand. He presses gently, and the boys' voices rise with their father's or sing in counterpoint. It is riveting. "The day of judgment is here!" rings like a clarion call. Silence returns with the end of the prayer's first section: "Thou makest all living souls pass before Thee,...fixing each creature's lifespan and inscribing their fate."

The three then lead the worshippers into he next section: "On Rosh Hashanah one's destiny is inscribed, and on Yom Kippur it is sealed." The *hazan* continues, in a low voice: "How many shall pass away and how many shall be brought into existence; who shall live and who shall die.... Who by fire and who by water; who by the sword and who by wild beasts; who from hunger and who from thirst.... Who by the plague.... Who by strangulation...." The words are searing. I turn to glance at the assembled men: they sway in prayer; faces taut, pale in the yellow light; intense, anguished stares. The Germans... It's clear it's the Germans they see. I see them too: behind every fateful decree in the *Nessaneh toikef* looms, in the distance, a helmeted German, legs spread, the barrel of a rifle pointing upward, a hand clasping the shoulder strap. The soldiers' faces are washed out, blank. I spot Isaac, my mother's cousin; a tall man. He is standing in the rear, in the dense crowd of men without a seat, looking at me. He is holding his two-year old girl on his arm; she has beautiful brown eyes and peachy-red cheeks, the kind that draw smiles from grown-ups. I cannot see his six-year old boy. He must be pressing against his father.

Isaac stares back at me, searchingly. His face is pale and tense. His lips are not moving. I get the feeling that he is wondering whether my brother and I will fare better than his children. Isaac's affection for us has always been tinged with envy. I cannot sustain his unwavering stare and break off eye contact.

The *hazan's* hushed recitation of the *Nessaneh Toikef* continues, unrelenting: "...who shall rest at ease and who shall wander about.... Who shall be serene and who shall be tormented.... Who shall be demeaned and who shall be raised." The congregation at the Moriah roars the response: "But repentance and prayer and charity will deflect the evil decree!" I hear my father's voice; it is as loud and insistent as the other voices.

I read the words without pronouncing them: wishful thinking, they are... None of it will keep the Germans at bay... God is squatting, right there, in the dark recess, straight ahead, to the left of the Ark; it's clear to the naked eye. He is making Himself invisible. He is cowering. I don't like Him. My father points with his middle finger in my *makhzor*, the High Holidays and Festivals prayer book. He must have noticed that my lips were not moving. I mumble, "But repentance and prayer and charity will deflect the evil decree."

✡ ✡ ✡

The decree of September 25 barring Jews from the parks of Greater Antwerp deprived our community of a precious bit of outdoors. Decked out in their Sabbath clothes, the people from the surrounding streets and the nearby Jewish quarter had packed, on Saturday afternoons, the park benches on the tree-lined roadway along Quentin Matsijslei, ogling, gossiping, minding their children, feeding them. They would stroll, relax by the grass and flower beds, watch the ducks and swans glide over the pond's shimmering, rippling surface. On Sundays the park was also well frequented. During the week mothers would take their children there for play and fresh air.

The city park became a quiet place, even on weekends. Save for the lone burgher taking it easy on a distant bench, or an occasional pedestrian, the park's outer roadway along Quentin Matsijslei looked deserted. "It no longer is the *Jodenpark*," I reflected — the Jew-park, so called by antisemites. "Theirs. Always was. Why are they still keeping away?"

I shrugged off the prohibition: my weekend routine had changed even before the decree, leaving much less time for the park. There was the Talmud hour with my cousin Shloimeh on many a Shabbat afternoon. On the way home I might drop in at Menda's. I spent Sundays reading or catching up on the subjects that had been covered on Saturday.

Once, Menda and I realized with a jolt that we had been walking in the park on our way to classes. We took off and raced, breathless, to the nearest exit, the corner of Quentin Matsijs and Quellin.

And there was that one quiet morning on my way to school — I was not in my usual rush — when I noticed for the first time the birds' exuberant chatter emerging from the bushes and the trees: "Theirs. Theirs only. The park belongs to *them*."

✡ ✡ ✡

Yom Kippur was upon us, my first since assuming as a bar mitzvah the yoke of the commandments.

The fast was the central event. It got easier after the midday hunger pangs: the gnawing at my stomach eased as the day progressed, though the minutes kept getting longer. I had a taste of how hunger could become an all-consuming torment. To take my mind off the craving for food and the slow movement of the clock's minute hand I concentrated for a good while on the liturgy, keeping up with the *hazan*, as my father had done all day long. It worked. I even enjoyed it. The *Nessaneh Toikef* sentence "On Rosh Hashanah one's destiny is inscribed, and on Yom Kippur it is sealed" had reverted to a liturgical phrase.

Ne'eelah, the concluding service, was conducted early, like *Kol Nidrei* and the evening service on Yom Kippur eve, to allow people to be home before the curfew. The shul-goers folded their prayer shawls as they exchanged wishes: "May our prayers usher in a good year." "Amen." Handshakes, inside and outside the *shul*. More resounding good wishes.

"And may this be the year of their defeat."

"Oomeye'n!"

"And may our enemies die a tortured death. This year."

"Oomeye'n!"

Amen. Amen. Amen.

We left *shul* in the waning light of day. The cool air was invigorating. My hunger had receded. I felt light and upbeat, even capable of continuing the fast.

My mother was at home with my brother. My father waited for nightfall to say, at top speed, the weekday evening prayers. It marked the passing of the Day of Atonement. In normal times it was recited at the synagogue. I abstained. I had prayed enough.

My mother served cake and coffee to break the fast. I waited with my father for her to sit down before touching the food. Finally, the first bite: O, the pleasure... It was worth fasting for that moment. Yet two thin slices and half a cup blunted my craving for food. I found to my disappointment that the intense pleasure anticipated for most of the day had lasted minutes only. My stomach was back to normal. Of the four-course meal my mother began serving half an hour later I ate only the fish and the soup: I was full. Soon it would be time for bed. And back to school the next morning. Nothing had seemed more remote only hours earlier.

✡ ✡ ✡

November 25, 1941:

A German decree institutes the *Judenrat*, a council of Jewish notables, with local councils in Brussels, Antwerp, Liège and Charleroi, the four cities where Jews are allowed to take up residence. In Flemish and French it is called the "Association of the Jews in Belgium." (*In*, not *of*, Belgium.)

I turned the word over in my mind: *Judenrat*, council of Jews. Our spokespeople. Or was it *Judenrat*, the Jew-council, like the Jew-register, another *Jude*-word dripping with venom when crossing German lips, a trick? There was a trace of contempt, and discernible distrust, in the way my parents, their friends and acquaintances pronounced "*Judenrat*," contempt and distrust for the "*Rat*," the "council" part of the word, the *makhers*, the doers, the officials, especially the German Jews among them who managed somehow to get appointed. They had no visceral ties to the *Ostjuden*, as they sometimes referred haughtily to us, the overwhelming majority of our community. Would their German-ness, the mother tongue, give them a prominent role?

To me, the *Judenrat* was some kind of ghost committee. It did not come up in conversations with my friends. I did not give it another thought.

We got on with our life.

December 1, 1941:

By decree, Jewish students beyond the mandatory school age (fourteen) are barred, as of the following school year, from non-Jewish institutions.

The *Judenrat* shall ensure the education of the children of mandatory school age. In Jewish schools. With Jewish staff.

There were, in December of 1941, about 1,200 boys and girls in Antwerp's Jewish day schools and 2,800 in the city's public schools.

I was thirteen, unaffected, unaware even that I might have to leave my school after the present school year. Though the news about the decrees traveled fast, I knew only of those that affected us or that were discussed at home.

✡ ✡ ✡

There was still an hour to while away before the evening meal when my father walked in. My mother came out of the kitchen. They kissed.

"Big news," he said with a grin and a gleam in his eyes.

"Yes...?"

"America is at war."

"Oy, you are joking..."

"Joking?... *Es iz YONTIFF in shtetl* (the town is in a *holiday* mood)."

"What happened?"

"The Japanese attacked America."

"The *Japanese*? Attacked *America*?"

"Yes, those little cross-eyed makers of *Dreckmaterial.* And England. Imagine."

"England too? How did they get involved with England?"

"Some colony or other. Whichever way you turn there is an English colony."

"Does that mean that America is at war with Germany?"

"Not yet. But that will lead to it."

"Well then, that is good news."

"Good news? This is a *momentous* development. America and England, allies, against a member of the Axis."

"Where did they attack?" I asked.

"Somewhere in the Pacific Ocean. You will probably look it up on the map."

"Yes, of course."

"What kind of people are the Japanese?" my mother asked. "Are they as capable as the Germans?"

"As capable," my father said dismissively. "Adventurists! Like the Germans. *They* attack Russia, and *they* attack America. The chutzpah! They will all come to a miserable end."

"The Germans first. Soon. Soon."

"Amen."

He put his hat and coat away. My mother returned to her evening chores in the kitchen.

Days later, the unimaginable happened: Hitler declared war on the United States! He compared himself to the "degenerate" Roosevelt — red blood (his) versus blue blood (Roosevelt's). "While they are stuck in the snow," my father exulted. "While they are freezing their hands and feet off looking at Moscow from the distance. Such folly. *Unbelievable.*" And, in a more deferential tone: "Could only have come from Above."

"Finally. Roosevelt. America. With us," my mother said with a deep sigh. "A balm on the soul." Her hand rested on her heart. She was close to tears. "Those little cross-eyed people," she got hold of herself, "they did us a big favor. We owe them thanks."

"I am grateful to them, and I wish them from the bottom of my heart a crushing defeat," my father said cheerfully.

✧ ✧ ✧

Winter was upon us. Night came as early as half-past four. We would usually be home by nightfall, or shortly thereafter: the blackout, the rain and the cold would drive people indoors. On moonless, overcast nights one would hear a lone pedestrian long before making out in a sideways glance a pale, barely perceptible patch of skin. In the trams, the ghostly light of the blue-painted, blackout-compliant ceiling bulbs gave the riders a pallid, sickly look: somber figures dressed in grays and browns, heading home, or to a late shift.

In the coziness of our home the evening hours flowed seamlessly past curfew time. I would be finished with my homework before supper. After the meal we gathered in the dining room where the coal-burning stove gave off a pleasant glow, for some reading, or an occasional game of cards. My brother would get into his pajamas right by the stove: the bedrooms were frigid. I kept the window in my tiny bedroom open a crack; it was healthy, my father had advised.

Dreary weather, early nightfall, the desolation of the deserted, dark streets and the curfew, combined to bring us and our young neighbors closer together. We had gotten friendly with them. They would drop in on us after supper, more often as the days had grown shorter. The Janowskis, the ground floor tenants — the parents now of a baby girl — would join us almost each time they heard the Rosenzweigs, who occupied the top floor of our three-family house, climb down the wooden stairs. By now they were converging on our apartment every Saturday night, and sometimes for a shorter visit during the week as well, after my brother's eight-thirty bedtime. They were two handsome and elegant couples. The Rosenzweigs were tall and dark, with big brown eyes. He had an easy smile, self-confident yet friendly; she was a serious gossip. Sitting upright and looking down into her plate or her hand of cards, she would let go of one tidbit, then another, reluctantly, it seemed, and with perfect timing, in Polish when the item was too strong or too sensitive for a young mind. I recognized enough words to decode the secrets. The Janowskis, recent — late-1930's — immigrants from Poland, were fair, with distinguished features and a dignified demeanor. They spoke a sonorous Polish. They would leave their apartment door open on a crack; ours was also kept ajar. Every so often Mr. Janowski stepped out into the hallway and listened. They would take leave when the baby cried. It happened rarely. The visitors brought cheer and color into our dining room.

Stories, reminiscences and jokes — my father was an accomplished raconteur — animated those evenings. The men would lean back between sips from their glasses of burning-hot tea. They occupied half of the dining-room table at one end, allowing them to sneak in a fast game of poker while the women had their asides — in Polish, quite often, especially when I was not supposed to understand. I was paying attention to the men's side of the table. Smoke from a lone cigarette, my father's, would snake its way up from the ashtray and thin out into a light-blue haze in the glow of the chandelier.

I looked forward to Saturday night, the long hiatus between the two Sabbaths. The women would join the men in a game of cards. My mother served cake with the tea. My brother was allowed to stay up. He would stand by my father's side, with an occasional trip to the cookie plate; he knew the polite interval between helpings. The men, more dexterous with cards, dealt for themselves and for their wives. The long wait for one's turn in the six-hand, slow-paced game of Rummy allowed for snippets of cross-conversation. I was standing in the middle between the men and the women, leaning, at times, with my elbows on the table, watching the game and listening in.

"These Japanese," Mr. Rosenzweig mused one Saturday night — a round of Rummy had just come to an end. "Still unstoppable. Entire chunks of the British and the Dutch empires in just weeks. And the Philippines. Frightening."

"It won't last," my father opined. "They'll fare like the Germans."

"How will the Allies get it all back? Where will they counterattack from?"

"From China," I joined in. "And from Australia."

"The question now is, whom will they finish first?" Mr. Janowski wondered. "Japan or Germany? They can't pursue victory on two fronts at the same time."

"God forbid Japan first," Mrs. Janowski said. "We can't wait that long."

"Europe comes first," my father stated emphatically. "Afterwards, those other territories. Roosevelt has been itching all along to help England defeat Germany."

"Thank God we have Roosevelt," my mother said.

"Imagine," Mr. Janowski mused. "This war has spread like wildfire. Every continent a battlefield, under occupation or at war. Mind-boggling."

"What's left? Honolulu?" my mother asked.

"Honolulu is where the Japanese attacked," Mr. Rosenzweig said laughing.

"I thought Honolulu was a funny name for a place at the far end of the world."

"It *is* at the far end of the world."

"So what were the Americans doing in Honolulu?" my mother asked between peals of laughter. "I will never understand politics."

"Madame Grünstein," Mr. Janowski said, turning serious, "politics is the acting out of human folly, that's all it is. I mean... two world wars in one generation. A Kaiser and a Führer."

"That's Germany," my mother pointed out. "I meant Roosevelt and Churchill. Politicians. Statesmen."

"The politics of a Roosevelt, a Churchill, or a Wilson is to try to contain human folly," my father said. "Unfortunately, they emerge only when the fire is already raging. They don't prevent it. They didn't stop Hitler."

"Why, in the beginning they even abetted him, with that *Ostpolitik* of theirs," Mr. Rosenzweig said.

"What *Ostpolitik*?" Mrs. Janowski asked.

"Hitler's Germany was to become the West's bulwark against communism."

"Indeed," my father said, "the politics of balancing evil with evil. They played with fire. They saw their mistake, though, soon after the Spanish civil war. Churchill sounded the alarm, like a prophet of ours. Nobody listened. It's as if peace cannot be sustained. Or prosperity, for that matter." Addressing Mrs. Janowski, "As your husband put it, 'Human folly.' Or human nature; same thing. It makes me think of the strife and the breakup of the Jewish kingdom after the long, peaceful reign of King Solomon. Solomon overtaxed the people to feed his passions and reward his cronies. They rebelled against his successor who wouldn't lighten their burden. The Czar and his aristocrats, leeches all. Even America, before Roosevelt stepped in: bread lines and soup kitchens in the land of plenty. It seems as if corruption and injustice are endemic; and when they are rife, things get ugly."

"America, at least, produced a Roosevelt. Germany produced a Hitler," Mr. Janowski remarked.

"That's Europe," Mr. Rosenzweig said. "Rotten to the core. One dictatorship more sinister than the other."

"You cannot lump the West with the rest of Europe," my mother countered.

"Madame Grünstein, when you say the West, you really mean Belgium, don't you?" Mr. Janowski said teasingly.

"In a way, yes. To me Belgium stands for the West," my mother answered. "But I recognize the other... members," she added with a faint smile.

"Like?"

"Holland... and England... and Switzerland..."

"And Luxemburg," my father added helpfully.

"You are setting very high admission standards," Mr. Janowski said, smiling. "How about France?"

"They haven't changed since Dreyfus," my father snapped.

"There are few places left where one can live like a human being," my mother said, "and they are beyond reach. I remember, coming to Belgium from Poland, how we walked the streets, like convalescents on their first day out in the sun. Such a blessed little land. *Schluss.* It had to come to an end. This hatred. It's driving us forth with no letup. We must always be prepared. Ready to pick up and go." I heard a faint echo of many a hand-wringing aside — my father was staring at the packet of cards in his hand. "We have no solid ground under our feet."

"After the war, God willing, we'll have solid ground under our feet," he said. "In *Eretz Yisruel*" ("the Land of Israel").

"After the war," my mother repeated with a sigh.

"After the war," Mrs. Janowski said in Polish.

"How far is Rommel from Palestine?" Mr. Rosenzweig asked.

"Not a chance," I said. "They would have to take Suez first."

"*Nu?* Is that so far-fetched?"

"The English will fight for Suez like they fought for England. With everything they have. *La route des Indes*," I added sententiously.

"Suez is pretty safe," Mr. Janowski opined. "The Germans have their hands full in Russia. And they must maintain troops along the Atlantic coast to guard against a possible invasion."

"At least they know now what war really tastes like," my father said. "Their cities are getting bombed into rubble. In Russia they are bleeding in the summer, freezing in the winter."

"Sad, though, that our furriers in Brussels are helping them stay warm," my mother said.

"Yes, sad," Mrs. Rosenzweig agreed. "Jews getting rich doing work for the Wehrmacht."

"Sad. True," my father concurred. "But frankly, when the German tells you to deliver a certain number of fur jackets, what can you do other than procure rabbit pelts, hire workers and get down to work? Say 'no' and face the consequences? Don't the workers at the Fabrique Nationale produce arms for the Germans?"

"They jumped at the opportunity, I heard," Mrs. Rosenzweig responded. "They can't deliver fast enough. Piecework."

"At least they are not doing it on the back of others," my mother said as if to herself.

The four diamantaires. A clear allusion for people in the know. It was equally clear to me that neither my parents nor the Rosenzweigs would mention the foursome: Mr. Janowski was not of the trade.

"These furriers and their workers must feel secure," Mrs. Janowski said.

"Yes. Secure. As long as the Germans need them," my father replied. "By the way, that whole fur jacket business was rush-rush. Russia was to fall before the onset of winter. Their hands and feet will freeze off. Napoleon's fate."

"Why couldn't he have..." my mother began. I looked up surprised, "been stillborn?" she finished — "rotted in his mother's belly?" she had meant to say; I knew: I had heard her say it before.

She got up to pour more tea. My brother helped himself to another cookie.

"Let's play," my father said on a higher note. "The scores are still quite low. Let's see who breaks loose of the pack." He proceeded to deal. The cards flitted around the table.

"Henia, you open," he said to my mother.

I followed the game. My mother won, smiling. "Only temporary," Mr. Rosenzweig, who was caught with a full hand, promised.

"What do you make of the *Judenrat*?" Mr. Janowski asked as he gathered the cards. "I can't figure out its real function."

"To be the Germans' mouthpiece and servant," Mr. Rosenzweig replied. "They will use it to rule us."

"But they already rule us with their decrees."

"Yes," my father interjected. "They decreed, for example, that Goyishe teachers can no longer teach the State curriculum in Jewish schools. And they assigned the *Judenrat* the task of replacing them with Jews."

"Why do they even bother assigning that task to anyone?" Mrs. Janowski asked. "Since when are they concerned about the education of Jewish children?"

"They should live so long. You see," my father explained, "Belgian law mandates that all children be taught the State curriculum. They are just abiding by the law of the land. Doesn't cost them anything."

"At the same time they are further isolating us from the population," Mr. Rosenzweig said.

"May it not get worse," my father offered.

"One should hope," my mother muttered. "In Poland, they are driven into ghettos."

"And where does one find Jewish teachers?" Mr. Janowski asked.

"The *Judenrat* has appealed to the high school graduates in the community," my father answered. "Scores have volunteered. They are getting six months of teacher training at Tachkemoni, till the end of the school year. Then they must pass some sort of qualification exam in Ghent. In September, they will take over from the Flemish teachers. The *Judenrat* arranged for all that."

I was impressed: young Jews who had completed the long journey that lay ahead of me, stepping into the breach. Men. To be a man. To be of service. Some day, I, too, would do such manly things. I tried to glimpse the future: a blur; brightly lit, like an overexposed photograph; at the end of five long years of high school. An eternity.

"And where will the money come from?"

"I don't know. The *Judenrat* may have to raise the funds in the community. Perhaps the State will contribute."

"And what will happen to the dismissed Flemish teachers?"

"They are not dismissed; they are idled by a German decree," my father said. "The Belgian State has an obligation towards them. I'm sure it will maintain their salaries if they are not reassigned to other schools."

My father was well informed. As a member of the Tachkemoni committee, he met with his colleagues in the school's office and came in frequent contact with the State-appointed Flemish staff and its director.

"It almost sounds as if the *Judenrat* is a good thing," Mrs. Janowski exclaimed.

"Yes," my mother said. "For the *makhers* [officials]. They'll know how to take advantage of their positions. They'll be the last to suffer, if at all."

"Sure. But especially a good thing for the Germans," Mr. Rosenzweig responded to Mrs. Janowski. "The *Judenrat* is their creature. It will facilitate their work. And their aim is not philanthropy or the education of Jewish children."

"How will it facilitate their work?" Mr. Janowski asked. "What work? The robbing and other heavy work they like to do themselves."

"The real question is," my mother said warily, "what do they have in store for us?"

"Forced labor?" Mrs. Janowski wondered. Her husband was young and vigorous. So was Mr. Rosenzweig. It weighed even on my mother's mind, though my father was at the ripe age of forty-two, and with a family. "Papa is not *Arbeitsmaterial* [labor timber]," my mother had once expressed her anguish to me. "He would not hold out."

"There was no forced labor for the Jews in Limburg," my father remarked.

"Well, take Limburg, since you mention it," Mr. Rosenzweig said. "They had the Flemish police serve the evacuation orders. And *they* sat smugly in their *Kommandantur* while the Jews boarded the trains. Then in Limburg they had the local police and municipal employees keep tabs on the deported. Or take the Jew-register: the municipal employees did the registering. They need proxies to do their work for them. That's all I am saying."

"Less intimidating also than Germans," Mr. Janowski said.

"So what work do they have cut out for the *Judenrat*?" his wife asked.

"The devil knows."

"The German Jews kept warning us," my mother said ruefully. " 'They mean what they say. Run. Flee while you can.' Alarmists, we thought. *Yekkes.* Gullible."

"They are up to no good, no doubt," my father agreed. "But they are treading more lightly in the West. Look, there have been no more attacks on Jewish shops by the Flemish thugs. The Flemish police clamped down with an iron fist. Only hate propaganda."

"True," said Mr. Rosenzweig. "But that propaganda is further isolating us. We could disappear tomorrow and the Goyim wouldn't even notice."

"Or give a hoot," Mrs. Rosenzweig added.

"The corset maker would," my mother said wryly. "She is making a fortune off the Jewish matrons."

"I hear that they are besotted with her," Mrs. Janowski said. She was not corseted herself, that was clear from her free-flowing dress and more laid-back poses, ("though she could use one," my mother once remarked. "After childbirth..."). Mrs. Rosenzweig did not need one.

"Yes, a shrewd one, the corset maker. Charges twice as much as the store on Quellin Street. And she herself is round as a barrel and does not wear one," my mother filled in. "Sits there, and ministers to the Jewesses." She switched to Polish, and I picked up enough key words to understand that some Jewish women entrusted the fat lady with fortunes (*majontek*) for safekeeping until after the war. The things my mother enumerated eluded me, but money and diamonds were not among them. It had to be furs and rugs, silver and china and crystal and things, I surmised.

My father took a puff of his cigarette.

"We'll slug through, with God's help," he weighed in in an upbeat tone. "Herr Janowski, your turn to deal."

After another round:

"Has anyone heard from the Buchfelds?" my mother asked. They had hired a smuggler to take them to Switzerland.

"No," Mrs. Rosenzweig answered. "But it may be too soon to hear from them."

"I can't understand why they did not take her sister along. A woman alone." My mother looked pained.

"The smaller the traveling party, the less conspicuous," Mr. Rosenzweig commented.

"Maybe she was too frightened to join them," Mrs. Rosenzweig said. "In fact, I saw her yesterday on the Isabellalei."

"What did she have to say?" my mother asked.

"She was in a *konverzatsia*," Mrs. Rosenzweig continued in Polish — I cocked my ears. "I didn't want to..." I missed the last word.

"With whom?" my mother asked in her low, for-adults-only tone. I expected a coded reply, a roundabout identification.

"Schein," Mrs. Rosenzweig answered, oblivious of tonal nuances.

My mother looked at her.

"*Ona lubi co kazda lubi*" ("She likes what every woman likes"), Mrs. Rosenzweig dropped.

That was clear as day to me! Hanky-panky! But what exactly went on?

"Who is Schein?" Mrs. Janowski asked.

"An enticing man," my mother answered.

"Enticing," my father repeated dismissively. "Some belly he has," he continued in Yiddish. "Can't put a sentence together. Hems and haws more than he talks."

"True," my mother said. "No intellectual. But his timing is flawless. And the women whose attention he gets listen more to the pauses."

"Also true," my father conceded. The men chuckled.

"Women who listen more to the pauses. Flawless timing." I turned the words over in my mind. How, and where, did one get to understand those things? Clearly not from school: had nothing to do with Latin or geography.

"This reminds me of a story," my father said as he put down his cigarette. His features relaxed into a sly grin. "A ravishing Catholic girl goes to confession...."

I watched and listened and soaked it all in. My brother had gone to bed around eleven, of his own accord.

The guests left. My parents got busy clearing the table.

"The Rosenzweigs won't hang around much longer," my mother said.

"I had the same impression," my father agreed. "Spring, maybe."

"The Janowskis will also take the jump."

"What makes you say that?"

"Just the way they both kept asking questions and taking it all in, quietly. He especially. And she strikes me as someone who is capable of taking risks."

"She is nursing a baby," my father probed.

"She is afraid of losing him to forced labor," my mother replied.

Shortly thereafter, in March of 1942, the Occupation Authority would score a coup when Interior's new secretary-general Romsée, a pro-German Flemish nationalist, got *Het Belgisch Staatsblad* and its French counterpart, *Le Moniteur Belge,* the government's publications of ministerial orders, to carry the German decree instituting the *Judenrat.* It stipulated that the councils bring all Jewish institutions and organizations under one roof to enhance their cooperation in the service of the isolated Jewish communities;

tend to the social and educational needs of the Jewish population;

register the Jews in their cities and outlying boroughs, and keep the information up-to-date, including changes of domicile; and,

facilitate the emigration of the Jews.

The *Judenrat*'s mandate may be expanded.

The decree's publication in the government's organs conferred legal status to the *Judenrat* and legitimized its mandate. "It is the first time in Belgian history that a decree based on race appears in *Het Staatsblad,*" rejoiced the pro-Nazi *Volksverwering* (Defense of the People). "The country will soon be cleansed of Jews."

✡ ✡ ✡

March 1942:

The occupier orders the liquidation of all Jewish enterprises. (They were identified and registered in accordance with a May, 1941 decree.) Commercial and industrial activities shall cease. Inventories shall be turned over to the Belgian offices of the respective trades at prices set by their officials. "They want us to wither away," my mother mutters. "Perish. They want us to perish."

Most of the more than seven thousand Jewish enterprises were small businesses and family stores serving the end consumer: an immigrant community's economic toehold in the host country. Only a few hundred firms were deemed worthy of transfer into Aryan ownership. Of the hundreds of leather and fur businesses, about forty continued their activities under Jewish management and German supervision.

The forced liquidation of hundreds of diamond firms spelled the end of the Jewish presence in the diamond industry. The elimination of the Jews from the only sector of Belgium's economy where they had played an influential role had begun in the previous year, with raids on the diamond exchanges, and with the institution of a Diamond Control Office where merchants had to deposit the stocks they had declared and through which all "official" trades had to be funneled. The clause that barred foreign nationals from the diamond broker's trade eliminated virtually all Jewish brokers.

The Jews' precarious foothold in the economic life of the country was shattered. A large swath of the Jewish population was left without income and with limited means of subsistence. Many went on the dole or became dependent on public or communal assistance.

The economic decree did not affect us. My father had stopped doing business ever since the war broke out, except for a few transactions to raise cash. My parents continued to draw on their savings. And as a diamond broker my father was not assumed to have a stock of merchandise. I became aware of the deepening hardship in the community: collections from door to door and appeals on behalf of the needy increased sharply.

More people with means turned to smugglers. Switzerland had become the favorite destination ever since the Vichy government took on the "Jewish Question" and its militias and police began enforcing its decrees against the Jews, especially the foreign Jews, across the entire French territory.

We retreated within an ever tighter perimeter. All our needs could be met within a short walk from home. The food stores were nearby; the Jewish shoemaker, the Moriah *shul,* my brother's school and mine, within walking distance. High school was the furthest, a twenty-minute stroll away.

Purim at the *shul. Ma'ariv,* the evening prayer, had come to a close with the concluding *Ahlaynu.* The reader ascended the podium and proceeded to cantillate the Scroll of Esther. Each time he pronounced "Haman," the name of the villain who schemed to annihilate all the Jews — men and women, young and old — in the ancient empire of Persia and Media, a din broke out and filled the sanctuary: the children twirled their noisemakers, excitedly, the men thumped on lecterns, fiercely and sustainedly. To drown out his name. The latter-day Haman was on everyone's mind.

✡ ✡ ✡

The Rosenzweigs left, then the Janowskis. Each couple came for a brief, subdued goodbye the night before their departure.

"Running borders with a tot," my mother had sighed after the door had closed on the last handshake.

"You never know. A young woman with a baby in her arms can soften a man's heart."

"A German's heart?"

"A Frenchman's heart. The French police are the more likely ones to intercept fugitives nowadays."

"Yes. And they do no harm. They just turn them over to the Germans."

The Rosenzweigs returned after the war, from Cuba.
The Janowskis were never heard from again.

The Janowskis' apartment remained empty. The Rosenzweigs' top floor apartment — it rented for less — went to a strange couple: a short, jowly, hunched-over octogenarian from Wallonia who spoke only French, and a tall, wiry *Reichsdeutsche* in her fifties who spoke only German. She would lead him up the stairs, one step at a time. He growled each time she exchanged a few words with my parents on the landing, at our floor. She would flash a devil-may-care smile and move on. At times it sounded as if furniture was being shoved back and forth overhead. And sometimes the old man would let out a long string of roars.

"What can that be?" my mother had wondered the first time we heard him. We had stood still and listened, alarmed. Now we just nodded each time he roared. "This old man is as strong as an ox," my mother remarked.

One morning, there was a knock on the door. Our German neighbor handed my father a brown bag and said, "I know it's harder on you people." She turned around without giving my father the time to thank her and proceeded upstairs. The crumpled brown bag contained half-a-dozen spring potatoes, the size of plump grapes.

"Odd," my mother mused.

"At least it's a friendly gesture," my father replied. "Might not be a bad thing to have a real German for a neighbor."

"Our guardian angel," my mother muttered.

Once, the tall *Reichsdeutsche* came to borrow two cubes of sugar "Only two. Until tomorrow."

"Oh, please, don't take the trouble," my mother said as she poured sugar cubes into her cup. "A little bit of sugar. Really, it's not worth mentioning."

"Oh no. Tomorrow," the *Reichsdeutsche* insisted and left.

"Tomorrow," my father said, "she'll be standing at the door with her cup of sugar like a soldier at attention."

"No, she won't," my mother said.

"What are you talking about? A German? It wouldn't be *Korrekt.*"

"You want to bet?"

"How much?"

"Just betting."

She never knocked on our door again. And just "*guten Tag*" and "*guten Abend,*" in passing.

One day, he came down to tell us that she was gone. He seemed lost. No, he needed nothing. Then, a few days later, he was gone, too. We remained alone in the house.

✠ ✠ ✠

There were *matsos* for Passover. In Poland, the Germans had apparently forbidden the baking of the unleavened bread. Some people had sent boxes of *matsos* to their relatives in the old country. A rumor had it that the Germans had dropped bread crumbs in the boxes after checking their contents, rendering the *matsos* unfit for Passover.

We had our Seder in the dining room. White table cloth. Dark red wine in sparkling glasses. Passover set of dishes and silverware never touched by leavened food. The Passover plate. Embroidered satin coverlets. Silver cups, my father's and the prophet Elijah's. The host of little rituals: the dippings, the melodies, the incantations, the blessings, the wine, the delicious morsels on a ravenous stomach — *kharoset* (crushed apple and nuts soaked in wine), hard boiled egg, the first bite of *matsoh*, the sharp, white horseradish, the Hillel sandwich; the long recitative of the *Haggadah* leading up to the meal. We raised our glasses as we sang the *Vuh-HEE sheh-amdah*, "And it is *this* that has stood by our fathers and us, *this*..." I had grasped it as I pronounced it; as if it were part of me. *This*: our clinging to the Torah, our not letting go, not "letting them," our saying "no," stubbornly. "And it is *this* that has stood by our fathers and us, for not one alone has risen against us to annihilate us, but in generation after generation they rise against us to annihilate us, but the Holy One, blessed be He, delivers us from their hands." The melody was cheerful. It felt good, uplifting. The *Shfokh khahmatkhah* (Pour forth Thy wrath) after grace, was somber, even awesome, by contrast. We stood around the table holding the fourth glass of wine; my father had opened the door to the hallway, to welcome Elijah from the gaping darkness. "Pour forth Thy wrath upon the nations that do not recognize Thee.... For they have devoured Jacob and devastated his habitation.... Let Thy burning wrath overtake them... and destroy them from beneath the heavens of the Lord." My father's forceful intonation lent the stark verses a sense of immediacy: they'd get their due, soon, very soon.

Cheer replaced solemnity as we launched into the songs after the recitation of the *Hallel*; from devotional to whimsical, they signaled the home stretch. I managed to hang on as my father revved up the speed, playfully, my brother chimed in with the last verse or the last words of each stanza, my mother sat quietly, pensive. Finally we recited emphatically "Next year in Jerusalem."

My father, observing the last custom of the night, read the Song of Songs to himself. We sat back, relaxed.

The second night's Seder — a custom of Exile — was less of a ceremony, more of an exercise. There is no such custom in *Eretz Yisrael*. How sensible, I thought. How cavalier. How Free. Never-never land.

✡ ✡ ✡

May 8, 1942:
Jews are barred from drawing unemployment compensation and other social benefits provided by law.

They are to accept work assigned to them by the Belgian labor offices.

They will work in separate groups and be housed in reserved centers.

The Germans began carrying out the decree in June; they needed manpower to work on the fortifications along the English Channel. Their targeting the "asocial elements" — foreigners, as it turned out, mostly young men idled by the snuffing out of Jewish livelihoods who had become a burden to the State — did not cause a stir among the country's administrators whose principal concern was that Belgian citizens not be taken out of Belgium to do compulsory labor. The Germans even secured the cooperation of the local authorities. They kept in the background while the Belgian police took over, from scouring the police files for "asocial elements," to serving them with the summonses, to standing guard over them at the assembly points before their departure for the North of France. (It was reported that in Brussels a Belgian functionary of the Labor Office found it "inadmissible" at a meeting with representatives of the *Feldkommandantur* and the *Judenrat*, "that only 86 Jews showed up when 450 had been called for work.")

A first notice summoned the recipient to a physical checkup in the city's Labor Office. There he was met and examined with summary dispatch by functionaries of the *Organisation Todt*, the German builder of the Atlantic Wall, the coastline fortification along the English Channel that was meant to thwart an Allied landing.

A subsequent notice set the date and place of departure.

There were seven convoys, four from Antwerp alone with more than 1300 recruits, and one each from Brussels, Liège and Charleroi. Over 2000 men altogether. They were sent over a period of three months — from mid-June to mid-September — to a string of labor camps along the English Channel. They were promised wages they never got. Their work stint, they believed, would guarantee the safety of their families. Their kin expected them back: they received, for a while at least, small payments "deducted from the men's paychecks."

✡ ✡ ✡

Yizkor, the memorial service for the dead, on the second day of the Shavuot festival, in late May: Those of us who had no close relative to mourn flocked into the hallway of the Moriah *shul* — we no longer spilled out into the street. A gathering of Jews in Sabbath attire might draw undue, even hostile, attention.

A man with deep brown eyes, wearing a beaten, wide-brimmed, dirty-gray homburg, was explaining to a group of youngsters — I was among them — the nature of the "Jewish problem." The Jews, went the argument, were expendable *Luftmenschen* (Yiddish for people engaged in marginal activities; literally, air people).

That's why everyone could push them around with impunity. It would have been different if the Jews in Belgium had been coal miners. The Germans could not tangle with a contingent of coal miners 15,000 men strong and risk losing all that production; not to speak of the reaction of their non-Jewish comrades and the broader solidarity between all workers. Belonging to the proletariat was the ticket to survival.

I sensed the perversity in what he said but was unable to articulate it. I finally dared asking him:

"Why aren't *you* a coalminer?"

"I was a coalminer before and at the beginning of the war," he answered.

"A communist," my father said with scorn when I recounted the incident. "The brazenness, the baseness of it. Doing away with the soul of a people, their own people, to fit their ideas. The arrogance of these street intellectuals. Interesting, though," he reflected, "showing up for *Yizkor.*"

"He stayed outside," I pointed out.

"They are standing up to the Germans," my father continued, "one must hand it to them." Then, sharply: "Don't be seen near him."

It turned out, after the war, that the man in the wide-brimmed, dirty-gray homburg who spoke French with a Yiddish accent had fought in the Belgian communist underground.

✽ ✽ ✽

June 1942:

All Jews age six and above must wear a yellow star in public. It is to be procured where one has been registered as a Jew. Non-compliance will be punished. British and American subjects, and nationals of neutral countries, are exempt.

My father fetched the stars for the entire family — three per person, one franc a piece — at the designated public school. The city clerk checked off our names in the Jew-register, and, deferring to the local *Feldkommandant,* stamped my parents' identification cards with a red star — a companion sign to the big-lettered, red "JOOD-JUIF," (a procedure not called for in the decree).

In Antwerp, about fifteen thousand Jews six years and older received the stars, as recorded by the city's Jewish Registration section. The registrar's office also reported to the local

Feldkommandantur, as ordered, the names of those who failed to comply.

Brussels refused to distribute the stars "out of concern for fellow Belgians and commitment to the dignity of all men without distinction," the mayors of the capital and surrounding boroughs declared in a letter to the military occupation authorities. This was a Belgian administration's first break ever with the politics of passive execution. The Germans did not demur: the *Oberfeldkommandantur*, then the *Judenrat*, handed them out.

The stars had a bold, black border line, and a bold black **J** in the middle, in the form of the Hebrew letter Nun. Black on yellow. I sewed mine with great care onto the breast pocket of my jacket, keeping the six-pointed black border line an even width.

My brother, by now eight years old, wore his to Tachkemoni. He didn't seem bothered in the least. I wore it, conscious of belonging to a different community, the People of the Torah, the nation that Scriptures identified with faith and learning. The Chosen. I saw the passers-by on the wide sidewalk of the Quellinstraat glimpse my yellow star, then look away, past me. Were they embarrassed that this was happening in their midst? On their street? Or did they wish that I would just go away? Was *I* the one who made *them* feel uncomfortable? Or was it my imagination? My Christian classmates and teachers reacted, if at all, with sympathy and friendliness. On the first day we showed up wearing our stars, Marcel Janssens got up from his bench at the head of my row and walked up to shake hands with each one of us in front of the whole class.

"Are you made to feel uncomfortable by your classmates?" my mother once asked.

"Not in the least," I said. "On the contrary." And I related Marcel Janssens' reaching out to us.

My mother was moved.

"That's exactly how one would be made to feel in Poland," my father said dryly.

"Yes," my mother chimed in. "With their *numerus clausus*" — the quota system for limiting admissions of Jews to universities.

I knew about it. Jews were relegated to the rear of the classrooms, taunted and harassed by their Polish classmates. "Bloodied, that's how one or the other would come home sometimes," my mother had recounted. " But back they went, the very next day!" I sensed the fierceness and the pride. "I didn't want you to grow up there," she had continued. "I pushed and pushed to leave that country. It took two years: papa was running his mother's leather and shoe business."

I even appeared on the stage of our high school auditorium with the yellow star on my chest: both Menda and I got parts in a play, *La Farce de Maître Pathelin*, along with Roald Bingen and a fourth classmate. I was conscious of it when I turned to face the audience with the professors in the front row, but forgot about it the instant the four in our cast got into the act. One sunny day in June of 1942, coming home from school, I caught sight of the street photographer on the fashionable De Keyserlei and, on the spur of the moment, gave him the hand signal: I wanted a photograph of myself with my star. I had my book bag under my arm and was feeling chipper in my gray, short-pants suit, white shirt and tie, high knee socks and shining black shoes, and my black velvet school cap with two stars. The camera captured my impish smile. It also caught in the background a poster showing an angular, helmeted face with the caption *"Vlamingen op!"* ("Flemings arise!") exhorting the young to join the Flemish SS. Many did, among them the son of the Flemish principal in charge of the State curriculum at Jewish Tachkemoni. The boy left for the Russian front with the blessing of his pro-German father. He did not return.

The sight of men and women, of children holding hands and old folks leaning on canes wearing the yellow star brought the hitherto submerged plight of the Jews to the public's embarrassed attention. That such a violation should be perpetrated in their midst... the barbarity of it! Strangers greeted Jews on the street, stood up for them on tramways. Gentiles wore yellow Stars of David or patches of decorative yellow. A store on Isabellalei, near our home, sold six-pointed stars printed in the colors of the Belgian flag. Children were instructed to be friendly toward their Jewish classmates. The sudden groundswell of solidarity with the Jews against the common enemy stirred Gentiles throughout the land into helping the hunted escape capture during the two years of Occupation that followed.

☆ ☆ ☆

Jews in the healing arts, from physicians to masseurs, dentists, veterinarians, nurses, midwives, dietitians, physical therapists, medical assistants, may dispense their services to Jews only. Jewish pharmacists may no longer dispense medication. Jews are not allowed to make or distribute pharmaceutical products.

✿ ✿ ✿

June 14, 1942: The first convoy of labor recruits left Antwerp for the North of France.

In Brussels the contingent was marched across town from the North Station to the South Station (there was no rail link between them). "A pathetic procession," the clandestine *Libération* wrote, "of two hundred to three hundred Jews deported to labor camps abroad, with a compassionate and angry crowd lining the route." A gaffe the Todt Organization did not repeat. Henceforth the labor recruits would be transported in covered trucks.

A harsh regimen awaited them, survivors recounted: long hours of hard labor, inadequate food, one Sunday of rest per month.

✿ ✿ ✿

Posters of the *Feldkommandantur* inform the public that Jews are barred from cinemas and theaters, from sports events, from public facilities.

On city trams, Jews must use the platform at the front of the trailer car.

"So we won't go see *The Dybbuk*," my father said with mock earnestness, recalling the performances by the visiting Yiddish theater troupes from Poland my parents had delighted in, before the war.

"Opera we need? Traviata?" my mother echoed.

Vanished as well, like chocolate and exotic fruits, ever since the invasion, the westerns I had feasted on, the Walt Disney cartoons, the movies with gangsters, Tarzan, Stan Laurel and Oliver Hardy.

A decree with no teeth.

"Having to stand on the open platform of the tram, that is a slap" my mother said at supper that evening. "Imagine, the people of Berchem and Gitschotel [municipalities of Greater Antwerp] riding the tram into town to shop or see relatives, standing outside on the platform with their yellow stars. What a spectacle. While the Goyim sit inside."

"There will be Goyim joining them," my father said. "As a gesture. There are principled people around."

"My classmates would do it," I joined in. "Well, a good many of them."

"Well yes," my mother conceded. "A show of sympathy. I agree."

"That's all we can ask for," my father said in a subdued tone of voice.

"I agree. I agree," my mother said. "I myself, were I a Flemish woman, would not give up my seat for fear of drawing attention to myself."

"Not even to a pregnant woman with a star?" I probed.

"That, yes."

"A woman with a child on her arm? An old woman or man?"

"You are missing the point: such instances could not be seen as blatant acts of defiance. Luckily," my mother continued, "everything we need is within walking distance. We won't have to stand exposed" — her voice trailed off — "like branded cattle on that open platform."

"I *want* them to see my star," I said. "I want everyone to see it."

"Nu-nu. Don't be a hero," my mother admonished.

One sunny day Maurice Zalcman joined Menda and me on the way home from school. The conversation meandered into religion. After listening to some ponderous remarks of mine about true monotheism, idolatry in Catholicism and the like, Zalcman said casually:

"Well of course, it's all nonsense. There is no God."

For a moment, he had us speechless: A heretic! A live heretic! I had never met one before. And a classmate reared on the Torah in the old Tachkemoni days, of all people! How reckless! Not since the invasion did something come down so unexpectedly. In a common reflex Menda and I rallied to God's defense, putting ourselves out of danger:

"Who made the universe!?" I blurted out.

"And who made God?"

"Whoever made the god that made the universe is the real God. This is turning into a joke."

"It isn't. Man made God."

"That's crazy! It's the other way around!"

"No one made us, we evolved, species evolve all the time. If you read Darwin..."

L'homme descend du singe et le singe descend de l'arbre" ("Man descends from the ape and the ape descends from the tree"), I interjected. It was too tempting a line.

"Come on," Menda broke in. "This pun has a beard. Listen, Zalcman, if you mean *B'raishit* [Genesis], there is no contradiction: the Torah is not about evolution, the Torah is about the Creator of evolution." Menda was hemming and hawing, as was his habit, but he would always come up with the precise word, the lapidary sentence.

"That's too easy," Zalcman riposted, "like with the age of the universe, five thousand seven hundred and two, then come the rabbis and play with the clock, 'Yes, a day of Creation is not to be taken literally,' then you have Metushelakh who lives to be almost a thousand. No, *B'raishit* and evolution don't go together. God created Adam from the soil, Eve from Adam's rib, blew life into their nostrils, that's what the Torah means. But that's not even the point..."

"Right now it is. What's the point in talking about the first amoeba when we weren't ready for it? It is written: '*Dibbrah Torah bilshon b'nai adam*' ['the Torah speaks in the tongue of the people']. How else could God have made Himself understood?" Menda was warming up. The sentences were flowing faster.

"He didn't, because God is a fiction. That's the whole point. The Torah was written by people. God appears in the third person. He is jealous, fearsome, kills, and wants to be loved. Don't you see, he has been fashioned in the image of man, not the other way round. All religions, at bottom, are the same: fear and love, reward and punishment, hell and afterlife, because they have all been fabricated by priests who use religion to control the life of the people. I agree with Diderot," he continued while Menda and I were reeling from his broadside. "Man will not be free until the last king is strangled with the entrails of the last priest."

"Catholic priests. I can agree with that," I contributed.

Dour Zalcman cracked a smile. Menda chuckled: "Rabbis were not so dear to his heart either."

"He meant all of them," Zalcman weighed in with his deep drone, "including the High Priest who wanted to make us believe that only he could enter and come out alive from the Holy of Holies on Yom Kippur. All fabrications. Trying to scare people. Just like in synagogue the children are scared to look at the *kohanim* [priests] as they bless the congregation. The fathers cover their children with their *tallith* [prayer shawl]."

"So you are going to synagogue?"

"No more."

"Your father lets you?"

"Yes."

"He knows about you and God?"

"Yes, I told him."

"Oh là là..."

Almost like converting to Christianity. I imagined the tempest in the dining room. Confronting his father, I thought, was even more awesome than doing away with God. A formidable loner Zalcman had appeared to me that day, unafraid, and unconcerned about what people thought of him. He didn't care about grades. I had seen him once play the piano, with all ten fingers, and I knew that he played for his enjoyment, not to please his parents or to impress others.

Like Menda, he was inept at sports. He and Menda and Maurice Holtzer, a bespectacled threesome, would stand in the schoolyard at Tachkemoni during recess, out of the way of the wild-running bunch, and talk. Flatfooted, he couldn't even run. Menda could not run either, or Holtzer, for that matter, but he could outdistance Zalcman by gearing up into accelerated lumbering. Neither could throw a ball halfway decently. Zalcman never drew attention to himself. In class, he didn't excel at anything. Menda was the star, excelling at everything effortlessly, with time to spare for daydreaming or reading up in our anthology or history book way ahead of the class. Yet when our music teacher in high school played on the piano Schubert's *Die Forelle* — "it's about a trout and a fisherman" was all he said before playing it again — and gave us ten minutes to write down the thoughts and images the music evoked, then asked for a volunteer to read his comments aloud, it was Zalcman who read his in a literate, perfectly accented Flemish. He continued extemporaneously about a carefree trout frolicking in the shimmering waters of a river, about the sudden appearance of a fisherman, the sinister foreboding, the trout's spasm and agony, about the quiet that returned without the joy. My sheet of paper had remained blank. I realized then that music could be more than pleasing sounds, more, even, than a reflection of the soul; and that fishing was killing.

Zalcman's argument about God was tightly reasoned. He had read an amazing number of authors, including some famous ones the less serious readers amongst us used mainly for name dropping, such as Rousseau, Voltaire, and other French philosophers. It was clear that he had set out on that awe inspiring journey on his own: those miscreant authors did not find him; he found them. When he assailed the originality of the Torah, mentioning the appearance of a flood narrative in other, earlier traditions, and the Hammurabi Code, Menda came barreling in:

"Hammurabi. Hammurabi. Did the Hammurabi Code order a master to free his slave after six years of servitude?"

"I didn't notice. But..."

"Did the Hammurabi Code order the authorities, when taking the nation to war, to assemble the men and exempt the newlywed, the one who built a house but had not yet dedicated it, who planted a vineyard but had not yet eaten from its fruit, the faint-hearted?" Menda was launched. "Did the Hammurabi Code forbid you to cut down your enemy's trees when you are laying siege to his city" — trust Menda to remember that one — "let alone harm his civilians?"

"Go tell Amalek," Zalcman snapped. "We wipe out the entire nation of Amalek, men, women and children, as ordered by God. But guess what, Saul spares *one* life: their king Agag! So good old Samuel goes into a rage, 'God has taken the kingship away from you!' and slices Agag to pieces."

"Samuel, uh, yes..." Menda stammered. "Amalek, uh, attacked us, uh, without provocation when we were weak and disorganized. We had just gotten out of Egypt..."

"Imagine," I interjected. "That was the only time we were all there, in one place, with nowhere to go. Could have been 'Adieu Jewish people.' That'll teach them."

"Amalek represents our mortal enemy, whoever, wherever," Menda continued, brushing past my remark. "They had to disappear. In fact, uh, Haman is supposed to be descended from Amalek, according to the *aggadah* [legend]..."

"Yes, *aggadah*," Zalcman grumbled. "Like all the rest."

"Never mind," Menda countered. "That's beside the point. The Hammurabi model..."

"That too is beside the point," Zalcman interrupted. "So the Torah is a better code of law. So what? That still does not prove the existence of God. Nietzsche..."

"Did you read *Nietzsche*?" I blurted out.

"Some, yes."

"Wasn't he an antisemite?" I asked, recovering fast from the shock.

"I don't know. He did say that the entire New Testament isn't worth one page of the Old Testament."

"Did he really say that? A great man."

The debate raged on, Religion is a crutch, Science can't explain everything, You can't explain one mystery with another; God the Almighty and free will are contradictory, Faith is an act of reason and free will. Around in circles we went, standing on the sidewalk, on the way home from school, with the Jew-star sewn over our hearts.

I was getting used to Zalcman's ideas, but I would not leave Menda in the lurch. Since I had never been unduly preoccupied with the existence of God, I decided to remain comfortably on the Almighty's side. I admired Zalcman's guts, though.

"Had I been born a Christian," I said towards the end of our tortuous street-corner debate, "I would be an atheist. But a Jew?"

"Wait a minute," Menda exclaimed, jumping with obvious delight at the opportunity to demolish my logic. He always had. "Does God's existence depend upon the religion you are born into?"

After Zalcman had parted from us I said, in a pondering tone: "God may not take kindly... to that atheistic..."

"Oh," Menda broke in with a chuckle. "If anything, God will be amused."

"Not if Zalcman is right."

Menda gasped, then laughed resignedly. I enjoyed my logic. We got home late.

* * *

My father stopped intoning hymns at the Sabbath meals. He would no longer recline. Gone was the smugness, the peace of Shabbat. We ate mostly in silence. My father would praise the food, as always — my mother was a good cook. She would get up for every course, bring, apportion, serve. I would plead for less, "Enough-enough, after the fish and the soup, I can't eat so much." She would cut off a piece of chicken breast and spoon off half a potato. "Still fussy," she would mutter. "In wartime. You need strength. Who knows..." We ate without looking up. My parents were wrestling in silence with their preoccupations. From the dessert — fruit or rhubarb compote — straight to a hurried recitation of grace. My father would mumble it by heart.

* * *

July 14, 1942: the second work contingent left Antwerp for the North of France.

Unlike the men in the previous group, they were not on the dole, and not without means. Most of them, though foreigners, grew up in Antwerp. Complying with the German decree was, to them, the way to avoid trouble and ensure the safety of their kin. A few young men even volunteered, to show that Jews were not afraid of manual labor. Carrying their bags full of the prescribed work gear, clothes and provisions, they made their way through sleepy streets to gather at the Central Station at the appointed time, set early — before the 7:00 AM lifting of the Jew-curfew — to prevent mothers and wives from accompanying their sons and husbands. The emotional family scenes might arouse the sympathy of the population.

But Antwerpians noticed and were shocked. The clandestine paper *De Roode Vaan* (The Red Flag) wrote that a crowd surrounded the Jewish men and slipped them packets and tobacco, prompting the German military police to hurry the draftees onto trucks. They were taken to a camp situated inland, near the French village of Charleville, by the Belgian border.

Their letters, we heard, described humane conditions: adequate food and accommodations, manageable work — cutting trees for the production of charcoal. They could get packages from home, walk to nearby Charleville. Some heads of households could bring their families to the village. Once, a team of workers and the soldiers guarding them engaged in a game of soccer. With the cold season drawing near, a camp committee got permission to dispatch three men with a truck to fetch the bundles of winter clothes the relatives back home had been asked to bring to the *Judenrat.*

The talk in town was of Charleville only: Livable. Close to home. Reassuring. Charleville became the hoped-for destination of those summoned to the Labor Office.

The selection of able-bodied men by an engineering and construction outfit like the *Organisation Todt* for a vital project in the North of France misled Jew and Gentile alike. It got many Jews to take at face value that other summons, the *tsetl* to Mechelen, when it made its appearance in late July and was issued mainly to men and women between the ages of sixteen and forty. "For work," it read. "Bearable," many felt. "The lesser evil." It guaranteed, they thought, the safety of those left behind. No one had an inkling of the Germans' intentions. A clandestine paper in Liège, the *Churchill-Gazette,* declared: "The *Boche* [epithet for German] of 1914 is at it again," — implying compulsory work only, outside the country — and went on to assail the complicity of the Belgian authorities. The secretaries-general became wary of a World-War-I-type deportation of the country's men only when alerted by the *Judenrat* that a number of Belgian Jews had been summoned for the medical checkup at the Labor Office. They signed a letter of protest. The Germans pledged not to send any more Belgian Jews out of the country. "What is happening today to the Jewish citizens," wrote *België Vrij* (Belgium Free), the voice of the Underground in Antwerp, "may happen tomorrow to everyone." It did. About a year later. Yielding to Berlin, the Military Authority began calling up Belgian men for work in Germany. Dodging was widespread. Men went into hiding. Monsignor Van Wayenbergh, rector of the Catholic University of Leuven, went to prison for refusing to release the roll of first-year students to the Germans.

✡ ✡ ✡

I did well on my exams. Bunched up at the top of the class was the uncontested threesome with Janneke Peeters holding on to his first-year title, Menda Zangen second, Roald Bingen third. I came in fourth.

I knew summer boredom of a new kind, one laced with a sense of dread I was picking up from my parents. It blocked out the horizon. High school was beyond the horizon; it did not even come to mind.

✤ ✤ ✤

Aunt Surtshe wrote from the ghetto: "This is my last letter from Kolbuszowa. Don't send us any more packages. We are all leaving tomorrow. We don't know whereto."

"Who knows whether I will ever hear from her again," my mother said, looking into the distance, letter in hand.

Surtshe, her husband and their two children were taken, with most of Kolbuszowa's Jews, to the annihilation camp of Belzec.

July 22, 1942: German police have hauled Jews off the trains on the Antwerp-Brussels line. Picked them off at the exit of Antwerp's Central Station. Random arrests of men and women; of people commuting to work. Also on the Pelikaanstraat, by the station, in the Jewish quarter.

Flight fever erupted. People made frantic arrangements. I glimpsed the fear in my parents' eyes. They were having whispered asides. Silently they would file back into the kitchen.

Letters from the arrested came, days later, reassuring; they had no fruit; packages were allowed. The return address: Dossin barracks in Mechelen.

They inaugurated the internment camp. The office workers among them, the women especially, were to become the in-house secretaries of the deportation.

✤ ✤ ✤

Jews in the employ of the *Judenrat* are delivering call-up notices on letterhead of the Military Occupation authorities ordering the recipients — men and women, mainly between sixteen and forty — to report at the Dossin barracks in Mechelen, for work duty. They are to bring, among other items, nonperishable food to last fourteen days, work shoes, and identity papers. Failure to show up at the specified time will be punished by deportation to a concentration camp and the confiscation of property.

Ten thousand people — at the rate of three hundred arrivals per day — was the quota set by Berlin. "They will be put to work in the German Reich," Anton Burger, Adolf Eichmann's roving emissary, in Brussels to launch the deportations to the East, told the Jewish notables of the *Judenrat*. "German and other heroes are spilling their blood to defend Europe."

Only about three thousand heeded the notice. The fear of deportation, the notables explained when summoned to the Gestapo. This was compulsory work indeed, the Germans assured them, not deportation, and ordered them to so advise the recipients. Which they did in a cover letter attached to the *tsetl*, adding that noncompliance might result in dire consequences for kin and for the entire Jewish population of the country — the Gestapo chief had threatened to seal off the streets and haul everyone to Mechelen without consideration of age or health and to be done with the Jews in one night.

The admonition on the letterhead of the *Judenrat* signed by its president, the chief rabbi of Belgium, and the heads of the local *Judenrat* offices swayed many people into complying with the work notice.

In early August the first train of deportees, people who had complied with the *tsetl*, headed East. The state-owned Belgian Railway Authority had laid a spur track that led from the front gate of the Dossin barracks to the main track. The passengers could leave their compartments at station stops on the way, to limber up, or to buy refreshments. A teacher from Tachkemoni mailed a card to his colleagues and the members of the school committee in Antwerp where the all-Jewish staff and administrators were getting ready for the upcoming school year. " 'In the rolling train car,' it began, in Hebrew," my father told us, "*Ba-qaron ha-nossay-ah*." That's all I remember. It held a few words and greetings in Hebrew, not somber or anguished judging from my father's rather amused expression.

Sixty years later a Jewish woman from Poland told me that she happened to be at the Warsaw station when a train stopped there, with Jewish passengers on board — "Jews: just one glimpse into the compartment and you knew." The year was 1942, almost a year after she began her clandestine life as a Christian. She saw them sitting, "well-dressed; they seemed calm," she reminisced. "I talked with one of them, in Polish. She was seated by the open window. She wore makeup; a necklace. They were from Belgium, she told me, they didn't know yet where they were going to live. I knew what was awaiting them. I could not make up my mind whether to tell her or not. It haunts me. What... what would you have done?"

A survivor recounted that a German woman boarded the wrong train, with her child. Her protestations in Auschwitz fell on deaf ears.

Entire families are getting the *tsetl*: "To keep them intact," a concession made to Queen Elisabeth of Belgium who had appealed to Hitler, through the agency of the king of Italy (her daughter was married to the Italian crown prince), that girls of working age and women be left with their families.

The trains rolled. The compartment doors were locked from the outside. People broke windows and jumped off.

✡ ✡ ✡

I ran into Goldenhar. Open shirt collar, rolled up sleeves. Tall, with an athletic build, dark eyes in a pale longish face ending in a strong chin, jet-black hair in mild, rakish disarray. He would speak unhurriedly, switching between schooled Flemish and the Antwerp dialect. He lived in the Jewish quarter, had been in the Flemish section at Tachkemoni. Always the last one left standing in a game of *balle de guerre*. The toughs from the public school who had occasionally dogged us on the way to Tachkemoni — they followed me once; I was scared, but did not run — gave him a wide berth. I have always admired him. He enrolled in the commercial section in high school, not one to bother with Latin conjugations. He had planned on starting work after the compulsory school age of fourteen: "The real world; life."

Goldenhar told me that he was looking forward to getting the *tsetl*: "To travel," he said with the glint of adventure in his eyes. "Life in Antwerp is boring."

I was taken aback. Adventure?... A vast gray void was all I could see out there, a no man's land. I did not respond.

We had little to say to each other after that. We parted.

Goldenhar, David, left Mechelen August 18th, 1942. In the Dossin barracks bookkeeping that was recovered after the war, he was listed as number 603 of *Transport* IV. His mother was number 602, his father, 601.

Strassberg and Zalcman were both taken away on the following *Transport*. It left August 25. Strassberg, Bernard, was number 304. Zalcman, Moszek-Isaak (he called himself Maurice), was number 662.

More people are turning to smugglers. They are facing the challenge of slipping by the German Security agents, the Vichy police and militias, and the Swiss border guards who are turning fugitives back — only nuclear families with children six years of age and younger are allowed in. The children, we learned after the war, were placed in foster homes; men and women were interned, separately; they could visit each other and their children once a month.

The transfer of all Jewish hospital patients to a separate ward at St-Erasmus, in Greater Antwerp's municipality of Borgerhout, was set in motion, as ordered.

✿ ✿ ✿

The shoemaker had been recommended for his expertise; a tiny man with a constant twinkle in his eyes. With sharp, dexterous strokes he was fashioning cavities in the heels of my fine black-leather shoes: they were to contain the two diamond rings and the two packets of diamonds my father had on him.

I was sitting in my socks, fascinated by the craftsman's precise movements, his sure-handedness. Shoes seemed a prized object in his hands; he often ran his fingers over the leather. My father had a good relaxed time with him. He liked shoemakers and their craft, from his days back in Kolbuszowa when he ran his mother's shoe and leather business.

"You could do this with eyes closed," he remarked.

"I have done a number of those jobs," the shoemaker said with a smile that rearranged the wrinkles on his face. "That and leather straps. The tailors also have a business going. But shoes are the better way."

"I think so, too."

A solidly-built young man on the tall side popped in with a snap greeting and left after rummaging in a tool box.

"A son of yours?" my father asked.

"Yes."

"*Unberufen!* [Touch wood!] A guy like a tree."

"Takes after my wife's family."

"Any more?"

"Four more like him, *tse lange yoor'n* [may they enjoy a long life]."

"Are you teaching them shoemaking?"

"Yes. A trade in the hand. Important. Afterwards they can do what they want."

The valuables fit snugly, a ring and a little cloth packet at the center of each heel; they seemed to belong there. It reminded me of the little pouch of valuables that hung on a long string around my neck, during our flight to France in 1940. Once again a palpable threat hung in the air, and my parents were taking precautions. Was that shoe operation pointing to a move, like a dash to Switzerland?

The little troves disappeared under two sturdy pieces of leather. New heels emerged, with perfect, glistening curves. The metal tips came last. I was standing now in my shining black shoes.

"How does it feel?" the shoemaker asked.

"Fine," I said. "The heels are a bit thicker."

"Right," he said with an appreciative smile. "Now, don't go around teasing your friends, 'Guess how much my shoes are worth?' "

"Oh no!"

The two men laughed.

To find some diversion from the boredom of the long summer days, I had joined a Talmud class at the Moriah *shul*. I would hurry on my way to the *shul*; I felt marked by the yellow star. With high school closed for the summer an empowering embrace had gone limp.

The class was held in a bare room above the sanctuary. Menda also attended, and Mayersdorf. Like Menda, he would grasp the thorniest math problem, the most intricate talmudic argument, at first hearing, sometimes even anticipating the teacher's explanations. Like Menda, he couldn't throw a ball.

Once, he missed a Talmud class. It took him ten minutes, the next day, sitting by himself in a corner, to catch up with the rest of us. Our *rebbe*, a small, soft-spoken man with a pointed, graying beard, instructed his son, a young rabbi who helped the slower ones amongst us, to quiz Mayersdorf and fill him in. Mayersdorf read to him the previous day's *gemara* — about a fifth of a page — explaining the main propositions in broken, German-accented Yiddish, and answering each of the few questions with a spare key word or two. It turned into a colloquy between peers. He then rejoined the class. The *rebbe* looked at him with affection. Mayersdorf had a reputation; he and Menda were beyond envy. I had lost the thread in that same passage, the day before, with the most patient of teachers, and had let my mind wander.

A few days later Mayersdorf told our *rebbe* that he and his mother had received their *tsetl*: the day's class would be his last. At the end of the lesson the *rebbe* closed the tractate of the Talmud and told Mayersdorf:

"You are allowed to eat *trayfuh* [ritually impure food]. You must remain strong. They'll want to humiliate us by giving us pork. You can leave a scrap on the plate, to show your contempt."

He then blessed him. It was a solemn moment. And poignant: we were losing him.

I went down with Mayersdorf into the street. We were friends. He had invited me to his bar mitzvah and he had come to mine. I wanted to say something important to him, something that would make a difference.

"Mayersdorf," I said, "it's more important to eat than to show contempt."

He looked surprised. I felt embarrassed.

"Finish your plate if you are still hungry," I pressed on. I was launched, unstoppably, on the do-good path. He nodded. We shook hands and went our separate ways.

I felt pain and regret, and shame. There I had stood, in expensive shoes whose hollowed out heels contained diamonds and rings (it kept me from joining, after Talmud class, in the single-goal soccer game on the *shul*'s tiny, walled-in courtyard), telling a hapless but composed friend how to eat in captivity, knowing that he and his widowed mother, refugees from Germany, had to heed the *tsetl* because they were without Flemish friends and without means. At her son's bar mitzvah party in April, Madame Mayersdorf had served the five boys sitting in her kitchen a cookie and a small dish of a thin chocolate pudding, "non-dairy, for it would be too soon after your *flayshig* [meat] meal." I didn't touch the pudding; it looked too gelatinous. It hurt her feelings. I have always been a finicky eater. She gave me another cookie. "Would someone want another dish of pudding?" she asked. Menda nodded his head, reached for my dish with a grunt, and wolfed down my portion with a relish that was meant to signify to Madame Mayersdorf that her pudding was delicious. She smiled: her creased face rounded out and radiated, as if dropping a mask. Mayersdorf had the same gleam in the same brown eyes when he smiled. I knew, when I was saying good-bye to him, that my journey would be different from his: my parents were old-timers; they had money for a smuggler, for bribes. Facing each other in tense, hushed conversations they desperately tried to conjure a way out. A way out... I had felt protected.

Mother and son were listed as numbers 996 and 997 of *Transport* VI. It left Mechelen on August 29th, 1942. She was 50. He was 13. His voice was changing.

I stopped going to Talmud class.

✳ ✳ ✳

August 13, 1942:
Romanian Jews were rounded up in the middle of the night and hauled off to Mechelen. Repatriation, it was said. They had felt relatively secure as citizens of a country allied with Germany.

A Flemish maid my mother had hired for the day told my parents that she had lost her employer.

"To single out Romanian Jews," she said, indignant. "And the other nationalities? *Das toch nie sjust!*" ("downright unfair!").

My mother glanced at my father who nodded, incredulous.

The officials of the land had appealed, at the behest of Jewish notables, on behalf of the thousands facing deportation. The

Occupation Authorities turned them down, but they exempted the Belgian citizens among the Jews from work in the East, thereby signaling that the population at large was immune from World-War-I-like forced labor in Germany. It appeased the country's administrators and assured their continued cooperation — indispensable to the Germans — in running the country.

Cardinal Van Roey's wish, conveyed through an emissary, that Jewish converts to Catholicism be exempt from compulsory labor abroad, could not be granted either: "It is a race issue. Only Belgian nationals are exempt."

To me, Jews holding the green ID card of citizenship were like rare birds. I knew only one, Monsieur Kahan, the bookseller. The Kahans were family friends. He was born in Antwerp. Jews, as a rule, were born in Poland, or Lithuania, or Russia, Poland mainly, or in Germany, and Austria. The green card was like a shield; magical almost. I had never seen one.

"A 'Belgian' couple, putting their trust in the green card, went out and bought new furniture," my father informed my mother. She shook her head in disbelief.

My cousin Shloimeh stopped by with a request. A Flemish police officer had served him with a summons to appear at the Labor Office, for work on the Atlantic Wall, and he needed a packet of coffee beans "to send my heartbeat soaring" at the medical screening.

He brought back the rest of the coffee. "The caffeine kicked in too early," he informed my mother with an embarrassed smile. "*Arbeitsfähig*" ("Fit for work").

Rookhel, his younger sister, prevailed upon him to try for Switzerland. She even found a smuggler. Shloimeh was nabbed at the rendez-vous in Antwerp along with a small band of would-be fugitives. The smuggler collected from the Germans as well. Rookhel turned herself in, out of guilt, to share her brother's fate.

Brother and sister were listed as numbers 977 and 978 of *Transport* XIV. It left Mechelen on October 24th, 1942, more than two months after their arrival at the Dossin barracks: it was taking the Germans longer and longer to fill a train.

He was twenty eight. She was nineteen.

Their mother, Aunt Rakhtshe, was taken off the street and left on *Transport* XI. Number 1342.

Uncle Avrum hid for two years — until the liberation — in a damp cellar.

Lotti has dropped in after seeing her younger brother off to the train station, on his way to the Dossin barracks in Mechelen. She needed to collect herself before returning home to her parents.

She is standing by the dining table, slender, beautiful Lotti in her loose summer dress — it betrays, in draping them, her breasts; mysterious little peaks. The afternoon light highlights her cheekbones.

"I packed his valise," she continues. "It is too heavy. I packed several bottles of his asthma medicine, he can take a swig when he is plain thirsty. Such a long trip. He is so thin."

Her eyes, like pools, fill up. They sparkle.

"You did right," my mother says reassuringly.

"I packed his tuxedo." She looks anxiously at my parents with her big blue glistening eyes rimmed with black eyelashes. "Where there are Jews there will be weddings." She moves a sleek hand. "Then again he can barter it. It should fetch a lot in Poland, don't you think?"

"*Nu sicher*" ("But of course"), my mother says softly, using the German pronunciation for emphasis.

"He didn't want to hear about Switzerland," she says. "To keep us out of trouble."

She pauses. Two teardrops break loose and roll over Lotti's high cheekbones.

"And you, Lotti?" my mother asks.

"I am staying with my parents. They have no one else." Her father is infirm.

She bids us goodbye and leaves.

"And they say there is a God in heaven," my mother mutters.

My father was still going to his committee meetings at the Tachkemoni school: the fall opening with an all-Jewish staff was still on. Mr. Govaerts was assisting them. He was pro-English and pro-Jewish. He never had the slightest doubt that the Germans were headed for defeat, as in the first world war; that the Jews would see the hanging of Hitler — Govaerts had an almost mystical belief in the indestructibility of the Jewish people, a belief that

Tachkemoni would flourish again, with him as the new Flemish principal replacing the discredited pro-German one.

Mr. Govaerts was also procuring false — green — identity cards and was scouting for hiding places.

Tachkemoni would open in September to a shrunken student body.

Saturday, August 15: the third contingent of men slated for work on the Atlantic fortifications left Antwerp. A privileged bunch: they drew the better *tsetl*.

The fourth and last convoy of labor recruits from Antwerp left on September 12, the first day of Rosh Hashanah that fell on a Sabbath.

The *Organisation Todt* laborers ended up in Auschwitz. Two *Transporte* with 1314 men were detoured via Mechelen, one late-October night — to pick up more people. 241 men jumped off on Belgian soil. Seventy seven Dossin inmates escaped from the next two convoys. Boxcars then replaced passenger cars. German soldiers with submachine guns were posted at the front and the rear of the trains. Deportees kept breaking out. Some made it.

On Saturday night, August 15, the Jewish quarter was sealed off and raided. Hundreds of families were hauled off in trucks in the middle of the night. They were dropped in various empty buildings — the Moriah *shul*, a military depot, public schools.

The Antwerp police, by order of the Gestapo, had come out in force, lists of addresses in hand — the quarter's population was mixed. The targeted families were given ten minutes to get ready. The more zealous cops crashed their way into apartments when the knock on the door went unanswered; others did not insist. The loading onto trucks was brutal. Cries filled the air. Families got torn apart. Parents lost children. Some Gentiles took in a neighbor's child. Most watched or just listened. A few complained about the ruckus: they had to go to work the next morning.

The following day the more than one thousand people caught in the dragnet were crowded into moving vans and taken to Mechelen. A complete *Transport* — number IV — in one night. It left August 18 with 998 men, women and children; old and young, healthy and sick.

My parents were shaken: suddenly, everyone was seizable.

The Saturday night raid was the first of several. They were to make up for the growing number of people who ignored the *tsetl*; the trains — three so far — had been running behind schedule.

My father stopped going to Tachkemoni.

No news from Menda.

His family got the *tsetl*, on August 18, he told me years later. They fled. They were caught at the Swiss border. "*Ich führe keinen Krieg gegen Kinder*" ("I don't make war on children"), the local German *Kommandant* had declared, and handed Menda over to the Red Cross. The Red Cross handed him over to the French *Judenrat* in Paris, the *Association Générale des Israélites de France* (AGIF). He escaped from a children's home run by the AGIF, hid for three months with a French doctor's family, moved between clandestine children's homes run by a Jewish underground organization. He ran into a couple of French policemen who, fortunately, turned a blind eye, as did the Italian military stationed at the Swiss border — they would observe, unnoticed, the smuggling of Jewish children into Switzerland. They even urged the Underground, after Italy's defection from the Axis in September 1943, to rush their charges across before the Germans assumed patrol duty. Menda ended up at a high school for Dutch refugees near Montreux in Switzerland after a yearlong odyssey across Central, South and East France.

His parents were deported to Auschwitz from Drancy.

On August 27 Flemish policemen distributed mimeographed leaflets alerting the Jews to an impending raid that night, urging them to take evasive action. An irate Gestapo chief called off the raid. Then, the next day, he abruptly reinstated it and ordered four precinct chiefs to haul in 250 Jews each from four districts with high Jewish concentrations, and to use force. Women with babies under one year of age and Jews with Belgian, British, United States and Swiss citizenship were exempt.

The Jews were roused in the middle of the night. Many resisted arrest by Flemish policemen, more so when noticing the absence of Germans. They locked and bolted themselves in, hid in cellars and attics. The police branched out into adjoining streets to make the quota. Some neighbors were reported to have directed the agents to Jewish residences.

The night's tentacular haul netted over 1,100 souls. Streets with few Jewish residents were not visited.

The arrests by Belgian law enforcement personnel of people who had committed neither crime nor public offense violated the law of the land. Yet the mayor, who was sworn to uphold the Constitution, did not oppose or even protest the enlistment of his police force in the devastating raids. (When mayors in other municipalities took a firm stand, the Germans relented — the lesser evil — rather than send ripples through a civilian administration that excelled in running the country's affairs. In such cases they turned instead to local SS and other collaborators.) Not until November 18 did the district-attorney advise the police commissioner of Antwerp that further unlawful arrests would be prosecuted, and that he was to refer to his, the district-attorney's, letter of advise if confronted with similar orders from the occupier.

More than 14,000 people were deported in the first three months, another 11,000 in the following two years of unrelenting manhunt by the Gestapo, the Flemish SS, the pro-German militants, and the informers, both Gentiles and Jews. More than 25,000 Jews were sheltered by the population — from the working class to the aristocracy, by the Underground, the clergy, in convents, in Catholic and secular child welfare institutions.

✻ ✻ ✻

Silence hovers over the meal.

My mother lets out a deep sigh. It sounds like a concluding thought.

"It's too late for blaming ourselves or for regrets," my father responds. They had emerged, shortly before dinner, from another of their hushed dining-room conversations. "We did not have the courage to go when Avrum sent us his smuggler. God knows how much more dangerous it is today."

"I would have gone had I felt more *kapitalskräftig* [strong financially]," my mother says blandly.

"Courage, more than *Kapital*, courage was what we needed."

"*Kapital* gives courage." My mother is looking down at her hands.

"Are you now blaming me for the lack of *Kapital*?"

"You were never ambitious."

"I have never hankered for riches. That's different. And I never will," my father says, indignant. "I have provided amply and honorably. And God willing, I will do so after the war. That's all I have ever committed myself to."

"Unfortunately, it is not enough. Not in light of the present circumstances."

"These circumstances have engulfed the entire Jewish people."

"Not those with a bank account in America." Avrum was one of them; it gave him and his family the right of entry.

"I am ready to share the fate of *Klal Yisruel* [the community of Israel]." My father has raised his voice. "I am no better than other Jews. I am ready."

"I am not ready. *Klal Yisruel* is with the living."

"A guarantee is what you want. I can't give you such guarantee. You married the wrong man. I'll give you a divorce whenever you want."

"It's too late for that."

"... At least, I know where we stand," my father says, sobered.

My brother and I are sitting at the long side of the kitchen table. We are facing the sunlit window, waiting, heads bent, for the squall to blow over. I feel for my father. I want to be with him, be one with my people. I wonder: "The fate of *Klal Yisruel*. What *is* that fate?" I realize that we are swept up in a historic event.

My parents are facing each other from the two ends of the table. I glimpse them, my mother, grim and pale; my father, angry and shaken. There is silence. My mother covers her face with her hands.

"What has come over us?" she whispers in a tone of despair mixed with disbelief.

"We'll slog through, God willing," my father says with conviction. "Have courage. Have trust."

"We'll slog through, I hope," my mother echoes, without conviction.

She gets up and begins clearing the table.

———————

My father makes discrete trips to the balcony. He surveys the street in the direction of Charlottalei, from where he thinks the black sedan and the green, tarpaulin-covered truck might come. Streets with just a few Jewish residents, like ours, have not been importuned, yet.

I also gravitate to the balcony: to be out — I don't want to hear what my parents may have to say to each other. Standing, rigid, hand on the concrete enclosure, like my father, I am looking down towards the Charlottalei. The sun-drenched façades, the cool, bluish cobblestones, radiate a newly-sensed sweetness. A man is walking, unhurried, with a package under his arm, a woman leads a little boy by the hand, a poodle on a leash is strutting in front of a matron in flat heels and rolled-down stockings: the simple routines, the minutiae woven into life's sturdy fabric. Our routines only serve to hold up the unraveling fabric of our existence. ("Why dust off?" I had asked my mother a few days earlier. "Is it really necessary?" "Yes," she retorted. "We must go on living like *menschen*. In fact, I meant to ask you to do it for me." I did. Every day thereafter.) Poodle, then matron, turn the corner into nearby Breughelstraat. I look up: the sky is a serene blue, like on Friday, May 10, 1940. And as on that Friday morning before the flight to France, the birds are chirping, carefree, mocking.

I feel hemmed in and move off the balcony into my parents' bedroom.

My mother is putting away some laundry in the armoire. She closes the door and turns around when she stops, as if struck: "This is death," she says tersely. No panic nor self-pity in her voice. "With the Pole, under the German..." — in her eyes, a savage look hardening into defiance — "we may as well throw ourselves in the *Schelde*." Cupping her face with her hands, "How will one get milk for a child?" she mutters. "Or medicine?" She is looking into the distance as if seeing Poland, or death. I know at that instant that we will not heed the *tsetl*.

CHAPTER 4 — TO BELSELE

We piled up in a small room above the Flemish butcher shop across the street — the butcher had offered it as a refuge to my father a while back — as soon as the friendly police chief of our precinct, walking up the street and spotting my father on the balcony, waved him away. My father took the hint.

The butcher and his wife had given shelter to several Jewish families in the spare rooms of their small house. It was a crowded, unsafe place, but it bought time. Each family had to procure its own food. There were tense trips to the corner bakery — without the yellow star. My mother would scurry across the street to our apartment to boil a pot of potatoes, some eggs, to sauté the cutlets we bought from the butcher. The previous Friday she baked a cake for the Sabbath. She had rushed back with a flushed, almost glowing face, like someone who has returned from a dangerous mission.

The vertical sun stripe on the drawn curtain — the blacked-out window was open a crack — and the sparkle on my father's spectacles — he was watching our house across the street through a finger-wide opening in the curtain — gave the low-wattage bulb in the ceiling lamp an off-color, feeble glow. My mother was sitting on the bed, her hands in her lap. My brother was sitting on the only chair. I was standing. We were waiting for two women from a Flemish village. Mr. Spingarn, a colleague of my father on the Tachkemoni school committee, had told him of Flemish villagers who had taken in the children of an acquaintance of his, a certain Madame Sobolski. "She is happy; her two little boys are well cared for. And she told me that there is room for more children with some of the relatives." My father asked his colleague to ask Madame Sobolski that she recommend us to the Flemish villagers. "Could she arrange for them to meet with us in Antwerp?"

My father consulted his pocket watch. The gold Schaffhausen reflected a ray of sun. "They shouldn't be long," he said. He had pulled it up frequently in the last half hour, clicked it open, glanced down, snapped it shut, gently, and slipped it back into his vest pocket. The familiar sound punctuated the tension in the room.

"There they are!" he said with a start and rushed out. I spotted two women dressed in black in front of our house. Moments later he crossed the sun-drenched, peaceful street and let the visitors in. A Jewish dwelling was no longer safe, but my mother had insisted that the meeting take place as planned: "I want them to see the home the children come from." She crossed over next. My brother and I were to wait until my father would signal us from the balcony door. My parents wanted some time alone with the two women. A few minutes, and it was our turn. A brisk walk across the sparkling cobblestones, the glowing sidewalk. I locked the front door behind us. We climbed the stairs and entered the dining room.

The four adults were seated in an intimate circle off the dining table. The two women were dressed in their Sunday church-going best; one wore a hat with a veil. We said *"goeden dag,"* I, with a respectful nod. Our parents were smiling approvingly. The woman with the hat returned our *"goeden dag."* The other, seated further back, a petite woman with deep-set, dark eyes, black hair, high cheekbones and a strong chin, greeted us with a smile covering her entire face. Her name was Alice Van Damme.

On a Saturday of that August, 1942, Alice had come to visit a friend in Antwerp and had happened to witness how hundreds of families were driven and kicked with rifle butts into the covered trucks and moving vans that were ringing Koningin Astrid Square, near the Central Railroad Station. Traffic was stopped. As she later recounted it, she had stood there, frozen. It was the sight of a little girl crying as she was lifted by a soldier, her arms extended to her mother, that jolted her: she resolved to bring a little girl home.

"This is horrible," she overheard a woman say to another bystander. "One should do something to help."

"If that's what you want," came the answer, "go to the *Jodenraad* [*Judenrat*] in the Lange Leemstraat."

Alice turned around — back to her village, Belsele — without seeing her friend. She pleaded with her parents to shelter a Jewish girl, won their consent, then pleaded with the members of the *Judenrat* and, after repeated trips to Antwerp, won their confidence. She obtained the name of a Jewish pediatrician,

Dr. Content, who was facilitating the placement of Jewish children in Flemish homes. The apartment where she had hoped to pick up a little girl was sealed — a sign that it had been raided — to secure its contents for eventual shipment to Germany. (The *Möbelaktion* — furniture drive — from Belgium and France filled hundreds of trains.) At the next address a surprised Jewish woman, Madame Sobolski, suspicious at first, warmed to Alice, stepped out of the living room and returned with two little boys, Marcel, four years old, and Johnny, a year-and-a-half. Mrs. Sobolski wanted her "saving angel" to take both children. Alice was to bring one little girl only, but she could not turn her back on those little boys. She prevailed on the mother to come along and see the children's new home.

Alice's parents, stunned at first, took to the Jewish woman and her children. They even offered her shelter as well. But Mrs. Sobolski returned to Antwerp to wait for news from her husband who had been drafted into the *Organisation Todt* for work on the Atlantic Wall. She told Mr. Spingarn, my father's colleague, about the Flemish haven. It led to the meeting with the two women in our apartment. Shortly thereafter Mrs. Sobolski was picked off the street by cruising German police. She was deportee number 46 on the twelfth convoy that left Mechelen on October 10. Mrs. Sobolski never heard from her husband. He was deported from France.

Alice, the daughter of the village blacksmith of Belsele, was twenty-two-years old. Her action sparked a wider rescue effort: her sister and her sister-in-law, both childless, offered, each with her husband's consent, to harbor Jewish children. They had put off having their own children until after the war.

✡ ✡ ✡

My brother and I were standing side by side, closing the circle. The lady in the hat and veil was Alice's sister-in-law, Adrienne Van Damme. She had a serious mien. I felt scrutinized.

"Well, yes," she said. "Two big boys." Hers was the standard Flemish, without a trace of a local accent.

Her remark was not the polite compliment I mistook it for — my brother and I were on the short and slim side. She had expected to find little children; big ones might be trouble. My father made us two years younger, "six and twelve," to soften her disappointment. And she wanted siblings; a child alone, separated from its parents, would be lonely, she felt. There we fit the bill. She agreed to take us. She was impressed with my parents and would not turn us away. All this had transpired before the two of us walked in.

"Sensible children," Alice chimed in. "And well-behaved."

"I can see that," Adrienne Van Damme said. And she smiled at us, a warm and playful gleam in her dark eyes.

"What is your name?" she asked.

"Henri." I had adopted it when I started Tachkemoni. "Henek" was too Polish. Nobody called me "Hersch," my name at birth. My mother could not pronounce the French nasal sound "en" in "Henri" and took to calling me "Harry," the name of my cousin from Frankfurt.

Adrienne Van Damme looked at my brother.

"Sylvain," he said. A freshly-minted name. "Salomon" would be a dead giveaway.

"Nice names. Would you like to live in the country?"

"Yes, Madam."

"Yes, Madam."

"*Goed. Komt maar af*" ("Good. Just come on down").

I smiled. My father also; it was clear that he liked the two women. Alice was beaming. I pictured green meadows against a backdrop of dense foliage, a luminous sky — would I get down to working the land? My mother's constant worried look had not left her.

My father said, "A Flemish teacher, Mr. Govaerts, will bring the children on Saturday." For we would be less conspicuous in the larger Saturday crowd, among folks visiting their kin or shopping for provisions on the farms. My father also went by the hunch that the Antwerp Gestapo who had become familiar with our calendar and customs might be less likely to stop and search us: that Saturday was also the first day of Rosh Hashanah, a holy day in the religious calendar when, as on the Sabbath, Jews are to refrain from traveling.

As Adrienne was writing down her name, address and directions my mother had a brief aside with my father, whereupon he said to the two women:

"We want to tell you... just in case you don't see the children on Saturday... we may try for Switzerland. We were considering it. We need a few more days to think it over."

My mother was the one who wanted to think it over: Adrienne's husband was a blacksmith, *koval* in Polish, a term often used to signify a brute. It conjured memories of drunkenness among the rural class of her native Poland, of their brutality, especially to wives and children. Adrienne and Alice did not look like the kin of a violent drunk. In fact, my mother seemed taken with them. Still, she was apprehensive. She needed more time. Govaerts, she had wanted to believe, might find us all a place.

I knew then and there that it would be Belsele for my brother and me, an impression called forth by the friendliness in the room, by my father's almost cheerful air, by my first foray in the light of day since we had fled our apartment. The mention of Mr. Govaerts sealed it in my mind.

The visitors rose to take their leave. All stood. Adrienne Van Damme towered over Alice; in her high heels and hat she struck a tall pose.

Back in our hideout my father told me that when he had brought up the question of living expenses Adrienne Van Damme surprised him with the modest sum of 1,500 francs a month. " 'That's not enough,' I told her. I offered her right away 2,500 francs, to cover eggs, milk, butter. You should each have an egg for breakfast. *'Dat komt well in orde'* ['no problem'], she said. They live right next to a farm. I told her to write down every expense she incurs for the two of you. She nodded. She will most probably exceed that amount. They are not looking to gain, but I don't want them to lose. A fine woman."

"Yes," my mother concurred. "An upstanding, reliable woman."

"I also told her that if we send you there, Govaerts will visit you regularly, bring money for your upkeep, clothes, whatever is necessary."

✳ ✳ ✳

My father was facing the wall, in prayer. His back got the light of the naked bulb. I revisited the afternoon's interlude in our sunlit dining room with the two emissaries from the country in their distinct dress, with their calm demeanor; confident, secure, free to move, to see Jews in the city; offering shelter in their village.

The lone bulb's pallid light dissolved into the shadows floating around the room. We would propagate them as we moved.

The towels hanging on the brass railing at the foot of the bed cast darkness beyond it. Even the colors would fade, the patterns blur, into shades of light and dark. My mother and brother had a pasty complexion.

We ate: a hard boiled egg each, then potato salad, holding the plate in the left hand and working the fork with the right; and a piece of cake. Our parents sat on the high-legged brass bed — it took up most of the space; baggage was stashed underneath. My brother sat on the chair, I, astride a valise.

We took turns washing up in the corner sink of a half-bathroom down the hall. My parents and brother lay down to sleep on the bed. I stretched out on an improvised bed on the foot rug: the bedspread folded up three times and a pillow. I found the quiet and darkness of night soothing. It was a long day.

Mr. Muehlstein dropped by our room. The Muehlsteins, acquaintances my parents used to have coffee with in town, before the war, and their daughter Dora, the accomplished skater, also occupied a room in the butcher's house.

"Greenshteyn," he intoned, "*mir zennen farloyr'n*" ("we are doomed").

"Not yet, Meelshteyn," my father responded. "In a pickle, yes. But not doomed."

"Where does one get your optimism?" Mr. Muehlstein said, nodding incredulously.

"Have you given up on Switzerland?" my father asked.

"No... We are going to risk it. I am shaking like a leaf. I haven't slept in two nights."

"When?"

"Thursday. Two more nights. And you," he asked, looking at my father. "What are you thinking of doing?"

"We are thinking of placing the children."

"Where?"

"In a Flemish village."

"How did you meet these people?"

"They were recommended. And we met two women from the family. They made a good impression."

"Farmers?"

"*Kovals*," my mother answered.

Mr. Muehlstein did not speak right away. "*Nu yah*," he said, "it's easier with boys. And you?"

"Here, for the time being," my father said. "Until we find something."

We stood a while, silent and motionless. Mr. Muehlstein reached for the door handle, prompting an effusive exchange of good luck wishes.

"May the hour [of your departure] be a felicitous one".

"*Oomeye'n*. For you as well. For all Jews."

"*Oomeye'n*."

"A millionaire, and couldn't help himself," my mother said when he was gone.

The Muehlsteins did not make it.

✡ ✡ ✡

Mr. Govaerts was due around nine, after nightfall, way past the Jew-curfew but well before the general curfew at eleven. He would take me and my brother to his house in Merksem, a borough of Antwerp, for the night, on the first leg of our journey to Belsele.

My father was saying the evening prayers ushering in the Sabbath and Rosh Hashanah. My mother was laying out on the bed underwear, socks, shirts, pyjamas, for my brother and me, just enough to fill a little overnight suitcase that would not draw undue attention to us. My brother and I hardly moved. The silence was oppressive. Even our shadows moved slowly across the walls of our hideout.

My father put his prayer book aside. He pulled a slip of paper out of his vest pocket and turned to me:

"This is the address of my brother Chaim in America," he said. "He calls himself 'Hyman'; he spells his name with two e's, Greenstein."

Uncle Chaim, who in 1905, at the age of fifteen, had set out for the New World, had urged us to leave "the boiling cauldron called Europe," more insistently after Kristallnacht; he would send us an affidavit. But the cauldron would not boil over, "The world will not allow," most people in our community had liked to believe, especially those unable to reach the safety of distant shores or, like my parents, unwilling to uproot themselves again in the midst of the depression.

"Keep this *tsetl* and guard it," my father continued. "If you don't find us after the war, contact him as soon as possible."

"If you don't find us after the war." It hit me: our parents were sending us to safety, even trying to ensure our well-being after the war, when they themselves faced the possibility — the likelihood? — of not making it, while I was looking forward to a vacation of sorts, in the country. I saw the tiny, stifling room: a trap waiting to spring. To take that scrap of paper was like accepting my father's fateful scenario as matter-of-factly as it was broached. I demurred.

"It's too dangerous to have that *tsetl* on me," I said. To speak my mind would have elicited a stern "Don't talk nonsense. This is no time to be sensitive." I knew it. And I would have backed down.

"Then commit it to memory."

No different from taking it: I looked at it without reading. My father put the slip back in his vest pocket.

"What will you do?" I asked.

"We don't know yet. Govaerts may find us a place."

"Why don't you give them the address of my folks?" my mother suggested in a challenging tone of voice. "Itshe. Esther. They know the children."

"Chaim is an old American, he'll know what to do. Besides, they'll be in touch; they will be seeing each other."

"Oh yes..." my mother replied wanly, "at weddings... at *simkhus* [joyful occasions]."

My father packed the few items my mother had prepared. He then showed me a pocket *siddur* (prayer book).

"I am giving you this *sidderrel* [Yiddish for little *siddur*]. You are going to an alien place, don't forsake *Yiddishkeit* [Jewishness in the religious sense]. And show your brother, he should know where he comes from."

"Yes," I said, ashamed. I had already left *Yiddishkeit* behind: I had stopped praying and putting on *tefillin* (phylacteries) in our cramped hideout. My father, who never relaxed his observance of the daily ritual, had kept silent about my lapse. I already had one foot among the Gentiles. Packing a prayer book had not entered my mind. A betrayal of sorts.

"I am also giving you a *tillimel* [Yiddish for little *Book of Psalms*]," my father continued.

A Jew's constant companion. My father never moved without his: a dog-eared pocket psalter. He read the daily portion of the weekly cycle after the morning prayer, in his prayer shawl. I had never read the *Book of Psalms*.

"Yes. I will also take my *tefillin*," I offered in a mumble, to atone for my breach of faith.

"*Tefillin!?*" my mother exclaimed. "Among Flemish villagers!?"

Incongruous indeed; I felt guilty *and* foolish.

"And you shouldn't give them a *sidder* with a *tillimel*," she continued, addressing my father, "a search, and..."

"A search, God forbid, would be the end, regardless," my father interrupted. "How can they leave without a Yiddish word? [meaning, a text from the liturgy or Scriptures]."

He slipped the hand-size prayer book and the miniature psalter into our little suitcase, under the change of shirts, socks and underwear. "No one will stop them, not with Govaerts." Mr. Govaerts looked indeed the ideal of un-Jewishness. He had a big, ruddy face — he scowled when he was serious — and sparse, carefully parted reddish-brown hair. His back was straight like a wall. He wore a tight suit — always the same — that exposed his ankles and large bony wrists and made him look even bigger.

"Yom Kippur is coming up," my father said. " Eat what you will be given. You are exempt. Don't fast. Besides, it will put off the Van Dammes so soon after your arrival."

"I won't."

Little was said while we waited for Govaerts. His arrival put my parents in a higher state of anxiety.

We said our good-byes in the narrow, darkened hallway of the butcher's house, shadows moving in the faint, cold light of the regulation-blue bulb. My mother hugged and kissed me. She then hugged and kissed my little brother. I joined Mr. Govaerts by the door. Suddenly she pressed my brother against her, clutching him, and sobbed uncontrollably. He started to cry. Troubled by her despair, I took a step towards them. But my father stepped in:

"You are making it hard on them. They are going to a safe place." And, gently, he pulled my brother loose.

My mother let go with a wail that hovered in the darkness: "Will I ever see them..."

Mr. Govaerts weighed in, calmly, in Flemish: "Madame Grünstein, a safe place in the country. How lucky they are."

"I beg you, get hold of yourself," my father pleaded. "God willing, we'll also find a safe spot for ourselves."

My mother snapped out of her spell. She ran her hands over her face, visibly embarrassed over her loss of control, and hugged us again, softly, as if to make up. "You'll be safe... Go in good health, my dear little lambs. You should be protected every step of the way." Then, as my father was kissing and blessing us, my mother turned away, and, in a voice still muffled, but with a fierceness I had never sensed in her before she let out:

"*Of Dahtshe Mitter! NOR OF ZEYE gezoogt!*" ("On German mothers! Let it befall ONLY THEM!").

My parents were standing back in the dark hallway, my mother with her hands to her face, my father with his arms dangling; somber statues. Mr. Govaerts opened the front door. I was last to step out. He closed the door.

The clicking of our metal-tipped shoes in the blacked-out, forbidden street kept piercing the silence of the moonless night. The pounding in my heart stopped after we sat down in the tram to Merksem: the few dispersed passengers looked haggard in the lugubrious blue light; they paid no attention to us. Mr. Govaerts spread his large frame and one arm across the seat, like someone at home. We looked normal.

✤ ✤ ✤

We left Govaerts' house the following morning, a balmy Saturday in September. He took us through bustling, sun-flooded streets. My brother and I were wearing our Sabbath clothes, jacket, short pants, white shirt and tie, but without hats, like Christian boys setting out for a weekend visit. Mr. Govaerts, large, gruff-looking and self-confident, was carrying our little overnight suitcase.

We walked in silence, looking straight ahead. I was avoiding all eye contact. Accordion music accompanying a few loud, cheerful voices wafted through the open door of a corner café. I recognized the *Sinjorenlied*, the Song of the Lords, as Antwerpians refer to themselves. I couldn't distinguish the words, but I knew the Jew-baiting substitution of the word *Joden*:

Chee-ree-O, chee-ree-O,	Cheerio, cheerio,
In Antwerpen zingen ze zoo,	In Antwerp they sing so
Weg met de Joden ["zorgen"	Away with the Jews ["wor-
in the original]	ries" in the original]
En weg met 't verdriet,	And away with the sorrow,
Zijn we Sinjoren,	Are we Lords
Of zijn we het niet?	Or are we not?

I felt as if Mr. Govaerts was taking two undesirables out of the forbidden city.

We went through the tunnel for pedestrians, under the Scheldt river, to the train station on the Left Bank. I felt conspicuous as we stood waiting for Mr. Govaerts to purchase the tickets. We climbed onto the train. Soon our car filled up with boisterous day laborers, villagers returning home after a week's work in the city and gleeful about the upcoming weekend. We attracted scant notice. People were not likely to suspect anything. To them, we were just city folks, of another social class. Many had their dusty, laced-up work shoes on, and their work overalls under open jackets. They were holding their bundles on their laps or at their feet. We waited, ensconced by the window. The first chug of the engine was liberating: Antwerp, receding in the distance, had been rendered harmless.

Lulled by the rumble and the clatter of the wheels, we watched the flat, peaceful countryside move by. The journeymen's good-humored banter and laughter filled the car with friendly noises. I would cast casual glances at them. Some were munching on sandwiches, washing them down with swigs of chicory coffee from their canteens. Now and then a worker's cap got lifted or came to rest on its owner's lap, exposing a white forehead over a tanned, weather-beaten face. They peeled off at the villages and townships along the way. Ours was the Sinaai station in the Waas country, halfway between Antwerp and Ghent. It served the village of Sinaai on the north side of the tracks, and, on the south side, an offshoot of Belsele, a hamlet called "Duizend Appels" ("Thousand Apples"), our destination. It was ten o'clock in the morning.

We followed Mr. Govaerts past lone-standing brick houses, sun-bathed gardens and orchards. An oasis, in another world. Yet Antwerp was only twenty-five kilometers away. An old woman, her small crumpled face perched over her scrubbing broom, watched us coming. Mr. Govaerts greeted her. She started, opening a toothless mouth. My brother and I mumbled *"goeden dag."* Her head swiveled along as we passed her.

We alighted on the tree-lined Lokeren Road, also called the Old Road. We crossed, slanting to the left, toward the last in a cluster of five small, two-story stone-and-brick row houses, the Van Damme residence at 12 Lokeren Road.

A boy was walking in front of us, barefoot. He was training with a thin branch a rusty bicycle rim, in a straight line; expertly, the way I used to run a thin, wooden hoop in the park. The rim stood chest-high. It made a grinding sound on the gravel-encrusted bicycle path. He wore a dirty, loose-hanging shirt; his pants were torn off at mid-calf. His ankles and feet were shades of gray. He walked briskly, absorbed in his game, his shadow trailing him on the sun-dappled bicycle path under the poplar trees. We were only steps behind him, Govaerts towering between the two of us, strangers spanning the bicycle path, I, in my polished shoes, *the diamonds! the diamonds in the heels*, my knee-high socks, my Sabbath clothes. *Shabbat, Rosh Hashanah.* I glimpsed the luminous sky and pictured the diffuse yellow light under our old synagogue's domed ceiling, a torch made invisible by the sun; I saw our *hazan* draped in his *tallith*, and the boys' choir, distant figures silenced by the new sounds. Flickers from the past. The next instant we surprised Adrienne Van Damme.

She gasped. She was not expecting us. To her and Alice, "Switzerland" had sounded like a polite way of turning her down. She had just finished wet-scrubbing the stone patio in front of her house. She threw a damp rag across the doorstep and untied her apron as she stepped out of her wooden shoes, and the three of us followed her down a narrow hallway into the kitchen at the rear of the house. By the time we faced each other she had recovered from her shock.

Mr. Govaerts introduced himself.

"I remember your name all right," she said.

He smiled.

She pulled three chairs away from the kitchen table, "Sit down, do sit down." She remained standing by the stove.

She inquired about our trip.

"Oh, simple," Mr. Govaerts answered. And he sat down between her and the window. He leaned back and crossed his legs. He felt at home. My brother and I sat at a corner of the table.

"You must have left early," she said. "Just getting to the Left Bank. Would you like a slice of bread with butter?" she asked the two of us. "It will be a while before we have our midday meal."

"No, thank you."

"No, thank you."

"You are at home. You know that, don't you?"

"Yes, Madam."

"Yes, Madam."

"Just call me 'Adrienne.' My husband's name is 'Gaston.' That's what you call him when he comes."

Mr. Govaerts smiled. I could see the satisfaction on his face, the pride, almost, in his fellow Flemings. He would have reassuring words for my parents, how my brother and I would thrive in the Flemish countryside. My father would smile. My mother's worry groove between her eyebrows would smooth out a bit.

"Mr. Govaerts, you certainly can manage a bite with a cup of coffee."

"No, thank you. But coffee, with pleasure."

"It will be ready in a short while."

"How are your parents?" Adrienne asked.

"Fine."

Mr. Govaerts described their situation briefly in a confidential undertone. She listened intently. They broke into a casual chat while she made coffee and prepared the meal. Mr. Govaerts seemed to enjoy himself as he sipped from his cup.

"You are eating with us," Adrienne said.

"Oh no, I can't. I promised my wife I'd catch the first afternoon train. I'd like to stay and greet your husband, and leave shortly thereafter."

Their relaxed conversation and easy laughter put us at ease.

Adrienne cocked her head: "Gaston." We heard the thumping of wooden shoes on the garden path alongside the blind wall of the house, then we saw him in the large kitchen window, leaning his bicycle against the window sill and kicking off one shoe, then the other — they landed with a clear sound on the rear patio. Through the adjoining pump house he went, into the kitchen, swift as the wind: Gaston, at five foot six a bit shorter than Adrienne, was powerfully built. He had a longish face, brown-reddish hair, deep-set green eyes, a bit slanted, over high cheek-bones. As surprised as Adrienne had been, he uttered the same direct welcome, almost word for word.

Govaerts had a brief chat with both. "I'll be back next Saturday," he said in parting, and hurried off to the train station.

We sat down to eat. Gaston had things to tell Adrienne, about a farmer who lost his horse, about the forge running low on some staple hardware. When she began serving the main dish I asked for smaller portions of potatoes and vegetables.

"I am not that hungry today."

"I can well understand," Adrienne said, taking back some and heaping it on Gaston's plate. "It's too little to save."

"Just pile it on," he said. Turning to me: "The country air will give you a giant appetite. You'll see. You'll go back home, two sturdy, muscular country boys."

"How about two sturdy city boys?" Adrienne asked.

"Country boys are sturdier. We all know that. We saw it in the army. The city boys were a bit more... delicate. Smart, yes. But, well, some were uncomfortable near horses."

"Okh, Gaston, you and your stories."

"Who is the smarter one of the two of you?" he asked us.

"I," my brother answered.

"I can see that. And who is the most learned?"

"He," my brother spoke up again.

"Well, now we know everything."

"Everything," Adrienne echoed with a smile at us.

"Sure."

"He talks big," she said good-humoredly.

"And I won't contradict her," Gaston confided to us. "I know better."

We smiled.

They talked some more about relatives and about pending chores. Theirs was a quaint dialect with local expressions, such as *van eigen* for "of course," and a predilection for the verb *peinzen* (to think), which they pronounced without the "n," over *denken*.

Their pronunciation of the Flemish "oo" sounded almost like a drawn-out French "u."

"Tell you what," Gaston said addressing the two of us, "if tomorrow's weather is as nice as today, the three of us will go bird-shooting."

I was taken aback: I did not know that it meant "bird-watching."

"But Gaston," Adrienne protested, "let them get used to the place first. I want them to go meet my parents. And they should visit your folks. The birds won't fly away," she said, smiling.

"But isn't that what birds do?" he turned to us.

"Well... Well..."

"You can say 'yes' to him," Adrienne said reassuringly. "I won't be offended."

"Yes," my brother said.

"There will be other birds," I said.

Gaston and Adrienne laughed.

Gaston cut his workday short. He and Adrienne busied themselves most of the afternoon to convert their garret into a makeshift bedroom. Theirs was a small two-story house. The upper floor consisted of a bright, nicely furnished bedroom facing the road, and the adjoining garret, a dark and narrow space in the rear. Adrienne cleaned it out. Gaston brought a brass bed and a horse-hair mattress from Adrienne's parents who lived nearby, off the Lokeren Road.

They finished readying the garret by late afternoon. Adrienne took Sylvain and me upstairs. "This is where you sleep," she told us, showing us into their bedroom. I was stunned by their hospitality, and embarrassed that they were putting our comfort ahead of theirs. Yet I took it for the order of things in that house, not to be questioned. This sleeping arrangement reflected the belief that we would be able to return to Antwerp in a matter of weeks, a couple of months at most; my father had said so to Adrienne and Alice during their visit with us in Antwerp. The Germans' turning on us was a clear sign of their impending defeat, so some of our Jewish pundits had argued: "They want to take us down with them."

When we came down Sunday morning, Gaston was in the backyard, chopping wood into kindling. Adrienne gave us breakfast, then took us to meet her parents, François and Célestine Spitaels, retired farmers who owned a big old house around the corner, on the Statiestraat, the street leading to the Sinaai station. In the afternoon Gaston took us to Belsele Village to meet his parents, Emile and Léontine Van Damme. We saw his sister Alice again, and met another sister, Maria, and the two boys they were sheltering, Johnny and Marcel.

✿ ✿ ✿

The following morning, after breakfast with Adrienne and Sylvain — Gaston had biked off at seven o'clock to the forge, Adrienne had gotten busy with the daily chores — I realized, with a shock, that I had nothing to do, nowhere to turn. A long day loomed, hollow. I stepped out into the backyard to get out of Adrienne's way. Sylvain followed me. A large vegetable garden separated our house from the neighboring farmhouse, an old, low structure. I watched the activity on the farmyard, answered a passer-by's greeting. We were exposed, I felt, standing there in our fine city clothes. How many people were wondering about us? The farmer's family, no doubt; and the proprietors of the café *Chalet* across the road from us; and to its right, in their gleaming tiled shop, the butcher and his wife; and, further up the road, in their one-story little house opposite the farmhouse, Irène and her widowed mother. Tall, slender, blond Irène had stood in her doorway when we had set out to Belsele Village to meet Gaston's parents, on Sunday. She liked to come babble with Adrienne, Gaston had told us. About matters of the heart. Women's stuff. And there was our next-door neighbor, Julia. She, too, had seen us on Sunday. We had given her a polite "*Goeden dag*" with a deferential nod of the head.

I returned to the kitchen. "Why don't you go for a walk?" Adrienne suggested. "By yourself. The two of you, together, would draw too much attention, especially on a weekday. Turn the corner onto the Waasmunster Road."

I walked alongside the cluster of row houses — five in all; the last one, at the corner of the Lokeren and the Waasmunster roads, was a café, the *Duizend Appels*, a dingy haunt. They were owned by the local beer merchant. Gaston and Adrienne had moved into theirs when they got married, in the late thirties. The other tenants had come from various localities. Were they following me from behind their drawn curtains? We did not owe them any explanation of our presence. Julia next door, Irène and the farmers across the vegetable garden were the only neighbors with whom the Van Dammes had a rapport. We had no explanation for them either and did not feel a pressing need to give them one: that we were two good Catholic boys went without saying; the villagers did not have Jews on their minds, and they were not aware of what was happening to us in Antwerp.

I turned the corner onto the Waasmunster Road. It ran south, in the opposite direction of the Statiestraat. I felt ill at ease trading glances or exchanging nods with the few men and women who came my way. I saw myself in their eyes: a stranger, a boy who should be in school or learning a trade. The less conspicuous I was, we all soon realized, the safer.

I would henceforth keep inside the house, or in the backyard, out of the public eye — I was too big to be idling about day after day. I had nothing to keep me busy. I would putter in the garden, trying to make myself useful, or watch the road, read the newspaper, and keep out of Adrienne's way as she was bustling about doing her morning chores. Bored, restless, anxious, I felt hemmed in and out of place. Stillborn was my hoped-for affair with nature, the walks in the woods, the hikes along the country roads, the rides on horseback.

✲ ✲ ✲

To keep up good neighborly relations Adrienne called our next door neighbor, Julia, to meet the newcomers. She walked in, a smile frozen on her lips, her eyes brimming with curiosity. She had her children in tow: two boys around Sylvain's age, bony, shy and a bit awed. Adrienne had warned us about them: "The minute she hears some gossip, or even a rumor, she barges in to tell me." Her husband, a mason, was a heavy drinker given to violence. A bit later another neighbor, Irène, came calling, to have a chat with Adrienne. She had seen us from her small, one-story house across the road where she lived with her widowed mother. Unlike Julia, who just looked at us, wide-eyed, then hung on Adrienne's lips, Irène addressed us, in Standard Flemish, repeating at times after Adrienne:

"...Henri..."

I nodded. Rather formal.

"...And Sylvain, yes. Nice names, two little gentlemen. Pardon, Henri, for you I should say 'a *young* gentleman.' "

I smiled.

"And do you like it here, so far?"

"Oh, yes."

"Yes."

"Must be a big change from Antwerp..."

"Yes."

Her polite yet genuine astonishment, her elliptical tone, her friendliness, everything about her was probing. In vain. She left. We looked at each other.

"How openly curious people can be," Adrienne said with a chuckle.

Just days later the family on the neighboring small farm also got to know us, especially Sylvain. Adrienne had taken him along on one of her errands to meet Simoneke, a girl his age. They became friends. He would dart across our vegetable garden in his wooden shoes and in the weekday clothes that Adrienne had sewn for him, to fetch some butter or eggs, or to play with the farm girl after school, or after Mass on Sundays. She often waved to him from the farmyard, or called out, or came running through the vegetable garden in her wooden shoes, to peer through the kitchen window, her nose squashed against the glass, or to dash into the pump house and burst through the kitchen door, "Where is Sylvain?" The two would run across our vegetable garden to play in the yard, or in the barn, or in the field. She would stay home from school with a headache or tummy-ache that disappeared as soon as they got together. Her folks didn't seem to mind: Simoneke was the only child among grown siblings and cousins in an extended, hard-working family. They were delighted with her spunky, neat little playmate.

✫ ✫ ✫

"If you boys want to visit the forge," Gaston told us a few days after our arrival, "tomorrow would be a good day. We'll be putting a rim on a big wheel."

Sylvain and I went the next day, right after breakfast.

Adjoining Gaston's parents' house in Belsele Village, the forge was a large, ill-lit structure crowded with a variety of workbenches, lathes, tables, vises, and cluttered with tools and metal parts. Raw materials such as bars, rods, plates were lying around in bundles. A suspended assembly of electrically driven pulleys and belts of different widths and lengths would start up with a mounting groan and settle into a loud rumble, with the joints in the belts flapping noisily around the pulleys. When the power was turned off, the clanking of metal on metal resonated pure in a rich gamut of pitches and amplitudes, from the delicate tinkle to the loud clang. The hammering on glowing-white, pliable iron, bending and shaping it at will elicited low, timbre-less thuds and drew sparks like tears from the contorted metal. Gone was the spirited music.

Gaston and his father, Emile, were going about their work. Emile, stooping but vigorous, moved deliberately. His dark, deep-set eyes were peering up from under bushy, graying eyebrows as if seeing something beyond the task at hand. The grime of the forge seemed encrusted on his bald head and darkened his crown of white hair. His graying moustache was yellow and brown under the nose from his indulgence in sniff tobacco. He would stop every so often for another pinch from his little silver box.

Gaston's motions were quick and purposeful. He was working the bellows. Beating like a mighty heart, it was blowing air into a bed of reddening coals. The fire, at table height, silhouetted Gaston's broad frame and spread a glow over his taut face.

I stood there taking it all in: the gray daylight seeping in through the dirty, slanted panes by the roof, the dull electric lights by the lathes and the workbenches, the dark colors in shades of gray and brown, the smells of metal and oil and coal, the coal fire in the dark corner by the large doors, the red hot metal, the rumbling and clanging noises, the thudding of bulky hammers with handles thicker than my wrist. And I knew that Gaston would never have entertained my secret wish to recruit me as a helper, even if we could have explained to the Flemish villagers why a twelve-year old French-speaking city boy on the frail side, using schooled Flemish with the deferential "U" for "you," was training as a blacksmith's apprentice. I was more disappointed with myself than with reality: how could I have entertained such a picture-postcard, vacationland view of a forge, of the trade?

"We'll soon be putting a rim on the wheel that's lying in the yard," Gaston said to me. "If you want to watch us, stand right there, well out of the way." And he pointed towards the middle of the front yard.

The metal rim, sized to insure a tight fit, had to be made larger to slip on the wooden wheel by making it red hot. Armed with metal pincers Gaston and his father slid, one segment at a time, the entire iron band through the burning coals. The glowing red segments darkened soon after they emerged from the fire.

Sylvain and I were standing at the designated spot. Emile and Gaston, both bending forward, stepped gingerly out of the forge with the dark-purple, live rim hanging horizontally between them from the four pincers. And we watched in awe as the two men dipped, in tense, carefully coordinated movements, the iron band into a basin of water, a segment at a time, sending up fits of steam, then hastened to position the rim around the wooden wheel lying in the dirt and forced it into place in a frenzied heavy-hammer, spark-drawing attack as the scorched wheel was belching smoke and small, blue flames leapt from under the metal and licked the wood for an instant before dying or being snuffed out by the hammer blows. Hurriedly the two men doused the smoking wheel with buckets of water that ran hissing and bubbling over the hot metal. A weak grip, a wrong move could have spelled physical harm. There had been no time even for a full-throated, tension-relieving curse. The job, once launched, had driven them.

When it was all over Emile took a leisurely pinch of sniff tobacco from his silver box while letting out in a low-voiced cross between growling and purring a string of curses that expressed almost lyrically how hard and hazardous and successful and gratifying that bitch of a job had been. With his big black thumb he pressed the brown powder up one nostril, then the other, wiped his nose — it was smudgy most of the time — with the back of his hand, wiped his thumb and forefinger at the trousers of his overalls and stepped into the kitchen for a few sips of black chicory coffee. Gaston remained silent, though not out of modesty: to this day, when facing down a barking, intimidating dog or facing up to a blunder I dip into the rich repertoire of curses I learned from him. Sylvain also learned fast and retained well.

✵ ✵ ✵

Hours of unrelenting boredom stretched day after day. I had nothing to read except the newspaper and a weekly magazine, *Het Vrije Waasland* (The Free Waas Country) — Belsele was at the heart of the fertile Waas region in the province of East Flanders. My high school kept popping up in my thoughts. It was the last place where I had moved freely. I recalled Mr. Van Bijlen taking us, in even tones and with few words, through theorem after theorem, like on a suspenseful climb; Mr. Velghe, with his booming voice, charting the evolution of a Latin word to the French words it spawned, like a thread running through the ages — a different kind of voyage; Mr. Govaert, the French teacher, and my assignment, "A stroll through Paris," based on a street map he had given me, the play he had staged, *La Farce de Maître Pathelin*, in which Menda and I had appeared with the yellow star sewn onto our jackets. I would visualize my Christian classmates, seated two by two, getting five solid hours of Latin and math a week, with lots of homework. And the new stuff, like Greek and algebra: what a big upward jump, that third year of high school. It had started weeks earlier without me and my Jewish friends. Would I return soon enough to catch up with them?

Afternoons brought a measure of relief. After the midday meal Adrienne would tidy up and wet-mop the tile floors in the kitchen and the pump house. I could then remain indoors, out of the neighbors' sight, without getting in her way. The three of us would sit down for coffee and cookies, or just Adrienne and I — Sylvain would not always wait that long when Simoneke was around. Savoring the treat while listening and responding to the bit of local gossip lifted the boredom and relieved the anxiety. I felt different: my presence mattered; I was company to Adrienne. I would look at her, when we spoke, when she poured the coffee, or when her attention was diverted by Milou, our cat. I admired her. Tall and slender, she had black, slightly wavy hair framing a longish face, and dark eyes. Her gaze was firm, warm and enveloping when she smiled. One afternoon she wore a thin, fitting cardigan she had finished knitting just days earlier. Its open collar showed to advantage her long white neck. I felt uncomfortable.

Soon after we drank our coffee she stood up and cleared the table, taking cups, saucers and spoons to the pump house sink. Time weighed heavy again.

Evenings in the kitchen were cozy and safe. Adrienne knitted, or darned socks. Gaston read the newspaper, or fixed a puncture in a worn bicycle tire while cursing under his breath. Adrienne decried his language. Sylvain and I watched him and savored it. We listened to the radio. Around 9:30 Adrienne would remind us boys that the evening was drawing to an end.

My brother and I would step out into the backyard and stand, spread-legged, watering the hedge. We would bid Gaston and Adrienne goodnight and start up the dark staircase leading from a draped-off opening in the kitchen wall to the upper floor.

We would alight to the night's faint glimmer and the shades of darkness in Gaston and Adrienne's spacious bedroom. Their space, not ours: I felt that we had dispossessed them by our mere presence. We had taken over their sprawling, plush bed. I felt small in it. Soon Gaston would check the front and back doors, turn out the light, while Adrienne would be coming upstairs, to the cramped garret. My unease would dissolve in sleep.

I began wetting the bed. One night. And the following. I would dread falling asleep. I would wake up from a pleasurable sensation of warmth and relief to a moment of sheer terror. I could not stop relieving myself even as I was pulling out of my dream. I would lie awake, motionless, in what felt like a puddle, hoping desperately to get the bed dry by morning with my body heat. I would doze off, overcome by sleep, and wake up in the morning, still soaking wet. Adrienne would put the large, shapeless, wool-filled mattress to air in one of the two gabled windows. No one ever said a word about it. My little brother slept fast and kept dry.

My nighttime agony stopped after a week.

It was a relief when, a couple of weeks later, Gaston and Adrienne reclaimed their bedroom — it had become clear that the Occupation would last at least into the following spring. The garret with its brass bed turned out to be a comfortable place to sleep, a room made to order for me and my brother. It felt right, from the first night. I would slip into that silent stretch the way one settles into a gently rocking train ride, oblivious of the place one left and unconcerned about the destination. The world was on hold.

Months later, a pleasurable and frightening release pulled me out of my dream in the stillness of the moonlit garret. I felt my pyjama pants: they were dry, except for a viscous spot. I rubbed it out. My penis was erect. Perplexed but relieved, elated, almost, I went back to sleep.

I would experience more of those rousing spurts in the middle of the night. The spot on my pajama pants would be dry and hard by morning, too small, I thought, to be noticed. Bed-wetting was a thing of the past. Gone even was the memory of it.

☼ ☼ ☼

Gaston and Adrienne tried to cheer us up. They would get into mock arguments provoked by Gaston's habitual peccadilloes. Adrienne would call him all sorts of unflattering names, he would make faces at her or clown behind her back, she would grab hold of him and kick him forcefully in the butt, he would feign a crippling injury. He and Sylvain had become pals and had adopted an "us against them" attitude. They would "shave together." Gaston would dab lather on Sylvain's cheeks, chin, and nose.

Once, angered by one of Gaston's pranks — he had snuck up behind her and, to Sylvain's great merriment, had loosened the knot in her apron — Adrienne poked the tin fork she had in her hand into Gaston's upper arm, a bit harder than she had intended, for she was herself taken aback by the result: the fork was bent. It led to a real wrestling match with the two of them rolling on the kitchen floor in a tight embrace. I was taken aback by the fury of the wrestling match. Adrienne was strong and did not hold back. Gaston only parried and defended himself, chuckling. My brother was laughing and cheering him on, "Gaston! Don't let her win! Use both arms!" He did, and got his legs around hers in a scissors hold. I was hoping that Adrienne would wrest herself free — a clear victory according to the unspoken rules of engagement. But Gaston didn't trust her and thwarted her every attempt. His strength was phenomenal: I had seen him restrain a large, restless horse while shoeing it. Adrienne relaxed her exertions and gave up. They looked at each other, he, admiringly, she, defiantly; her face was flushed. He kissed her on the cheek. They disengaged and got up. Adrienne straightened out the skirt of her dress and began tying her apron behind her back. My brother declared Gaston the winner. Adrienne shook her fist at him while holding the unfinished knot with the other hand,

"You just wait, little fella."

"We are not afraid, hey Gaston?"

"I don't know, we'd better keep our eyes open." And rolling his eyes in Adrienne's direction, "Rather fiery," he said to us while rubbing his upper arm.

"Oh, you nitwits," she said in her usual, calm voice.

She was back working at the kitchen table. I was glad it was over. I was in love with her.

✿ ✿ ✿

A few unusual activities pierced the shroud of diffuse anxiety.

Gaston took me and Sylvain hiking on a Sunday afternoon; we hunkered down in silence behind a thicket of bushes for some bird-watching.

We went digging and bagging potatoes, one evening, under the scintillating night sky — the four of us, in our wooden shoes, on the Van Dammes' little plot of land.

I saw my first ever circus show. Adrienne told me of a roving circus that had pitched its tent in Sinaai, the neighboring village to the north: "Why don't you go and see?" I found the wide open space with its encampment, bought a ticket, and took a seat. I felt safe and inconspicuous amidst the general excitement, the hoopla, the trumpeting, the grandstanding. And waited. The clown... clever, full of surprises. Was I the only one not laughing? What a way to hide, though; should have been a Jew. A column of look-alike doggies marched in, two abreast, cute: short, lustrous, light-brown hair; pointy snouts and ears; big, marble-like black eyes looking a bit nonplussed. A man emitted short, discreet signals and the little dogs split into two files looping back on themselves, merged, split, weaved, rolled over in unison. The man led them out to applause. The dogs trotted out gingerly, satisfied with themselves, or relieved. A man led an elephant into the ring, had him stand on his hind legs, then on one leg. The audience gasped; and applauded. What was an elephant doing in Sinaai, standing on one leg? What kind of men are driven to this sort of accomplishment? I felt alone and different. More acts, more suspense, more grandstanding and clowning and blaring music. I liked the magician. And the women, the beautiful young women in skimpy, glittering costumes: they climbed up the rope ladder, lithe as cats, swung from the trapeze; or performed on horses trotting around the ring: they stood erect, facing front or

rear, or on one leg in the airplane pose. Each statuesque acrobat would come into full view, just a few meters away, as she was
moving by. My eyes would feast ravenously on her, hold on to her
for another few instants, take a look at her face, Was she soft or
forbidding, or mysterious? Then tear away to catch the next one
in all her fullness. They went by too fast, and they returned in
round after round of excitement and frustration.

I had a memorable bike trip to Lokeren: Gaston took me along
to his hardware suppliers, De Beule, and Van den Abeele. I rode
Adrienne's bicycle: eight kilometers west of Duizend Appels, in
the opposite direction from Belsele Village, along the tree-lined
Old Road. The rush of pleasure I felt, the sense of power, pedaling vigorously, like a pro. I was a legitimate traveler with a destination, just passing by where no one knew us. I felt alive. Free.

The two spacious hardware stores revealed another world to
me, a world of iron and steel, the large and long goods neatly
lined up on the floor, by size and category, tools and hardware
of all sizes and shapes on running shelves and in countless bins.
A world of men, most in work coveralls, fully absorbed by the
size and shape, the feel of widgets and gadgets, as if protected
by an invisible shield from anything that might be the least dis-
tracting or untoward; no, no shield, they didn't need one, they
were invulnerable. They smelled of iron. The men I had known
in Antwerp, both Jews and Gentiles, from barber to physician,
had soft-skinned hands with clean nails and gave off city smells
of books and grooming, of beards and tractates, of English
fabrics. Except the Jewish shoemaker. So many of them wore
glasses.

After the visits to the hardware stores we stopped off at the
house of Gaston's married sister, Laura, who lived in Lokeren.
Laura and her husband Jules were hiding a Jewish girl from
Antwerp, Simone, another one of Alice's finds. She was on the
plump side, with big, serious, brown eyes. We exchanged a few
tidbits of information about Antwerp, the streets we had lived in.
We spoke in French while Gaston was busy chatting with Laura
and Jules.

"How do you like the food?" she asked me, searchingly.

"Not bad. I eat everything. For the first time."

"It must be the same where you are, meals without compote..."
Her voice had trailed off.

"Yes, soup and the main dish."

"Imagine..."

"Do you get out of the house?"

"Never."

I had been drawn to a workbench and the exposed guts of a radio set: Jules was repairing radios by day and projecting films in the local movie house at night. I had stared, baffled: did that spare tangle of wires and little objects capture and emit sweet music and clear speech from all over the world? Jules smiled.

"Does it interest you?" he asked.

"Oh yes! Is it complicated?"

"No, not really. Occasionally you come across a tough one, and it can get under your skin. Then I rely on a diagram if there is one, like this one."

I looked, nonplussed.

"You see these triangles, rectangles, and circles and things?" he continued. "These are symbols. They represent the different pieces." He touched a tiny, multicolored cylinder, "A resistor, it is called," and a tiny disk, "A capacitor."

"And the lines?"

"The wires... you see? Here, and here... connect the pieces. Allow them to work as one entity."

"Nice."

Thrilling, the knowledge that unlocks secrets and makes things happen. Another world, under a work lamp, on a small table.

Gaston, still talking with his sister Laura, had observed us.

"This one," he said, pointing at me with his chin, his face drawn in a serious, almost severe expression, "wants to know everything." I detected a touch of pride. "The little one," he continued, "is more like me: he wants to do everything. Making mischief included."

I pedaled back from Lokeren, keeping doggedly up with Gaston, flush with the pleasures and the discoveries of my trip.

✻ ✻ ✻

On the second Sunday of our stay in Duizend Appels Adrienne took us, Sylvain and me, to church in Belsele.

"I want our busybodies to see us," she said. "There is no mistaking where we are going, all decked out, twenty minutes before High Mass."

"We might even run into some of them in church, or on the way," I ventured.

"No. They themselves never go, except for the mistress of the *Chalet* and the butcher's wife. But they attend Low Mass. They are too busy, afterwards, serving beer and slicing meat."

"And Gaston?" I asked.

"He rarely goes," Adrienne said. "He always finds things to do. I myself go mostly to Low Mass, and not every week. I like to have my long Sunday mornings, prepare the Sunday meal, putter around the house."

The soaring space, the resonating chants, the organ music, the measured incantations, were all-enveloping. The Latin lent mystery. The congregants would respond in unison: a rolling rumble would fill the church; it sounded dutiful, without fervor. An impressive ceremony; yet distant. The monotone incantation of *Dominus vobiscum* made the words sound empty. Altogether not threatening. How different from our informality: we would shout our prayers at Him, roar our responses, address Him as "you," try to force His hand.

Adrienne, I observed, did not kneel on the straw seat or sign herself every time. Sylvain performed like a good Catholic boy. I could not bring myself to kneel or make the sign of the cross, but I did not feel conspicuous: we had come a few minutes late and had filed into the last row in the rear. To show devotion I leaned with my forearms on the high back of the chair and bowed my head.

The sermon, delivered in a homiletic tone, was boring.

"We have to steer clear of the priest," Adrienne said on our way home. "Priests from the surroundings gather occasionally in Belsele. Two of them, the brothers Phillip and Cyriel Verschaeve, advocate openly for the Germans and their beliefs; from the pulpit, no less. Firebrands. They write books. This very street is named after them. It used to be the Dorpstraat." A wide, short, tree-lined stretch of more recent stone and brick houses and some villas, leading from the old village to the road. "They know what's going on in the land. Anyway," she continued on a lighter tone, "you did well." And, with a smile: "You Sylvain, you'll be a film actor."

✵ ✵ ✵

Days only after our arrival in Duizend Appels, Adrienne told me that she had talked to her mother about my parents and the possibility of sheltering them:

"She can give them a room of their own. It's a large house, empty, so to speak. They can use the kitchen. Much safer and more tranquil than in the city. And a stone's throw from us. Don't you think they'd like to come?"

"I'm sure they would," I said.

"Why don't you suggest it to them in a letter? Mr. Govaerts will take it to them."

I did. Govaerts came to visit us on Saturday. He brought us clothes, and my less expensive, roomier shoes, to spare my treasure-bearing pair; Adrienne put those away. I never wore them again. Govaerts took my letter and relayed the offer.

The following Saturday we heard through the kitchen wall a rumble of footsteps towards the backyard. We then saw filing past the window, in quick succession, Govaerts, my mother, and my father. They burst into Adrienne's kitchen, their faces flush with excitement from their fifteen-mile journey, the same journey Sylvain and I had made two weeks earlier. Their arrival caused a joyous tumult. Govaerts was smiling, proud of his repeat performance. Once again he had waited until Friday night, and, under the cover of darkness, he had taken them from the hideout above the butcher shop to his house in Merksem, to chaperone them out of Antwerp the next day, when the somewhat denser weekend crowd on their way to visit relatives or fanning out in the villages for provisions provided better cover. My parents had dressed down, trying to look ordinary: my mother had worn a head-kerchief and flat shoes; my father had donned a worker's cap. Govaerts had bought the train tickets and done the talking: their foreign accents would have given them away. Gaston's arrival triggered a new round of laughter and embraces. He soon took out the glasses and poured the brandy.

Adrienne asked my mother, "Were you still frightened once you had left Antwerp?"

"Every time someone looked in my direction."

"You had nothing to be scared of," Gaston remonstrated, reassuring, "you look like a real Flemish peasant woman."

My father and Govaerts laughed.

"Some compliment," my mother mumbled to me. We were sitting next to each other.

It was then, amidst the banter and the clinking of glasses that my mother told me under her breath of Hitler's latest speech: " *'Einen anderen Purim werden sie NICHT haben'* ['Another Purim they will NOT have']. That's how he expressed himself." A declaration of war. In our language. Turning our symbols on us.

I had heard Hitler on several occasions, the first time when I was ten, before the war: I had accompanied my father to the apartment of Mr. Saphir, our landlord on the Simonsstraat; his was the only radio in the house. I had understood very little of Hitler's ravings and retained nothing, except "*die Juden.*" But I remembered the cavernous echo of his voice, as if he were speaking under a dome spanning all of Germany, and the thunderous *Sieg Heil's* from what sounded like the entire German nation. I recalled in Adrienne's kitchen the pall of that distant threat reaching us in the Saphirs' living room; Haman had been mentioned.

In the kitchen, an atmosphere of victory. My father, Govaerts and Adrienne were cracking walnuts, talking and laughing. My brother was leaning on his elbows over the table, helping himself every so often to a peeled walnut. Gaston, standing by the stove, was presiding over the celebration:

"*Allez*, Madam Grunstein, your glass is still full."

"My stomach," my mother pleaded. "I must wait a little while."

Mr. Govaerts looked at his watch: his train was due. He and my parents went out the way they came — from the rear, along the blind wall of the house: less attention-grabbing than stepping out the front door. They crossed the road and turned the corner onto Statiestraat. My parents disappeared into the house of Adrienne's parents, François and Célestine Spitaels. Mr. Govaerts continued to the Sinaai train station.

He came twice more, with clothes and other personal effects for my parents. Maintaining further contact might have exposed us all needlessly. He stopped coming.

☆ ☆ ☆

The next day, Sunday, Adrienne's sister, Palmyre, a factory worker, and her husband Lucien, a skilled mechanic, came on their bicycles from St-Niklaas, a town six kilometers east of Belsele in the direction of Antwerp. They were in the know. The two sisters were close, and Lucien did not drink. Gaston and Adrienne, Sylvain and I joined the party, an unusual gathering in the old couple's house. Another sister, Elvire, lived nearby with her family, but was not in on our secret. Adrienne and Palmyre were not on speaking terms with her. Moreover, she had two children — their ages between mine and Sylvain's — who might pick up something about us at the dinner table — a slip of the tongue — and repeat it in school.

Lucien enjoyed conversing with my father. He was eager to learn about diamonds and the related crafts. He made it clear that he and Palmyre would have liked to put up my parents in their house in St-Niklaas.

My parents were not about to move. They felt safe in their country hideout. The house was dark and musty, but spacious. My mother would be able to cook without anguishing forays into the street. And their boys lived nearby.

But their presence generated traffic. Adrienne liked their company. She brought provisions for her parents and ours. My brother and I went to see our parents every day, often out of a sense of duty and for lack of something else to do — for Sylvain, his get-togethers with Simoneke took precedence over all else. My mother's lavish hugs and kisses were, as often as not, suffused with sadness. Whenever she asked us solicitous questions with the familiar worried look, especially about food, I felt as if Adrienne was on probation. My father had retained a role, his only one, as the provider for his children's upkeep, with a monthly stipend to Adrienne who ran the Van Damme household of four. We had little to talk about. When my brother complained about my bossiness, my father admonished him:

"These are special times. We are not with you, so you must, at times, listen to your older brother."

"I must listen to Gaston."

"Absolutely. But you must listen to your brother regarding certain things that Gaston does not involve himself with."

"Like manners," my mother suggested.

"Adrienne is the boss of that," my brother retorted.

"Like saying a bit of a prayer," my father said. "I told Henri in Antwerp to teach you."

"We are not in Antwerp."

"We are Jews in Antwerp, in Belsele, anywhere in the world." And turning to me: "You should teach him with mildness." And to both of us: "Remember, these are special times. Go now. You can't stay long." The neighbors might wonder what two city boys who had come to the country for fresh air were doing in the house of an old, retired couple other than paying a courtesy call? And so often?

☆ ☆ ☆

September 1942 was coming to an end. It was clear to Adrienne that to our neighbors the uninterrupted presence of two well-bred French-speaking city boys was a deepening enigma: we did not go to school; our parents had not made an appearance yet; we had traded bourgeois city comforts for modest working-class country living — our next-door neighbor Julia, whose house was identical to ours, knew that we slept in a converted garret; we drew water with a hand-pump; the stench in the outhouse, welling up from the cesspool, could be overwhelming; square pieces of newsprint served as toilet paper. Our neighbors' curiosity had shone in their eyes from the first day.

Adrienne had tried to come up with a story that would satisfy their curiosity. When Julia finally came out with a question about the parents, Adrienne alluded to family problems back in Antwerp. Her tone intimated that more confidences might follow.

"And school," Julia pressed on.

"Nothing to be concerned about," Adrienne replied. "They'll catch up in no time. Smart boys. They will get lots of help. There is money. Just that happiness is one thing money can't buy."

Irène's elliptical comments betrayed the same questions.

Most conspicuous was our idling about. But enrolling Sylvain in the village school and me in the high school of neighboring St-Niklaas would have exposed us to a wider and more dangerous circle of people without lifting the mystery surrounding our presence in Duizend Appels. It would have required a stack of false papers — birth certificates, proof of mandated inoculations, medical histories, school records — and the connivance of school officials we could not trust: a number of school teachers in Belsele (and throughout the Flemish land) had embraced the German cause, as Flemish separatists or as opportunists.

Going to the village school would also have brought Sylvain to the priest's attention. He was associated, Gaston and Adrienne felt, with the brothers Philip and Cyriel Verschaeve, two fiery priests who had embraced the New Order in their teachings and from the pulpit. Cyriel Verschaeve was a writer and a teacher at a Catholic seminary. His advocacy of an independent Flanders in a German-ruled Europe — he professed a blind trust in Hitler — and his image, among extreme nationalists, as "Flanders' spiritual Führer," led many Flemings to collaborate with the Germans and adolescent Catholics to volunteer for the Eastern front in the ranks of the Flemish *Waffen SS*. We were fearful of the lot: teachers and priests were more informed than the other villagers, and the Nazi-sympathizers among them more attuned to antisemitic propaganda and to the Germans' actions against the Jews; they would be more apt at perceiving a dissonance in our story. Fortunately, Duizend Appels, though within the village limits of Belsele, was at a distance that kept us out of their orbit.

Adrienne was worried: "Who else is blabbering about us? If it becomes a topic of conversation..."

The implication was clear: speculation about us could reach the wrong ears, with disastrous results, given Belsele's share of Nazi-sympathizers and collaborators, even Blackshirts.

The same day she brought it up with my parents.

"They are coming right out with their questions," she said. "Polite, yes, but direct."

"And what have you been telling them?" my father asked.

"I have been hinting at family problems."

"So now we have to think of some problems to satisfy their curiosity."

"But how long can I keep Sylvain out of school on account of family problems?"

"Tell them that Sylvain is sickly," my father told her. "The doctor prescribed a fresh-air cure and ordered that he stay out of school for an indefinite period of time."

Adrienne liked that.

"And the phantom parents?" she asked.

My father's bushy eyebrows moved up his large forehead and he started laughing, as if savoring in advance an off-color joke:

"Tell them that the mother is demented."

Adrienne gasped, then laughed.

"Most interesting," my mother said whimsically. "And you? What prevents you from visiting the children?"

"Tell them that the father is too busy," he said with the same glint in his eyes. His eyebrows shot up again. "A skirt chaser... Women and work. No time nor mind for the boys."

My father and Adrienne were laughing heartily.

"My husband should have been a writer," my mother said to Adrienne. "Such a rich imagination."

"I think so, too," Adrienne laughed. "Women and work," she repeated. "And what kind of work? They *will* ask me."

"School inspector." The choice of profession had been inspired by his service on the school board of Tachkemoni.

After Adrienne was gone, my mother said in a low voice, in Polish, so I should not understand, though I did,

"Playing games. For our life."

"Have trust," my father inveighed, in Yiddish, "we are all in a good place, among fine people. The children are well taken care off."

"I do thank God for that," my mother said, almost in a whisper.

That evening at supper Gaston listened intently, eyes half closed in a taut face, as Adrienne told him the whole story. He was not amused.

"You handle it with the women," he said perfunctorily.

Adrienne liked my father's suggestions and fleshed them out into a good story, that she fed craftily, in titillating tidbits, to Julia and Irène, and to Simoneke's parents. It became the tale of an unhappy family: the mother was quite frequently hospitalized — mental institutions, was the ever so subtle intimation — and was unable to care for her children; the father was a highly placed school official, rich, handsome, with a busy life and a passion for the fair sex that left no time or concern for his boys; Sylvain was a bit sickly — quite understandable; he wasn't putting on weight, and needed a change in family environment, the fresh country air and a complete absence of stress, meaning no school — doctor's orders. Do not worry about the smart little boy falling behind, she assured the neighbors, not with his father's pull. As for Henri, he was Sylvain's only comforting presence from home. Not to mention that he welcomed the respite from the stressful family life in Antwerp. Well, no, not all that glittered was gold.

Leaking "our family secrets" left nothing for the villagers to decode, there was no need to pry. It deflected the poisonous sting of envy: our misfortune overshadowed our affluence and the Van Dammes' apparent connections with classy city folks. It turned their inquisitiveness into sympathy for our plight. What further ingratiated us with our neighbors was our switch from French to Flemish. I spoke the formal, schooled Flemish. Sylvain picked up the local dialect within weeks and spoke it like a village boy. Hearing him argue with me in fluent, rapid-fire dialect, with snap repartees like "In Duizend Appels, *I* am the boss!" was theater for them. Our story caught on. It got us accepted unreservedly.

Fifty-five years later I and three other Hidden Children (that is what we call ourselves today) repaired to the home of Ed and Carla Lessing in Hastings-on-Hudson in New York. We had come from the burial of a friend, Eddie Strauss, a child survivor from Belgium. The conversation turned to how we and our rescuers explained the absence of parents. I related my father's idea to portray my mother as a deranged woman, calling it clever and imaginative.

"Not so original, Hirsch," remarked Ed, who had hidden in Holland. "My mother was crazy too."

"My mother was crazy too," Sanne Spetter, the other guest, chimed in. She was also from Holland. I leaned, almost lurched, forward, dumbfounded, from Ed to Sanne.

"Well, my mother didn't get crazy right away," Ed noted. "First she broke a leg. It got infected. Had to be amputated. She suffered a nervous breakdown. Well... it's a long story."

I turned to Carla, also from Holland:

"And your mother, of course..."

"No, my mother wasn't crazy," she hastened to say, smiling.

"Not crazy? Was... was something the matter with her?"

"No, she was fine," Carla said, laughing, "We hid together, the whole family. But that also is a long story."

✿ ✿ ✿

For days after my parents' arrival in Duizend Appels the
weather remained clear and mild. With the solicitous encourage-
ment of Adrienne's mother, they gave in to the temptation of
lounging in their hosts' orchard at the rear of the house, under
the trees' low-hanging, leafy branches. They felt hidden from
the public eye by a tall and dense hedge. Pleasure would spread
across my father's face. He would still crack a joke or tell a story.
And they were close to their children.

After some time, Adrienne's mother, Célestine, began to notice that people would slow their pace and peer over the rear
gate and through the hedge as they walked by on the earthen
path along the orchard. Once she saw a villager bending over
with his face smack against the hedge. Did someone glimpse my
parents? From the gate, when they stepped out of the kitchen?
Or through the hedge? Then a neighbor remarked to her how
lively her place now seemed. A little war council was convened
one night: my parents had already stopped going out into the
orchard, even after dark; Gaston, who had rarely set foot at his
in-laws' home before my parents' arrival, would stop coming;
Sylvain and I would be dropping in on Sundays only, after Mass.
We were bunched up in one spot, with members of the same family; a mishap in one household could have repercussions in both.
On a subsequent visit Lucien, Adrienne's brother-in-law, offered
to shelter my parents. They consulted Adrienne, who counseled
that they go:

"It is safer. A town. People can't be as nosy. And it's a comfortable house. I would take them up on their offer. We'll come visiting with the children."

Distance was a friend. I sensed it too.

My parents took the train for St-Niklaas in the company of
Lucien, one October night.

"He stole them from me," Adrienne's mother complained —
my parents were company, and they were paying rent.

Their stay with Lucien and Palmyre would become a nightmare. Their hosts, amiable at first, turned callous and exploit-
ative. They wanted ever more rent money — diamantaires had
to be rich — and more of the clothes that Govaerts had brought

on his follow-up visits to Duizend Appels — "They are of no use to you." Eventually, my parents drew the line for both money and clothes, my father at a prosperous-looking wide-striped, gray-blue suit that Lucien coveted more than anything.

Lucien and Palmyre relegated them to the attic. They supplied them with bread only, under the pretext of late working hours and long commutes. Adrienne ended up bringing my parents potatoes, from Duizend Appels, at night; she could handle a forty-kilogram sack on her bicycle. Occasionally she got them some other provisions as well. My parents would know unceasing, gnawing hunger: dry, most often stale bread and cold potatoes; my mother would boil them late in the evening, to avoid Palmyre. They spent all day in the attic, quietly, communicating in whispers and gestures. The seamstress on the other side of the thin party wall was home all day.

✡ ✡ ✡

The October days grew ever shorter: Gaston sped off to the forge, and returned after work, in total darkness. The hope — wishful thinking, really — that our stay in Belsele would be brief had given way to the realization that the Germans were not about to loosen their grip. The Occupation was nearing its third winter with no end in sight.

Our story of woes had taken hold. But now, my open-ended stay and idling about became a perplexing issue. How long would I be providing a family presence for my brother at the expense of my education? Especially since Sylvain seemed to prize Simoneke's company much more than mine. In fact, it was plain that he was thriving. "Look at the color on his cheeks," Irène would say with a touch of pride: Belsele's healthy living. My presence could no longer be explained. I had to go into hiding. Stay inside. That was the inescapable conclusion that Gaston and Adrienne reached in consultation with my parents. Back to Antwerp, the story would go. I could no longer delay my studies.

The logic of hiding was compelling. I couldn't think of another solution either; in fact, I couldn't think at all. I just looked at the tips of my shoes — my reflexive stance when perplexed or annoyed and without emotional elbow room. Everyone must have perceived me as capable of enduring such a regime. Indeed,

I had always been compliant, eager to please, ready to meet the challenges that were set out for me.

It was decided that I was to spend my days in Gaston and Adrienne's bedroom, for the neighbors might surprise me in the kitchen. They would come in through the front hallway or through the pump house in the rear, sometimes without even the perfunctory knock on the door, and proceed to the kitchen while calling out for Adrienne; moments later they would be inside. Doors were left unlocked during the day. Locking up would be a change in old neighborly habits. The neighbors would have found it perplexing, and it would have been one more thing for Adrienne to explain. I was to refrain from making any noise that might seem strange to our neighbor Julia — a thin wall separated the bedrooms in the two identical houses.

And so, on a Sunday evening in October of 1942, I took off my shoes and put on the sturdy slippers Adrienne had sewn from the salvageable remnants of Gaston's discarded work overalls. We all wore such slippers in our wooden shoes and indoors, but mine, suddenly, felt different: they had become my only footwear, distinctive, like a prisoner's. My shoes had become an item to be stored away. I had taken the evening train to Antwerp, so the neighbors would be told. Antwerp. The forbidden city. To me, it was no longer real, existing in name only, like Sodom after Lot's flight.

It was time to go upstairs. Adrienne came in from the pump house with a pail half filled with water: it would serve as my indoor toilet. The sight of her climbing the stairs with the pail pulling at her shoulder shook me out of my brooding haze. I would henceforth live differently from everyone else, and alone, in silence. I climbed the stairs behind Sylvain.

CHAPTER 5 — HIDING

I woke up to sunlight slanting low through the garret window, and to the thought, like a cloud, that I would be staying upstairs all day.

The sounds of morning bustled in: a door handle snapping loose, a pot coming down in the pump house sink, the clanging of the pump, and, drifting in through the open garret window, the moo of a cow, the low thuds of wooden shoes on the dirt path, a dog's bark. That morning the sounds rang sharper: I was the outsider listening in. I noticed for a few intense moments the dense, carefree twitter of the birds.

Sylvain was still sleeping. I woke him up when Adrienne called from the kitchen. Gaston had already biked off to the forge at seven, his usual time, about an hour before daybreak on that late October day.

We got up. I handed my brother the pocket *siddur* opened at the *Sh'ma* (Hear, O Israel) and watched, hawk-like, over him — we both stood in our pyjamas — as he whispered, with obvious displeasure, the Hebrew words. He had felt imposed upon ever since I had foisted the prayer routine upon him, my way of complying with my father's charge to me in our Antwerp hideout, "Teach your brother." I had chosen the *Sh'ma*, the oft repeated prayer, the hallowed expression of our creed, words, we were taught at Tachkemoni, that Jews had invoked throughout history in the face of persecution and death. I was also holding onto whatever shreds of authority I had over him. We went through our morning routine, he, mumbling hurriedly and mispronouncing; I, correcting him in whispers, *"oo-vuh-shOkh-buh-khah,* O! Not AH." He read on, unperturbed.

Sylvain finished the *Sh'ma* and hurried downstairs with his clothes slung over his shoulder. From the weaker clank of the pump handle I knew that he was washing up — face and hands.

I washed up in the garret — a vanity held a three-piece porcelain set consisting of a washbasin, a pitcher and a soap dish. It was the first departure from normalcy and a disconcerting reminder that my day would be different. The narrow pump house, wedged between the kitchen and a little stable, was too exposed: it opened onto the back yard through a glass-paned door.

I came down for breakfast like a stowaway among accomplices, on the alert for approaching footsteps, ready to bolt and dart up the staircase.

The time came for me to go upstairs. Pulling aside the heavy drape that hung over the opening in the wall, I faced the dark staircase — it spiraled to the right and climbed along the common wall between Julia's house and ours — and I saw in a flash the emptiness of the unseen space above, of the day. It caused a surge of anguish, squelched by the all-absorbing attempt to tread softly, as traffic on the creaking steps would be heard clearly next door. The staircase led to a landing. On the right was the door to the garret; straight ahead, a door opened onto Gaston and Adrienne's bedroom. The two rooms covered the top floor of the two-story house.

I entered the garret. I picked up the *siddur* and began reading, without moving my lips, my usual, abbreviated version of the morning prayers, from *Barkhu* to *Ahlaynu*, the same portion — it contained the *Sh'ma* and the *Ameedah* — that Silberstein had us recite at the start of class at Tachkemoni. It took about ten minutes. Prayer before class was not school policy, just a ploy by some of the Jewish teachers so they could chat in the hallway about "the situation" — would it lead to war? — about staying put or emigrating, about money. We would race through the prayers. Some of my classmates would skip entire passages. When Silberstein appeared at the door the class would be a-buzz.

The prayers, that morning, sounded distressingly irrelevant, especially the supplications in the *Ameedah*:

"Forgive us, our Father, for we have transgressed; pardon us, our King, for we have sinned,..." Forgive us, for what? For flipping on a light switch on Shabbat? For some pitiable Jew biting into a cold chicken drumstick on Yom Kippur? I couldn't bring myself to beat my breast twice, once for each confession, nor could I ignore the custom altogether. I just held my right fist to my heart.

"...And may all wickedness disappear forthwith, and may all the enemies of Your people perish speedily,..." German wickedness, disappear forthwith! Sitting on His haunches, like a solitary and distant Sphinx, was how I imagined Him, waiting for things to sort themselves out on earth. Sidelined, the God of my prayers.

I remembered Maurice Zalcman declaring to Menda and me that there is no God. *No God... Could he have been right?... Unafraid, yes.* I felt diminished in the sudden solitude of the garret.

"...The sprouting seed of Your servant David may You speedily make to grow..." I looked with near detachment at the familiar words in the ancient tongue: they sounded flat and stilted under the patch of scintillating blue sky in the half-open garret window, amidst the chirping of the birds, the cackle from the neighboring farmyard, the noises from the kitchen. They drowned in a sea of un-Jewishness.

I rushed through the *Ameedah* to the concluding amen and glossed over the short imploration that follows; it rated the smallest print in the *siddur* and read like an afterthought: **"May it be Your will, O Lord our God and the God of our forefathers, that the Holy Temple be rebuilt speedily in our days...."** *The temple, speedily in our days... sheer fantasy.*

There were only a few steps from the garret to Gaston and Adrienne's bedroom. My haunt, from now on. I took the steps with trepidation, as if entering the unknown.

The blankets, sheets and pillows were airing in the two windows. The wool-filled mattress was turned over and fluffed out. I stood, motionless. *What now?...* My heart was pounding, that's all I heard. *What now?... What now?...* I felt a strange void, as if time had been sucked away. Timelessness in the bedroom, like stillness in the eye of a hurricane. *What now?...* I stared at the massive armoire. I looked down at the tips of my slippers. I looked sideways: between the door and the glass-topped night table stood a straight-back wooden chair, *for me,* hard, empty. Final. I sat down, closed my eyes. Brilliant dots flared up and died. My mind churned, empty. I felt again in the grip of a never-ending moment. It was dizzying. I opened my eyes and noticed the slow-moving white puffy clouds in the blue sky. Soothing.

I moved to the shady corner near the left window, where no one could see me. The road below was quiet. I stared at the tightly meshed gray cobblestones — they fanned out in successive, curving rows from a number of center stones. I looked at the three freestanding houses on the opposite side of the road: The café *Chalet* — it faced our windows; its top floor had an off-white,

Swiss style, gabled façade with wide brown stripes at various angles; the lone upper window was tucked under a sharp-angled roof. To the right stood, massive, the butcher's house, its black roof panes glistening in the sun, the red bricks, aglow; and, to its right, dwarfed by it, Irène's little one-story dwelling. The white-tiled butcher shop was empty.

I turned back, sat down, got up, shuttled between the middle of the room and my chair. The aimless moving about brought me close to panic. I picked up the newspaper I brought from the kitchen and tried reading. The printed words drew blanks.

I took up position in the shade near the window. A villager walked on the dirt path along the road, on the opposite side. I followed him until he moved out of sight. *He'll get there. Where? There. It will be later then. Later. How much later?* I kept following him in my thoughts. A cyclist appeared from the opposite direction and disappeared. The mistress of the *Chalet* — svelte, with a head of dark hair — served a lone patron a glass of beer, then moved out of sight. I heard the clatter of an approaching horse and the rattle of steel-rimmed wheels on the cobblestones. Horse and wagon and driver — a mustached farmer under a collapsed, soiled worker cap — passed by and disappeared. I listened, motionless, to the fading sounds, until they slid into silence. It was soothing. I snapped out of this fleeting trance: *Horse and farmer will get there. There. The patron will empty his glass and leave.* I decided to watch him finish his beer. *My day will end with theirs.* The café patron glanced at his pocket watch and wound it briefly: *it will all come to an end, the savoring of the beer, the horse and wagon ride, the bailing of hay, the plowing, the planting. Their day. My day. The week. The war. It will pass. All goes by. Egypt. The Dynasties. The Pleistocene... The... The Cambrian, nom de Dieu! If I were doing something significant, time would pass. Something... The Germans can't hold out much longer. Their days are numbered.* It rang hollow. *I'm trapped!*

I returned to my chair. Once again my mind ran in all directions. I jammed my fists into my trouser pockets and remained seated. *They won't last long.* I latched on to these words, *They won't last long.* Wan hope. Thoughts telescoped into each other, flotsam cresting on the waves of my inner turbulence. A Jewish pundit's pronouncement popped up, "Their end is near, their turning on us is a clear sign of it." Another one, "You can't defeat the Bank of England and Fort Knox." "Our clever Jews, fooling themselves,"

I heard my mother say dismissively. The short, stocky, German Jewish plumber who fixed the drain in our kitchen sink with his gleaming German tools: "A Jewish Hitler in Palestine, that's what we need." A miracle worker, Hitler was; "Our bad luck he turned out that way; the Germans will do *anything* he says"; *got out*; *America*; *left the boiling cauldron called Europe, uncle Chaim's boiling cauldron.* "*Einen anderen Purim werden sie NICHT haben*" ("Another Purim they will NOT have"), I could hear my mother muttering to me in Adrienne's kitchen. *Hiding. Like Marranos. Modern-day Marranos. No, like quarry. The only way. No more Switzerland. Never-never land.* My parents: they whisper in the dining room about Switzerland. My mother is wringing her hands. *No decision, ever.* I imagined us sitting in the train compartment, my mother and I facing my father and my brother. My father blanches at the sound of heavy steps in the corridor — someone, unhindered by baggage, is approaching. We are waiting, frozen, for the German to darken the doorway, for the word *Kontrolle* to drop, for the steely look at the cornered family, oh, so unmistakably Jewish. The scene freezes at *Kontrolle*. My cousin Shloimeh, in our dining room, with the remainder of the coffee: "It kicked in too early. I passed muster." For work on the Atlantic Wall. Nabbed him in Antwerp, with the whole group. The smuggler betrayed them. His sister, Rookhel, hooked him up with that smuggler, felt awful, turned herself in. *How did she do that? Did they let her in the Kommandantur? She is stubborn*:

"I want to be with my brother!"

"*Na selbstverständlich. Komm' ja 'rein*" ("But of course. Come on in").

I saw her, slender, yet filled out, with a roundish face, lustrous brown hair, full lips, big blue-green eyes, her father's, my father's, our grandmother's eyes. *Where is she? We are safe here in the countryside.* Antwerp seems so far away, beyond the horizon, swallowed by the earth. *They can't last much longer, not against the Allies.* A high-moving, light-gray cloud dimmed the sunlight. I simmered down.

I felt the need to move about, to get out of the bedroom. The garret was confining: in the bedroom part, the brass bed that Sylvain and I slept in, the vanity holding the porcelain wash-set, and a chair, left just enough room to open the door from the landing. The shallow space behind the shoulder-height curtain was used to store odds and ends, like tools, empty cans and jars. There also stood the galvanized iron pail half filled with water: my toilet. Next to it, on the floor, the toilet paper: cut up newsprint.

The only clear daylight in the garret was under its window; the light weakened as it seeped deeper into the room, barely touching the corners. The garret window was raised halfway, a horizontal glass cap over the square opening in the slanting roof. Standing in the foot-wide space between the bed and the curtain I could see the black, bare treetops in the distance; they were beckoning, more so when swaying in the wind. Sitting on the bed I could see a sliver of cloud and sky.

A sudden burst of sunshine set the patch of sky aglow and sent a beam of sunlight streaming in through the garret window, irradiating a fine cloud of dust particles. They swirled, tumbled and rose, floated in and out of the light. Arresting spectacle. Unending. Numbing. I started, self-conscious, from my seated, hunched-over position. The garret, suddenly, felt like a vault. I returned to the bedroom.

I had my first break when Adrienne came upstairs with an issue of *Het Vrije Waasland*. She also handed me a couple of Hedwig Courts Mahler love novels in Flemish. Pointing her thumb toward the neighbor's house she whispered, mindful of the thin common wall, "Fireworks, last night," and brought her hand to her mouth in a drinking motion. With Gaston and Sylvain out of the house the mere inkling of a conversation would have puzzled our neighbor Julia; a jarring note that might cling to memory. Poor woman. Her husband the mason would be gone all week on a construction job and return on Saturday, make the rounds of the cafés along the Road, and stay drunk till Sunday night. He would leave early on Monday morning without a trace of a hangover.

Adrienne made the beds and tidied up the garret and the bedroom while I sat still on my chair by the night table, to keep out of her way and at a safe distance from the open bedroom window. Her presence, her busying herself, restored a sense of living, of time passing. When she went downstairs with my toilet pail both rooms were spotless. Transformed. Especially the bedroom: with its two gabled windows facing the road, it was a bright space, wide — sixteen feet between the two outer walls, and thirteen feet deep from the landing to the front of the house. It was mine, fresh, soothing.

I sat for a while and took in the change in environment. Time, once again, had ground to a halt. I picked up *Het Vrije Waasland*. The print no longer drew a total blank; often, though, a sentence, or an entire paragraph, required a second, even a third reading. I picked up the two decks of cards that Gaston gave me and started building castles on the foot mat by the bed. It was absorbing at first. I soon tired of it and felt let down: building card castles as recreation or in a contest used to be fun; as a major activity it was a time killer that left me feeling empty. I opened a Hedwig Courts Mahler novel. In it a solid young man and a beautiful young woman who are strongly attracted to each other suffer a disappointment due to a misunderstanding which, when cleared up, leads to a kiss and a proposal in marriage. Bliss follows. The story was short, easy to read, easier to forget. It left no memory, like bland food. *I must do something meaningful. I must make time count.* The thought intruded, persisted. *I must make time count. This is an important time, like the Inquisition. This is History. A Flemish bedroom. Jewish history. I am in it.* Yet I felt so removed from my people, from life.

I needed to relieve myself. I moved to the garret and squatted over the pail without bearing down for fear of tilting it or falling inside. The sloping ceiling was just inches from my head. The image of the big white-and-gray rabbit crouching in its dark cage in the little stable adjoining the pump house (Gaston was raising rabbits for food) flitted through my mind.

Relieving myself restored a sense of normalcy. I noticed an empty glass jar whose label featured a mature woman. A simple dress accentuates the troubling, erect fullness of her breasts and the firm, shapely forms of her long legs. She has a young face framed in a wavy brown *permanente*. She is standing by a tree and reaching up at a low-hanging branch weighed down with bunches of red cherries. To touch her, the real live woman...

I knew that it was noon when I heard Gaston's voice. Adrienne sent a whispering sound up the staircase, accompanied by some tapping on one of the lower steps: she was motioning me down for the noonday meal. Henceforth, two taps would suffice to bring me to the landing.

"How are you doing?" Gaston asked me.

"Fine."

"Do you have stuff to keep you busy?"

"O yes."

"If you need anything, just say so."

"Nothing, really..."

"It won't last long. *De Mof* [an epithet for 'the German'†]," and he made the wringing motion with his clenched fists.

"I know."

As we were eating the main dish — boiled potatoes with a vegetable — we heard the turning click of the front door handle. I bolted behind the drape as Julia called out, "Adrienne?" "Yes, Julia, come on in." Climbing quietly two steps at a time I was in the bedroom before Julia shuffled in her slippers to the kitchen door. Our neighbor had come to borrow half a cup of sugar. After she left, Adrienne was about to serve me a fresh portion on a clean plate: Gaston had emptied my plate into his, stacked the two and had gone on eating. I stopped her:

"I don't want anymore. I was not very hungry to begin with," I said.

"You ate some, at least," she said. "I can understand it. The first day..."

I felt a pang: "the first day."

"And with Julia barging in," Adrienne continued. "But you must eat well to retain your strength."

"I will," I said in a dull voice. "Tomorrow I'll be back to normal."

"Keep in mind that you are growing."

Growing. How odd, when life was at a standstill. Hiding, I suddenly felt, meant remaining small. My Christian classmates, they were growing. I saw them, as in a snapshot, seated two by two, hunched over their work, forging ahead, concerned solely with the mysteries of algebra and Greek.

It was a tense meal for all. It was decided that I would henceforth have both breakfast and the noon meal, the main meal of the day, upstairs.

Minutes after eating, Gaston left on his bicycle with Sylvain running alongside him in his wooden shoes. A routine of theirs. Gaston would pick up speed at the far end of the vegetable garden. Sylvain would then peel off and turn back. Sometimes he would wait for Gaston's return and run at his encounter. The two would then ride in together, with Sylvain sitting on the straight bar and holding on to the handlebar, or sitting in the rear, on the baggage rack; he had become adept at hoisting himself onto it while the bike was moving slowly.

I climbed back up. Gone was the morning with the busy sounds of house work. Soon Adrienne would be wet-mopping the large black and white floor tiles of the pump house and the kitchen and be done with the after lunch chores. I felt calm. Slouching in my chair with my hands in my trouser pockets, to keep them warm, I settled into a slump, head bent, eyes closed. *I must make time count. These are important times.*

I came out of my torpor and drew myself up in my seat. Time had passed, but it was slowing down again. I went to my look-out post near the window. The road was as animated as in the morning. The afternoon sunlight made the cobblestones glisten; it brought the off-white façade of the *Chalet* to life, it bounced off the red bricks of the butcher's house, infused warmth into the earthen bicycle path.

I heard the tapping sound and a short noise: Adrienne had put a saucer holding a cup of chicory coffee and cookies on one of the lower steps. I fetched it in total silence. Looking at the sky while savoring the treat was, up to this moment, the high point of my day. There was a different feel in the air. The sounds from the outside, the greetings, the loud *djurr*'s (local corruption of *bonjour*) launched from opposite sides of the road, the light filtering sideways through the windows, cheered me up. I surveyed the bedroom for the first time, taking in every piece, every detail, like an exploration. *Voyage autour de ma chambre!* The book by Xavier de Maistre I had received in second grade, at Tachkemoni, as a year-end award. *That's it, Voyage autour de ma chambre.* In it the French monarchist describes the room he was confined to, its furnishings, his movements and imaginings during a forty-day house arrest in Turin. I had slogged through the thin little book from cover to cover the week I had been confined to the house because of a festering wound at the ankle. I had retained little of the prize that was meant to enrich a schoolboy's summer.

I would make time count: I would draw the bedroom in Belsele as the pictorial part of a record that would become my

Voyage autour de ma chambre, a record that would render memorable the otherwise empty days ahead. I would apply the rules of perspective I enjoyed practicing in drawing class in high school. I would draw the bedroom with its oak-veneered furniture as I saw it almost all of the time: from the rear, facing the left window, with the large bed at the center. I would bring out the diamond stitching in the dark-green, sumptuous-looking satin bedspread. I would profile, at the outer left, where it stood along our common wall with Julia, the large, three-tiered armoire with a curving door on each side. The top of the Swiss-style, gabled façade of the café *Chalet* would appear in the window facing me. The pattern of brown stripes around the window under the café's roof had suddenly become intricate and interesting. The upper structure of the butcher's brick house would appear in the window to the right. I would sketch in the two black metal anchors neatly wedged into the side wall. I didn't understand their use, but they reinforced the impression of solidity. A separate drawing would show the bed's curving headboard lining the back wall that divided the upstairs between bedroom and garret, the two glass-topped night tables, and my chair between the left night table and the door to the landing. I might also draw the road as seen sideways from the left window with the intricate cobblestone design. I had the outline of a big project, a voyage beyond the confines of my room, a record of hiding. Belsele in Jewish history. *Tomorrow, I will start tomorrow.* I had licked a nasty problem. I could wait out the day now; calmly.

The afternoon began to fade early: the days were short. I watched the light thin out and gray. The sky darkened, slowly. Dusk was enveloping the earth. A period of grace.

Adrienne liked to wait until dark before turning on the light. She locked the front door, then stepped out into the back yard and closed the shutters of the kitchen window before calling me down. We heard Sylvain's distinct patter as he came running in his wooden shoes from the neighboring farm where he played almost every day with Simoneke.

Gaston came home at seven, the usual time.

"How was it?" he asked.

"Fine," I answered.

––––––––

We had supper. Adrienne cleared off the table. We moved our chairs to their usual place around the stove. Adrienne knitted by the shuttered window; Gaston, facing her from the other side of the stove, read the paper, uttering every so often some grumbling comment about one piece of "nonsense" or other. Sylvain and I sat in the middle, facing the stove. I had blanked out of my mind the mood swings and the feelings that had befallen me upstairs. Yet the experience I had emerged from set me apart. I had wrestled with timelessness, and I would remain locked in that struggle. I had stepped into a double life: the kitchen life, outwardly the same as everybody else's, and my solitary life upstairs. A member of the cell, and a dweller apart. It was brought home again, later in the evening, when Adrienne came down with my toilet pail, emptied it in the outhouse, rinsed it, replenished it with water, and took it back up to the garret.

I welcomed the long night, that sweet cradle and silent buffer.

✡ ✡ ✡

The next morning I woke up with the anguished intimation that a long wait had begun. I lay still and listened to the sounds of the world ushering in a new day. Adrienne called. Sylvain and I got up.

I ate breakfast alone, in the bedroom, without appetite. I felt relegated to the upstairs, yet I did not miss being in the kitchen where my presence was a burden to others, where my heartbeat would quicken at the sound of approaching footsteps and the click of a turning door handle would make me bolt behind the drape. The upstairs had become my dwelling place and my refuge. I sat motionless, resigned yet relieved, and waited for Adrienne to turn the untidy bedroom — the bedding was airing in the windows, the wool mattress lay pummeled shapeless — into my spotless and undisturbed realm. A grace period, until my grappling with the day would begin.

I remembered my project, "Voyage autour de ma chambre," with a surge of pleasure. I asked Adrienne for a pencil and paper which she brought to me — a thin pad of grayish, newsprint-quality sheets — as soon as she had finished the upstairs cleaning. My sketch was to show the bedroom at its immaculate best.

But I couldn't get beyond a few lifeless lines. My failure to draw stung. I gave up on the project, image and word. Just writing did not occur to me: it was a school activity, with the teacher assigning the subject. And the idea of keeping a journal was unfamiliar to me — explorers and adventurers did that, and people caught up in unusual, action-packed events. I could see little that was worth recording in a normal, ordinary life, much less in a life of hibernation. I felt swept up in the maelstrom of Jewish history, a latter-day Marrano, with nothing to say.

I was back to where I had been the previous morning. The bleakness of a long day, of many long days ahead loomed, depressing. I sat without moving for a long while, shifting position, shaking off the numbness that had settled in. The first day went by; so will this one, I told myself. I will find something to do. Something with a purpose. I will find ways to kill time till noon, till cookies and coffee, till evening. I felt less impelled to move than on the previous day. I sat for longer intervals, watched the road with less trepidation, made sense out of the newspaper. Daydreaming was less jagged. I got lost in my thoughts and tried at times to retrace their meandering flow, a challenging, often frustrating exercise.

I was first to get the soup of the midday meal — Adrienne brought it up before Gaston's return from the forge. It felt like a special treat. Picking up the main dish off a lower step of the staircase while the three of them were seated around the kitchen table made me feel left out. I put my empty plate down on the floor of the landing and went back to my chair.

Adrienne waited for Gaston to leave before picking up my plate and getting busy with the cleanup chores. I slipped into an after-dinner torpor — disjointed thoughts flickering and dying, like lazy fireflies, the precursor of slumber — to regain consciousness at the sound of an iron pail handle hitting the rim with a clank: Adrienne was wet-mopping the kitchen. I remained seated in a backward slouch, staring the minutes away.

The cookies and the hot coffee induced a sense of well-being, a vague feeling that sometime, somehow, I would be turning the days to come into a meaningful interval between life interrupted and life resumed, a milestone on the road to Jewish manhood.

The day was on its downward course. Just waiting, becalmed, for darkness to erase the day.

It got too dark for reading. The silence and mystery hanging in the deepening shadows stemmed the inner churning. The windows were darkening slowly into blackness, like drawbridges coming up for the night. The day had been my prison; time, the warden. Night came as a deliverance, a relief felt more deeply even than on the previous, the first day of hiding.

Adrienne turned on the light in the kitchen, closed the shutters and locked the front door. I sat a while longer, taking in the transparent darkness of the bedroom. Before going down to the kitchen I stopped by the garret window to stare at the firmament. Its depth, unfathomable and vertiginous, like death, induced a feeling of loneness and utter insignificance. It cleansed my mind from the day's preoccupations. An unexpected moment, both disquieting and soothing. A minute later I was in the kitchen, joining the fold, squinting, relieved.

✿ ✿ ✿

Weeks later. Liberation had become a mirage. A routine carried me from sunrise to dusk.

Morning no longer entailed coaxing my brother into reciting the *Sh'ma*. He had become increasingly reluctant to mouth under my hawk-like and resented supervision the words that bored him, infuriating me with his sloppy pronunciation, until, one day, he flatly refused to read past the first, the shortest of the prayer's three sections. That led to an argument in which my angry whispers degenerated into hisses that were heard in the kitchen. When Adrienne wondered aloud what was going on Sylvain ran downstairs and complained that I was forcing him to read prayers in Hebrew.

"In Hebrew!" Gaston exclaimed in a low voice. He was indulging in a leisurely morning, that day, before taking off to the hardware store in Lokeren. "Can *you* read Hebrew?" he asked Sylvain.

"Yes."

"I'd like to hear that."

Sylvain ran upstairs, grabbed the *siddur* without looking at me and scampered right down. He read the *Sh'ma* clearly and faultlessly, as if he were on stage, articulating every syllable. Without head cover. I was picturing Gaston and Adrienne surrounding him and peeking at the Hebrew prayer book as they listened. I was trying to imagine how Hebrew would sound to them: pretty awful, I thought, with those repetitive "ah" and terminal "khah" sounds. I stood there, tense, humiliated, and fuming over the profanation of the *Sh'ma,* of the *siddur.* Sylvain stopped after the first section, waiting for their reaction. I also waited, with bated breath.

"Ah *potverdekke* [a sanitized curse], have you ever heard something like that?" Gaston said. "Is that Jewish?"

"No, this is Hebrew. Jewish is like Flemish, what people speak."

"And Hebrew is what?"

"The language the Bible is written in. And the prayers."

"And do you understand that?" Gaston asked, incredulous.

"No."

"Who would..."

"Gaston, to each his own," Adrienne intervened. "Do we understand the Latin of the Mass?"

Gaston grumbled under his breath, his way of conceding a point.

"And does Henri understand that?" he asked.

"Yes."

"*Mill-YAAR-de!*" Gaston exclaimed, impressed.

"Gaston, what's so unusual about it?" Adrienne countered, "we have boys who study Latin in school. It's the same thing."

Some more grumbling under his breath.

"He knows Latin too," my brother filled in.

"*Mille grijze!*" Another sanitized curse.

"Gaston! Stop swearing! Tell you what, my boy," Adrienne said in a congenial tone, "you don't have to say these prayers; you are excused until the end of the war. And no more quarreling upstairs. You'll pray all you have to when you go back to Antwerp." She had raised her voice slightly, for my benefit.

Sylvain ran back up, put the siddur on the vanity in the garret with a defiant look at me and disappeared just as fast. My brother resented my bossiness; he had always stood up to me. I took this *Sh'ma* episode as a betrayal and a defeat.

———

I would start the day with an elaborate ritual. Standing half-naked in front of the vanity mirror, I washed down to the waist with soap and cold water, as my father and I after him used to do at home. I braced myself, in the chill of the garret, for the cold, wet wash mitt to land on my bare chest. It was the act that ushered in the day. I ran the washhand over every square centimeter of my upper body. The initial shiver would yield to a feeling of soothing coolness. After lathering the wet washhand I put the wet soap bar — an almost latherless ersatz — on another, dry washhand to be used the next morning: a soap-saving tip I picked up in *Het Vrije Waasland*. Rubbing myself dry turned my torso a light pink. Washing myself from the waist down completed the ritual. I brushed my teeth, got dressed and combed my hair. I felt invigorated, clean and alive; a member in good standing of the human race.

Breakfast would follow almost immediately — bread and butter with a slice of cheese, an occasional soft boiled egg, and coffee with milk and sugar. I ate it in Gaston and Adrienne's unmade bedroom.

Next I would fetch the *siddur*, the *tillimel* and the two packs of cards from the garret. I had kept up the recitation of the morning prayers despite the sense of unreality they had induced on the first day of hiding: they were imbued with my people's presence, they spoke in a shared tongue of a common past. Our future would well up, irrepressible, from our past. I knew. Stopping the prayers would have felt like leaving the fold; a betrayal of the deported. I read the same short portion, without moving my lips, as both an act of will and an act of submission, but without the breast-beating at the passage imploring God to forgive us for our sins. I would just hold my fist to my heart, in a reluctant gesture, the same as on the first day of hiding. I would be done praying in less than ten minutes.

I would then sit in silence, and wait with anticipation for Adrienne to come and tidy up the bedrooms. I would cock my head at the sliding sound of the curtain rings on the wooden rod and listen to her ascending footsteps.

Holding two brooms — a shaggy one for the hard, shining bedroom floor, a dust pan and cloths, she would peek through the bedroom door and whisper:

"*Alles in orde?*" ("Everything all right?")

"*Ja, alles in orde,*" I would whisper to her.

A cheerful interchange between co-conspirators. Her appearance gave me a thrill. Being alone in her presence induced a titillating tension I had felt ever since the first afternoon's coffee treat in the kitchen.

She would do the garret first. I knew the routine by its sounds; I would anticipate them: from the squeak of the garret window's rusty hinges as she raised it for more air, the gush of water as she emptied the wash basin into the toilet pail, the thud of the heavy horse-hair mattress as she overturned it, the rumble of the bed's metal wheels on the wooden floor as she moved it away from the wall, then back, the knocks of the broom against the walls and the legs of the bed, the rattle of the lid on the porcelain soap dish — she would dust off every surface, to the final squeak of the window's hinges as she lowered it one or more notches, depending upon the weather. And throughout, the sound of her busy footsteps.

She would enter the bedroom.

She might pause first for a whispered bit of gossip, like, "Julia, poor thing." I knew the rest: husband gone or drunk. Another blowup next door, no doubt; or "Irène..." I caught on right away: this had to do with their conversation in the kitchen the day before; I had tuned out when I heard them talk about the price of meat and eggs, "is she desperate for a man." Had I known what they would be talking about... Not just wanting to get married. *Desperate* she was. For a man. Wanted to be kissed, like... no, not like the prim Hedwig Courts Mahler girls. Like Jeannette MacDonald, or Danielle Darrieux, or better even, like Annabella, the sultry, brooding actress. Kissed, and coddled. And more — I didn't know exactly what. Choosy though, Irène was. She had turned down quite a few of them. I pictured her: taller than most men, a straight, thin figure, almost flat, head held high, like Adrienne, thick, blond hair, fine features, long fingers.

I would watch Adrienne as I read: swift, energetic, lithe; moving, unconcerned, in front of the windows as she circled around the large bed, bending over it, shaping and dressing it into a dark-satin, calm-inducing pristineness; shaking out the foot mats in the window, dusting off every surface, including the window sills and frames, the bed's head and foot boards; yet moving deliberately from one spot to the other, from one task to the next; an ordered, almost choreographed work. She had moved it up ever since I went into hiding. I had felt flattered. All this ado... for me, sort of. I was reading distractedly while stealing glances at her. "Remain seated, just lift your feet," she had whispered the first time she came near with her shaggy broom. I wanted to kiss her. I craved an embrace. And felt distress for harboring such emotions, the desire. I would hide it all under a studied casualness. "I'm getting out of your way," I whispered after a few days, and left for the garret. But not right away as if I wanted to avoid her. Nor did I want to miss that occasional bit of local or family gossip.

I felt freer in the garret, with a space all to myself. I might even take *Het Vrije Waasland* along. If my mind wandered off the page, it was because of Adrienne's presence in the adjacent room — a sweet distraction. Sunlight slanting in through the garret window, brightening up a swath of blanket at the foot of the bed, made the tidy space even look cozy. It was a normal wait, like others in a free man's day. Easy. Pleasant, almost.

"All done," Adrienne would whisper from the landing.

Sometimes she would take a brief but close look at me. Was it concern? She would smile. I would force a smile.

That was the last time I would see her until the afternoon coffee, which I took downstairs sometimes, or until dark. She went down with my toilet pail. She came up twice more, with a fresh pail of water, and with a full porcelain pitcher for my use the next morning. The upstairs was mine.

Like the morning ablutions, the transformation of the large bedroom into a pleasant space gave me a feeling of renewal. I felt fresh and at my keenest, charged: an expanse of virgin time was stretching out in front of me, like a promise in the air. Real hiding — a Jewish imperative, an occupation, almost — could now begin.

Sitting by the door I would luxuriate in the newness of the day — it lent itself to prolonged moments of anguish-free contemplation — and take in the sights: the off-white gable of the *Chalet* straight across the road from us, the upper part of the butcher's massive red brick house with its black-tile roof, the patch of sky above it, the clouds as they drifted by, the bare treetops in the distance. I would listen to the matinal sounds: the clomping of wooden shoes — low and muffled on the dirt path along the road, high-pitched and loud on the cobblestones; the crunching on the bicycle path of gravel under tires; the expansive greetings — the loud *djurr's* — sent ringing from one side of the road to the other. A new day in Creation had begun, stirring when the sun shone and the air was limpid, favoring laziness and day-dreaming when the sky was gray.

After a while I would engage with an anticipation of pleasure in one of my routine activities. I might pick up the newspaper and start searching for indications of the inevitable German defeat, a mere question of reading between the lines: they were crowing over little gains; and every retreat was strategic, as if they had a choice. The Germans seemed to be the only dupes. Scouring the papers for news about the hostilities and the fickle front lines had been an addiction ever since the lightning conquest of Cyrenaika by the British in January of '41.

The war communiqués of late were bland. That was good news: no movement meant that the Germans were standing still and depleting their resources while the Allies, we all knew, were getting stronger by the day. Two months after I went into hiding the news was exhilarating. The Germans were stalled at Moscow, Leningrad, and Stalingrad. The Russian winter would certainly finish them off. Could victory — could Liberation — be at hand?

One day in December — the battle of Stalingrad was at its height — Adrienne caught Hitler's distinctive bark on the radio. She tapped on the stair and motioned me down. Gaston was with her. The speech was long, I was straining to understand, and they were getting impatient.

"What is he saying?" Gaston asked testily.

"Well... they won't get Stalingrad," I said with a smirk.

"That's all he said? It sure took a long time!"

"He said that Stalingrad must and will fall, not because it bears the name of his archenemy, but because it is of the greatest military importance."

"A small difference."

"Yes, but they have been at it since the fall, and still, nothing. You don't take a Russian town in the winter. And he is telling the Germans that he is not doing it out of personal pique. They must be falling like flies." I was full of glee.

"What else did he blabber about?" Gaston asked.

"The usual. The American plutocrats. The Russian communists. And the Jews who are responsible for the war... And there were things I didn't catch. It's a double disaster, first the military defeat, then Baku... Stalingrad would have opened the way to the oil fields of Baku, in the Caucasus."

I was trying to allay their irritation at having suffered for so long what must have sounded like barked gibberish to them; most of it had been incomprehensible to me also, but I had been unwilling to admit it to myself: after all, I *knew* German.

"How do you know all of that?"

I sensed that I had sounded off-key. I had shown off, like a little know-it-all smart aleck.

"From school... *Koninklijk Atheneum*. We had a famous geography teacher, Dr. de Roeck." A solid Flemish name. I was eager to produce Flemish sources for this superior knowledge. And indeed, Dr. de Roeck had published a great atlas. In his class the topics were land masses, the effects of ocean currents and mountain ranges, of trade winds, evaporation and condensation on climate and soil formation, on human habitation and growth. It had sounded as if geography was destiny. Baku I knew from Tachkemoni.

The scope of the German defeat at Stalingrad would be mind-boggling. *"Ah-SHER hakhi-LO-tah Lin-POL"* ("Once you have begun to fall"), I remembered Zeresh telling her husband Haman, "You will fall down before him." The BBC commentators were exulting: "A turning point in the war." We would listen to the forbidden British radio as we sat, on the long winter nights, around the glowing potbelly in the kitchen, behind locked doors and closed shutters.

But the victory at Stalingrad was like a bright shooting star in the dark night. Soon thereafter the war resumed its plodding course.

After reading the newspaper, I might consider a game of solitaire. No hurry: the pause only sharpened the desire. One of the two games I played — I discovered them both in *Het Vrije Waasland* — was easy and led rarely to gridlock. The other, starting with all cards turned face up, required the ability to project ahead, much like analyzing the chess board. I played game after game, trying stubbornly for the ultimate stacking-up of the cards by suit and in the proper sequence. Each opening configuration held the same fresh promise. Some games were doomed from the start: they allowed for few first moves and even fewer second moves before ending in gridlock. But quite often the opening configuration allowed for a number of moves whose further ramifications were too numerous to tabulate mentally. I would play until I tired of it. Rare, but gratifying, were the successful games.

Before discovering the games of solitaire I had built card castles. The look-alike, ephemeral structures had brought home the emptiness of my day; a stultifying exercise, like counting peas. Even Milou, our cat, an occasional visitor, had stopped paying attention to the rising and crashing structures. The first time he had seen me erect a house of cards, he watched my every move. Mystified, he had raised a hesitant paw as if to touch — or test? Or join me? But he didn't come near the construction in progress. Would Milou ignore, or bring down, perhaps, the finished castle? He did not. Then, with a flick of a finger, I had caused the structure to collapse. Milou was seized with a slight, backward tremor. He looked at the heap of cards, extended a paw, touched a card at the edge, then backed away to go down on the mat and avert his gaze, as if the thing had never existed. I had been aware of my role as the higher intelligence manipulating events around the startled, grappling subject. Was someone manipulating us? I wondered, like loosing the Germans on us? Treacherous territory. I dropped the subject. Milou gave subsequent "séances" scant notice. I stopped them, stopped altogether building card castles.

I became fond of our cat's undemanding, discreet presence. He would pitter-patter up the stairs, often in retreat before Adrienne's wet mop; make his unhurried entrance from the landing; rub against my leg with an occasional arching of the spine; and go down in a sphinx-like pose on the mat. I would sit on the floor and stroke him, pick him up, get back on my chair and stroke him some more. The cat would nestle on my lap and purr, a somnolent look in his round, halfway shuttered eyes. His body warmth was soothing. My thoughts would not range far afield. A peaceful time. A couple of times it had been the two of us, silent and immobile, while Julia, or Irène, was in the kitchen spilling the latest gossip.

Some noise or other would make him prick his ears, jump off, saunter out and pitter-patter down.

The morning freshness waned as the minutes crawled by. I would close my eyes and fantasize.

I have escaped into a forest from pursuing German soldiers, climbed into a tree and am biding my time while the search proceeds at ground level: they look behind every tree and rake every bush with machine-gun fire. Eventually a soldier stations himself right under me. I knock him out by coming down with both feet on his shoulders, Tarzan style, use his rifle to finish him off with one crushing blow to the neck, and climb back up the tree with his rifle and ammunition. A patrolling soldier discovers the body. I shoot him straight through the heart when he is bending over his dead comrade: the wound will suggest that the shot was fired at ground level. The Germans multiply, lurching from tree to tree. I pick some off, judiciously, when they are all at a good distance, unable to locate the elevated source of the fire.

Spinning fantasies had become a mainstay. It worked like a narcotic. It relieved the anguish, the boredom; like Milou's company. And killing Germans was a staple fantasy. I would slip into it as into a favorite sweater. It was also an entertaining mental challenge. I would take my time, repeat the moves, refine some scenes, like the jumping-off point with the first soldier: in addition to his rifle, ammunition, grenades and belt, I would also lift his ration and canteen, his greatcoat for a hammock, and his helmet for elimination — feces on the forest floor would give me away. The tree bark would absorb the urine which I would let out in a long, slow trickle; it would not reach bottom. A timely downpour would wash away all incriminating scents and thwart the bloodhounds. I had kept dry, though: I would be nestled quite snugly under a cover of overarching, leafy branches. I had not left the choice of my perch to chance.

The fantasy would wear off. I would reread an amusing story in *Het Vrije Waasland*, linger over a striking sentence or paragraph, try to recall it verbatim, feel frustrated when I could not remember the pithy expression, the humorous turn of phrase. Vexing. *Menda* could have. I remembered the time I had to elbow him out of his daydream — he was gazing out the window — in

Kahn's sixth grade class at Tachkemoni, when it was his turn to read from the Hebrew anthology. He recited from memory while running his finger over the page to find his place. He had read the whole piece long before it was his turn and became bored. I would return grudgingly to that elusive phrase in *Het Vrije Waasland*, enjoy it again, wish I had said it.

I would leaf once more through one or other magazine Adrienne had subscribed to since our arrival. I would reach for a Hedwig Courts Mahler novel. No. For the afternoon; a more conducive time for romance, when the day was winding down, when restlessness gave way to resignation, when I felt more mellow. I was rationing them, not knowing how many more of those love stories Adrienne would find. There were no other books around. Adrienne and Gaston did not read. To get books from any source was beyond the realm of anyone's thinking, and unsafe for being out of the ordinary.

Morning was the longest stretch in the short days of late fall and winter. I would move around, to overcome inertness, to fight the boredom. I would stand in the shade to the side of the window and stare at the road, the *Chalet* and the butcher shop, at the horizon, at the open, free space beyond. I would stand and wait for the passer-by, the bicycle rider, the farmer on his horse-drawn cart, the carefree. They were of the Flemish land, like the trees; they were beyond envy.

I would move to the garret. On a sunny day the light was soft in the bedroom part, bright in the crawl space, bursting under the garret window. And out yonder, in the scintillating patch of sky, the sun, embarked on its east-west arc, was sitting still. I would feel suspended above ground. O, to walk the earth and bask in the sun. I would close my eyes, see a myriad dots of light, open my eyes, run, half-blinded, my hands over the blanket under me, survey my cell, slowly, noticing ever more clearly the walls, the three-piece porcelain wash set on the vanity, the low curtain with the opening in the middle, the covered toilet pail under the sloping roof, the dust particles swirling in the beam of light under the garret window. *What am I doing here? Trapped.* I would return to the bedroom. On a sunny day the northern sky in the gabled windows was a serene blue, and closer. I would regain my inner composure.

———

The noon meal signaled the end of the long morning stretch. The second half of the day with its more tranquil mood could begin.

Slouching on the wooden chair and keeping my hands warm in the pockets of my trousers, I would drift into a slight after-meal torpor induced by a lazy daydream or a stream of disjointed thoughts dissolving into a haze — a siesta of sorts. Or I would settle straight away with the female acrobats in skimpy costumes under the tent in Sinaai — that was all I would recall, in hiding, from my visit to the circus. Eyes closed, I would lose myself in imaginary, endlessly repeated kisses and caresses. The faces were blurred, but the shapely, bare legs, the voluptuous thighs and the gentle swelling of the breasts above the bodice were etched in my mind with photographic precision. I remembered two acrobats: one was athletic; she had black hair and dark eyes. The smaller one had blond hair and a lissome body; I felt freer with her, more playful, but powerfully drawn to the more austere woman with the black hair, the strong, shapely legs and the full, half-naked breasts.

My penis would swell but remain trapped in the crotch of tightly fitting briefs and pants. Occasionally I would respond to what I thought was the call of the bladder — a sensation at the tip, like a very light, pleasant burn — by coaxing my penis downward into the pail until the urine could flow. That ended my state of arousal. I knew next to nothing about things sexual, had never heard of masturbation and didn't stumble into it in hiding. Most of the time I would end up tiring of the sexual reveries or snap out of them by moving my body and opening my eyes to reacquaint myself with the bedroom, the two houses across the road, the sky and the clouds in the windows. With the onrush of fresh sights and thoughts my penis would shrink, and I would feel a sense of relief, like coming out of a fever.

I have read all there is to read, I have my fill of solitaire, the fantasy has gone stale, the sky is gray, the road is deserted, and Milou is not around. I sit. And sit. Time is all there is, trickling by, worthless. During the first, pre-hiding weeks in Belsele time was precious, and I felt its loss keenly as I was idling about with almost nothing to do. High school, in those early days, became the focus of my feelings of lost happiness. I had imagined my

Christian classmates studying new, awe-inspiring subjects that propelled one on the road to manhood. I had kept track of the days and weeks passing, determined to come up from behind and pull abreast. The class I am seeing now has fallen silent. The teachers have faded away. Latin and math have become irrelevant. Greek, algebra, and physics have lost their mysterious appeal. My classmates appear to me like inhabitants of a different world. Some day they will be rid of the Germans, a repeat of World War I. They can count on it. Until then they can walk the streets, go swimming, borrow books from the library. Each day enriches their tomorrow. Liberation is my only tomorrow, unfathomable and remote now, like the coming of the Messiah, when everything will look and feel and sound different — I cannot imagine how. A blinding light in the distance, like a mirage, is all I can see with eyes closed. It is filling the sky. I know that in the end my people will prevail. We always have. But when? Will I be among them?

To outlast the Germans... I must.

The mid-afternoon coffee breaks lifted my spirit. Adrienne's frequent gesture made me feel remembered even when her absences or callers in the kitchen prevented her from treating me downstairs. Door-to-door salesmen, neighbors, relatives not in the know and long-time acquaintances who happened to be passing by were more likely to call in the afternoon, after the day's major chores, when a housewife would be more amenable to indulge in gossip or listen to a sales pitch. Insurance salesmen were the most obdurate, pleading for a few minutes of attention to explain the virtues of their offer whose acceptance then became a mark of prudent practice and good judgment: the target was on the defensive or downright unreasonable. "They want so badly to gain the upper hand," Adrienne told me once after dispatching another such visitor. Especially on an attractive woman, I sensed.

On an occasional quiet day, with Sylvain gone playing, Adrienne would call me down for the afternoon treat. All doors were closed to keep the cold out. A caller had to open two doors to enter the kitchen, whether coming from the front through the hallway or from the backyard, past the large kitchen window, through the pump house. This gave me enough time to jump behind the heavy drape that curtained off the opening to the staircase and scurry up the stairs into the bedroom. Adrienne would drink her coffee before calling me down or after I had gone back upstairs: time might be too short for disposing of the extra cup and saucer in the pump house sink.

Adrienne would sit at the long side of the table, opposite the wall, with the window further down to her left. She could spot anyone coming from the rear. I would sit sideways at the end of the table, to Adrienne's right, with my back against the wall, and close to the staircase — a shady spot. No one could see me even with their nose flattened against the window. The sound of approaching footsteps, the crunching noise of bicycle tires on the gravel path alongside the blind wall of the house would have me take up position behind the drape. A knock on the front door, or Adrienne's quiet "*trap 'et af*" ("scram") would propel me upstairs. I had become adept at going up and down the dark staircase without making it creak: I had learned where and how to place my feet, and which steps to avoid altogether. It was a challenge that required total concentration. I enjoyed it. Once, our neighbor Julia could not contain herself with the latest bit of gossip: one perfunctory knock on the front door, the short, loud click of the handle — and she was rushing down the hallway calling out for Adrienne. I was not even half way up the stairs when I heard the kitchen door handle turning. I froze. I was stuck, afraid to shift my weight on the creaking staircase.

Visiting downstairs felt safer and cozier in bad weather. The large black and white tiles of the kitchen floor would still be fresh from the wet-mopping. The stove's black top would shine. Adrienne would knit or sew and tell me in a low voice some of the latest gossip, or drop a remark about an unwelcome caller: "This gendarme. Came visiting again, yesterday. For the third or fourth time. Was going on and on. If Gaston heard that drivel..." I had caught one sentence of his convoluted discourse: "A mouth can stay open, an arm cannot stay outstretched." I had understood that it was about the man-woman thing. (The first time the gendarme had stopped by, on his way to St-Niklaas, was to inquire about Gaston with whom he had served in the military. Adrienne had given him the address of the forge in Belsele. He never made the ten-minute bike trip.) "I don't think he'll come again," she continued. "I didn't even offer him a chair to sit on."

And after a pause, as if to herself: "Men can make such asses of themselves." I never will, I resolved.

I would drink my coffee, unhurriedly, and listen, chuckle, ask a question, wait for the next tidbit. I admired her without letting on. I felt comfortable with my secret love. After a polite wait I would get up, calm and restored, part from her with the usual exchange, "*Tot straks*, Adrienne" ("See you later"), "Ja Henri, *tot straks*," slip behind the drape and climb the stairs in my practiced, silent way.

I knew the day's progress by the luminosity in the air. On a sunny day the afternoon light streaked in from the west and, diffracted by the glass panes, broke in rainbow-like hues on the distant wall. The windows and the sheer curtains were aglow, the dark-green satin bedspread sparkling. The rays of light widened and faded in their slow progression across the back wall and the bed's headboard, their sharp edges blurring as the sun hung lower and the afternoon wore on. The white clouds turned red and purple and blue. The corners of the room, then the walls turned gray and disappeared. A soothing penumbra erased a day whose passing had made no dent in the seemingly endless stretch of hiding ahead.

The windows were last to give up the gray remains of the day. They slowly turned pitch black, blocking out the entire world. Night had overcome day once more. I had made it through another day, ensconced in my world of shifting thoughts and haunting memories, of yearning and fantasies.

I loved the evening's widening veil of safety and rousing mystery.

I would often dally upstairs, trying to pierce the young darkness yet still be of it. On a clear night. I would gaze through the half-open garret window, my opening to the outer reaches; it held a patch of firmament. The swirls of scintillating stars would grow denser and finer the more I stared, their uneven brightness giving the darkness a vertiginous, accelerating depth. I would keep staring until I felt the frightening pull of the celestial abyss; it dwarfed my fear of the German. I would reach for the bed behind me and plant my feet firmly on the floor, feeling the reassuring planks holding me down, and keep staring. I had a glimpse of the infinite: it was cold and without consciousness of our world, of me. Were the Germans also awed by the night sky? Could they also be seized by a sense of their own insignificance? How could they? They wanted to lord it over the world. *Deutschland über Alles.* Too busy cleaning their rifles in their barracks.

I would return to the bedroom and see, silhouettes darker than the night, the *Chalet* and the roof of the butcher's house. I had returned from the alien, unfeeling universe to the familiar, nurturing earth.

I would come down the staircase, quietly, quieted and expectant, and alight, squinting, from behind the drape. Adrienne would be setting the table for the light evening meal. We waited for Gaston. He would signal his approach with characteristic noises: without dismounting from his bicycle he would slam open the wooden front gate and make a ninety degree left turn onto the narrow gravel path along the side of the house, toward the rear, dismount with low thuds of his wooden shoes, enter the pump house adjoining the kitchen with a loud "*djurr*", park his bicycle, slip out of his wooden shoes, lock the backdoor to the pump house and open the door to the kitchen. It was a familiar and reassuring routine that allowed me to stay put. It would take him a while to wash off the grime from his hands and face.

Some days Gaston would be home late. We knew the cause as soon as we heard the steady thud of wooden shoes and the muffled noise of a metal wheel turn onto the path along the blind wall of the house: a flat tire. I pictured stony-faced and stiff-lipped Gaston walking his limp bicycle in the dark as if it were a naughty boy he couldn't punish — the image of comic frustration, and I would struggle to hold in the laughter. He would park the bike with a spiteful knock against the wall, under the kitchen window, to vent his frustration as much as to signal his presence. "Some juicy cursing tonight," Adrienne would announce. She would not decry his cursing, not on a week night when, after supper, he was trying to subdue a recalcitrant old tire, made of ersatz rubber, that would go flat on him all too often. Sylvain and I had mastered Gaston's entire repertoire, with the art of combining the curses into long purple strings. The operation would take place in the kitchen. Sylvain and I would assist by handing him some tool or by pumping air into the immersed inner tube to locate the puncture: it was exciting to see the tiny jet of air bubbles rise from the hole in the red rubber tube; a small victory. I found everything about the mending job clever and ingenious, from the tricks and techniques to the tool-and-supply kit.

Save for the tire-fixing episodes, during which Gaston would commandeer half of the kitchen, evenings were quiet. We would take our places around the stove. Gaston would read the paper, grumbling now and then. On occasion we listened in a hush to the BBC for the unvarnished truth and the commentary about special events, like the Germans' move into the French Unoccupied Zone, the sinking, by the British, of the French navy in the port of Toulon before the Germans could secure it, or the battle of Stalingrad. Adrienne would knit, or darn socks, but stop for the BBC broadcasts. The mending on the sewing machine, like patching up work coveralls, pants and shirts, she would do in the afternoon light at the large kitchen window.

Some evenings Adrienne would entertain us with readings from a small bundle of brochure-like feuilletons: true stories, culled from the newspapers of years past, about colorful local thieves and robbers who had struck in the surrounding countryside. Cops and robbers stories.

"Are the doors locked?" she would ask as she picked up a fascicle.

"Yes."

"Yes."

She read with animation. We were in her thrall. Some stories were hilarious. She would stop, occasionally.

"Now, this is gruesome."

"Adrienne, keep reading," Sylvain would plead. "We are not scared."

"You'll have nightmares."

"I never dream."

"I don't dream either," I echoed.

"Yes, but *I* may fall out of bed," Gaston complained.

"Come on... Come on."

"Well then, I'll continue."

She read to us a long tale about a string of suspenseful robberies, of a farmer and his wife found bludgeoned to death — there was blood even on the ceiling lamp. The murderers were caught days later; they were so stupid. We could relax.

On very cold nights in the deep of winter the fire in the coal burning stove that was lit three times a day, for cooking only, was kept going into mid-evening. We would sit around the red-hot potbelly with our feet on the stove's warm, chrome-and-enamel-covered ornamental base. The rest of the drafty house would be cold. Late on some such desolate and moon-less night I would venture out for a brisk walk. A protective darkness enveloped the hamlet, obliterated the horizon. I would hug the trees along the deserted road and adjust my pace so as to find myself hidden by a tree from the light beams of an approaching lone car. I would step up in the direction of Lokeren — an emptier stretch of road — past the café owned by a woman famed for her beauty: *'t schuun Yvonneke* (the beautiful Yvonne) was how she and her café, *'t Pallieterke,* were known. Her establishment was the most prestigious among the many that dotted the road east and west of us — they were run by accommodating women and had earned Duizend Appels, far and wide, the sobriquet *de Warme Landen* (the Tropics). I had never seen the mysterious woman who attracted the wealthy few to savor a good vintage wine or an aged cognac, and more. I would walk vigorously along the shielding trees, feeling alive, retrace my steps, reenter the kitchen, flushed, smiling, gleeful, remove my shoes, and take my place at the stove for what remained of the evening. Gone was the alienation of the first evening of hiding. I had long since rejoined our cell, as a full member. I no longer brought down, after dusk, the upstairs bottled up inside me.

Ahead of us lay the dark night. It held Christian and Jew alike in its embrace. I slept tight. To wake up in the middle of the night was a treat: I could tell, from one look at the garret window and the contours of objects in the dark, how much sleep, like a safety blanket, lay ahead: hours, sometimes, clocked equally for all earthlings. The more, the better; real time, passing; to dissolve, later, in the light of day. My brother, curled up and facing the wall, would always be sound asleep.

✥ ✥ ✥

One day Adrienne handed me a couple of thin fascicles. "From your father," she said. "He'll send you more when he is through reading them." The title page read, in German:

HAEUSSER METHOD
Self-teaching letters
for the learning
of the English language

authored by
Professor E. Haeusser and Professor Dr. R. KRON
with the collaboration of
CHRISTOPHER DARLING, M.A. (Lond.).

Complete in 27 letters.
First (sample-) letter.
Price 50 Pf.
Sixth edition

I had not known my father to have that bundle of *letters*. I pictured him in a flash, sitting in his relaxed reading pose, in the stillness of hiding, head bent towards the page, absorbed in the study of English as he had been in the study of the Torah portion on Shabbat afternoons. A strong profile. A reaffirmation of our faith in the Americans and the English.

I looked at the two lines,

zur Erlernung
der englischen Sprache

English — that prestigious language shrouded in myth, like the British empire, like America, the language of Churchill and Roosevelt, of Shakespeare, that mysterious Englishman who personified England. I had known only two men who knew English: the first was a distinguished-looking man I had seen once before the war. He and my father had doffed their hats while passing on the street. "A diamantaire. Travels to London. He knows English," my father had informed me. I had imagined that tall, elegantly dressed diamantaire with deep-set dark eyes to be very rich and influential. The other was our high school principal, Dr. Adhémar De Smet: it had become clear to me that he knew English when he told a packed auditorium what to do in case the alarm sirens went off at the approach of British aircraft, the "RAF" — he had pronounced it as a familiar acronym; "RAW-yel

Air Force," he then expounded with a full mouth, declaiming it almost, sounding that difficult English "R" like in the movies, delighting in it. Knowing English, let alone showing it as he did was a sign in those days of one's sympathy, much as choosing to learn German, or a Gentile's study of Hebrew, was a clue to someone's leanings.

I turned the promising title page... and got bogged down in a massive foreword spanning seven crowded pages of lengthy German sentences replete with clauses and sub-clauses whose verbs would often be found dangling at the end. Caesar had been easier to parse. The sentences I did manage to wrestle down turned out to be unenlightening. I gave up and leafed on. I noticed in passing that the foreword's Part Five, "Hints for Studying," began with a short sentence: it suggested to the reader to get one or two study mates.

The *letter*'s first section, "About the English pronunciation and our pronunciation encoding," was no less forbidding: *six* double-column, dense pages, in Gothic typescript to boot.

Finally, the First Lesson:

I have a house. We have a nice house. Our house is a large and fine building. My father built our house three years ago.

I was astounded: it read almost like Flemish or German. *Large* was French. Only *nice, ago* and *built* looked foreign. As for *building*, I had forgotten that it was an English word. Below each line of English ran the phonetic transcription studded with intricate notations, and below that, in small Gothic characters, the German translation.

The pronunciation! Knowing English, to me, was being able to understand the American movie actors, Errol Flynn, Victor McLaglen, James Cagney, Nelson Eddy, and speak like them. I leafed back to the section, "About the English pronunciation and our pronunciation encoding." Reading and decoding it turned out to be a pleasant exercise. The sentences were short and clear. I deciphered the Gothic alphabet as I went along, deducing the sound of the characters that did not look like their Latin counterparts from the words they appeared in. The Haeusser *letter* was brimming with precise instructions regarding lip configuration, opening and widening of the mouth, position and curvature of the tip of the tongue, area and degree of contact between up-per teeth and lower lip.

Thus, for the pronunciation of the English "w" (that sound does not exist in German): "the mouth positions itself to pro-nounce the [German] 'u' sound, but pronounces instead the vowel that follows." Its phonetic notation? A "u" crowned with a tiny "w." Except for a few abstract signs, such as the ones denot-ing long and short vowels, the Haeusser notations were clever, self-evident almost. There was much more information about the English "w" sound, a refinement in pronunciation, exercises, even a paragraph about the English "wh" sound (with its own no-tation) as distinct from the "w" sound, a trifling distinction, the professor concluded, whose absence in no way denotes plebeian speech; altogether almost half a page. The various pronuncia-tions of the English "r" rated two full pages, of the "th," one page. Even the "l" sound rated a long paragraph.

I returned to the two lines of English about "our house," and, using the line with Haeusser's phonetic notations, practiced my pronunciation ceaselessly, honing each sound.

The lesson was followed by columns crammed with remarks, pronunciation pointers, personal and possessive pronouns, aux-iliary verbs, and dialogues exercising every English word many times over: **"Have you a house? Yes, Sir, I have a house. Have you a nice house? Is your house nice? Is your house large?"** Everything German was in Gothic typescript. I closed the bro-chure, satisfied with my "Englishmanship." The veil of mystery had been pierced. English, I felt, was within my grasp. I felt ready for some light, entertaining pieces and short stories, each with its appended snippets of grammar and vocabulary of new or dif-ficult words, like in our Latin reader.

The next day I did the *letter*'s only other lesson, about George Washington and his hatchet, with the same attention to every nuance of pronunciation — I lavished minutes on "George" and the "Wash" in Washington.

The Haeusser Method stuck.

My father sent over several more *letters*; they dealt, in succes-sion, with family, house, furniture and housewares, men's and women's clothing, laundry, crafts, jewelry and the like, the hu-man body, arithmetic operations.

They were boring. Haeusser had swamped them with one-liners featuring uninteresting words that would not be found, I was sure, in Stefan Zweig's passion-soaked novellas: the various kinds of wood (**oak** was the only word I understood in German translation) and other furniture-related items like **glass chiffon(n)iers;** a bewildering array of clothes and related items such as **single-breasted** and **double-breasted** coats, **lace trimmings, petticoat, apron, morning dress** and **mourning-dress, morning coat** and **frock-coat.** The tedium got to me. I gave up. (In his ponderous 7-page foreword I had stopped slogging through early on, the professor had prided himself on covering every practical aspect of life that would engage the educated traveler and worldly business man.)

Adrienne took the Haeusser *letters* back to St-Niklaas. My father stopped sending more. Did he also tire of them? Did he deem it unsafe for Adrienne to be carrying them on such long bike trips? Was he waiting for me to ask for more? I soon forgot my foray into English.

✡ ✡ ✡

It was my first day out, a Sunday, three weeks after going into hiding. I came down in the morning with my shoes in my hand. Sliding my feet into the supple, shiny black leather, straightening out the tongues, tightening the shoelaces just right and tying them, released a flush of anticipation: in those shoes I would be moving about like everyone else; I would tread this earth.

Dressed up in my city clothes, I was standing in the doorway, surveying the road and taking in the morning air before breakfast; and signaling my presence. I had already gone to the outhouse. Using it openly gave me a lift, despite the stench. Afterwards I had stood for a while in the vegetable garden and had looked in wonderment at the horizon beyond Waasmunster and the sky above — I got only forty centimeters of each in my garret window.

Irène, tall and wiry, with her pretty face and shiny blond hair, walked out of her little house.

"Well well, a visitor from Antwerp," she exclaimed as she crossed the road in my direction. "Good MOR-ning, Henri."

"Good morning, Irène."

"It has been a while... And for how long?" She used the standard, schooled pronunciation.

"Just for the day, I have school tomorrow."

"*Okh yah.* To see Sylvain, that little rascal."

"And Adrienne and Gaston. And to enjoy the good air," I added with a smile, giving Duizend Appels its due.

"*Van eigen*" ("Of course"), she said, with a slip into local parlance. "And did you get here this morning?"

"No, last night." That made it quite plausible for me to have arrived unnoticed.

"Oh..."

"You know, school until noon, the Left Bank, the slow train ride, stopping everywhere..." That answered her unarticulated question about traveling late.

"*Ja, van eigen,* the days are so short. You really want to take advantage of the day, don't you?"

I grinned.

"I'll hop inside for just a moment," she said. "Adrienne!? No disturbance?"

"Come in! Come right in."

After the exchange of greetings and other niceties, I heard Irène say to my brother, in the local dialect, "Must *you* be glad, having your brother *all day*."

"Yes, and I'll be just as glad when he goes back to Antwerp," he retorted.

I walked smiling into the kitchen. Everybody was laughing, except my brother who was playing up his act. He would often add spontaneously a deft, true-to-life touch to our cover story. He was nine, yet he never had to be told what to say or to hide, or how to behave. He would blurt out "*Jood!*" ("Jew!"), the common epithet for someone caught cheating or lying, as naturally as his occasional village playmates.

Irène left. We had breakfast.

My "visit" was unfolding according to script. I had come down after dark, the night before, grinning, nervous, and brimming over with the excitement that precedes an unusual voyage. Gaston had trimmed my hair, expertly.

"You are moving as nimbly as Louis," — the village barber on Statiestraat who had cut my hair before I went into hiding — I had said as Gaston circled around me with comb and scissors, the tip of his tongue sticking out and curled upwards.

"I can ply almost any manual trade," he had answered. "I can slice raw meat as evenly as a butcher. You saw me skin a rabbit and stretch its pelt. I watch the craftsman once, carefully; that's all I need. And I can do it."

Next, I had put on my white shirt and tie, to appear like a visitor just off the train, in case a neighbor were to come in. None of the villagers who knew us traveled that late on Saturday night, so would not be left to wonder why they hadn't seen me at the station. The laborers would be back from their week-long work stint in the city by noon.

My Saturday evening had ended with a carefree, noisy climb up the creaky staircase, and without the toilet pail half filled with water. I had used the outhouse. I was of this world again.

And on Monday Adrienne would tell the inquiring neighbors that I had returned to Antwerp on the Sunday evening train, to take in a full day of country. The laborers would return to their city jobs early Monday morning: they spent Sunday night at home or in the cafés along the road.

Adrienne had thought of such "visits" to break up the oppressiveness of hiding. They even reinforced our cover story by casting me more firmly as the mature brother providing a family presence to Sylvain. And it was no secret that I also enjoyed the change of air.

After breakfast Adrienne told me to drop in on her parents: "It will also give more neighbors an opportunity to see you. Then you are free until noon. No church, not on such a short visit."

"After seeing your parents I'll go for a walk down the Waasmunster Road," I said.

The countryside is bare but welcoming. I go off on back roads and solitary dirt paths. The earth is rough and uneven, it bears me without a murmur, impervious to the tracks I am leaving in my wake. I embrace the horizon and feel the sky above me.

I cover long stretches without seeing a soul; the fewer strangers come my way, the calmer I feel. I gorge myself with the bracing air, sniff out the earthy smells and hold on to them, inhaling deeply. The crunching sounds, underfoot, of the bare earth, of the gravel spiking the earthen paths, of sand, puncture the whine of the wind, the chirping of the birds, the distant lowing of a cow. I stop and listen, stop and smell, soak up the autumn sunshine.

I am back on the road. A man appears around the bend. I look at him searchingly: will he look at me inquisitively or with benign curiosity? I try to make eye contact when we are a few steps apart. He stares past me. I abort the nod that should have elicited the *djurr* I would have answered. Unnerving: he saw me; why did he avoid contact? Beyond a certain passing distance, such as from opposite sides of the main road, it was within protocol for two strangers to ignore each other. But the Waasmunster Road was narrow. We *should* have exchanged greetings. But he did not give me a chance. Why? Was I the odd, the not-fitting-in stranger? What was the matter?

A distant bark jolts me into hastening my pace. Dogs make me nervous; they are suspicious and attract attention with their barking. They can smell things. The trees are my friends, especially the old, gnarled oak trees with their tangle of low and far-flung branches. I want them to know me. They are reassuring — they can keep a secret. I slow down for some, even stop, and look at them intently. There, at the end of a short and narrow tree-lined path is the big old venerable oak I met weeks ago, before going into hiding. I step up and touch him, then move on with my secret.

Another man is coming my way. He greets me with a bland, rather formal "*djurr,*" the kind that is meant to acknowledge, fleetingly, a stranger's existence. That is reassuring. I respond with a "*djurr*" at a somewhat higher pitch. Responding with a lower pitched, less open *djurr* would sound gruff and grudging, and may leave a more permanent memory of my existence. I move on, relieved but still wary: is he looking back? The thought that his suspicious gaze may be following me is bothersome. But I cannot allow myself to look back. A resounding *djurr* from him would have been the most satisfying: it would have given the impression of a man who was not holding back or keeping score, of someone who liked greeting people, who liked the sound of his voice. I learned to gauge greetings and respond in kind in the early days. I can modulate my *djurr*'s with the best of them. My *djurr*'s will become more resolute, I know, with each encounter, and I will walk the land with more confidence.

I am in open country, off the road again. The sun is shining, shining on everything, on everyone... on me too — what bliss. And all of a sudden it erupts, my secret: *Here goes a Jew! A Jew. I AM A JEW... A Jew is walking the Flemish earth! A Jew is breathing the pure Flemish air... The sun is shining on a Jew... What are you going to do about it, sales Boches!?* (dirty *Boches*, French epithet for Germans), *vuile Mof!* (in Flemish). Glee seeps in with the gush of hatred and contempt, *Ama-LAYK!* Biblical Amalek, our mortal enemy, *Sof-KHA kuh-SOF Ama-LAYK* (you'll end up like Amalek). It burst forth in Hebrew, pithy, damning, how good it feels to say it in Hebrew, to form Hebrew words to curse the German, here, under God's sky, *Ha'a-ZEE-noo Ha-sha-MAH-yim* (Listen, ye heavens), Moses' parting song before the crossing of the Jordan, "Listen ye heavens, and I will speak; And let the earth hear the words of my mouth." I recite as I walk. The first two verses were all I remembered. I repeat them till they flow seamlessly, taking delight in their rocking clauses, in their images of dew and young grass, of squalls and soft rain, their soothing music. The pounding inside my head has abated. *I am here in spite of you, Amalek. WE will write your history... Long after you are gone.* I know. I am stepping at a vigorous pace, an interloper no more, to cover distance, to be somewhere else, farther, it's my first day out in the open air, on the dark brown earth, in the shining sun.

I am back on the narrow, winding Waasmunster Road, retracing my steps to the house. A woman appears. Slender, hardly older than I... No, she is older. I feel so much more relaxed with a woman. She is my height. I stare at her. I can do that: women are held to standards of modesty that do not apply to men; they will avert, often drop their gaze and break off eye contact as soon as it is made, or avoid it altogether.

She passes me with a blank, distant look in her eyes. I can sense her desire to put some distance between us. Because of my staring, I know. I would not greet her, wouldn't think of it. You don't greet a woman you don't know. Had she only smiled at me, opened her arms. I like women. They are not threatening, like men; just hard to know, like philosophy... no, like poems in which each verse, each word almost, has meanings. How do you know when you can kiss a woman?

A matron. She looks straight at me. I hasten to say politely *"Goeden dag."* *"Goeden dag, mijn jongen"* ("Good day, my boy"), she says. And I feel put back in my place. Still, a safe place.

I come to the end of the Waasmunster Road and turn right onto the bicycle path of the Old Road where we live. I throw a glance through the open door of the café, the *Duizend Appels*, a rather dingy *Warme Landen* establishment — it takes up the ground floor of the small corner brick house. It is run by a scrappy old couple and their five daughters: sullen females, some, so I heard, amenable to entertaining patrons upstairs. I glimpse one of them. A man is sitting at a table — rumpled suit, no tie. Another man is standing at the counter. A lifeless scene in a dinky place, on a sunny, vibrant Sunday morning.

Right next to the corner café the door is open on a dimly lit single-room dwelling. I get my first glimpse of the fat woman — she rarely steps outside. She is sitting on a bed against the wall, a mound of flesh and flab topped by bursting cheeks around a recessed pointy little nose. She gives me a vague, mocking smile — she has small pointy teeth, and from two little bright eyes shining behind the padding on the cheekbones darts a strange glint, sneering, sustained. Unsettling. Is that the look she casts on the traveling salesmen? "Adrienne," Julia once announced as if it were headline news — she had stormed into our kitchen, leaving the street door open; I was upstairs, listening — "the young salesman who called on us earlier this afternoon has been in that shack for two hours and the door is still shut tight." I wonder, as I recall Julia's words. I am out of the fat woman's sight. The eerie, brief encounter with her felt like a challenge, or did she aim a rebuke, a curse perhaps, at the pampered city boy? One room; one bed. Her large brood of small children — it grows each year — run in rags. Her husband, a clean-shaven, athletically built man, a mason by trade, supports them. He takes his children for walks — some of them went barefoot in late summer and early fall — and thumps in his wooden shoes past his neighbors sitting in front of their houses, with his nose up and an extinct rolled cigarette dangling from his lip, letting out a loud fart when it so moves him, never the first to extend a greeting. No drinking. A tribe unto themselves.

I catch sight of Julia standing in front of her house. A few more steps and I greet her with a polite smile, a deferential nod of the head and a formal *"Goeden dag"* — the well-bred city boy through and through, a bit shy. She smiles like someone who has received a box of chocolates. An upper front tooth is missing.

"Glad to be back?"

"Oh yes. What a change from the city."

I open the front door and bring a whiff of the outdoors into the house.

To mark my visit from Antwerp, Adrienne prepared a special midday meal of vegetable soup, rabbit in a wine sauce with flour potatoes and apple sauce, and vanilla flavored rice pudding for dessert. Sylvain would later say, to Julia's great amusement, that the rice pudding was the best thing about my visit. Gaston had a beer — Adrienne sipped from his glass, Sylvain and I had Spa water. We had moved the table up toward the window. The sunlight fell on the bright table cloth, on the glasses and the cutlery. After dinner Adrienne cleared off the table, washed the dishes and ran a wet-mop over the tile floor. She then set out four cups and saucers, milk and sugar, and cookies. The kitchen, spotless, was filled with the aroma of the coffee.

We sat around for a while, lazying about with a newspaper, listening to one thing or another on the radio, gossiping. Adrienne was knitting away. I reflected more than once, with a sense of relief, that I would not have to lurch towards the stairs behind the drape and scurry up to the bedroom at the sound of approaching footsteps. Yet Simoneke's footsteps, heard an instant only before she appeared through the kitchen window, gave me a start — she was quite light-footed in her leather shoes; I was used to hearing her little wooden shoes signal her trotting approach from the far end of the vegetable garden. I made myself look relaxed before she came through the door. She left with a cookie and without Sylvain — more grumbling — on account of his brother having come for the day. I was already less jumpy when I heard Julia, the only other caller, at the front door.

Around mid-afternoon we crossed the road to the *Chalet*. Unlike the many *Warme Landen* cafés, it was owned and run by a staid, middle-aged couple. Sunday afternoon was family time. Many patrons sat in their overcoats. They were dressed in their Sunday best; the women wore hats, the men and the boys wore clumsily knotted ties.

The place was animated, with people greeting each other, ordering drinks, wending their way between chairs. Men sitting at neighboring or even distant tables would trade jocular remarks. Such casual exchanges would occasionally draw in more patrons firing off wisecracks and repartees, veering often into sarcastic hints at one big-time shenanigan or another. The men would listen intently, nod with an informed smile or chime in — more hints at yet another shady affair. The women countenanced their men's indulgence in silence. I was in the dark. The spontaneous, undeclared and rather brief jostling had its own unstated protocol about the appropriate moment for taking the floor, about the limits on volume and explicitness of contents. A distinct social pecking order emerged, discernible in the tone of the respondent, the loudness and the length of his retort, in his deportment. In a nonchalant pose of low-key authority one might merely tilt one's head or lean slightly back in the direction of the previous, unseen entrant and proffer a one-liner. Some betrayed their insecurity by their eagerness to chime in, their high pitch and rapid-fire delivery. Others would vie for position in the contest by assuming the tilted-head pose — a tad too much of a tilt: they would talk straight to the ceiling, a bit fast and loud; the authoritative nonchalance was missing. Tone, much more than tenor, held my attention. There was a fickleness about those exchanges that made me nervous: I felt like the onlooker who got stranded in the middle of a fast moving ball game.

Gaston, slouched in his chair and leaning on the armrests, stayed out of those bouts: our secret ruled our public and private lives. We were in the same lifeboat, concerned solely about the temper of the ocean and the seaworthiness of our craft. "They won't get *me* alive," he had said once, with an unsettling determination. Someone sitting closer by followed up his little peroration, something about bending land use regulations — a riddle to me — with a "Wouldn't you agree, Gaston? What do *you* think?" My heart jumped; the ball had landed in our midst. Gaston, lifting his chin, his eyes half-closed, tossed off a medium-pitch one-liner — it also went over my head — with the muted authority of the man who is his own boss, the village blacksmith serving the farmers who depend on him. The fickle exchange flitted about at a safe distance from us before subsiding. They are not taking notice of us, I noted with relief, it's about land, and the crooks in their midst, their own crooks, not about money changers in the temple, nothing to do with who got Jesus nailed to the cross. Thank God for Flemish crooks.

A woman at the neighboring table turned to Adrienne and inquired about me — Sylvain needed no introduction.

"Oh, the older brother... and visiting for the day... how nice." And turning to me:

"Young man, the truth," the word "truth" gave me a jolt, "are the people in Antwerp as friendly as here?"

I smiled and kept silent.

"He is not going to let Antwerp down, for sure," Adrienne said, laughing.

"And right you are, my friend, you stick up for Antwerp."

"But *I* am sticking up for *Duust Appels*." That was my brother, in top local form.

We laughed. My identity of visiting brother was of one piece.

Sylvain and I finished our soft drink. Adrienne drank her cup of chicory coffee and Gaston his one glass of beer: he was not a drinker, and he was thrifty. He didn't smoke either. He had one cigar which he kept for a special occasion and found, one day, charred at the tip: Sylvain had gotten to it first.

We returned home. I felt the rush and the relief that come with having done well on an important exam. And there would be more Sunday visits. Also, the Christmas school vacation was coming up; I would be spending it of course with my brother, in the country, lucky city boy that I was — both Julia and Irène had smiled broadly, approvingly.

The light went on in the kitchen. Gaston took off his tie. All got into their slippers. I kept my shoes on: my train wasn't due yet. Gaston closed the shutters and locked the outer doors. Adrienne began setting the table.

There were a few casual comments about the day's events. Adrienne remarked how taken Julia and Irène had seemed with my visit. I smiled.

"What were the men talking about in the *Chalet*?" I asked Gaston.

"Oooh," he said, blowing air, "showing off... foolishness."

"Gaston, there *is* a lot of hanky-panky going on," Adrienne said in a remonstrating tone, "and the more they have the more they steal. And they act so smug, as if they had the pope's blessing."

"Yes, and the more they steal, the more they have. I am not arguing with you," he hastened to say before Adrienne could take him to task for his flippancy. I repressed a smile, "but to spout off like schoolboys, come on."

"Men are only men — overgrown boys. What do you expect?"

Gaston raised his eyebrows and rolled his eyes but kept silent; that would always make us laugh. Turning to Sylvain:

"You also played it just right today." And with raised thumb, "First class."

The compliment took my brother by surprise as much as it made him feel proud: playing his role, brother-bashing quips and all, came to him as naturally as "hello" and "thank you."

"I thought so too," Adrienne said smiling, " 'that little devil,' I kept saying to myself." Then, in a tone of playful admonition, "I wonder what you are going to be when you grow up."

"A diamantaire like my father or a blacksmith like Gaston. I haven't decided yet."

Gaston and Adrienne laughed.

"You have plenty of time," she said. "I think you'll end up a diamantaire."

We drank our coffee, then moved our chairs to our usual places around the stove. We sat around, whiling away the evening. I was myself again, back in hiding. My train had left.

The time came for Sylvain and me to go to bed. I paid a last, sneak visit to the outhouse. Then, with my shoes in my hand, as on that first Sunday night, I climbed up the stairs, quietly, into the night, my refuge. No thoughts or feelings until morning. I fell fast asleep. I did not remember dreaming, did not remember a single dream, ever.

✣ ✣ ✣

On Monday morning, my Sunday visit seemed like a short-lived extrusion from my shell. As soon as I entered the unmade bedroom, after the bracing morning ablutions, I felt the emptiness of the day ahead, much like on the first day of hiding. I ate my breakfast. I then recited the morning prayer. The words tumbled out of my brain — my lips were not moving — as though they had a will of their own. Bringing my fist to my heart without beating my chest — my half-hearted mea culpa — as I rushed

through the *Ameedah's* **"Forgive us, our Father, for we have
transgressed; pardon us, our King, for we have sinned"** was just
a reflex. I then waited for Adrienne to tidy up the bedrooms
before easing myself back into hiding, like someone who has returned to his drab, workaday environment from an exhilarating vacation. My journey back began with a glance at a magazine, followed by a desultory game of solitaire; mere dabbling
in the usual activities. Everything felt a bit different, more flat.
Even the lady in the crouching space had lost her pull, the circus women their rousing appeal. And my mind teemed with disjointed thoughts akin to those preceding sleep. They left me feeling empty. I broke away by moving silently around the upstairs,
looking through the windows at the horizon, staring through the
garret window at a patch of sky, sitting down in the bedroom, settling into daydreaming.

I am hiding in the crevice of a mountainside overlooking a
vital pass. I am loosening boulders on armored cars and tanks,
causing collisions and back-ups, halting entire convoys, sending
scores of vehicles off the escarpment to a thunderous and fiery
end.

I tire of hitting at the ceaseless flow of tanks and vehicles. My
mind wanders, when... I find myself in the Siberian steppe, like
Jules Verne's Michel Strogoff. A large pack of famished wolves
have picked up my scent and are pursuing me across the snow-
covered countryside. I manage to climb up a tree just in time.
They surround the trunk and howl at me, raging. I break off a
branch, lean down and gash one of them with the sharp end.
Wolves nearby, gone wild at the smell of blood, tear the one I
wounded to pieces and feed. Covered with blood, they in turn
arouse the frenzy of a yet bigger circle.

The wolves keep coming back and I keep stabbing them, until
the feeding frenzy leaves the snow covered with mutilated wolves.
The few surviving ones, sated, traipse away. And I am off on my
trek to the nearest town where my appearance in the doorway of
the crowded saloon strikes terror in the heart of the two large villains who had thrown me off the fleeing troika — a hush descends
on the boisterous patrons, even the cigarette smoke clears away.

In a variant of the finale I make my way into the nearest town,
a Far West kind of locale — I remember those places vividly from

the thin *Le Far West* booklets we would swap in the Tachkemoni days; the good-guy cowboy riding into town would say "By Jove" or "By George" when he meant business. I manage to go unnoticed until I can wreak cruel vengeance on the fearsome, dangerous pair by ambushing them in the dark.

Calm filtered down as the afternoon progressed. The treat of cookies and chicory coffee gave me the usual lift. Dusk, the gentle messenger, brought peace and tranquility. The firmament in the garret window stirred in me the familiar feeling of insignificance in a cold, awesome and unfathomable universe. The bed, the plank floor, the tight enclosure of the garret, the wailing wind, the sounds of the kitchen and the road restored to me the presence of the world and the awareness of my place in it. *I shall come out of the darkness!*

I rejoined the fold in the lighted kitchen, a-squinting, and expectant once again.

On Tuesday I was back to normal.

✡ ✡ ✡

On the next "visit," in early December, I stayed on for an extra two days. The special treat was justified by the fair the town of St-Niklaas was hosting for an entire week in honor of its patron saint and namesake. It was drawing big crowds of town and country people. Missing a few classes was something a school inspector's son could do with impunity.

"Since you are staying over for a couple of days," Adrienne said to me that Sunday morning, "it behooves that you make an appearance in church. Julia or Irène will see you going, or coming. And if they ask where you are, I can say 'in church.' "

"Are you going?" I asked, knowing — and dreading — the answer.

"I usually go to Low Mass. Gaston likes to tinker on Sunday mornings. Go by yourself," Adrienne said casually. "It will show familiarity and devotion."

"I... Well..." I mumbled, wary of my lone participation in an hour-long rite where I would have to cross myself.

"Okh, there is nothing to it," Gaston said. "And when you do the sign of the cross, just mumble under your breath," and he signed himself as he pronounced, *"Kus-m'n-kluu-te"* ("kiss-my-balls"), planting one syllable in each of the four cardinal directions.

"Gaston!..." And turning to me: "You don't have to say a thing," Adrienne declared. "Just do like the others."

"Well, yes, do like the others. And you don't have to listen to the priest," Gaston continued. "No one does. He is a bore."

"But Gaston," Adrienne remonstrated, "the lad may find it interesting, not like those peasants who fall asleep."

"Well yes, interesting..." he mumbled.

I went to Mass as to an exam I had not studied for. I selected a seat in the last row, by the aisle and near the door, where the least number of people could see me and from where I could make a quick exit. I mimicked the worshippers — *I am a Marrano, a modern-day Marrano* — but could not bring myself to complete the sign of the cross or kneel on the straw chair whose tall back was turned towards the altar: I had drawn a line. Legs straight, head bent to hide my face, I would lean with my forearms — hands clasped — on the back of the chair. I relaxed upon spotting a few villagers who had also stayed off their knees.

The profound silence, heightened by the Latin resonances tumbling out of the priest's mouth and the responsive rumble of the congregants, was suddenly broken by the tumult of the many chairs being turned around and the noise of people sitting down. The priest ascended the spiral stairs to his finely sculpted wooden perch, and he held forth, as if nothing had changed since Jesus was crucified, as if nothing was happening twenty-five kilometers away, in Antwerp: the Jews were the villains, the good guys were called Samaritans and Galileans, and the Romans were neither good nor bad. To my relief, the villagers coughed and fidgeted throughout the sermon, and many dozed off, their heads bobbing uncomfortably.

I would attend High Mass a few more times. The priest's gaze never veered in my direction. And I ended up feeling less threatened by his occasional diatribes against the Jews.

In the afternoon Adrienne took us to the fair. The event in the huge, cobblestone-paved marketplace dominated by the Church of Our Dear Lady and the old town hall — the many booths, galleries of all sorts, rides, shows, displays and attractions, the milling throngs worked by colorful and voluble hawkers — was overwhelming at first and, after a while, numbing. A street photographer aimed his camera at us, clicked, and handed Adrienne a slip. She picked up two prints a week or so later. She gave me one. Sylvain and I looked camera-conscious. Adrienne, tall in her high heels, her dark coat and light gray hat, looked her confident self.

After the fair we dropped in on my parents at Adrienne's sister's house. They came down to the little dining-sitting room in their bedroom slippers — my father, tie-less; he no longer had the dark-brown mark, below his adam's apple, from the stud in the *faux-cols*, the detachable, stiff, white collars he wore in Antwerp.

Sylvain reciprocated my mother's first kisses, then submitted to her effusive hugging and kissing. I was at an age where I felt less comfortable with my mother's show of emotions. I felt my father's tenderness in his subdued embrace.

My mother asked none of her usual questions about food. She offered us cookies, mitigating the impression she and my father made at first of inmates having visitors. I nibbled on a cookie. Sylvain put his hands on his round belly: the jelly puffs we had at the fair were weighing on our stomachs. My mother felt reassured.

The conversation, at first, was halting: I did not want to speak Yiddish in the presence of Adrienne. To address my parents in Standard Flemish felt unnatural. I answered a few questions about my "visit": when it would end, how I kept busy in the open.

"Take advantage of the good air," my mother urged in Yiddish-accented Flemish.

"I do. I do."

"He takes long walks," Adrienne chimed in.

Sylvain picked up the slack in a fluent local dialect, as if he had been raised in it, telling about the fun at the fair, the picture the roving photographer took of us. My father and Adrienne were amused.

"Will you pick them up?" my father asked her.

"Why not?" she replied.

My parents ended up conversing with Adrienne, inquiring about her parents, the extended Van Damme family; about the mood abroad.

Nothing was said about hiding, theirs or mine.

————

The Christmas recess brought relief. I was not only a visitor and family stand-in, but also a vacationer. Plying the country roads, I would look confidently at strangers, exchange *djurr*'s with men, nod at women or greet them with a polite *goeden dag*. I saw myself in their eyes: the city boy spending his school vacation in the country — a prized treat in wartime. It gave me added legitimacy. I forayed into Sinaai and ventured into the woods of Waasmunster, feeling less apart from nature; less voracious of the bracing air, the stroking wind, the wafts of earthen smells from the bare fields and the ground cover of dead leaves. A relaxed two weeks. I visited Gaston's parents, dropped by the forge, biked along the road. Went to High Mass with Gaston, then stopped off for a beer at the bustling, sun-flooded café *de Oude Zwaan*, in the church square. Being in a throng of good-humored, noisy strangers who took my humanity for granted was uplifting. It burned away, like morning mist, the emanations of the age-old antagonism I had felt during Mass. I biked to St-Niklaas, alone, for another visit with my parents. They looked worried, with more of an inmate air about them than on the previous visit. The lift I had gotten from the bike ride dissipated. The conversation languished about food, "Sylvain and I are eating well," about the war, "No end in sight." I took leave. "*Es verrt zeyn ghit*" ("It will be all right"), my father said, "we'll make it, with God's help." My mother echoed my father's words, without his conviction.

After supper on Sylvester night, Adrienne, Sylvain and I went to Gaston's parents' house. Rain hung in the air. We were walking on the tree-lined Phillip and Cyriel Verschaeve Street when something hit my nose, like a big drop of water. But it did not run off: it clung to the right nostril and it was lukewarm.

"A bird shit on my nose!" I exclaimed.

"Oh, you nitwit," Adrienne said, "what are you going to imagine next?"

"Adrienne, you don't understand." That was Sylvain. "That bird knew that my brother would be coming by."

"Yeah... you too are some bird," Adrienne said, laughing.

"Well," I countered like someone who is willing to wager big, "I won't touch it. I'll show you who is right."

"You do that."

I was a big sensation. All, except Johnny and Marcel, the two little Jewish boys that Gaston's parents were hiding, gasped, then burst out laughing. Marcel, the oldest — he was four — looked a bit puzzled but offered a shy smile. Adrienne told, laughing, what had happened, and I stood there, as if on stage, deadpan, holding my head high. My performance drew more peals of laughter. Gaston walked in. He sensed the mood, saw me, opened big eyes and turned away in disbelief and mock disgust: I knew that I had handled it right. I moved toward the mirror without changing my posture or expression. The bird dropping, with shades of brown and green, and a streak of beige, had dried up. Smack on the tip of my nose would have made it perfect, I thought. But I was satisfied. I had only wanted to show Adrienne wrong, and I had turned out a good performance to boot. I finally wiped my nose. As the laughter was dying down, Gaston, pointing at Sylvain, said, "This little one is some rascal. But that one," he said, wagging a finger at me, "a still water...runs deep." That was my first stunt. My brother had already racked up a few: he had tried smoking Gaston's cigar; and in the fall, he and Simoneke had played with matches, hiding behind a haystack. Only that one haystack went up in smoke, thanks to the farmers' quick intervention. Simoneke's parents accepted at face value her assertions that she and Sylvain had nothing to do with the blaze, "Probably because of the compensation the shrewd farmer must be getting from the insurance company," Adrienne had mumbled to me.

It was a peaceful evening in a blessed Flemish haven. We sat in the rarely used sitting-dining room. There was a small Christmas tree with trimmings, the first one I had seen in a home. Everybody wore fresh clothes. Gaston's father, Emile, was leaning back in an armchair. He had Johnny, the two-year old, on his lap. His crown of straggly hair was snow-white; it was usually gray, from the grime in the forge. Gaston's mother, Léontine, or his sister Maria must have lathered that crown over a basin and rinsed it, pouring warm water from the kettle. His striped shirt was already rumpled, his flowing black bow tie was drooping to one side. The old man was beaming; his dark, twinkling eyes darted all around. Gaston's mother, Léontine, was busying herself; she wore a black dress with a white lace collar and white cuffs. His sister Alice was helping her mother. Maria was holding Marcel on her lap. We had round sugar cookies with real coffee instead of the usual chicory. I must have looked pensive amidst the banter and the small talk. Gaston's mother looked at me:

"Henri, my lad, we *will* get rid of them."

"I know it. I wasn't thinking of them."

That was one of the first things she would say, in a determined tone, every time she saw me, as if renewing a solemn pledge. Léontine Van Damme was a small woman, strong-boned and lean, with big, brown eyes, high cheekbones and gray hair pulled back in a bun; a country woman, a devout Catholic. A fighter. Her mind was on the struggle. Her house would become a way station for Jews and for Flemish work dodgers.

At midnight, the lights went out. We moved around, shadows revealed by a handful of Christmas lights, kissing each other, exchanging wishes of good health and freedom. I was too inhibited to kiss Adrienne in the intimacy of darkness.

"What must I think of that?" she asked when the lights were back on, "kissing everybody but me? I got such a fat kiss from Sylvain."

Gaston looked at me reproachfully.

"I'll kiss you now," I offered sheepishly.

"It's too late now. It will no longer do."

CHAPTER 6 — PSALMS - I

La langue c'est la foi (Acadian saying).

The haze induced by an afternoon torpor lifted from my eyes to reveal the *Chalet*, the butcher's house, gray clouds streaked with charcoal racing across the sky, bare treetops swaying fitfully on the horizon. Lazily, I surveyed the bedroom: the filtered winter light gave the walls a grayish tint and deepened the color of the green satin bedspread.

I glimpsed the *tillimel*, the little *Book of Psalms*, on the night table, next to the pocket *siddur*. I would bring it along each morning in deference to my father's unspoken wish when he slipped it into our little suitcase — he had made a point of showing it to me — the night Sylvain and I left our hideout in Antwerp. I had never read the *Book of Psalms*, and had been putting it off, day after day. Boring, I thought, devotions that pious old Jews recited for the souls of the departed, or to implore divine intervention in times of distress, or for the sick, when the doctors had given up. I felt that I fulfilled my duty as a Jew by praying. The *tillimel* had become a mere prop on the night table. Leaving it in the garret, though, would have felt disloyal to my father.

I reached for the tiny psalter, lazily, to finger it. A miniature Bezalel edition from Jerusalem, it fitted in the palm of my hand. Its front and back covers, made of olive wood, were beveled and glossy. The front cover was painted with a view of the Holy City, the back cover featured palm trees. I liked the feel of the graceful little artifact.

I opened it to the first page for a desultory glance. The small Hebrew characters, the vocalization signs and tropes stood out, black and sharp, on the thin, parchment-like paper.

"Happy is the man who did not follow the counsel of the wicked, and did not stand in the path of sinners, and did not sit with the frivolous."

It is a galvanizing moment: the words are simple, direct, and beautiful; the verse pulsates with poetry, its music quickens the heart. It has laid bare my love for the Hebrew language and for Scriptures, the feeling of kinship with the Children of Israel that Silberstein's Bible class had nurtured. Once, he punished us by simply stopping a reading of Exodus. That day we were riveted to the passage in which Moses, holding the tablets, was descending from Mount Sinai while the Israelites were sacrificing to the Golden Calf. The story was coming to a climax, with Silberstein's spare comments heightening the suspense, when red-haired Maniel Fuss, the class clown and iconoclast, mumbled a smart-alecky comment that elicited giggling around him. It broke the spell. Silberstein responded impulsively, ordering us to close our *khumash* (a book from the Pentateuch): we were not deserving of such lofty fare just then. "Grammar time," he had said in anger.

I read again the psalm's opening verse, in wonder. The language and the pace are different from what I was used to in the Pentateuch, in Joshua and Judges, Samuel and Kings, in the books of Ruth and Esther. It is about a man's conduct. About me.

"And he shall be like a tree that is rooted near abundant waters, that brings forth its fruit in due time and whose leaf does not wither"; trees by the water's edge. There is safety under their cover. I can tread without fear, lie down, stretch out and close my eyes. I feel the stroke of a soft spring breeze. It sends a ripple across the shimmering pond. *My time will come.* I feel a softening inside, hope coming down like dew, spreading like a balm. *I also will bear fruit... My sons? My deeds?* **"And who succeeds in all he undertakes."**

I pause. I feel challenged to become that man. I want to grow out of the boy I am and break out into the world, explore and create. How does one become a man? With age? Who will I become? Questions that I had asked myself every time I saw, in passing, my reflection in the large display window of the prosthetics store on the Quellinstraat in Antwerp; I would raise my head and straighten my posture to look strong. *I WILL become a man. Do great things. In Eretz Yisrael.*

"Not so the wicked, — the Germans, the collaborators, the predators — **for they are like the chaff that the wind drives forth."** A verdict. Final. One poetic verse. Nine crushing Hebrew words. I am exulting. Appeased.

I read the psalm again, more slowly than before. The same thoughts and emotions visit me, as if on cue. I can hold on to them or let go, by slowing my pace or moving on. The second reading is even more intense than the first.

I pause. Hiding, suddenly, feels different.

Ps 2, **"Why are the nations in uproar?...** I am taken aback by the sudden shift in emphasis, from the just and accomplished man and his lofty rewards to the rogue nations of the world, scorned and called to account; by the shorter cadences and the use of poetic word endings, by the different sounds and the brisk pace. The second psalm speaks in several voices but I am unable to identify them. It is a different genre of poem altogether. I know the words and sense the power yet am thrown off-balance. I give up. I realize that the *Book of Psalms* will not always be easy reading.

"Break them with an iron staff, smash them like a potter's vessel. Bracing language, not a plea. I have grown weary of the supplications in the daily liturgy, especially the eighteen invocations in the weekday *Ameedah*, the prayer one recites while standing, feet joined, and in silence. I read again, **"Break them with an iron staff, smash them like a potter's vessel"** for the sheer pleasure of hearing the thunder. And I think of the Allies, especially the Americans, as God's punishing staff. They will crush the Germans and bomb their cities to smithereens.

I caught the opening verse, **"A psalm of David upon fleeing from his son Absalom"** (Ps 3) as I was about to lower the *tillimel* into my lap and take a breather. From homilies to King David's plight! The story that had captivated and mystified me in Silberstein's class. What a surprising collection of poems, the *Book of Psalms*!

"O Lord, how many are my oppressors, many are they who rise up against me. The verse is so familiar....

"Many are they who say there is no saving his soul.... The prayer before bedtime! I have not recited it in years. Like running into an old friend. My eyes glide over the lines. A single word brings an entire verse back to mind.

"And You, O Lord, are protecting me. You raise my head.

"I call to the Lord, and He answers me... I sense the passion. The cry from the heart is my own. I am letting go, with the Psalmist.

"I lie down and sleep, in the Flemish night, **I awake,** in the garret, under a patch of gray sky, **for the Lord sustains me.** David trusts. I trust.

"I shall not fear the hostile multitudes that surround me. The Waas country is my buffer, the house on the Lokeren Road, my shelter.

"...Rise, O Lord, save me, my God; for You have stricken all my enemies on the jaw, You have broken the teeth of the wicked." *Absalom. He couldn't have meant Absalom.* "My son, my son Absalom," David had cried out, "would that I had died instead of you." I understand why the prayer book left out the opening verse. The scene in Samuel springs to mind, of Absalom killed as he hangs, defenseless, by his tangled hair from a branch of an oak tree; killed by Joab, the king's general. David is stricken, and victory turns into mourning. "A father does not want to survive his son," Silberstein had commented — I see myself sitting in the front bench, looking up at him. So then, it had crossed my mind, my father would give up his life for me. Reassuring; and awesome. Mysterious. "As a father has compassion for his sons thus, O Lord, shall You have compassion for us," Silberstein had quoted, by way of explanation. "And the mother?" I had wondered. I had waited for him to say more. But he motioned us to read on.

The class scene reawakened the mystery. "As a *mother* has compassion for her children," flitted through my mind. My mother, she would lay down her life for us, all of us, fiercely, without hesitation. No mystery there. Like Madame Zangen, my friend's mother, "If I could put Menda on an airplane to *Eretz Yisrael*, I would dance all the way to Mechelen," she had said to my mother. I see her, lighthearted, arms spread, on the road to Mechelen.

"Thy blessing be upon Thy people, Selah." The prayer was a psalm.

I would get reacquainted in the days to come with the many psalms that had become part of the liturgy: the psalms welcoming the Sabbath, the cluster comprising the festivals' joyous *Hallel*, the psalms in the Sabbath and Festivals morning service, the ubiquitous *Ashray*, and others. The individual verses from the *Book of Psalms* that studded the liturgy also sparked flashes of recognition. Our traditional, Hebrew-only prayer books brought from Poland did not mention the source of the prayers; the verses were not numbered; often, the psalms' introductory verses were omitted. I had read those prayers assiduously in *shul*, on the Sabbath and the Festivals, enjoying the Hebrew and the challenge of keeping up with the men.

Those psalms elicited my attention as never before. They embraced me like dear friends of old, even the arcane ones.

I did not find Psalm 4 inspiring. My attention began to flag. I started leafing through the *tillimel*, skimming, just plucking opening verses. **"A Psalm of David,"** almost all of them said. And I remembered: David is the author of the Psalms, the Tradition teaches us. David took leave from his people as "the sweet songwriter of Israel"; Silberstein had lingered on those words, *"Ne'im zmirot Yisrael."* David, the Psalmist, not just the gifted harpist who could dispel Saul's dark moods. I recalled his rending elegy to Saul and Jonathan. How smitten we had been, in Bible class, by the tragedy unfolding in the North, the crushing defeat of the Israelites at the hand of the Philistines. Yet they soared aloft on the wings of David's poem, the fallen of the Gilboa. "Saul and Jonathan, loved in their lives, and not separated in their death; swifter than eagles, stronger than lions..." — fragments were welling up — "How the mighty have fallen in battle..." From the day we crossed the Jordan no one graced the pages of our ancient history like David. When Silberstein had assigned essays to some of us with a post-Pentateuch biblical figure for topic, I landed David. My scholarship and skills had not matched my enthusiasm and I had ended up reading in front of the class an incomplete essay in Hebrew that impressed no one. I felt a twinge of shame at the memory of that disappointing performance. Menda, who had been assigned the dour character of Samuel, read an essay that made Silberstein raise his eyebrows and turn his head as if to have a fresh look at his pupil. Menda could have written a learned piece on Balaam's ass.

Leafing through my *tillimel* I came across psalms whose introductory verses touch upon David's life on the run trying to escape Saul and the Philistines. The Book of Samuel came to life. "David picked his hiding places well," I remembered Kahn — we had him after Silberstein — telling us with an approving smile: we had just gotten to Ein Gedi with David. I saw again the wistful expression on Kahn's face as he recalled the oasis by the Dead

Sea. He had lived in Palestine in the early thirties and had been to some of the places where David had hidden from his pursuers. He had liked talking about the Land and its peoples, the Kibbutzim, the Bedouin encampments, the Arab markets. I recalled his story about the Arab egg sellers and buyers: squatting in the marketplace, they would keep track of the number of eggs that were slowly changing hands by repeating each number in a chant, until the seller found the next egg nestled in the straw. We enjoyed Kahn's rendition of the singsong, in Arabic; he knew the language. The similarity to Hebrew had struck us. Precious moments. Even tense, irascible Kahn was relaxed, at ease with himself and the class.

Sitting with the *tillimel* in my hands I imagined the desert heat, the shimmering sand, the palm trees of Ein Gedi, the luminous sky. Within the span of a thought I vaulted from David's Ein Gedi to the orange groves and wine cellars of Eretz Yisrael. I remembered the sepia picture postcards from Mandate Palestine, from places with poetic, reassuring names like Rishon Letzion (First in Zion), Zikhron Yaakov (Jacob's Remembrance), Petakh Tikvah (Gate of Hope). I was singing to myself the song that Nathan Bistricki taught us in Silberstein's class. The Hebrew poet, short, stocky, with a leonine face, a pepper-and-salt mane, warm dark eyes and a booming voice had visited our class months before the German invasion of Poland. The song, an alphabetical acrostic of towns and settlements, rang in my ears: Artoof in Judea, Beit Alpha in Yizre'el, I forgot the place starting with the letter *guimmel, Menda knows, remembers everything,* Deganiah in the Galilee, Herzliah in the Sharon. That's how far I got.

The words and cadences of *sheer ha'aymek*, the Song of the Valley, welled up in me, about the moonlit night stretching across dew-covered fields of the Valley of Yizre'el, from Beit Alpha to Nahallal. "Rest, o valley, land of splendor, we are standing watch over you." The melody lingered for a while. We sang it for Bistricki. I continued, in my head, with a song — the opening words to grace after a meal — I had picked and written for him on the blackboard in a fluid handwriting and with the correct spelling. Silberstein had eyed Menda, the class whiz, when he called for a volunteer, but I had promptly raised my hand. Bistricki, standing right by me, had watched intently every stroke of my hand. He had smiled. I had felt the glow. Menda, then, at

Silberstein's behest, cleaned up the vocalization, turning a *patakh* into a *kamats*, inserting a *daguesh* where called for. Bistricki was impressed. If only he could take us all with him to his kibbutz, he had said wistfully. Silberstein was beaming.

I was reveling in a proud past. I saw a bright future. For my people, for me.

I paused. My mind, idling and unfocused for so long, was churning with memories and desires. I had found a vessel for my emotions and my hopes in the mother tongue of my ancient and distant birthplace. I had discovered a letter addressed to me personally, that had laid unopened too long. Its message spanned time and space; it carried the old sounds, the longing for a long-lost dwelling.

✫ ✫ ✫

The next morning I got up looking forward to a rewarding day. I washed up, got dressed, ate my breakfast in the large bedroom. I didn't rush a thing, except the morning prayer which I mumbled even faster. The Psalms had become the stronger bond that tied me to my people, to our history and our homeland. Every activity, including the morning prayer, and every pause felt real, like in normal life. All ushered in a meaningful day for which I was preparing myself. I waited for Adrienne to make the beds and tidy up. Alone again, I sat down in the bedroom, ready and eager. There would be no interruption until the midday meal. I no longer felt shipwrecked in the sea of time.

I started from the beginning. The first three psalms elicited the same emotions as on the previous afternoon. I revisited, even anticipated, the images, the memories, the moods, the thoughts, like the ordered steps of an entrancing ritual. I gave each step its full stride, reading the psalms as slowly as before.

I reread Psalm 4, the uninspiring one, having resolved not to skip a word. And moved on. I had embarked on a voyage of discovery, verse by verse, psalm after psalm.

Ps 5, **"Listen to my cry, my King and my God, for to You I pray.**

"Lord, mornings You hear my voice, mornings I lay it out for You, and I wait, expectant."

He prays with *kavanah*, with intent and fervor, David does; he is committing his soul to his words.

Ps 6, "A Psalm of David. O Lord, don't admonish me with your anger and don't inflict pain on me with your wrath. Another stalwart of the liturgy.

"Be gracious unto me, for I am despondent,... and You, O Lord, until when? The question, ever-present, if muted, even drowned out at times, surged in a visceral upswell. *Until when?*

"...For there is no remembrance of You in death; who will render homage to You from the grave?

I sense the silence, the abyss. I glimpse a barren landscape, the vast body of Jewish learning plowed under, a world without the atmosphere of Shabbat and the sound of Hebrew. Running my fingers over the sharp Hebrew characters I feel like the lone keeper of an irreplaceable, secret treasure. *"Einen anderen Purim werden sie NICHT haben"* ("Another Purim they will NOT have"). Hitler's pronouncement. My mother had related it to me, in an undertone. It had sounded ominous amidst the laughter and the clinking of glasses in Adrienne's kitchen, when my mother whispered it to me. It sounds unsettling in the stillness of the bedroom. From my mother's tone and mien that day I had sensed that, to her, the deadly game of hide-and-seek had only begun. Its outcome, uncertain. To win this game "For Your sake, if not ours," David seems to say; like Moses in the desert, when, after the Golden Calf, God wanted to wipe out the Children of Israel and make him into the progenitor of a new nation. Moses downright shamed Him: "What will the Goyim say?" And it worked! God with a Jewish inferiority complex!

"I am tired from groaning, every night I make my bed swim...." He did, with his tears... I did... The memory, buried deep, of my bed-wetting in Adrienne and Gaston's plush bed, shortly after we arrived in Duizend Appels, surfaces in a haze of shame and vanishes.

Ps 8, "A Psalm of David. Lord our Master, how mighty is Your Name in all the earth, — a new voice, an exalted mood — **You whose majesty fills the heavens.** A song of praise. I felt its quickening touch like a breath of fresh air.

"From the mouth of babes and sucklings.... the babbling and gurgling of the innocent; myriads of delicate sounds rolling and tumbling over each other, forming gentle waves and running together like rivulets, a constant murmur under the sky. They bring to mind Guido Gezelle's poem *"Muggen"* ("Mosquitoes") in which the Flemish poet sees a profound meaning in the seemingly random and purposeless buzzing to-and-fro of mosquitoes in droning swarms: they are composing a song of praise to the Lord. "How Jewish," I remember thinking in class when our teacher read and explained the poem to us. Gezelle could have been trusted, I ponder, despite his having been a priest. He, of all priests, must have read the Psalms. In Flemish? In Latin? How could a translation capture their music? I feel smug knowing Hebrew and about my kinship with David. Chosen.

"From the mouth of babes and sucklings You established strength... to silence the enemy and the avenger. From soft harmonies to vengeful enemies, all in the same verse... Strange... I know every word, so why is the meaning eluding me? If others understood it, why don't I?

"When I behold Your heavens, the work of Your fingers, the moon and the stars... A fellow gazer, from a cave's opening — so I imagine — in the Judean desert, where he is hiding from his pursuers. The spell is back.

"What is man that You remember him? — He, too, muses about man's insignificance — **...yet You crowned him with glory and made him rule over Your handiwork... the beasts of the field, the birds in the sky, the fish of the sea.**

Six swift verses take me to the sky and back to the soft meadow, from the celestial bodies moving in the outer reaches to the birds aloft and the creatures coursing in the oceans.

"Lord our Master, how mighty is Your Name in the whole earth."

Dusk descended. Peace.

✵ ✵ ✵

I find myself plodding through a string of psalms that do not hold my attention. So many words I don't know. Oftentimes I know the words but do not understand the verse, and, just as vexing, fail to understand the psalm when I grasp most of the verses. I see that failure as a reflection of my limited ability and lack of insight. Yet I don't skip a word for fear of missing a gem, and for the sheer pleasure of hearing the ring of Hebrew. Would Menda be getting it? More than I am, no doubt. And Mayersdorf, to whom the Talmud, in Aramaic no less, was an open book? When will I be able to read without the help of a teacher? What is that special something beyond language and vocabulary, beyond mere knowledge that enables one to crack the arcane, to understand? What enabled Rashi, writing with a quill pen on parchment, in medieval France, to comment on the entire Bible and the Talmud, and in such concise, elegant Hebrew? He had to read it all — that alone takes a lifetime, understand it, collect his thoughts, and write them down. A genius.

My mind wanders. I put the psalter away, and look up at the milky-white sky hanging over Duizend Appels and distant Sinaai.

An evening like many others. We were having supper. Adrienne stood ready to serve out of the pot.

"The gendarme came home drunk again," she spooned out with the potato and vegetable purée. "Okh, the misery of some people."

Julia had babbled again. The gendarme, her next door neighbor and newcomer to Duizend Appels, was accusing his young pregnant wife — a former prostitute — of carrying someone else's child, and he would beat her mercilessly. Julia heard it all through the thin party wall just the way Adrienne and Gaston could hear the drunk mason's homecomings and Julia's screams in the wee hours of weekend nights. She *had* to be aware that Adrienne knew. How did that make her feel? Embarrassed? Jealous of Adrienne? Jealous, no doubt. The more reason to be on our guard: misery and jealousy, I sensed, were a dangerous mix. I could see her bursting in at Irène's, were she to find out about us, with an expression of disbelief, "Jews... Jews... Hokum, that whole story," dousing her glee with a dose of self-righteousness, "How *could* she..."

Gaston was chewing slowly in angry silence. He despised violent drunks.

"I'm off to Lokeren tomorrow morning," he mumbled. "Ordering some stuff."

I asked, "At Van den Abeele?" A bit of name dropping, alluding to the trip the two of us made to his hardware suppliers.

"No, De Beule. Van den Abeele doesn't carry these goods."

De Beule and Van den Abeele. Music to my ears: De BEUL' en VAN den a-BEE-le. *Yzerwaren* (Ironware). Tough. Durable. Men in overalls, at ease with the hard stuff. I could no longer see their faces.

✳ ✳ ✳

Ps 14, **"The Lord looks down from heaven on mankind to see if there is a sensible man seeking God.**

"All have strayed... there is none that does good, not even one. Much like before the Flood. So, what next? Three difficult, obscure verses. No, I won't return to this one. Then, taking me by surprise:

"O would that the salvation of Israel came from Zion, when God turns back the captivity of His people; the exile. Clearly, the exile. Way after David's time. So, he did not write all the psalms. **Jacob will exult, Israel rejoice."** And we will sing as we dance the horah! Big circle turning fast, turning before my eyes: guy, gal, guy, gal, arms locked, hands gripping shoulders, faces shining, feet thumping the ground in unison. The words resonate in my head,

"We shall yet remember the horah,

"We once danced,

"The horah in the Galilee."

The round gives way to the pounding rhythm of the Hebrew line, Thus we will tread on the soil of the motherland and we shall sing, It is great to be alive.

I dream on.

After some more dry reading I knew that only the occasional psalm would pulsate for me with poetry and passion, unlock memories or make me dream. The passages that I was unable to understand or appreciate were slowing me down. I would slip into daydreaming, or pick up the cards for a few games of solitaire. I soon fell into a reading pattern that was to stay with me until the end of the *Book of Psalms*: a session in the morning, another one in the afternoon. Reading the Psalms became my occupation. Like shoemaking to the cobbler. Some days I opened my *tillimel* only once. I would start each reading by revisiting one or more of the psalms that had gripped me. I would read them slowly, often more than once, with unabated intensity and enjoyment. I would then move on through new text, sometimes at a trudging pace, in anticipation of the next "peak" psalm or passage.

✡ ✡ ✡

Ps 19, **"A Psalm of David. The heavens recount the glory of God and the firmament proclaims His handiwork.** The celestial canopy, entrancing and awesome, the populated, terrifying void that pulls me, after nightfall, like a siren's song.

"Each day speaks to the next, and each night informs the night that follows.... A cosmic, unbroken link. Passing on, **with no speech nor words, without the sound of a voice,** that which we shall never capture.

I sense for the first time the majesty in the opening verses I had read so often in *shul.* They heighten the spell when I stand at the garret window, staring at God's firmament: immense and silent, it pulsates with mysterious intimations. I no longer see the cold, life-threatening vastness I had glimpsed through the garret window. I feel insignificant and safe. Alive. And free.

"...He has assigned a dwelling for the sun.

"And it is like a bridegroom alighting from his nuptial tent, rejoicing, like a strong man, to run the course. His hair, like Samson's, is flowing in the wind; he is prancing in the celestial glow. I take flight with him.

The firmament and the sky, my companions; the sun, the moon and the stars. They replace boredom with awe. They loosen the shackles of timelessness.

I am alone with my poem in the silence of the bedroom, with the psalm I knew as a prayer. A mere glance, now and then, and the verses spring forth from memory, sparkling, cadenced:

"The law of the Lord is whole, restoring the soul....

"The precepts of the Lord are right, rejoicing the heart....

"The fear of the Lord is pure, enduring forever....

"More precious are they than gold,... sweeter than honey....

The light is reflected off the page of my *tillimel;* the sharp, handsome Hebrew letters hop, the words dance, the verses glow, down to the last one which also concludes the *Ameedah* prayer,

"Let the words of my mouth and the meditation of my heart be acceptable to You, O Lord, my Rock and my Redeemer."

Ps 20, **"A Psalm of David. The Lord will answer you in a day of trouble....**

"He will send you help from the Holy Place, and from Zion He will support you....

"He will give you according to your heart's desire....

As if a voice in the distant past had foreseen my predicament, my neediness. Still, I counted in my days of trouble only on the tanks and planes of the Allies, on their resolve to crush the Germans.

"Some in their chariots, others on horseback; The Romans, the Assyrians: the memories surfacing from Bible and Jewish History class evoke destruction and deportation. I see in the distance a dense agglomeration of shimmering white houses and domes, the radiance of civilized life. The barbarians attack. To be civilized is to be under siege. There, I came up with a definition. A good one. But we always knew it, we Jews, without putting it in these words. Didn't Velghe, immersed in Cicero, and Van Bijlen, who mentioned Euclid with reverence, think so too, deep down?

"But *we* shall invoke the Name of the Lord our God. I see Silberstein, sitting behind his desk and brandishing a *khumash*, a book from the Pentateuch, "This is our shield. Stronger than a tank. Cannons cannot destroy it." I had pictured a cannon firing at his *khumash*, and a Jew in a black caftan, with a white beard, facing a tank with an open Torah scroll held aloft, like in *shul* after the reading of the weekly portion, on Shabbat. I had wondered, how would the Torah protect us? Had Silberstein truly believed it? After all, rumor had it that he listened to the radio on the Sabbath. In real life, it seemed to be the other way around: we were the protectors of the Torah, often at great sacrifice. I had listened intently, trying to sort it out: books endured, sure, learning got transmitted. But tanks and cannons had loomed so awesome.

"They have come down on their knees and fallen, but we have arisen and gained strength." *They will come down on their knees and fall. And we shall rise up and gain strength.* I know. How good it feels to know. I close my eyes: *We shall prevail. We always have.* Hope surges.

Psalm 22 opens with a bucolic image: the doe of dawn, as I understand the Hebrew. The meaning eludes me, but I savor the words, the rhythm. Then, gushing forth, without warning, *"Eli, Eli, lamah azavtani?"* ("My God, My God, why have You forsaken me?") *THAT'S where Jesus got it from.* To see it in Hebrew characters... A real Jew was Jesus.

"AYlee, AYlee, LAH-mah azav-TAH-ni? — WHY have You forsaken me? — Too far away to save me, out of earshot.

"My God, I call by day, but You don't answer; and at night, in vain. Does He care?

"Our fathers put their trust in You; they trusted and You set them free. He didn't lift a finger during the Inquisition, the pogroms. Today, He is nowhere to be found. Except in the Psalms. David has brought Him out of hiding.

"To You they cried out and they escaped; they trusted You and were not covered with shame; unrelenting is David.

"But I am a worm, not a man... despised by people. No false pride, not David. He danced without restraint before the Ark of the Covenant, rejoicing with the peasant folk, like one of them. His wife Michal, Saul's daughter, was embarrassed and dismayed.

"All who see me mock me... they shake their heads. Where was he? On the lam? Fleeing from Saul?

"...my heart is melting into my entrails." I know the feeling. Unending is the litany of his troubles. And the Lord answered him. Him.

I sat back. Quiet reigned. I had regained my footing with three resonant psalms in short succession: an ode to Creation, a hymn of hope and victory, a cry from the heart. Three poems, one voice. I was plying again the *Book of Psalms*. The tedium of hiding had lifted. My mind wandered on for a while, in distant places, in times gone by. Relaxed, I took a long break with a few games of solitaire, then put the cards away, and watched the afternoon darken into dusk, and dusk thicken into night.

It was a good day.

☆ ☆ ☆

I was absorbed in a promising game of solitaire when I noticed Milou's watchful, cold eyes: they followed the movement of my hand, glanced at the cards — they formed a rectangular frame — then gazed at me as I was pondering my next move. I wondered what went through a cat's mind as it was eyeing a human bent over an array of cards when an image struck me, of a German in *Feldgrau, Those are the eyes of a German* — head and shoulders was all I saw — staring with the same uncomprehending eyes at a frail, bearded Jew in a black caftan, with a skullcap, sitting cross-legged on the floor and bent over an open tractate of the Talmud. German eyes, looking, coldly, at a specimen. The Jew remains immobile, his body riveted to the floor, his eyes focused by an act of will on the text and the frame of commentaries. He won't look up so as not to cause a ripple on the placid surface of the feline eyes. A disturbing scene, in the flicker of a thought.

I thrust a fierce, steely look into the big, gray-green eyes, and kept boring into them, until the cat got up and walked out, head low; as if heading for the wilderness, like the biblical he-goat, bearing the sins of Germany. I followed the paws' patter on the stairs down to the bottom. And paused, trying to calm down.

Still roiled, I resumed the game; forced myself, to erase the image.

No win.

✠ ✠ ✠

Ps 23, "A Psalm of David; the Lord is my shepherd, I shall not want." My heart jumps. I read again. And again. A calm descends over me. I feel safe. I trust. I surrender. Someone is looking out for me. I shall not want a thing: walking the streets, running on the beach, diving into the cresting wave, friends, books. The Lord is my shepherd, I shall not want.

I detach myself from the opening verse and read on, slowly:

"He will make me lie down in pleasant pastures; the grasses are dense and fresh, a deep lush green. **He will lead me by tranquil waters.** I see a distant lake's shimmering surface. Tall majestic trees line its shore.

"He will restore my soul.... Quiet reigns, a balm on my heart. No secrets to weigh me down.

"Though I may walk in the valley of the shadow of death — a *Transport* is rolling to the East in the silence of total darkness — **I fear no evil....**

"You set a table before me against my oppressors... — they can't get near me.

...my cup is full to the brim. I breathe in, deep.

"Only goodness and grace will follow me all the days of my life." There is a spring in my step. O, freedom.

In the weeks that followed I repaired to Psalm 23 like a pious Jew to the Sabbath. The reveries might come with some variations, but the ethereal mood would not change. I anticipated the poetic phrases and found them ever more moving. I felt removed from danger. The tongue of the Psalms and their poetry had become, for me, the carrier of hope, of the urge to believe, of faith.

Reading the Psalms had become my occupation. It was a journey and a refuge. A vessel to navigate time. A buoy.

Ps 27, **"The Lord is my light and my salvation, whom shall I fear?...** I do not fear. Not in Duizend Appels.

"When the foes set upon me to eat my flesh, my oppressors and my foes, *they* **stumbled and fell.**

"Though an army should surround me, my heart shall not fear; even if war were to break out against me — it has — **still I will be confident."** To have confidence. Like tasting freedom.

Ps 30, **"What gain is there in the spilling of my blood, in my going down to the grave? Will the dust praise You? Will it declare Your truth?"**

Sounds familiar. I leaf back. There, Psalm 6:

"For there is no remembrance of You in death; who will render homage to You from the grave?"

The old image popped up again, of our patrimony buried under, of the sun beating down on parched land.

Ps 31, **"You have seen my misery, You knew the troubles of my soul, but You have not delivered me into the hands of the enemy...."**

Ps 32, **"Be not like the horse and the mule, devoid of understanding...."**

I glimpse villagers trudging about in fields and barns, un-comprehending of the war unleashed by the Sons of Darkness against the Sons of Light. Devoid of understanding. At peace.

✵ ✵ ✵

I am coming out of a hypnotic killing fantasy with the usu-al letdown: no sooner have I felled a German from my perch than another one steps into full view. There is no end to it. The Germans don't sit and fantasize: they conquer and kill. "Thou shalt not kill" is drivel to them. They want us to be his-tory; and the ten commandments, an ancient relic, like the Rosetta stone. Like the Hammurabi code. Zalcman read the Hammurabi code. He read everything. Even Gilgamesh. Or about Gilgamesh.

"We didn't invent anything, you know, like morality, or the Flood," I remember him saying during our meandering street corner debate. "We just dipped into what was there."

"So what, Zalcman," I am telling him now. "We dipped deep, deep. But then we raised it high, high. While they were still dan-gling from the trees by their tails. By their tails, Zalcman."

"Hammurabi was not dangling by his..."

"I meant Europe, of course. The Germans."

"You know, Gruni, if Moses hadn't come down that smoky mountain amidst all that fanfare, then Hammurabi would have been the famous chap today."

"Uh..." Why did I have to make him say that? "Hammurabi, you see, wrote his code for his people, just for them. On clay tab-lets. The nation went under, so went the code. The tablets were found. Pure luck. Nice tablets. Moses carved our code into stone tablets and raised them for all the world to see. That's what God picked us for. The fanfare was to get everybody's attention. And sure enough, our commandments have circled the earth. Look here, the whole world counts to seven."

"What do you mean?" he asks.

"The Sabbath is what I mean. We gave it to the world. The sev-enth day. Sure, this tribe or that nation had some sort of screwy days of rest to honor this or that ridiculous god. Or take the French revolution. They wanted to make every tenth day the day of rest. Le Directoire, as you know" — I had to show off. "But seven it is, even in Berlin."

"Tell me, Gruni, do you really believe that God chose us to proclaim the ten commandments?"

"What difference does it make? We did."

"Do you believe in God? The truth."

"I... We have to, Zalcman. It is not as simple as you make it out to be."

Why did I get into that gray area? Not to believe in God. In the present circumstances. What a dangerous leap. We *have* to believe. Everything is happening just like we read in Silberstein's class. I mean the curses in *D'varim* (Deuteronomy): "Morning, you'll wish it be night. Night, you'll wish it be morning." The fear. The hunger. The diseases. The humiliation. The deportations. It's all in there. The blessings, just a few verses. The curses, pages and pages of them. The relentlessness. The fury! I remember how awed I was: We will be scattered among the nations, oppressed in our places of exile, demeaned into worshipping idols... But no, we are not idolaters. We are still the bearers of the tablets. *That's* why we are hounded. That's why... Will it ever end? How?

Ps 39, "Let me know, O Lord, my end, and the measure of my days, what it is; I want to know when I will cease to live."

Awesome, Godlike knowledge. Why does David want to know? Because he knows what he has to accomplish. He wants to squeeze it all in. What do I want to accomplish?... To know the day... The exact day... Disquieting. Like a death sentence, almost... To wait for death. How does one die?

I am back in my tree. Sated by the carnage and trapped in it, and looking for a way out, I wait for the Germans to give up their search. I come down, slip away, and meet a shapely woman — much like the petite blond acrobat of the roving circus — who falls immediately in love with me and offers to hide me in her house. Her features and hair color are indistinct; but she is my height. I know, as we walk side by side, that I will play an active part in our new life, a life of danger and wile, excitement and gratification.

We devise hiding routines and escape strategies. We spend a lot of time in bed, even in broad daylight: I like to see her breasts and her nipples, and her legs, everything that I am touching and kissing. We eat from the same plate, use one knife, and drink from the same cup. Thus there will not be the slightest delay in answering the door and letting the unexpected caller, or a German search party, into the house. I will have plenty of time to scamper off, with the second spoon or fork in my hand, into my ingeniously designed hideout. She procures the extra food from another farm: buying more from her regular source would raise eyebrows and could lead to dangerous speculation. I have wasted no time in explaining that to her. She has sewn all the clothes I need. I keep them in my hideout; my shoes also.

She is an artist. Her drawings are astonishingly beautiful. People snap them up at whatever price she asks. She is not one to take advantage, though. I marvel at her mastery of the line, her freedom of movement on the sheet. I have never been able to reproduce with any grace an imagined object, however simple; a skyscraper facade — that's all I could come up with — when our high school arts teacher asked us to draw something we knew, using only geometric figures. But now, working alongside my female companion, I turn out great geometric compositions. She sells them as her own work — she gets praised for her versatility — knowing full well that I have cleverly hidden a star of David in every one of them: she will convert to Judaism after the war.

I would toy with my fantasy, solve problems such as how to wash men's shirts and underwear and hang them to dry without tipping our hand, or disposing of the bodies of the two German soldiers I killed — one of them, the sergeant, had had the nerve to make a pass at her — and secreting their motorcycle.

Somehow, the Germans' noose around me has gotten tighter. One day, she announces to neighbors and acquaintances that she is going to live with relatives. Skipping town and waiting for her, unnoticed, at the agreed upon place was another one of my major exploits. We settle in a quiet, far away place and pass for the sole survivors of a family that has perished in a bombardment. On the outside we are Christians, a woman and her younger brother. On the inside we live like Jewish husband and wife: sharing my life and the prospective conversion make her into a de facto Jewess. Modern Marranos, with a twist.

I never knew her name. We never called out for each other, that would have been too dangerous. And when we were together, there was no need to address each other by name. In my fantasies, none of my female protagonists ever had a name or a distinctive face. The places had no definite identity either.

Our secret drew us together, our lives were in complete harmony. The more I basked in the glow of her unshakable loyalty, the less avid and intrusive my kisses became, edged out by the warmth of our partnership. The circus women remained anonymous, expressionless, inert, and rousing in the extreme every second they were around.

✢ ✢ ✢

Ps 42, **"As the deer craves the springs of water, so does my soul crave You, O God. My soul thirsts for God, for the living God; when will I come and be shown into the presence of God?"**

I read again:

"As the deer craves the springs of water, so does my soul crave You, O God. My soul thirsts for God, for the living God…"

I close my eyes: "As the deer craves the springs of water, my soul thirsts."

Ps 44, **"You hand us over like sheep to be eaten,** me too, if they catch me. I, a sheep waiting — a sensation in the chest, like blood draining from the heart; **and You scattered us among the nations.**

Galut! (Exile!)… Again. The first? The second? I turn to the opening verse: this psalm is written for the Sons of Korakh. Levites. Officiated at the temple; must be the second temple, after the Babylonian exile.

"You turned us into a taunt to our neighbors, a laughing-stock to those who surround us; to this day.

"All this has come over us, yet we have not forgotten You; we have not reneged on Your covenant. Circumcised, we are.

"Our heart has not turned back… Shabbat. We have kept Shabbat. *We* are the faithful ones.

"For Your sake we are killed all day, we are thought of like sheep for the slaughter. Again. Sheep. Us.

"Wake up, why Lord do You sleep?" He is afraid to look. Helpless.

The pope. What made me think of him? I lost my train of thought. I see a frozen figure in ceremonial garb with a high, wide, pointy hat and a scepter, in an ornate, lifeless hall of the

Vatican. I see him clearly: the lean frame, the stony, longish face with the dark eyes behind the wire-rimmed glasses. Popes. They inspired the crusades, they presided over the Inquisition. I remember our reading in Shimon Dubnow, in Silberstein's class — the Hebrew made the account more intimate and searing — about the devastation the crusaders wrought on our communities in the Rhineland, along the route to the Holy Land. We fled east, out of their way. The Spanish Jews scattered too, across the Mediterranean, to Holland, to Turkey. Fled Torquemada's burning stakes. Those who stayed converted, and practiced the faith in secret; in cellars. I would not have converted. Well... maybe... What's a little water and some mumbo-jumbo? It's a blot, though; I would not have told. Nonsense. Baptism took place in a church, in the open. People knew, especially the faithful in the cellars.

Anyway, out of the question; today a Jew is a Jew, even if he is a Catholic priest. To Mechelen he goes. And we can't run either: the Germans are sitting on all of Europe. Jewish Europe, anyway. Sweden and Finland, Spain and Portugal have no Jews. Switzerland has a handful of its own, maybe; and the few who made it there. The continent is sealed off. Could they succeed where the crusaders and the inquisitors have failed? The pope must be exulting at the prospect of a Europe wiped clean of Judaism, that age-old thorn in the Church's side. What if he calls down damnation on the Christ killers? What if he calls on the faithful not to come to our help? In a papal letter — or is it an encyclical? — to all the priests, to be read on the same Sunday in all of Europe.

I can picture our priest reading from the pulpit, I can hear the unctuousness that permeates his sermons. And the professions of love now and then, the love of Jesus. Would his flock be dozing and coughing through the encyclical as they do during his sermons? Would he change his tone and try rousing them? How many Christians might be dissuaded from helping Jews? How many would even turn informers, out of Christian duty? It would not affect Adrienne and Gaston, I know — it is the four of us against "them." They have stopped going to confession, to keep out of the priest's sight and mind: he must be aware of Sylvain's presence, and could bring up the subject with them. They don't trust him. An image pops up, of the priests I had seen sitting at a round table in a garden near the church in Belsele, hatless, still forbidding in their black garb, well-fed and contented, schmooz-ing. Had the brothers Philip and Cyriel Verschaeve, the pan-Ger-man priests, been among them? Those men in black cassocks and white socks, with their wide-brimmed, round-topped black hats had always made me feel uneasy. What animated them, I would wonder, beside the desire to convert us? Each time I had passed an open church, in Antwerp, I had imagined Jesus, the dreaded personage issued of our people, to be lurking high from his cross in the dimly lit vastness, like a reminder of a never end-ing, implacable hostility. Only on Sundays, when I would espy the relaxed, neatly dressed crowd of worshippers, missals in hands, chatting and smiling in front of the church, much as we did on the Sabbath in front of our synagogue, could I see a human face to Catholicism.

Will the pope speak out?... He hasn't, so far... What's hold-ing him back?... He won't. He knows how the winds of war are blowing. Only idiots and Germans believe that Germany is win-ning the war. Battles, yes, but not the war. He won't call for our demise. He is evil, but smart... Or have the Allies taken up our cause and cowed him into silence? Makes no difference.

Not to worry. He'll shut up.

✡ ✡ ✡

Ps 51, **"A Psalm of David. When Nathan the prophet came to him, after he had consorted with Batsheba —** ah! That good story.

"Be gracious unto me, O God — no story.

"...For I know my transgressions, and my sin is always be-fore me. Mea culpa, he is so good at that. "The prophet entraps the king and gives him a tongue-lashing," Silberstein said. "Can you think of an Assyrian king or a Roman emperor letting a Nathan live and go free?" Come to think of it, none of the king-lets of Judea and the break-away North would have shown much contrition either.

"Against You alone have I sinned... And the transgressions against his fellow men? An entire platoon gets wiped out in that intentionally ill-conceived, suicidal assault that was meant to fell Batsheba's husband, Uriah the Hittite. Shouldn't David have appeared before a judge? Or the High priest? And he gets to keep her, the fruit of his crime. Marries her. The future mother of Solomon. The king is above the law, after all, even in Israel. "Against You alone..." Shouldn't God have been angered by such a lopsided confession?

"Wash me and I shall be whiter than snow.... Chutzpah.

"Save me from blood vengeance... from the relatives of Uriah and his comrades who were killed because of his scheming instructions to Joab? Doesn't he owe compensation to their families?

A letdown, that psalm.

Ps 52, **"A psalm of David, when Do'eg the Edomite came and told Saul, and said to him: David has come to the house of Akhimelekh."**

Ps 54, **"...of David, when the Ziphites came and told Saul: David is hiding in our midst."**

Unsettling. Both instances. I close the *Book of Psalms*.

Milou appeared in the doorway, tail curling up. He brushed against my leg and went down on the foot mat. I went down on my knees and stroked him, took him on my lap and stroked him some more. The cat purred, living up the moment. It took the edge off my bout with time. We are friends again.

✧ ✧ ✧

The day has begun and has trickled along like many a day past. As I pull out of my reverie and stare, listless, at the sun-reddened bricks and glistening black roof tiles of the butcher's house, I realize with a familiar dread: time has stopped. It stagnates. It fills the air.

The house is quiet. Nothing stirs. A rough spot; another time pocket. They creep up, unexpected, in the hollow stretch of occasional afternoons without a coffee break.

It will pass, I keep saying to myself. It will pass, I know. It always does. When it becomes unbearable. But I must sit it out. I will then move to the garret, stare at a patch of sky, come back. I will pick up, listlessly, a magazine, or a pack of cards — not the *tillimel*: the Hebrew would sound flat, out of place — and wait for dusk.

It will pass. I think, therefore it will pass. *Cogito, ergo...*uh... Never mind. The day will pass. I also know that tomorrow

Liberation will not feel a day nearer. I am not serving time. I am hiding from the Germans. From the world.

A cow's moo stirs the timelessness that envelops me, lone sounds rippling toward the horizon. The horse-drawn cart whose clatter gets stronger, then weaker, then fades into the distance, the truck that rumbles on and away, bring a bit of relief: they drag a smidgeon of time along.

I remember Joshua. He ordered the sun and the moon to stand still. I recite in silence, *"Shemmesh buh-guiv'on, dom; vuh-yaray'akh buh-aymek ayalon."* He needed more time to finish off the enemy, to squeeze in some more action. Must have gone by in a flash. Only in the bedroom is time standing still.

It will pass. *"Het gaat alles ten einde"* ("All things come to an end"). A hit song. I am running it in my head:

Het gaat alles ten einde,	All things come to an end,
Het gaat alles voorbij,	It all goes by,
Na ied're December,	After each December,
Komt weder een Mei.	Comes again a May.

I sing it again. Like a hymn.

I wrench myself off the chair, move to the garret, look through the window at the treetops in the Waasmunster sky, come back, sit down, pick up, wearily, a pack of cards. I can't even think of reaching for my *tillimel.* Fantasies would not take hold.

I play a game of solitaire. And another one. I read, once again, a magazine article I had liked.

Dusk.

✤ ✤ ✤

"...O that I had wings like the dove; I would fly away and dwell at peace. I would wander far off...." (Ps 55).

✤ ✤ ✤

Hiding where I can move about freely — the ideal refuge. I am dreaming. Mons comes to mind, from my geography class, a town in the rolling, verdant hills of Wallonia in the south of Belgium. I never heard of Jews living in Mons. The townspeople wouldn't know a Jew if they saw one. A safe place; must be. Not like Antwerp, where anyone laying eyes on me, a policeman, a schoolboy, would know.

Mons. I might even go to school there, under a false identity and a good cover: father Walloon and prisoner of war, mother Flemish and in a sanatorium. I am living with an uncle and aunt, we have the same family name.

"From where?"

"From Antwerp," I would say. The only place I know.

"Oh, Antwerp, I was there several years ago. That fantastic tree-lined avenue running down from the Central Station towards the Cathedral, you know..." and I would snap back,

"Avenue De Keyser," and in the same breath, "De Keyserlei," I would add in Flemish, in the low-key self-assured tone that comes with intimate knowledge.

"A lot of Jews there," he might remark.

"All gone," I would say matter-of-factly, "good riddance."

Why did I say such a dastardly thing?... Out of fear... A weakness, I sense it. He may not even be an antisemite. He may even have helped Jews. No, he didn't, he would not have mentioned Jews if he had had anything to do with them. He mentioned it because he is suspecting something. Still, why say "Good riddance"? I feel shame. Why couldn't I have said, "Yes, a lot of Jews"? Or just "Yes," period? Or better even,

"I don't know... not in my neighborhood." That's it, that's what I say.

"Where in Antwerp did you live?" he might ask.

No, that was the wrong answer. "Yes," period, that's all I should have said.

"Do you know Antwerp?" I ask.

"A little bit."

I am searching feverishly for a purely Aryan part of town. I only knew the center and the surroundings of the park where one couldn't help noticing the Jewish presence.

"Do you know the Harmonie, on the Chaussée de Malines?" Not on the out-of-towner's circuit.

"No. I have been in Antwerp a few times only, way back."

That's the end of it. Come to think of it, no one in Duizend Appels ever asked me, or Sylvain, a personal question. It's because of class, they are a bit awed by what Adrienne has told them, the rugs, the chandeliers, the father's pull; and because of the family story of tragedy and sin. They know all they'll ever want to know.

The sun irradiates the air outside the bedroom windows. My mind wanders. Sunny, charming Mons has vanished beyond the bright horizon.

Adrienne has slipped in some unusual reading material along with *Het Vrije Waasland* — she passes upstairs everything she gets: it is a religious society's thin tabloid of devotional writing on soft, grayish, low quality newsprint. There are advertisements for religious articles: votive candles, rosaries, a missal, clerical garb, and the like. I turn the page. There is a small drawing of a chubby monk and a pudgy, cute piglet trotting by his side. Both are smiling. The sun is shining overhead. The title reads: *Sint Antoniusbeestje* (St Anthony's little animal). The column of print underneath waxes sentimental over the saint's adoption of his lovable four-legged companion; it exudes Christian love... Christian love for an animal that gets bled to death for its meat *and* blood amid cheery Christian onlookers. I like the drawing, though. More text. And advertisements.

I turn the page. A young man and a woman are drawn in profile, in bold, spare lines, over the entire left side of the centerfold. She is sitting on the floor, her legs bent to one side. He is down on one knee, head slightly bent; he is looking into her eyes. She is reaching up to him with bare arms, her head tilted back. The folds in her long flowing dress — tight from the waist up, with a décolleté — underline her shapely breasts and round hips. His loose garb which covers only one shoulder, his athletic build and strong features evoke a Roman legionnaire without armor. I am envious.

I read: He has killed her son. She is forgiving him in the spirit of Christian forgiveness.

I am revolted by her betrayal, repelled by the "Christian" spirit, disturbed yet fascinated by her desire, her rank desire; her surrender.

✠ ✠ ✠

I was biking to St-Niklaas, to see my parents, on a Sunday morning, when their hosts were at home — I had "arrived in Duizend Appels" the previous night. I had started out in the

direction of Belsele Village — a routine destination. At the fork
dominated by a castle I had borne to the right onto the New
Road, climbed the railroad overpass, and was pedaling on across
the land — a bracing, six-kilometer trip into a gentle head wind.
I felt alive and free.

When I arrived, my parents filed down from their mansard
room. They looked gaunt. We had the little dining room to
ourselves: Palmyre and Lucien had closed themselves off in the
kitchen. We spoke softly.

My mother hugged me in a lingering embrace.

"Are you all right?" she asked.

"Of course I am. Couldn't be better." A less than glowing account might have aroused concern.

My father kissed me.

The visit was short and strained. We had little to tell each other.
My mother's concerns — about diet and health, about safety —
were reflected in her anxious look, inscribed in her pinched lips,
locked in her joined hands.

"Are you taking advantage of the outdoors?" she asked.

"And how," I answered. "Just this round trip by bicycle, the
vigor it gives. And," I hastened to add to allay any worry about
over-exertion, "I wasn't out of breath, didn't even perspire."

The conversation sputtered.

"Purim is coming up," my father said.

"Purim," my mother said, her voice trailing off. How incongruous, her tone intimated.

My father would inform me, throughout hiding, of upcoming
Jewish holidays. I took it for granted that he knew how to track
them. I never asked him how he did it. I knew that he wanted me
to recite the special prayers associated with the holidays, the only
way we had to mark them in hiding. He never asked me if I did. I
would forget the dates. I prayed the bare minimum.

My mother said: "The English radio reported that Jews are
sent away never to be seen again." She sighed: "My sisters. Their
families. Antwerp."

There was a pause.

"We'll soon be free," I said to break the silence.

"Free," my mother muttered. "Yesterday," she continued, "I
spied the woman from across the street sweeping the sidewalk in
front of her doorstep. In the shining sun. She had a cheap, loose

dress on, like a night gown, almost. I was overcome with envy. I told papa that I'd give everything, give up all material goods and comforts to be a street sweeper; with just the dress on my back. Oy, to feel secure. To live without fear..."

"Henia," my father said soothingly. "We see them as free. The Jews who were taken to Mechelen would see us as free."

"Nu yah..."

"This won't last," my father continued. "You will not be a street sweeper and you will wear nice clothes." His tone, still gentle, grew firm, "We will survive them," and sharp now, "they will lie deep in the ground."

"I know that," my mother concurred. "I hope we'll be there to see it."

"We'll be there. We'll be there," my father said reassuringly.

"We'll be there, maman," I seconded my father. "We'll get our revenge."

"We'll leave that to the Russians," my father observed. "They know best what to do."

"Staying alive is the best revenge," my mother muttered.

The conversation languished.

It was time to leave. My mother held me in a clinging embrace. My father held me tight while kissing me on both cheeks.

"Go, take advantage of the fresh air."

"Go in good health."

Not a word about the ordeal of hiding. Mine had receded into oblivion, Psalms and all, the moment I put on my shoes.

My father never mentioned the *siddur* and the *tillimel* he had slipped into our overnight case before sending us off to Belsele. "Teach your brother," he had instructed me that night. Now, just a few months later, Sylvain was speaking only the local dialect.

✣ ✣ ✣

Boredom has driven me out of the bedroom. In the garret the gray light dims as it penetrates the narrow space, leaving most of it in semi-darkness. I sit on the bed, lean back on my elbows; watch the drizzle cover the glass panes with dew-like droplets; swing a leg through the opening in the curtain; look at it like a doctor administering the knee-jerk test; swing and look once more; glimpse myself, in a disquieting flash — I see someone with a hollowed-out existence. An upswell of anguish, an intimation of endless confinement, drive me out. No, I will not assume that pose again, I shall not let go.

I get a lift upon reentering the spacious bedroom. I restart the day, becalmed; look at the tranquil sky, at the horizon pierced by the distant treetops of Sinaai where the sky meets the earth; I start a game of solitaire, the easy one; read; daydream; reread a psalm; or just sit back and listen with renewed attention to the noises from the road. The world is moving again. I will be of it. Some day.

I am sitting still and gazing straight ahead. At the sliver of sky above the Café *Chalet*, at the triangles on its Swiss-style gable. Triangles. The base angles of an isosceles triangle are equal. Van Bijlen. His lapidary exposition of the Euclidian theorems. Euclid, a Greek. The Greeks gave us geometry. Wait a minute: the base angles of an isosceles triangle have been equal ever since the world came into existence, even before... Were there triangles before the... Let's not go there. Let's say that the Greeks *discovered* geometry. Wait a minute. Everybody knows intuitively the basic property of an isosceles triangle. Yes, but the Greeks drew our attention to it and built on it, theorem after theorem, like Van Bijlen in geometry class. They *developed* geometry. Yes, *that* they did. And they postulated the two postulates, the jumping-off points. What else are they famous for? Hippocrates. The first modern doctor. No reciting of Psalms to force God's hand. Quite understandable: whom should they turn to, Zeus, or a deity issued from his thigh? How can intelligent people countenance such nonsense? Oh well.

And tragedy. They invented tragedy, we were told in Ancient History class. Sophocles. Euripides. Invented... Really? The expulsion from Eden then, just a picnic? And Cain and Abel? David and Saul? And Absalom? And the rape of Tamar in King David's household? And Yiphtakh's daughter? And blind Samson bringing down the building on himself? Slow down. David and Samson, that's history. Greek tragedy is a literary genre, yes, a genre, that's what the prof said. Plays, on the stage. The characters, or... or their actions, can be invented. Like in Corneille and Racine. On the other hand, Adam and Eve is a divinely-inspired... uh... cosmogony... That's not the word, idiot. Well, let's put it this way: we all have the same father and mother. In the

Bible, if you walk in God's paths, you will relax under your vine and under your fig tree; if you stray, you'll end up in shit. That holds for beggars, kings, and nations. In Athens, God did not preside over history, starting with Herodotus. The first historian. He wrote about the Greeks like Shimon Dubnow writes about us, today, without mentioning God's role; only our faith in Him, at most. So *we* are learning history the way Herodotus taught it, and *they* have adopted the ten commandments, including the Sabbath. Did the ancient Greeks have a Sabbath? Our prof never mentioned it. And did they have to set their slaves free after a certain period of servitude, as we had to after six years? Velghe talked only about their literature and intellectual prowess. Never heard of Athens in Jewish history class at Tachkemoni, only of hellenized Syrians, a corrupt bunch of idolatrous pleasure-seekers who ran naked in their sports meets and who got kicked out of our land by the Maccabees, with the help of God of course, to give us Hanukkah. And our high school profs never mentioned Jerusalem. Strange.

I move towards the window for a peek at the *Chalet*: a patron in a relaxed pose, one hand resting on the table, a glass of beer in front of him, is talking with the proprietress in the glassed-in porch. She presses with both hands a tray against her knees. Her upright, slender frame is at ease. I can tell when she is speaking. I wait. And wait some more. I can see by the slight sideway motion of her head that the conversation is about to end. A nod and a gesture of the hand, a pause, and she turns around to disappear inside. I return to my chair.

Ps 69, **"By David.**
"Save me, O God, for the water has risen to the soul.
"I am drowning, me, in time, **... and there is no foothold....**
"I am tired of crying out; I am hoarse; my eyes are failing me. He is desperate, the Psalmist. Not me. Just that his cry has touched off my anguish — it has risen, is flooding the soul.

"More numerous than the hairs of my head are they that hate me for no reason....

"Pour out Your wrath on them, and let Your burning anger overtake them." So *that's* where the Haggadah got it from! Straight from the psalm!

———————

Ps 72, **"The prayers of David the son of Yishai have come to an end."** I am taken aback: Is he taking leave from us? With this one short verse at the end of the psalm? Right smack in the middle of *The Book of Psalms*? How final; somber almost. Sure enough, the following psalm is by Asaph, and the next one, and the next, a whole slew of them. I am leafing through my *tillimel*, picking out the opening verses. After Asaph, the sons of Korakh. Look here! David's name popping up again. More "Sons of Korakh." Ethan the Ezrahite. David again! Well, never mind, there must be a reason for that shuffling.

I reread Psalm 72: **"Lee-Shlomoh"** is how it starts, meaning clearly, "To Shlomoh, or for Shlomoh." David implores God to grant his son judgment and righteousness, **"That he may judge the poor of the people, save the children of the needy, and crush the oppressor."** Crush the oppressor!? Solomon turned oppressor himself with his exorbitant taxes to feed his passions! Leeches all, the king and his cronies. It led to the split-up of the kingdom and civil war. "Unwise," my mother would have opined. "Very smart, King Solomon was, yes, and clever. But not wise."

King David then steps into the background: his prayers have come to an end. Like passing on the scepter?

CHAPTER 7 — PSALMS - II

Dreary weather closes in, like a protective shroud. I am sitting still, feeling safe and stranded and dully aware of the worthless minutes that trickle by, of the countless minutes and days to come, until Liberation, that momentous event, forever receding... like the coming of the Messiah. The Messiah... how unreal. I cannot grasp it. Yet Rambam (Hebrew acronym for Maimonides), the great Rambam, believed in his coming. He had made it an article of faith, *"Ah-ni ma'a-min"* ("I believe"): **I believe with total faith in the coming of the Messiah; and though he may dally, I do believe.** The savior. He will transport us to Jerusalem, the city of palaces and palm trees. The sky will be aglow, the air, soothing. He is dallying, just dallying.

The Messiah will come, I suddenly remember, if all Jews as one observe one single Shabbat. It is written in the Talmud. Silberstein told us. Every single Jew, just one Shabbat. The talmudic saying takes hold. But how do you get Jews to agree? All the Jews... Zalcman comes to mind... And the watchmaker of Kolbuszowa... And Madame Eichel... These three alone: how could they be made to sanctify the same Sabbath, abstain from carrying money, tearing paper, touching a pen? Is it possible? I set my mind to the task.

Zalcman. I could win him over. I would listen to his scientific explanation on the origin of the messianic idea and say,

"Now, Zalcman, let's assume that you are right. One Shabbat, one single Shabbat, what do you have to lose?"

"Nothing doing, I will not be part of some damn foolishness."

"But if you don't participate, nobody will know that you are right, they'll just blame you for holding back the coming of the Messiah."

Faux pas, wrong thing to say to Zalcman, he would shrug off such a silly accusation, or it would raise his hackles and he would defy the lot of them, arms across his chest. He is not afraid. One day on the Tachkemoni schoolyard, he had handed his eyeglasses to Menda and, in a cold fury, had turned on the boys who picked on him and Menda and Holtzer — the threesome who would stand and talk during the long morning and afternoon intermissions while the rest of us were running wild. Using his arms like battering rams, and swinging them clumsily — he couldn't throw a straight punch — he had given a drubbing to a couple of the tormentors. They never came back. No, I must not provoke Zalcman into squaring off with the Messiah crowd. I would say to him, "So what if you feel silly for one day, nobody will know, you are doing it for a friend, I would do a silly thing for you," and he would nod and say, "*Bon.*" We would shake hands. He was a man of his word.

Now, how do we win over the watchmaker of Kolbuszowa? "A consummate craftsman, a learned Jew, engaging," was how my father had described him. "And a big *appikkoirus* [heretic]," he had dropped in a confiding, almost conspiratorial tone. "One day the watchmaker told me," my father had continued with a glint in his eyes, "that he left the more challenging repair jobs for *Shabbas*: 'I can concentrate much better,' he explained. 'It is so peaceful, with our benighted Jews in *shul* all morning, rocking in prayer, and sleeping off in the afternoon their fat, heavy meal. No one around to bother me. It's a great day for special work. But the rare piece needing the most delicate attention, you see that antique clock over there?' " — my father was smiling — " 'I keep for Yom Kippur. A blessed day; long and quiet; an inspiring stillness envelops the *shtetl.* Not to mention Yom Kippur that falls on a *Shabbas.*' " I wonder, would the watchmaker sabotage the messianic redemption?

I imagine my father saying:

"The mensch in you cannot let the community down." My father was a master at appealing to the mensch in people. "I know, I know, it's nothing but superstition, you'll tell me."

"That's exactly what I'll tell them when they come bothering me."

"No. You can't. This is no time to go against the current. They know your opinions and beliefs. Set them aside, just this once. They will be touched by your show of solidarity. Besides," my father would add, and I can see the mischievous smile on his face, "you have no choice, if you want to have the last laugh."

They are both laughing. I am laughing too. They shake hands and say, "*mazel 'n brookhe*" ("good luck and blessing"), a formula as binding as an oath or a signed contract.

"I will do it for you, Bentsee'n [Yiddish pronunciation of Benzion]. But that miserable little *Moshee-akh* of yours had better not come near me, with his cherub's face and his white beard. Or is he forever young with a bushy black beard?"

"We were never introduced." More laughing, the three of us. My father, though deeply religious, liked to poke fun at the sacred.

"And I will not eat of the *livyoos'n* [leviathan]," the watchmaker declares emphatically. "Just the thought of it turns my stomach."

"Come the Messiah, you will *love livyoos'n.*" They burst out laughing. I am feeling merry. A felicitous paraphrase: my father is so clever! "You will *kill* for a piece of the *livyoos'n.*"

"Don't say that. No killing in messianic times."

"God forbid. Figure of speech. An unfortunate one, I admit. No, come the Messiah we will all have hearts of gold and souls of silk. Everything will be perfect. Your watches, for example, all the watches in the world will keep perfect time. You will be a man of leisure. You will live like a duke."

"I would *loathe* living like a duke. I want to work on watches."

"No watches. Come the Messiah you will *love* living like a duke." I always tended to pile it on.

"I am sorry," the watchmaker says, "that I signed on to that *meshigahs* [craziness]."

"Too late, you gave me *mazel 'n brookhe.*"

"I know. I will go through with it."

I savor the laughter a while longer.

But Madame Eichel... How can she be made to comply? Her case appears hopeless. My mother had given her the sobriquet "*ja sobie kupie*" (Polish for "I shall buy for myself") — the two women conversed in Polish when they would meet on the street. Madame Eichel was constantly buying clothes, even on the Sabbath, and she would gush over them. "That's all she ever talks about," my mother had said, "what she will buy for herself next. 'Will *I* surprise my husband.' She buys by the kilo the first strawberries, baby tomatoes, cherries, whichever is the season's first and costs a fortune. Her husband must be a business genius, or else he must have a money-making machine."

"Or be a nervous wreck," my father had countered.

"No," my mother had replied, "it would show on her. She is always cheerful; not a worry in the world."

Madame Eichel had been beside herself when, in the spring of 1942, the Germans imposed the yellow star and allotted only three stars per Jew, "To restrict us to three garments! Which do you pick? For what occasion? How can one live that way?"

I imagine Madame Eichel with her painted doll's face getting the urge on *the* Shabbat for that exquisite bolero outfit, "to welcome the Messiah in. What? Not even a bit of rouge? I'm not going to *kiss* him." How do you restrain a woman like her? My mother — she can. Walking slowly arm-in-arm with Madame Eichel, she says in her low key, enveloping, convincing tone reserved for sensitive family matters, "*Pani* [Madame] Eichel, true, it's all a men's thing, that craziness, as you call it, but we must support them, they work hard and carry a heavy burden, and who knows, for once they might have seen beyond the tip of their noses and gotten it right, I mean they may really understand what's going on in the world. And these bearded rabbis with their strictly-to-be-observed *Shabbas* may know something after all. Who are we to judge?" The two women would end up discussing a program of strict observance of that fateful Shabbat.

Well now, if you can win over these three, you can win over any Jew. I feel satisfied with myself.

The communist! How could I forget? The Jew with the deep brown eyes, in his beaten, wide-brimmed, dirty-gray homburg. The street intellectual, my father had called him. I picture him as he held forth to a group of youngsters in the hallway of the Moriah *shul* during *Yizkor* (the memorial service for the dead) on *Shavuoth*: Belonging to the proletariat was the ticket to survival. A coal mining community, producers, not *Luftmenschen* (people who live by their wits; air people, literally), surrounded by the country's working class.

He was soft-spoken, with a thick Yiddish accent, the man in the dirty-gray homburg, but he had exuded the steely conviction of the religious zealot, like the one who told me to cover my head, that walking around bareheaded offends God and brings down His wrath on all of us. No one, nothing, would ever sway the communist to observe the national Sabbath. He would stand there and demur, tight-lipped, even if he knew that it would work, more doggedly so if he knew. He would have the Messiah shot by a Russian commissar.

This hard-bitten communist won't budge. *He* is the enemy. And he is free to think, free to do as he pleases. So are the cheats, and the plain foul-tempered contrarians, we have free will, God created Adam and Eve with free will, He has no control over us, He can only reward and punish. And what of the Nicholayevski soldiers, those ten- and twelve-year old Jewish boys who were snatched from their homes and pressed into the Czar's army, never to return? And the poor souls who don't even know that they are Jews? How do we get all of them on our side? We will *never* be able to bring the Messiah. Surely the sages of the Talmud knew, the Jews of yore weren't any more virtuous than today's, only a handful left the comforts of Babylon to build the second temple. I feel like the butt of a hoax. I never believed seriously in the coming of the Messiah; I had a vague, unreflected notion of it, like of the end of time. I am angry just the same. Bombs, only bombs and more bombs on German cities — let them be smashed to dust! — will hasten the coming of Liberation. O, the heavenly drone of the Flying Fortresses on their way to Germany! I see in my mind's eye the V-formation of silvery birds. I imagine the crew, tiny, up high, in their aviator jackets and gloves, their headgear and goggles. Godlike, almost. No, not the Messiah. An army... A Jewish army.

Ps 74, **"Why, O God, have You forever forsaken us, have You fumed with anger against Your flock?...**

"Why do You withdraw Your right hand?...

"You split the sea with Your strength, You shattered the heads of sea monsters....

"You made fountain and river spring forth, You dried up mighty streams. I am carried along, far, far away...

"Yours is the day, Yours also the night; You have created the stars and the sun.

"You have drawn the borders on earth, You made summer and winter....

"Remember the covenant.... We carry it in our flesh.

"Arise, O God, fight Your fight...." Don't be afraid!

✽ ✽ ✽

Ps 78, **"Listen, my people, to my teaching; incline your ear to the words of my mouth.** Like *Ha'azeenu* (Moses' parting hymn and admonition).

The Psalmist's spare lines retrace scenes of yore, bright Tachkemoni moments: the crossing of the Red Sea on dry land;

God's munificence in the desert — He provided water and bread and fowl to a yammering and rebellious nation.

"**He led them with a cloud by day, with the light of fire all night long,** the cloud, the column of fire, day after day, a divine act more signal even than the parting of the Red Sea where He used a raging wind to trace a dry path. "God uses natural ways to perform His miracles," Silberstein had explained; must have been shallow to begin with, I guess. No tricks though with a cloud that moves in like clockwork in the morning for forty years in a row, and a column of fire that rises as soon as you can count three twinkling stars. Awesome, the cloud and the fire. They must have gotten used to it, though, for backslide they did. And He punished them, of course, steam blasting from His nostrils.

"**Yet He remembered that they were but flesh, a passing breath,** despite their trying Him in the desert, forgetting His deeds in Egypt, the plagues — oh, the poetic rendering of the plagues, but then, in the middle of the retelling, the Psalmist interjects,

"**He loosed His anger against them, wrath and indignation, and trouble** — the verse we recite on Seder night! Never liked it: the smart-alecky rabbis in the Passover Haggadah used it to calculate that whereas in Egypt the Egyptians were smitten with ten plagues, at the Red Sea they were crushed by 250 plagues! Never got the point of that cockemamie exercise.

And after some more falling out and making up,

"**...the Lord awoke as one asleep, like a strong man recovering from wine.** God, a sympathetic drunk. He is not tongue-tied, the Psalmist. *Met een stuk in Zijn kraag* ("With a load in His collar"), as one would say colloquially, or *Menne stuk in Z'n kluute* ("With a load in His balls"), as Gaston would put it.

"**And He chose the tribe of Judah, Mount Zion which He loved.... And He chose David His servant, and took him from the sheepfold.... To be shepherd over Jacob His people, and over Israel His inheritance.**"

A long journey of old retraced in seventy two verses of swift, poetic narrative. To tell us... why... to be good boys of course, as in Moses' admonition.

In the old days, at least, God kept His end of the deal.

———————

The most improbable thought crossed my mind: the Germans have won and will remain in control of Europe, indefinitely. Downright silly: everybody knows, except the Germans, that they are doomed, for the simple reason that they have not won yet and the Allies are getting stronger by the day. Yet seeing myself as an older boy, as a young man still sitting, slumped in the wooden chair in Gaston and Adrienne's bedroom, shook me up. What had begun as a harrowing wait had turned into a life sentence — for Gaston and Adrienne also.

I erased the unsettling image. It was clear that the only way to live would be to lead a normal life under a false identity, but not in Belgium, where my fake background and forged identity card could readily be unmasked. Reticences or unforeseen gaps in my life story would arouse immediate suspicion in the climate fostered by the Germans' unrelenting antisemitic propaganda and the teachings of the Catholic Church. After a German victory, the Church would no longer remain silent. And time would be on the side of the enemies. It was obvious that I would have to leave Belgium. The France of Laval and Maurras, the country that spawned the worst antisemites, would be even more dangerous: the French police and informers, Vichy with its dreaded militia, were doing zealously the German's work. My parents had feared them as much as the Germans. Italy had the pope. Holland... Dutch Jews had sought refuge in Belgium.

I chose Trondheim — it had made the news during the battle of Norway. It is a small distant place way up north of the capital — big-city people are too much aware of what is happening in the world — where there could not have been any Jews and whose inhabitants would know Belgium only as a name on the map. I would simply be the Belgian, that pleasant, civil, law-abiding and work-loving foreigner. That would pre-empt all suspicion about my real identity: people who don't know Jews have such grossly distorted views about us. Some even think that Jews have horns. The Germans portray us as ape-like creatures with thick lips and crooked noses, incapable of doing real work, living off Gentiles and trying to harm them.

I am launched on another fantasy. What a life, in the green valleys, along the fjords, at the foot of snow covered mountains. It is alluring, even when projected into a world returned to normalcy, a world without Germans. I could live as a Gentile, forever. No more fear, not a trace of doubt about staying alive. How tempting, to bury my burdensome past deep inside me, and live without obligations, without restraints. I could throw off the yoke, with a beautiful woman by my side, always, free to eat any food, to do anything. I won't have to become learned, or become a respected businessman, or acquire a profession. I will just work, grow food, chop wood; or work in a trade, carpentry, perhaps. I will not have to be an example. I will walk away from it all and be free of the burden to perpetuate the faith, to perpetuate anything. Free to be. Norway, the siren call for cutting the ties that I would have been unable to sever in Belgium.

Enjoying myself in bucolic Norway reminds me of the Carthaginians in Capua, which brings to mind the Israelites in Moab. Capua was all fun: Mr. Velghe, our Latin teacher, had grinned, which caused chuckles to ripple through the class. In Moab blood flowed, Jews killing Jews, zealots killing men who had left their tents, in droves, to follow the Moabite women. The Book of Numbers was quite explicit. It was such an obvious trap, and the Israelites went so fast, like harkening to a siren call. We were in fifth grade. I remember Silberstein's dour expression. What was it about Moabite women? What spell did they cast to get grown men to make such fools of themselves and worship the first idol they came across? I would not have bowed to her idol.

I liked my Norwegian fantasy. It ran smoothly from the first time; there were no retakes, let alone rehearsals, no loose ends, none of the technical hitches I had gotten into with almost all of my staple fantasies. For instance, circumcision, the ultimate betrayer in uncircumcised Europe, hadn't even crossed my mind. It was implicit in my fantasies that no doctor would ever have to see me. As for kissing, only she would have to be naked.

Norway, eventually, lost its appeal. I saw myself ever more clearly as the bearer of an awesome secret, the perpetual outsider. Trapped.

I will not be free until I am free to be a Jew.

Ps 79, "A psalm of Asaf. God, nations have come onto Your land, they have defiled Your temple, destroyed Jerusalem.

"They have given the dead bodies of Your servants as food to the birds of heaven, the flesh of Your devout ones to the beasts of the earth.

"They have shed their blood like water about Jerusalem, and there is no one to bury them. Can it happen today?...

"We have become an embarrassment to our neighbors and a laughingstock to those around us. We are, to this day.

"...Pour forth Your wrath upon the nations that do not recognize You — the Haggadah again! — and upon the kingdoms that do not invoke Your name. For they have devoured Jacob and devastated his habitation"; an imprecation that was followed, in the Haggadah, by that other borrowing — I am leafing back... there, from Psalm 69 — "Pour out Your wrath on them, and let Your burning anger overtake them." Words that gave me a chill, on Passover night, when they were recited while standing around the Seder table, with Elijah's cup filled to the brim, and the door to the dark hallway, wide open.

✡ ✡ ✡

Ps 88, "...You caused my acquaintances to shun me.... Would they? Would my classmates look the other way if they saw me?

Roald Bingen. What would he do? He would not say, "Come to my house after dark." He could not do it without asking his parents. They would be scared, I know. I see his large family in the crowded house, his father — his trimmed beard is graying — resting in an armchair, smoking a pipe; his mother, concerned, energetic, but harried. No. Roald Bingen says, "Go to church so-and-so, street such-and-such; our priest is pro-English."

Vanderlinden, my bench mate. A blunt antisemite. He says, "Are you still around?" He might even try to turn me in. He is worse even than Jennart, the pro-German who belonged to the Walloon Nazi Youth. We got along. I can hear Jennart say, I won't turn you in, but I can't help you; I won't betray our movement.

Vande Wijngaert, Menda's benchmate. He sat across the aisle from me. He spoke little, smiled a lot. You never knew what he was thinking. No, I would not want to run into him either.

"...Is it for the dead that You work wonders?... How sudden. David is getting roused.

"Is Your mercy recounted in the grave, Your faithfulness in the midst of desolation? Piling it on.

"Is Your wonder made known in the dark, and Your righteousness in a — must be 'forsaken' — **land?**

Not one: *three* shake-Him-up verses, stronger than the if-only-for-Your-sake entreaties that had stood out earlier. I leaf back:

(Ps 6). **"For there is no remembrance of You in death; who will render homage to You from the grave?"** Rather weak.

(Ps 30), **"What gain is there in the spilling of my blood? In my going down to the grave? Will the dust praise You? Will it declare Your truth?"** A bit stronger.

No, David, there is no reasoning with Him. He hardly punishes the Golden Calf idolaters who witnessed His miracles in Egypt and on the Red Sea — they jumped on the only transgression that was available to them; but us, the faithful ones, He delivers to the Germans.

I was standing by the window, with my back against the wall, in a spy's stance, watching the road below. Now and then a villager ambled along; a biker pedaled by; unaware that a Jew was looking at them, a naturalist observing a familiar species: secure Flemings. They gave me cover by just being around, busying themselves in their drab work clothes, sitting like statues on their bicycles, or clomping pensively in their wooden shoes. They don't have Jews on their minds, I thought with a sense of relief, with gratitude almost. They are not infected by their religion. They doze off in church, thank God; those who go. Flemings, first and foremost. Christians by name. Non-Jews is what they are. Sunday is a workday; they chop wood, garden, work in the farm yard. The day of the Lord. The Messiah, the priests call him; he came to save mankind, they want us to believe. The ravages, ever since he showed up. A Messiah is supposed to usher in peace and harmony. A hopeless task, even for God. That's why we keep our Messiah locked up. We dangle him, like a carrot in front of a donkey. The Never-Never Messiah. He is in hiding. He'll never come out. Smart. Doesn't want egg on his face. The Messiah who shows his face is, by definition, a false Messiah. Theirs, the Messiah-Of-The-Other-Cheek with the film actor's face, the blue eyes gazing into the distance; drives the nuns wild. His brides. Much good it does him. He had Maria Magdalena though, when he lived, a loose woman before she fell in love with him. Washed his feet. Followed him around. He didn't mind. Claimed to have sprouted from the seed of David. That would make him a cousin of our Messiah. What a pair. And some pedigree the two cousins have: going up the line from King David, via Ruth the Moabite, his great-grandmother, you get to Lot who fathered Moab with his older daughter without even knowing it: she got him drunk. Wait a minute, this calls for some serious thinking. I sat down, cross-legged, in the shady corner by the window.

Let's start all over: the two cousins are the offspring of King David who is the descendant, via Ruth, of Moab, the son of Lot and his older daughter.

Now, going up the line via King David's great-*grandfather*, Bo'az, Ruth's husband, you get to Peretz, Judah's son from his daughter-in-law Tamar whom he mistook for a whore — she had disguised herself and tricked him.

Oh yes, to be picayune, going up the line from King Solomon's son and successor, Rekhav'am, via his mother, Na'ama the Ammonite, you get to Lot again who fathered Ammon, Na'ama's ancestor, with his younger daughter; also in a drunken stupor — the sisters were getting on in years; they wanted offspring. They had just fled Sodom before it burned and engulfed its inhabitants. We had to skip that passage. Simple: "We now turn to page such and such," you knew that Silberstein was hiding something. But "We are skipping the sacrifices," no hanky-panky there. And a big sigh of relief. If it weren't for the Romans we would still be slaughtering the bulls and the oxen and the sheep and the doves and the... How bloody. And boring. Wait a minute... Would we? All the peoples who stayed on their land changed big time. Romans, Greeks, Egyptians,... Phoenicians,... Gauls. Different everything: language; religion; names. Champollion, a Frenchman, deciphered Egyptian. The Rosetta stone. Hieroglyphics: a closed book to the natives. The Greek and Latin writings. The Moors studied them; preserved them for us. Velghe said so in Latin class. The monks scribbled them down on parchment. Highbrow stuff is all it is now, for the professors. The classicists. And for getting into medical school.

Wouldn't we also have lost it all had we stayed on our land? Wait a minute... We were exiled *because* we were losing it all. "And he did the evil in the eyes of the Lord." King after idolatrous Jewish king. "And because of our sins we were exiled from our land" — the festivals' *Musaf* prayer. Let's get this straight: We sit on the land. We forsake the Torah. We get yanked off the land. Then cling to the Torah, *etz kha'im*, as to the tree of life. We return to our land. Sin. Get yanked off. Wait a minute... What is this? Land and Torah don't seem to go together. The land is making us into a nation like all other nations. *Verboten*. But that's what we wanted: "Anoint a king over us, to rule us. He shall lead us into war. Like all the nations." Samuel gave in. Even crusty old mean-spirited Samuel — I never liked him — gave in. How do you prevent this land/morals thing? The Messiah. Eureka! *He* is supposed to break the vicious cycle. Come the Messiah, we'll dwell in our Land *and* remain virtuous. But he won't come, the bastard! By definition!

Here is a true honest-to-God messiah who won't show his face, and there is the blond, blue-eyed, so-called messiah who made things a thousand times worse. *Sie stinken Beide* (They both stink): Heine's verdict! Heinrich Heine! The disputation, back in the Middle Ages, between the rabbi and the bishop in front of the assembled Jews and Christians. In the presence of the king and queen of Spain. I recall Menda's mother reading excerpts of Heine's long poem to my friend and me, in her kitchen, one Saturday afternoon. The debate's loser was to adopt his opponent's religion, on the spot: the rabbi would get baptized; or the bishop circumcised. Madame Zangen declaimed the verses with obvious delight, exposing with a smile the comical strand running through the deadpan seriousness of the contest. The argument took an unexpected turn when the bishop denigrated *Toysfes Yomtov*, the talmudic commentary. Interesting, Heine knew of it. The name at least. Now that was too much for our rabbi to bear: to impugn the authority of *Toysfes Yomtov*! He rose to its defense. Argument drew counter-argument, the comical vein now clearly exposed. The debate dragged on. The public, including the royal couple, were growing weary. "Who do you think is right?" the king asked the queen. I see Madame Zangen grinning as she read to us the queen's answer, "I don't know, but I think they both stink."

Zalcman. Where is Zalcman?

I gazed again at the road.

A woman pedaled into view on the opposite side: Long hair, oval face, deep-set eyes. Full lips. The undulating depression in the middle of her ample skirt evoked long shapely thighs. Sleek ankles. Not from Duizend Appels. She disappeared.

I returned to my chair.

✡ ✡ ✡

Ps 90, **"A prayer of Moses, the man of God.** An oldie! From *shul*! Like a ray of sun brightening up the room.

"Lord, a refuge You have been for us in every generation; *ma'on*, an abode, huge, in my mind's eye, hewn out of the rock, where one feels safe, out of reach.

"Before the mountains were brought forth and You formed the earth and the universe, from eternity to eternity You are God.... From before, from *way way* back. There is no beginning and no end... timelessness... an endless void. Just God, timeless, sitting on His ass, everywhere and nowhere. Then, one day,... no, there is no day yet; then... no, there is no "then"; "then" is a point in time. Simply: He... Decides... To create... The universe. Voilà! That is when He started counting time: Day one. Day two. So then, His universe, the darkness I peer into at night, is not an endless void? Why not? Couldn't He have filled it with stars? Idiot! If it is endless, how can you fill it? It would take forever. Well then, our universe is just a floating ball of stars? Like dust particles suspended in the air? Is there a furthermost star? Wait a minute: Light-year: the distance light traverses in a year. There; a yardstick based on time. We have meters and light-years; minutes and eons. So the clock, *the* clock, started running at the beginning of Creation, and it will run forever because the universe will last forever. The minute hand, though, moves slowly... I give up.

"...For a thousand years, to You, are like yesterday... like a watch in the night. The ice ages. The Egyptian dynasties, thousands of years. And *galut* (exile), two thousand years of it; still going. Each one of them, a watch in the night.

And we, in comparison, are like **"grass, fresh and wholesome in the morning, to wither away and dry up in the evening.** Ephemeral. Gripping. Me too?

"...We go through our years in a whimper. Man: a blade of grass. His life: a puff of air. Sobering. It erases the fear of the German.

I read it again. And again. The Hebrew holds me in its spell. I continue:

"Our life span is seventy years, eighty, perhaps, if one is strong, and most of it is travail and deception; for it ends

speedily, and we fly away." Still an eternity. As long as the Germans don't get me.

Ps 91, "He who dwells in the safety of the Most High.... The liturgy again...
    "For He will save you from the snare that springs shut....
    "...under His wings shall you find refuge....
    "Do not fear the terror of night — my heart quickens; **the arrow that flies by day** — won't get *me*; **the pestilence that stalks in the dark;** *Kettev* — must be something terrible — **that rages at noon.** Then, gushing forth:
    "A thousand may fall at your side, and ten thousand at your right, it will not come near you. I feel invulnerable. But those fallen multitudes at my sides, the deported... No! Not my people! The Germans! He means the Germans!
    "Just look around and you'll see the wicked get their due....
    "No evil will befall you, and no plague will come near your tent, my hideout.
    "For He will order his angels to watch over you, wherever you go.
    "They will carry you upon their hands, I am riding high again, **lest you stub your foot against a stone."** And I am crushing underfoot a young lion and three fearful beasts I don't recognize. My heart expands.

Fifty years later, in the spring of 1993, I went to Belgium to take part in a joint eightieth birthday celebration for Gaston and Adrienne. The passenger sitting next to me on the flight from New York turned out to be a student and teacher of Sufi, a deeply religious woman. She seemed pleased when, in answer to her question, I told her that the open book in my hands was a psalter. She mentioned Psalm 91: did I know it? "Oh yes," I said, "this one I know almost by heart." She asked me to read it, and I began translating Psalm 91 aloud. A smile spread across her face. It soon gave way to a deepening seriousness. Gazing ahead, she would nod in recognition and chime in, helping me along. She knew the psalm by heart. After reciting herself **"A thousand will fall at your left, ten thousand at your right, it will not come near you,"** she told me that she had fervently read Psalm 91 every day of her son's tour in Vietnam, trying with all her might to deflect harm from his path. She saw the question in my eyes. "He came back," she said — I did not avert my gaze — "...unharmed." Her eyes were shining. The other question on my mind, irksome, like a parasite, about the thousand on the left and the ten thousand on the right, went undetected, to my relief; it dissipated, like mist, in the glow on her face. She had willed it. Just as I had, in hiding, when I would aim my verses like arrows, or deploy them like shields. I was moved to tell her about my reading of the Psalms in hiding. A few sentences. She listened with wide open eyes, then turned her face and bowed her head, as if to collect herself. Or to say grace? Confront once more the shadow of death? I waited. She drew herself up and looked at me, then nodded. I had never mentioned my psalm-reading to anyone.

✡ ✡ ✡

That fall and winter, a man from Drongen, a small town near Ghent, came to Belsele on Sundays, to court Gaston's sister Alice. His name was Maurice De Viaene, a shoemaker by trade. Alice was of delicate health and ate sparingly. Among other presents, Maurice brought every Sunday a delicious white bread with a brown glazed crust that he baked especially for his beloved. To get a taste of it was a rare treat.

One day during the Christmas vacation Gaston's mother, Léontine, came by our house. I was alone downstairs — Gaston was at work, Sylvain was at Simoneke's and Adrienne was out on a short errand. Léontine chatted with me as we waited for Adrienne's return. The conversation turned quickly to Maurice, "a fine man, a master shoemaker." His custom-made shoes were prized for their fineness and elegance, "real works of art," was how Alice's mother described them to me. "Fetching a lot of money these days." Maurice was a good man. She was happy for her daughter.

I said, "He knows about Marcel and Johnny."

"Yes."

"Does he know about me and Sylvain?" I already knew the answer. And Léontine knew the import of my question.

"Yes," she answered.

She looked at me with her big brown eyes, and lowered her voice. "Do not worry," she said, "he is one of us."

I kept looking at her, waiting for some credentials, or a reassuring hint.

"He knows English," she said.

Alice got married in February and moved to Drongen.

By casting me in the role of a responsible older brother, my Sunday visits, aside from giving me an invigorating break, had become a valuable prop in our cover story of the broken family. Julia and Irène came to expect my visits. Yet, Adrienne spaced them three, four weeks apart: they were, after all, a brazen exercise, and though it was highly unlikely that the visiting charade would be exposed — no one even asked Adrienne why I never arrived with the early afternoon train to enjoy more of the weekend — it was deemed safer not to repeat it too often. Adrienne was also thinking ahead: on the long days of spring, the late evening trains would arrive and depart in daylight.

My visits were also irregular. I would arrive unannounced; no fixed schedule; nothing for Julia or Irène to track or to expect. They only knew that I liked coming to Duizend Appels as often as the family situation and my school work permitted. They would tease Sylvain:

"Bet you Henri will show up tonight."

"Oh... again," he would say resignedly, drawing chuckles.

Their welcoming and unquestioning attitude allayed my nervousness. It emboldened Adrienne to call, on a rare Sunday, an extra visit, when the morning sky held out the promise of a nice day. She would knock on the stairs and whisper, "Dress up and come down. You got here last night." Once she called me down on a Saturday morning, giving me a long weekend. No one alluded to my skipping Saturday morning classes; a trifle, given my standing. It would also have been too personal a question: my schooled Flemish, using the formal "*U*" for "you," my politeness, greeting everybody with deference, my reserve, precluded all familiarity. My brother had no inhibitions. His was the Duizend Appels code of behavior.

"Hey Julia," he would blurt out, "what do you say of city folk who think that milk comes out of a bottle?"

She would burst out laughing, covering her mouth with her hand.

"Some rascal of a brother you have there," she would turn to me. "Taking some liberties, that boy."

"Henri, Sylvain is not going back any more," Irène once chided me. "All that freedom. And once he takes up with a local girl," she continued, "*allez*, you know how that goes." Lovesick Irène could be counted on to bring up affairs of the heart. She confided hers to Adrienne. And Adrienne told me.

The pleasure of the visit would grow as the morning wore on, to peak at the dinner table and the early afternoon coffee. Yet I didn't quite feel that I belonged, not on the back roads, not in the café, or on the front patio. I felt most comfortable biking where no one knew me. A bicyclist could be a stranger from a distant place, like Sinaai or Lokeren, just passing by; he would not be scrutinized like a pedestrian. My secret kept churning inside me. Coming out the front door in the morning to signal my presence, or quashing the reflex to bolt behind the drape at the sight of a visitor, got my heartbeat to spike. I felt apart even when the American Flying Fortresses would drone overhead on their way to Germany. In clear weather they brought the people out of their houses. I would also come out and stare at the glistening armada rumbling on high in the radiant blue sky. Awesome, that drone. Another bombing run. They were flying over more often. In greater numbers. To wipe out the German cities. I was exulting. A joy suffused with rage, the glee of vengeance. And conscious not to show it: the villagers were smiling and exchanging light-hearted remarks, judging by the tone of their voices. Were they merely entertained?

"*Schuun*" ("Beautiful"), Adrienne said under her breath the first time we had stood squinting aloft, with our hands shielding our eyes.

"*Ja*," I said, softly.

Our neighbors began to drift back indoors when the planes were still dots of light in the distance. I made sure not to remain the last one gazing.

Gaston, and especially Adrienne and Sylvain, seemed more relaxed than I was. For them, leading double lives had become second nature. Sylvain moved as if he had been born in Belsele. He even told Adrienne that he wanted to be an altar boy. Could she arrange it? "It will make me look even more Catholic." He had seen them in processions, and heard them sing at High Mass which he attended occasionally with her.

"Okh God," Adrienne said laughing, "they do look nice in their outfit" — a white garb with red trim. "No, Sylvaintje, you can't come anywhere near these people, from the priest on down. They'll wonder about you, start asking you questions."

"I'll know what to say."

"No, no, for God's sake. After the war, in Antwerp, you can do anything you want, wear any costume you like."

A short time after Alice's wedding, on the Saturday of one of my longer weekends in the open, Adrienne sent me on an errand to Gaston's mother in Belsele Village. I had a brief chat with Léontine, then dropped in at the forge, before heading back home. I was passing by the kitchen door in the back of the house, when two men in city clothes — top coat and hat — walked up the yard. They blocked my path. "*Gerechtelijke Politie*" ("Judiciary Police," the Belgian equivalent of the FBI), said the shorter one, his eyes boring into mine. He had produced an open, rather small, dark-leather wallet of sorts. I froze.

"Does the Van Damme family live here?" he asked. The other had stood back a step.

"Yes."

They left me alone and proceeded to the kitchen, in the rear. I hurried back to Duizend Appels and told Adrienne about my encounter.

Shortly thereafter Gaston walked in, with the story:

Two Jewish women the elder Van Dammes had sheltered, Mrs. Karfyol and her widowed mother, Mrs. Freifeld, were found asphyxiated, under a mattress, in their apartment in Antwerp. They had vacated their room at the Van Dammes' to accommodate guests at Alice's wedding. Mrs. Karfyol's husband had been deported. Her two children were sheltered in the township of Ekeren, in the vicinity of Antwerp. The two women would visit them every month and bring their rescuers money for the children's upkeep. They moved around quite boldly: their neighbor in Antwerp would let them through his house into his backyard where they climbed over the wall and sneaked into their apartment to get things and spend the night. "My parents' address was found on one of them," Gaston said. "The men reassured my mother that they are good Belgians, that they are on the good side." The Van Dammes' extensive involvement with helping Jews came to light. The agent who accosted me, Gaston told us, had boasted that he knew, as soon as he laid eyes on me, that I was a Jew.

"Oh yeah, the smart aleck," I grumbled. I found the remark offensive.

Gaston did not return to work that afternoon.

The agents intended to interrogate Alice as well, in Drongen. Léontine insisted on coming along to introduce them and reassure her daughter.

The men from Antwerp, Albert van Kerckvoorde and Gérard Beckers, were on the good side indeed: they belonged to a cell of the underground Socrates Group, operating out of the Ministry of Justice. Léontine Van Damme became a courier carrying money and ration cards for the Group. Her daughter Maria ran the household during Léontine's frequent absences. Shortly before the end of the Occupation the Germans discovered the cell. Van Kerckvoorde fled to Belsele, then to Drongen. Beckers was caught. He killed himself.

I am scouring *Het Vrije Waasland* for another tidbit when the sky darkens, suddenly. It is hanging low, hugging the windows like a gray, diaphanous shroud. In the unusual dimness the printed page looks a mottled gray. A godsend: I can quieten down, slump back in my chair and wait for it to clear; it will. A normal wait with an end. It propels the day forward. It takes me into a softly lit private library, a cozy island somewhere in the damp grayness of a big city. The private library in the big city has a sliding dark wooden ladder to reach the volumes way up by the ceiling, like in the movies. Books and books. About islands and continents, vastness and mystery, deserts and rain forests; about oceans and mountain ranges, explorers and civilizations; the history of nations. About everything there is to know. About the worlds I want to grasp.

The quieter, slower moving world under the heavy sky, the darkness in the afternoon, favor the tranquil indoor occupations. The library in my daydream becomes that of Mr. Van Bijlen, our geometry teacher. He brings me textbooks and class assignments, allowing me to keep abreast of my Christian classmates. I suddenly miss learning. I will resume my studies. I will.

Ps 104, **"Bless the Lord, O my soul. O Lord my God, You
are very great. You are clothed in glory and splendor.** Why am
I moved?

**"You cover Yourself with light as with a garment, You span
the heavens like a curtain.** It pulls me along.

**"...You who ride the clouds, who move on the wings of the
wind....**

"You established the earth not to be moved ever.

The entire earth is offered up in one riveting poem, high
mountains and lush valleys, oceans teeming with life where
ships sail, springs where the creatures of the field quench their
thirst, forests alive with the song of birds, where animals roar
for prey in the dead of night. The sun rises above the horizon,
when man goes forth to work — I picture a contented farmer in a
sunny place, as remote from Belsele and its toiling inhabitants as
Liberation is from the present moment. A glide through space.
The earth below is alive. I touch down and take off at will.

**"All of them wait for You, to give them their food in due
season.**

"You give, they gather in....

**"You hide Your face, they panic; You withdraw their breath,
they perish and to dust they return.**

**"You send forth Your spirit, they are created; and You re-
new the face of the earth.**

The God of Creation, the Master of the Universe,

**"Who looks at the earth, and it trembles, Who touches the
mountains, and they smoke."**

I recall our geography teacher's impressive atlas of the earth,
the huge maps of the continental land masses with rivers running
like veins, surrounded by the blue of the seas and the oceans, and
covered with color patches: various shades of yellow for deserts
and sandy soil, of green for fertile lands, alluvial plains and virgin
forests, of tan and brown for relief, with the Himalayas, the Alps,
the Rockies, the Andes stretching out, dark and imperious; the
maps of climates and rainfall. Interesting, but remote; a memory
of a bygone era. Only the geography of war is real, war on land
and sea; and, from the air, on German cities. The only significant borders are the moving front lines. The globe has become
a sprawling battlefield with a few inviolate places: Eretz Yisrael,
the nest I cannot fly to; mythical America, vast and impregnable,

shining in glory and wealth; and a few regions, mere names, like India, South America, the North and South Poles.

The psalmist's bird's eye view of the earth is the exhilarating one.

It is a quiet day. I sense the peace that emanates from the land, from the fields and the tree-lined meadows, from the woods, the hedged-off orchards and winding country roads. The land: stretching far, protective, sustaining. Lasting. Mystical. It is the Lord's, the Torah says. We are only tenants, from jubilee year to jubilee year: on the fiftieth year it reverts to its previous owner. I recall how puzzled I was: you pay for land, to return it a few years hence? Not so, Silberstein explained: you pay only for the number of harvests left until the jubilee year; so that no family in Israel can be dispossessed. Land remains, money can fritter away, could be stolen. Without the protection of the jubilee year, those forced to sell, for whatever reason, may end up destitute, they and their descendants, while some schemers amass vast land holdings and pass them on.

But how was it supposed to work? The tribes of Israel get a share of the Land proportionate to their numbers. Each member of the tribe is allotted a parcel. Now, that land belongs to him, his descendants and their descendants in perpetuity. The law of the jubilee takes care of that. Fine. The parcels get smaller and smaller. Can't feed all the mouths. One of the heirs can buy out his siblings. The land stays in the family. Fine. If they waste their money and become poor, well, too bad. No, wait a minute: they can buy a house in town; it's like owning land. Do the jubilee laws apply to a house? I don't remember. Silberstein did not go into details. Now, suppose someone dies without heirs... Never mind, the jubilee works: the antisemites would not have waited a minute to debunk it if it did not hold water. I never heard a bad word about the jubilee. One thing is for sure: if it were adopted, there would not be the few landowners on the one side and the host of miserable peasants on the other side, serfs really, like in the Middle Ages. Come to think of it: no more fighting over land, over territory; if the whole world adopted the Torah, that is.

I am launched: The whole world has gone Jewish. We are no longer Judaism's endangered guardians. We are the original, the Jews. The aristocracy. I see us with that smug, confident stride.

No, on the contrary, Don't flaunt it, our sages say. The sin of haughtiness. Will cause resentment. Antisemitism. Worse. No. "Be modest" is the watchword. I see myself practicing modesty: I keep my head slightly bent; I am ultra-polite; I deflect deftly, but not to the point of rudeness, *the* question, Are you an Ur-Jew? But then, of course, our names will give us away: Grunstein, Steinberg, Bergson, Sonnenfeld, Feldman. Can't do a thing about that.

A world where Judaism and Jewishness are the norm. What relief. A world familiar with the Bible and the Talmud, respecting our learning instead of burning our books. No more murderers and robbers; only crooks and thieves; and liars and hypocrites; and smugglers of gold and diamonds and currencies; and informers.

An all-Jewish world. How nice. But how dull! The lively African women — they go bare-breasted, someone said — covered from head to toe and turned serious, all of a sudden, worried, even. The daring, provocative Gentile girls who look so alluring on the back seats of their boyfriends' motorcycles, thighs bared and hair blowing in the wind as they zoom by us on our way to synagogue — turned modest and domesticated. An entire world headed for synagogue on Saturday morning, regurgitating the same old prayers, the same old passages in the Bible and the Talmud. We would lose the precious Sunday. The prayers — they would no longer call down God's wrath on the nations that seek to destroy us: everybody is a Jew. And the priests will no longer incite the mobs against the Christ killers. How stupid: there *are* no more priests. They have converted. Some will even want to become *rabboonim* (rabbis). They are all Jews now, even the pope, no, not the pope, God hardens his heart, like Pharaoh's before the exodus. He is made to watch how his erstwhile flock gets converted, he witnesses the circumcision of the Swiss Guard, one after the other, in St. Peter Square, without anesthesia — wouldn't be kosher; he gets apoplectic, dies of a heart attack, no, the fun would stop, he has to stay alive and fuming, like Pharaoh. How funny, the whole scene — I am pleased with my ingenuity; the divine equivalent of an off-color joke. No, God doesn't joke; dispenses bliss or visits calamities. That's all. No sense of humor. O là, I hit upon something that God does *not* have, a sense of humor; certainly not for off-color jokes: whom will He tell them to? To us, humans? Inconceivable. My mother had felt embarrassed when my father told a *risqué* joke on an evening with the Janowskis and the Rosenzweigs. "These are jokes for your cronies," she had told him afterwards.

Cronies: God hasn't any. No peers, no cronies. By definition. So, He can't tell jokes. And the Devil is not a peer, just a protagonist who can goad Him, rope Him into all kinds of unsavory business, like that bet at Job's expense. How heartless. As if Job's wife and children, the servants, the maids, the livestock were nothing more than chips at the gaming table. Silberstein told us once that the Devil represents our inclination for evil, our insubordination to God's law. In the Job saga, the real villain is God. He could have turned His bet into a farce, like Haman's. That would have spared the innocent. But then, God did not stage that farce: His name does not appear once in the Book of Esther. Of course not: no sense of humor. Besides, the Book of Esther is about Jews, not about the Children of Israel. God has nothing to do with the Jews any more. Some common mortal wrote Esther. Like Molière; *he* could have written it: the timing of the incidents including Haman's entrances, his puffing himself up, his stumble, his wife Zeresh foretelling his downfall, his hanging. Where was I? How did I end up with Zeresh?

I reach for *Het Vrije Waasland.*

☆ ☆ ☆

Ps 106, **"Halleluyah....**

"Who can express the mighty deeds of the Lord? — like the song, inspired by the psalm, no doubt: "Who can express the mighty deeds of Israel, who can count them?" Catchy, sung as a canon. It lingers for a brief while.

Then, after some more niceties, out of the blue,

"We have sinned just as our fathers have....

A litany of sins this long psalm turns out to be, our forefathers' sins from the moment they left Egypt to their settling down in the Land of Canaan:

"...They rebelled at the sea, at the Red Sea; "are there not enough graves in Egypt? To die in the desert is why you took us out of there?" is how they turned on Moses when they saw Pharaoh's horsemen closing in. Sounds so Jewish.

"And they lusted in the desert; for meat. The divine manna that sustained them just fine was... too bland.

"And they were jealous of Moses — Datan and Aviram, the insurrectionists.

"And they sullied their honor with the likeness of an ox that eats grass. What a putdown. The Golden Calf episode... The suspense it generated in Silberstein's class.

"And they scorned the lovely land... That had to be the spy fiasco, their defeatist report: "The inhabitants are giants, their towns are impregnable fortresses." **"And He swore that He would fell them in the desert,** the generation that knew slavery — forty years of wandering would do it — for losing heart, for suggesting that they return to Egypt. Servitude makes you weak and fearful, Silberstein had explained. Their children would inherit the land.

"And they attached themselves to Baal Pe'or; idol worship, God's worst fear. The Moabite women! The temptresses. God Almighty! Ditching Him, after forty years of His manna, and fowl, and water; and the cloud by day and the column of fire at night. A cuckold, you might say. **"...And a plague broke out in their midst.** Beat up on Israel, the unfaithful bride, like the gendarme, Julia's neighbor. Hold it: does God know what I'm thinking right now? He might. I'd rather be careful. Too late. Well... I am not afraid.

"And they angered Him at the waters of strife; and it was bad for Moses because of them. Slew the rock with his stick instead of talking to it nicely. The water gushed forth anyway. But he was barred from the Promised Land. "Because of you," Moses said in his parting address — quite ruefully, it had seemed to me. Lacks a sense of proportion, God does.

"They did not destroy the peoples that the Lord had told them. What? That too is a sin? Quite bloodthirsty, the Psalmist. They annihilated Amalek, they destroyed the Emorite, and the people of Bashan. Not enough? And why did Midian have to be destroyed? Didn't Moses find refuge in Midian when he fled Egypt? And a wife? Didn't Yithro, Moses' father-in-law, teach him how to administer a large, unruly flock without running himself into the ground?

"But they mingled with the nations, and learned their ways. "Learning their ways" seems to be the rub. As long as the others become Jews, it's fine. The proof: a multitude of non-Jews — *airev rav* — attached themselves to us as we fled Egypt. Further back even! Ephraim and Menashe, Joseph's sons from an Egyptian woman, the ancestors of two mighty tribes. And Moses' children from his Midianite wife, the daughter of Yithro, the high priest of Midian. And Ruth! Ruth the Moabite! David's great-grandmother, the Messiah's ancestor! A lot of mingling back then. Not like in our time; taboo stuff. We lose them when they marry non-Jews. Joseph, my mother's cousin, married a Flemish woman. He wouldn't listen to the relatives; not even to my mother. No one had him over since. He would drop by to talk with my mother, came by before leaving for Nice. His Flemish wife wouldn't go with him, "They are not after me." She was seen, after he was gone, walking arm-in-arm with German officers. "*Einfach eine Dirne*" ("A downright whore"), my mother had muttered. "A man goes and buries himself, with his own hands, *into* the ground. He wouldn't listen. 'Not if God Himself came down,' he told me. That's what one gets for going off the straight path." I got the message.

He had a deep voice, Joseph. Dark and tall, with delicate hands. I muse: a man in love is unstoppable. As mysterious a phenomenon, but without the dark, terrifying side, as an enraged man wielding a knife, about to kill. Murder is like crossing a fateful red line, never to return. Murder, I can't fathom murder. He took a smuggler to Nice, Joseph did, came to say goodbye to my mother. Made it to Cuba. Cuba... Freedom on a tropical island. The thought leaves me wistful.

"And they worshipped their idols....

"And they sacrificed their sons and their daughters to demons — to Moloch?

Some way to recount, and in gripping verse, a people's historic journey! Is this what is meant by "The Sins of Israel"? Was this what Mr. Dignieffe, a high school teacher of ours, meant when he chided a student — a Gentile — whom he had chastised: "You protest as if I were accusing you of all the sins of Israel"?

✡ ✡ ✡

Gray daylight filters feebly through the windows — blind eyes turned inwards. The printed page is a dark blur. The house is suspended in a mist; floating. It is eerily quiet. The world has slowed down. Dreary weather is conducive to mellower moods; it favors the inner life. I am relaxed.

Adrienne is walking up the stairs. "Rain on the way," she whispers in the doorway. She lowers the garret window; it squeaks and lands with a clang of the metal bar. Down the stairs she goes. She is gone.

It is raining. Timid drops: they leave thin streaks in a downward slant on the window panes. There is a faint flicker through the celestial shroud, followed by a much delayed whimper: a storm, way out in the distance. It lifts my spirits. I sit upright and wait, wishing the storm to come my way. The flashes get brighter, the rumbling in the sky, louder, like boulders crashing and rolling on. Then, after a suspenseful pause, right over our roof, a deafening conflagration sends tremors down to the foundations of the earth. The house is under siege. I am rattled, yet unafraid, excited even, by the fury unleashed from the sky. I have always been stirred by violent storms, by the massive waves, dark monsters crashing at my feet against the dike on the North Sea coast — I would hold on to the steel-pipe railing, battling the wind and catching the spray in the face; by blizzards and torrential rains. Inclement weather can only affect the free, drive them indoors. Doomsday weather would be the ultimate equalizer. I imagine people holed up, like me. Germans also. Not a good day for them to be out hunting for Jews.

The storm is moving away, leaving a torrential downpour in its wake — sheets of water, blasts of wind. The driving rain is pelting the roof and lacerating the glass panes. I listen intently to the dense score, above my head, of a myriad of high and low notes, with the insistent percussions of the heavy drops generating the base line and the soft tinkle of the smaller drops providing continuous harmonic variations. Gusts of howling wind change the score, taking it into higher octaves and generating bursts of stronger claps on roof and windows.

I move to the side of the left window. Standing with my back against the wall I watch the rain drops crash on the glistening cobblestones of the deserted road. The bending treetops seem pulled by their branches, like women by their hair. I stand awed by the violence of the elements. The treetops have swayed back, defiant. They bend over again, in fits, as if reeling from staccato blows, bowed but indomitable. I watch and listen, then pull myself away. I step into the garret, to experience the rainstorm in the narrow chamber. It is like being in a wooden box showered with marbles. I sit on the bed, head bent and eyes closed, open my eyes and watch the rain stream down the sloping glass panes, sensing almost physically the force of the downpour, feeling close to nature, without fear and without the rending desire to be out, to be free.

The rain is letting up. A faint thunderclap rumbles off in the distance. Light filters, then streams, back in. The show is over. I am standing in the doorway of the bedroom. I wait; and wait some more, and feel adrift again, longing.

Adrienne is coming up the stairs. She opens the garret window: I am not to do it, for a window rising on its hinges from the roof without Adrienne's head appearing through the opening — she might even be seen downstairs — would be a baffling sight to someone coming off the path that runs behind the backyards. It might just happen so. Adrienne is now in the bedroom putting some laundry in the armoire. A short exchange, whispered — Julia, our neighbor, is at home — and she is gone, like a summer breeze.

✠ ✠ ✠

Ps 113, **"Halleluyah; praise, ye servants of the Lord,
Praise the Name of the Lord.**

Familiar... Yes, it *is* the *Hallel*, a string of joyous hymns sung on the festivals by *hazan* and choir and the standing congregation. Six psalms — I counted them — form the *Hallel*. I know entire passages by heart.

Praise for His compassion:

He **"raises the poor from the dust."**

He makes **"the barren woman a joyful mother of children."**

Rejoicing about deliverance (Ps 114):

"When Israel went forth from Egypt, The House of Jacob from a people of alien tongue,

"The sea beheld and fled, the Jordan turned back;

"The mountains skipped like rams, hills, like sheep."

Ridicule for the nations' idols (Ps 115):

"A mouth they have but do not speak, eyes they have, but do not see.

The singing in *shul* would well up, full-throated, with "the Lord blessing the House of Israel, the House of Aaron" — I hear it — and resound toward the psalm's end:

"The heavens are the Lord's, but the earth he has given to the children of man.

"Not the dead will praise the Lord, nor will all who go down into silence.

Another tug at His beard, David, or Psalmist, whoever you are. You have said that before, more than once: He must keep us alive, it's in His interest. Sure enough, "We will bless the Lord henceforth and forever. Halleluyah." That last verse we would roar.

I am reading on, revisiting the familiar; down to Psalm 118, the *Hallel*'s last:

"Praise the Lord for He is good....

"From narrow straits I called upon the Lord....

"...I shall not fear; what can man do to me? Would have to find me first.

"...I will outlast my enemies.... I will. I know I will.

"The nations surround me....

"They surround me like bees....

"I shall not die, I shall live.... A life-and-death struggle. I am in it.

"He tormented me, but He did not deliver me to Death.... They will not get me.

"This is the day the Lord has made, let us be merry and rejoice in it.

Joyous even this, more somber, psalm. Then, to my surprise,

"Please, O Lord, rescue, please do; Please, O Lord, bring success, please do." The two supplications the devout would send aloft, shouting each plea twice — four fervent responses to the *hazan*'s lead. In the prayer book it jumped off the page, a prayer unto itself with its larger, boldface type. In the *Book of Psalms*, it is just one verse — the twenty-fifth.

I finish the psalm. I close my *tillimel*. Leaning slowly forward, heels resting on the front rung of the chair, head over knees, lips pinched and eyes closed, I beam heavenward:

"Please, O Lord, rescue, please do; ME... ME... LIBERATION...

"Please, O Lord, rescue, please do; MY PEOPLE... MY PEOPLE... FROM DEPORTATION...

"Please, O Lord, bring success, please do; TO ME... TO ME... AS A MAN...

"Please, O Lord, bring success, please do; TO MY PEOPLE... TO MY PEOPLE... ERETZ YISRAEL...

I would return to Psalm 118, make my way, deliberately, to verse 25, lean forward and fire off. One petition. The next. The third. The last.

I am ensconced in a tall tree with my arsenal, my provisions, and my hammock improvised from the immaculate greatcoat of a high officer I shot clear in the nape. Countless Germans lie dead, but their number never dwindles, depriving me of a sense of victory. The fantasy is about to peter out when an idea bubbles up. I climb down and appear, dangling by the arms from the lowest branch of a tree, a couple of feet off the forest floor.

The shock on their faces! By common reflex, a phalanx of rifles is leveled at me.

"Are you scared of me?" I say, with a smile, in a flawless German.

As if by common accord, all rifles swing upward, their barrels forming a thicket.

"May I?" I ask, just as politely, smiling. And I come down on the soft forest floor.

An officer breaks through the ranks.

"*Was ist denn das!?*" he barks.

I smile, as if to say, "You have three guesses, you *Dummkopf.*"

"Where are the others!?" he barks.

The others... that will be my trump card! The information I am presumed to have. To those Teutonic minds, it takes an army to engage one.

"I will speak only to your commanding general," I say, calmly but firmly.

"What!? You are refusing to obey a German officer!?" Pitch and volume rose, as if this time he had really meant to bark. And, with his hand reaching down to his holster, "*Du Saujude du!*" ("Sau" is German for "sow," meaning "you sow-issued Jew.")

It is my turn. Matching his pitch and volume, I shout,

"*Jawohl, du Saudeutscher du!*" He is stunned. I give him no time to recoup:

"Do you want to face a military tribunal, *du Sau Offizier du!?*"

His face turns pale.

"Well then, shoot an unarmed boy, *du Sau Feigling du!* [Coward]. And adieu vital information, *du Sau Idiot du!*"

It took a few retakes to line up the four "Saus." I had tried a number of permutations with the last three. But I had to kick off the series with "*Saudeutscher*" to match his "*Saujude.*" *Noblesse oblige,* sort of.

After a moment's pause to allow my tongue lashing to sink in, I shout:

"*Avanti!* To headquarters!" And I start moving. Then, "*Gegangen soll werden!*" I only have to shout the Yiddish for "let's get a move on!" in my cousins' Frankfurt accent to turn the Yiddish idiom into authentic German. Sure enough, the troops fall into step.

Germans are respectful of anyone who barks at them in German. In all my confrontations with them, I would go for broke and it would work. When words would fail me I would project my unspoken thoughts, precise repartees and diatribes like well trained thrusts of the blade. Hemming and hawing would have been disastrous.

"Surround him!" the officer barks. "And march him to my car!"

I am seated in the rear of a long, plush convertible. I feel like a dignitary, with a cowed lesser officer to my right acting more like an aide-de-camp than a guard. The chastened officer sits next to the driver. The three of us keep silent (the driver doesn't count; he is not supposed to open his mouth unless ordered to do so).

In the initial take I forget to enjoy the ride: I am too fixated on my confrontation with the iron-crossed general. But after I have made him bite the dust, in the presence of his subordinates including my own two officers, I retrace my ride from the edge of the forest, through a landscape much like the flat Flemish countryside. I wave and smile at the people lining the road — a lot of young women, and boys my age — and yell out "*Ich bin Jude!*" ("I am a Jew!"). They are stunned, eyes popping, as if their world has been rocked to its foundation. I smile reassuringly.

My odyssey is unfolding nicely. Onward.

Torture... I forgot torture. Just the idea of having my eyes, my ears, my mouth, my navel, my genitals, my nails mutilated makes me uncomfortable. I have to outsmart them into forgoing torture. Or I will have to find a way to kill myself when it will spite them most.

There I am, flanked by my impressive escort of bodyguards, facing the iron-crossed general again across the oblong table. He has his corps of officers lined up on both sides of the table. Everybody is standing.

"*Sind Sie der Haupt?*" ("Are you the head?") He uses the deferential plural "*Sie.*" Obviously, he has been briefed about me; they all have.

"*Je ne parle que le Francais, mon général*" ("I only speak French, my general"). *Mon général,* in the best of French military traditions, is my response in kind to his using the deferential "*Sie.*"

The general and his retinue seem to understand. All eyes turn on my officer.

"Herr General," he says in a civilized tone, "he does speak German... I..."

"Oh," I cut in, pooh-poohing, "I barked and he understood."

"Translation!"

An officer translates. The general also understands.

"But you understand German, don't you?" the general says gruffly, but without departing from the deferential plural. That will henceforth be the pattern, I know.

"*Oui, mon général,*" I say calmly. "But this conversation will be held in French or it will not be held at all."

That will take him down a peg, just to show who is in control. It will also give me time to think. I read about that two-way translation stratagem somewhere.

The general gets the point. His face is twitching. He repeats: "Are you the head of that infestation of thugs and cowards?"

The translation is superb. The translator's French is impeccable, with hardly a trace of a German accent. Sorbonne, no doubt. His tone and demeanor are low key. I detect a kindred soul, an ally perhaps, who knows?

I say, almost offhandedly, that I will not entertain a single question about our military or other operations.

"We have means to make the likes of you talk." Torture; there they go.

"You can't frighten me," I say quietly, with a contemptuous smile.

The verbal jousting gives me great satisfaction, for I have the upper hand.

But my fantasy is languishing. I may have to take it all the way back to my perch in the tree, when an idea comes to me: I'll tell all for one free hour in Berlin. The general is downright panic-stricken: he must choose between the humiliation of giving in to a captive Jew or a court-martial for having another elite division pinned down in the forest when it is so desperately needed on the eastern front. He throws an anguished look at the translator. The latter is rooting for me and counsels silently to accept my offer. I am going to Berlin! The same triumphant ride — a run identical to the trip from the edge of the forest, only faster. The iron-crossed general sits next to the driver and my chastened officer sits next to me.

I show up in Berlin, on the Kurfürstendam and Unter den Linden — those poetic sounding names and the Reichstag are all I know of Berlin — to arouse the German masses with my fiery speech, like a good Jewish prophet. I open their eyes and win them over to the civilized ways worthy of "the people of Goethe and Schiller" my mother mused about back in the days of the survivable decrees. Stunned by the courage of a lone Jewish boy in shirtsleeves, swept off their feet by my eloquence, an eloquence of conviction, not of words — for there is no need to articulate for myself in my Germanized Yiddish the things that I feel with such irresistible passion and moral superiority — stunned and carried away they roar their reconciliation and brotherhood with the People of the Book. A big crowd of Germans on the Kurfürstendam even raise a cry for conversion to the *Mosaischer Glauben* (the Mosaic creed) as some German Jews liked to refer to our religion, and they lift the tall wooden platform where I stand with my hands on the railing, and carry it along the Kurfürstendam.

The cheering stops, the images blur and fade, leaving a void that becomes resignation, gray like the sky weighing on the roof of the butcher's house and pressing in on the dull panes of the gabled windows.

✿ ✿ ✿

The rabbis of the Middle Ages have sprung to mind, pitted in public disputation against the Catholic bishops, in the public squares of Western Europe. And I see myself arguing down the likes of Gobineau and Céline, of the brothers Jean and Jérome Tharaud who have written so many books about Jews, all brimming with venom; Menda and I read several of them. I appear in

Paris to argue them all down in the presence of the assembled masses on the Place de l'Etoile and the Champs Elysées, with Menda and Zalcman at my side to provide me with ammunition when necessary. Menda knows everything and can summon it verbatim after only a brief, stammering hesitation. Zalcman is the debunker of religion, all religions, and he is right, except for the one true faith, but religion is not what counts in Paris. Like the Germans they hate us because we exist, most of all they hate the irreligious, the assimilated Jews, they execrate the Alfred Dreyfusses and the Léon Blums, they waved *le prépuce à Blum* (Blum's foreskin) in the streets of Paris. Rome is where religion counts, but showing up at the gates of the Vatican would be useless, they can't forgive us for turning down their Jesus, we killed him, so they say, yet they must know the truth in the Vatican. Zalcman is right, they fool the masses, promise in the world to come what they rob in this world, "not until the last king is strangled with the entrails of the last priest," — Zalcman's Diderot. Paris isn't as rousing as Berlin, though I prevail handily in the confrontation, a brainy disputation, a victory without cheer. The French crowd is lifeless, not like the Germans who can be roused to fever pitch (they *Sieg Heil* themselves senseless). If only I could turn this debate on the Place de l'Etoile into something good for Jews, it is important to drive the point home in Paris, Paris is the brain of Europe, *la Ville Lumière*... Not any more. Paris under curfew must be dark.

Sinister, the Rome-Paris-Berlin triangle, *Rome damns, Paris condones, and Berlin executes. They'll do anything they are told, they are born to kill. And we are born to be...* I didn't want to think it, but I did, I couldn't help it and my heart caved in, so debilitating, that feeling of helplessness, so humiliating, it hurt. I remained riveted to my chair, aware that I wouldn't be able to run were they to come for me. Like in a nightmare. Was this what we were chosen for, to stand out with the Tablets, with the Torah scroll in its velvet mantle and with its silver crowns, conspicuous and defenseless, and be killed, like Abel? And the German would live? And what if Zalcman was right? What sense did it all make then? I no longer felt on solid ground. A myriad thoughts collided before I could articulate one, leaving a littered void. It took me a while to pull out of it: Yes, it *did* make sense, in some obscure, frightening way... it had to... Zalcman right or wrong. That's why they were going to fail. They always had, the kings, the popes. *I am a Jew, and I will remain a Jew, come what may. I couldn't be a Goy, even if I wanted to.*

I looked up at the clouds and the treetops, and listened to the wind.

Ps 119, **"Happy are the upright, who walk in the law of the Lord.**

"Happy are they who keep His statutes, who seek Him with a whole heart.

"They do no wrong, they walk in His ways.

The short verses flow forth like little waves washing up on thirsty sand. The same words keep coming back, each one in its own verse; words like commandments, statutes, ways, precepts. Nine different expressions for God's law.

"Open my eyes and I will behold the wondrous things from Your law.

"I am a stranger in the land, hide not Your commandments from me.

I sense the fervor, the Psalmist's relentless search for God's word.

I read on. And I realize with the start of discovery that the psalm is composed of groups of eight verses; each verse in an octet starts with the same letter of the alphabet. From *aleph* to *tav*: twenty two letters, one hundred seventy six verses, playful variations on the nine words for God's law. A long, modulated, entrancing hum. The constant lapping of a gentle surf. A treasure trove. I settle in for a long and lulling voyage.

"And I shall always keep Your law, for ever and ever.

"And I shall walk in the open, for I have sought Your precepts.

My mind begins to wander. I take in ever smaller portions. The pauses get longer. I perk up and dally at the occasional verse that leaps out from the past, from the liturgy; bright, cozy spots:

"Teach me keen reasoning and knowledge for I have faith in your commandments.

"Do accept, O Lord, the utterances of my mouth, and teach me Your ordinances.

I stare at the sky above the black-tile roof of the butcher's house. Time passes, tranquilly. I hear Adrienne's tentative steps on the stairs. Soup time.

The early afternoon calm had set in — Gaston had left for the forge, Sylvain was out, Adrienne had finished with the after-dinner chores. I had come out of my sexual reveries. I recognized the dull sound of a full coffee pot being placed on the stove: it would soon be coffee time. I heard, after a while, the clink of porcelain on porcelain. Adrienne was having her coffee. Soon it would be my turn, barring a visit from a neighbor. I contemplated the sky, listened to the sounds of the road, examined the brown stripes on the off-white façade of the café *Chalet*. I heard the handle turn in the kitchen door to the pump house, then the sound of the porcelain cup and saucer coming down in the sink. Two knocks on one of the lower steps roused me to the landing: Adrienne was motioning me down, and I slunk down the steps to take my place at the end of the table, closest to the staircase.

The table's dark top reflected the light from the window at the other end of the kitchen. There was a saucer with cookies, and a porcelain dish holding sugar squares. A wisp of steam was rising from my cup. Adrienne was knitting — needles jabbing and twisting, embracing and clicking softly, in a ceaseless mating dance. She seemed at peace: her work was done, her kitchen was spotless, and there was plenty of time until the evening chores. She was in control of her time, of her realm. I admired her. The moment was precious. All my burdens had been lifted. Forgotten, the games, the psalms, and the wrestling with time. The minutes engulfed me as they flowed by, like the waters of a quiet river. They flowed alike for me and for the free in the land.

Adrienne put her knitting away and got busy clearing off the table. It was time to tiptoe back upstairs.

I was standing in the shady corner by the window, looking down at the road, following an occasional pedestrian, a bicyclist, a truck, a horse pulling a cart. My time was still flowing along with theirs. The glowing aftereffect of the visit with Adrienne was wearing off, though. I was looking forward to dusk and its mysterious balm. It would come, it was only a matter of time. Regular, palpable time.

I picked up my *tillimel*. Psalm 119 felt somewhat remote. Muted were the variations on God's laws and statutes and ways and precepts. I read on, detached, just to finish what I had begun. I was nearing the end.

"**See my affliction and rescue me, for I did not forget Your law.**

And, starting the next to the last, the letter *shin*, octet:

"**Rulers have persecuted me without cause, but my heart is in awe of Your words.**

"**I rejoice at Your word like one who finds great spoils.** I perk up: a jewel from the past, from the Festivals' liturgy. I always liked that verse. I am looking at it closely, turning it over, savoring it. "**Like finding great spoils.**" Well put, David, who doesn't understand that wicked joy? War. Booty, the yardstick, the gold standard. Even for measuring God's word. He also compared God to a drunk. David knew about drinking too. Which psalm again? I am leafing back... Ah, Psalm 78, "**But then the Lord awoke as one asleep, like a strong man recovering from wine.**" Another yardstick. Uninhibited, David is.

Back to Psalm 119: "**I rejoice at Your word like one who finds great spoils.**" Spoils. Batsheva. Nathan. More memories are crowding in: David roaming across the desert at the head of a band of toughs — that's what our teacher Kahn had called them; his tense encounter (ending on a happy note) with the wife of Naval — "smart woman," Silberstein had said with a knowing smile: she became his wife; his taking it easy by the springs under the palm trees of Ein Gedi — Kahn had journeyed there. I continue reading with renewed pleasure to the end of the psalm. And pause, satisfied.

Yet something in the psalm has caught my attention... O yes, the octet starting with the letter *vav*. I leaf back: sure enough, the first word of each verse begins with the conjunction *vuh* (and) or with one of its modified forms (in Hebrew, that conjunction and some prepositions are attached to the words they introduce): *And let Your mercy.... And I shall answer.... And I shall observe.... And....* The easy way out, I feel; like cheating, almost. I look up the *aleph* octet: only one repetition: the first two verses start both with the word *ashray* (happy). I give the *aleph* octet a score of 7 over 8. The *bayt* group scores 2 over 8: all verses but one begin with the preposition *buh* (in, with) or with one of its modified forms. I rush to the *lamed* cluster: did the psalmist take the easy way out with the preposition *luh*? (to, for). Three times only. And twice he started a verse with the expression *luh-olam* (forever). I give that group a liberal 5 over 8 score.

I am scouring the psalm, in search for a perfect 8 over 8. I find the letter *hay* group to be rigged in a different way: seven of the eight verses begin with the causative form of a verb, **Teach me..., Make me understand..., Lead me..., Incline my heart....** (In the imperative of the causative the Hebrew verb takes on the prefix *ha* or *ho*.) Score: 2 over 8. Poetic though, that array of lofty verbs; there is music in the recurrence of the grammatical form, even in the repetitive *ha* sound. Suddenly the counting exercise seems petty-minded. Yet I have to go through with it. The *khet* and the *samekh* octets are the only ones with a perfect score. My numbers fling is over, like a spent game of solitaire. I close my *tillimel*.

I wait for dusk, for darkness, for the night sky.

I did not open my *tillimel* on Saturdays. The air pulsated with the sounds and activities that precede a Sabbath: the house cleaning chores, the wet-scrubbing of the patios in front of the houses amidst the prattle of the women, the frequent ring of the butcher shop's doorbell, the sonorous shouts of the men. Even the clatter of horseshoes and the rattle of steel-rimmed cartwheels on the cobblestones sounded like the shaking out of the week, the last expectant run before the general partaking in the repose of the land. The massive beer wagon weighed in with a denser, arhythmic clatter of horseshoes — two Belgian workhorses were pulling it; its wide edifice of wooden beer cases was alive with the rattle of bottles. I would listen wistfully to the symphony of freedom and carefreeness heralding a different Sabbath. No psalm-reading in that heady air.

I could not pray either. Saturday had dethroned Shabbat the Queen, relegating her to a fleeting, at times, disquieting memory. Erased from the calendar, Shabbat no longer appeared as the culminating event in an immutable cycle. I would recall her majesty and serenity, the convivial atmosphere under her gossamer canopy, only in the languor of my weekdays.

I did not open my *tillimel* on Sunday. The house was noisier, more lively. Adrienne started with the preparation of the more elaborate Sunday dinner earlier than on weekdays. Gaston rarely sat still. He would chop wood for kindling, or repair a flat in a bicycle tire. He always made his presence heard. His slippers made a distinct, fast shuffling noise on the tile floor. Sylvain would be in and out, running an errand, or on the lookout for Simoneke. Adrienne would shoo them out of her way as she moved between kitchen and pump house. The life on the Road sounded different as well: churchgoers, café-goers, villagers in their doorways would exchange greetings; the *djurr*'s of the men, loud or lusty or perfunctory or friendly, high-pitched or dull, came in more densely than on weekdays.

By early afternoon a quiet would descend on Duizend Appels, punctured by the sound of footsteps or ruffled by the crunch of bicycle tires on the gravel path. People stayed at home, or visited with relatives, or sat in cafés. Sylvain would play with Simoneke or accompany Gaston and Adrienne. I was often alone in the house for a long stretch of afternoon. The atmosphere of the village Sabbath with its intimations of pleasure in the midst of freedom hovered in the air like a force of nature. It cast a seductive spell. I would listen, intrigued, to the rumble of a lone car from the moment I picked up its distant, faint hum to the moment it died out. No trucks. An occasional horse-drawn cart. No beer wagon. I would listen to the silence. The mooing of a cow, the crowing of a cock would come from afar, on ripples of melancholy. Sunshine exacerbated my restlessness, my feeling of imprisonment. I would move stealthily between the bedroom and the garret. A breath of fresh country air wafting in through the garret window caused the strongest, the most bittersweet stirring of all. I felt it in my entire body. I was agitated, unable to entertain coherent thoughts, riven with the desire to be out there, somewhere, in that un-Jewish world. Yet the thought of bolting never crossed my mind. Not even in my fantasies. Not even in my Channel crossing fantasy: it begins in Ostend — a port city and resort by the North Sea — as if I had been transported there by magic. In fact, leaving Duizend Appels would have been rather simple: with the spending money I had saved I could have boarded a train for the coast in 't Heike, a hamlet between Sinaai and Lokeren, during a Sunday visit. But stealing away was inconceivable, like jumping off a cliff. The guilt feelings alone would have squelched the impulse, had it ever surfaced.

In that fantasy I am pushing a stolen rowboat into the sea, after dark. I am rowing all night, avoiding detection. By the crack of dawn I am in friendly waters. British pilots spot me, British seamen pick me up and receive me with admiring smiles and vigorous handshakes. I announce my presence in London on the BBC — not my crossing, lest the alerted Germans make similar escapes impossible: a message in German for my parents and another one in Flemish for Adrienne and Gaston and Sylvain. I see them huddled around the radio. I imagine their relief, their joy; I can see the gleam in their eyes. And, in England, freedom, space, books, school, sports. I learn English in no time. My accent is pure, my diction, flawless. I experience anew the impatience to grow, the hunger for the unknown. I vacillate between going to boarding school — the British would arrange that, in recognition of my bravery — and living with a family. No women.

Crossing the Channel was a wish as much as a daydream, unattainable, yet feasible, it seemed: one day Adrienne came home with the news that downed allied pilots had made it to England. From Ostend, I imagined. The Channel was not that wide: one could see the white cliffs of Dover through a coin-operated telescope on Ostend's dike. The ferries, in peacetime, would take swarms of high-spirited excursionists across, every day. People had attempted to swim across. Unbeknownst to me, though, the fugitives reached England by way of France, Spain, and Portugal or Gibraltar.

The realness of the escape to England made the Channel crossing fantasy uncomfortable. I dropped it from my repertoire.

One cloudless Sunday afternoon close to the Easter vacation in 1943 — spring was in the air, I was alone in the house and felt alone in Creation — I could no longer restrain myself: I came down, one slow, practiced step at a time, skipping the creaky stairs and avoiding the creaky spots. Then, I scampered on all four, across the kitchen, to the low radio table in the corner past the window. The sunlight was streaming in, setting the half-curtain aglow. I crouched in the shade under the window sill with my head by the radio. I turned it on to a barely audible volume, so low that with my head only a foot away from the set I could no longer hear the announcer's voice. I felt safe. It was comedy time: jokes and spoofs on current events. I didn't stop laughing. I was totally absorbed, and happy. One spoof mocking the British stood out: relating gleefully their reverses at the hands of Rommel in North Africa — they had

had him on the run just a few weeks before — the announcer
followed up with a ditty, a series of puns on the name Rommel
and the Flemish noun *rommel* (clutter, mess) and the derived
words *rommelige* (cluttered, untidy) and *rommelen* (to rummage).
It went:

O Rommel, wat rommel,	O Rommel, what clutter,
Wat is dat met die Rommel,	What's the matter with this Rommel,
Die rommelige Rommel,	This untidy Rommel,
Die blijft steeds rommelen in de woestijn.	He keeps on rummaging in the desert.

I found it funny and clever. Some more lines dripping
with sarcasm for the befuddled British and extolling the swift
Germans, then the refrain — that ditty — again. I sang along
under my breath: I had it down pat. I was enjoying myself. The
broadcast came to an end. Amused and appeased, I crawled back
to the staircase and inched my way up to the bedroom. My inner
turmoil had dissipated. I waited.

Adrienne was upset and Gaston was angry when I told them
about the radio hour. Gaston didn't let me explain the elaborate
precautions I had taken and made me promise not to do it again.
I never did.

We had supper at the kitchen table and our evening session
around the stove. Taking up, at bedtime, the pail half-filled with
water ushered in the welcome night. A tranquil, reassuring week
lay ahead.

The next morning the weekday routine started again, for everyone. I regained my normal, more placid hiding disposition.

✧ ✧ ✧

Ps 120, **"Sheer ha-ma'alot** (a song of ascents). The opening
words — arcane yet all too familiar — jump off the page. No, it
is not the hymn we sang on Shabbat and Holidays prior to the
recitation of grace after meals.

I am turning the pages, skipping one song of ascents after
another. There. Psalm 126 — the goodies the *Book of Psalms* has
yielded! I read, stripping the psalm of its melody, trying, for the
first time, to grasp its full meaning.

"When the Lord brings about the return to Zion, we shall be like they that dream. Another psalmist; of the Ingathering. **"... Then they will say among the nations: 'The Lord has done great things with those.'**

"...Reverse, O Lord, our captivity — the Babylonian? — **like streams in the Negev.**

"They who sow in tears will reap with joyous song," the Psalmist reassures toward the end.

Jewish history. Family life, at the *Shabbas* table. Distant, both. I pause.

I am embarking on the songs of ascents, fifteen of them, I counted: Psalms 120 through 134. Short ones.

Ps 121, **"I lift my gaze unto the mountains: from where will come my help?**

A wayfarer, on a hazardous journey. His is an abiding faith in God:

"My help is from the Lord, the maker of heaven and earth.

I am that wayfarer. Above me rise majestic peaks. A lush valley stretches below dotted with peaceful habitations. I am passing through. No one shall know my name.

The Psalmist speaks to me; to my anguish, my hope:

"He will not let you stumble, on the trek to freedom; **Your guardian will not slumber.**

"Behold, He who watches over Israel will neither slumber nor sleep. Safe. Us. Me.

"The Lord is your keeper; He is your shade. I feel enveloped.

"The sun will not overcome you by day, nor will the moon spook you at night. I am invulnerable.

"The Lord will keep you from all evil, yes, from falling in their hands; **He will guard your soul.** I feel tranquillity setting in.

"The Lord will protect your going — out of hiding — **and your coming** — back to freedom; **henceforth and forever."**

I am reading the poem — eight short, even-toned verses — for the third time. It captivated me even in *shul* where the pace of recitation was swift.

Reminiscent of Psalm 91 is this song of ascents. There, too, I am exposed to danger. There, too, I proclaim my faith:

"I say to the Lord, You are my refuge, my fortress; my God in whom I trust.

There, too, I am heartened:

"...under His wings shall you find refuge....

"Do not fear the terror of night, the arrow that flies by day....

"A thousand may fall at your left, and ten thousand at your right, it will not come near you.

"Nothing bad will befall you....

"For He will order his angels to watch over you....

"They will carry you on their hands, lest you stub your foot against a stone."

Both poems hold me in their thrall.

Ps 122, **"I rejoiced when they said to me, let us go unto the house of the Lord.** Joy, from the first verse.

"Our feet are standing within thy gates, O Jerusalem. The city is aglow. Pilgrims ascend to give thanks.

"Peace be within your precincts, serenity within your palaces." To sojourn there. I will.

Ps 123, **"Be gracious unto us, O Lord, be gracious unto us, for we have had our fill of contempt.**

"Our soul is swamped with the scorn and the contempt of our oppressors."

The wretchedness, on the heels of the pilgrims' happiness. The wretchedness: blunt, familiar, yet cutting afresh.

Ps 124, **"If it had not been for the Lord Who stood by us, say ye, Israel;**

"If it had not been for the Lord Who stood by us, when men rose up against us,

"Well then, they would have swallowed us alive, in their rage against us;

"The waters would have swept us away, a stream would have washed over our soul;

"Well then, the raging waters would have washed over our soul.

"Blessed be the Lord Who did not give us as prey to their teeth.

"Our soul escaped like a bird from the snare of the fowlers;

"The snare broke and we escaped."

Ps 128, "Happy is each one who fears the Lord, who walks in His ways.

"When you live off the labor of your hands, bliss and goodness shall be yours.

"Your wife shall be like a fruit-bearing vine inside your house, your children like olive saplings around your table.

I am reminded of the righteous man in the first Psalm who shuns the paths of sin. He has prospered since, the man I wanted to be. He has a beautiful wife; the proverbial woman of valor, no doubt. And sons, and daughters. I see the glow of contentment lighting up his table.

"Behold, for thus is blessed the man who fears the Lord.

"The Lord bless you out of Zion, and may you witness the good of Jerusalem all the days of your life.

"And may you see children of your children. Peace be upon Israel."

Peace. In Jerusalem. I am dreaming again.

Ps 129, "Much have they persecuted me from my youth on, say ye, Israel;

"Much have they persecuted me from my youth on, but they have not prevailed against me."

Ps 130, "From the depths I am calling you, O Lord. The famous "de profundis!" De profundis... solemn; as moving as the Hebrew.

"*Mee-ma'amahkim* (from the depths) — from an open grave, from a deep narrow pit, from the entrails of the earth — I am clamoring to You, O Lord.

"Lord, hear me, listen to my supplications.

I am not letting go:

"From the depths I am calling you, O Lord.

"Lord, hear me, listen to my supplications.

I am moving out from under the spell.

"If sins is what You remember — mine are just peccadilloes — **Lord, who will remain standing?**

"For You grant forgiveness....

"I have hope, my soul is hoping....

"My soul goes out to the Lord — an upswell; like a flood. I am not holding back — **as I wait** — for Liberation — **more intently than the watchmen wait for daybreak.** He *must* come through. He must.

"Israel, wait for the Lord, for He is merciful.... That's all? To be told, no, *Israel* is told, to wait... for His mercy.

"And He will redeem Israel from all their sins." Never mind our sins! From the *Germans* redeem us! Bring back, bring back the trains of deported!

Ps 133, **"Behold, how good and pleasant it is for brethren to dwell together.** The canon we used to sing! In four voices. Another find. I intone it in my head. Yes, how good and sweet it is, for brothers in Israel to rock together in song.

"It is like the fine oil on the head, coming down on the beard, the beard of Aaron.... It seeps into the soul; I feel it entering the heart. The balm of serenity.

"Like the dew of Hermon that comes down on the mountains of Zion, for there the Lord has commanded the blessing; eternal life."

Dew, the gentle breath the earth exhales at dawn, the blessing, life eternal. I muse. The psalm lingers on.

I have reached the end of the songs of ascents. What jewels in this *tillimel...* I sit back, contented. The tiny psalter is lodged between the palms of my hands. I finger its smooth olive wood covers. I hold on to it for a while before putting it back on the night table.

✡ ✡ ✡

Now and then Adrienne took Sylvain to see our parents. She would pick a nice day and, dressed in their Sunday best, the two would be seen walking to the train station. They would board the train for Antwerp and get off in St-Niklaas, the second stop. Adrienne had the key to her sister Palmyre's house. She would first ring the seamstress whom she had known for years to reassure her about the noise she might hear next door.

"The mama was happy to see her boy," Adrienne would inform Julia or Irène. "She was at home. Doing better, poor thing."

Those visits, made out of sympathy and compassion, gave our cover story a needed boost: Adrienne had become concerned that prolonged parental estrangement, when the city was only a short train ride away, might resurface as a topic of conversation among our neighbors.

My parents were grateful to Adrienne for coming with Sylvain. At each visit my mother had something for her: a scarf, a pair of gloves, or a garment that looked flattering on her. The two women wore the same size clothes; they had the same complexion, both had black hair and dark eyes. The choice pieces of my mother's wardrobe were hanging, unused, in the closet ever since Govaerts had brought them shortly after our flight from Antwerp. Irène and Julia would compliment Adrienne on her new dress or fine patent leather shoes. "From the boy's mother," Adrienne would say: to purchase such items in times of scarcity and rationing would have been out of character even if it had been within her means.

Once, I was watching the road when Adrienne and Sylvain were due back from "Antwerp." I caught them turning the corner onto our stretch of road. Adrienne wore a stunning outfit for wartime Belsele — a stylish, well fitting light gray jacket and skirt, and a white fluffy blouse.

"Julia came out on her doorstep," she recounted later with a smile. " 'Adrienne!' was all she could get out of her mouth."

"From Sylvain's mother," I said. "Isn't it nice? We have the same fit."

"And you are already wearing it!" she said.

"Yes, it was much simpler to wrap my dress," I said. "The poor woman. So many clothes. Most of them just hang unused in the closet."

The neighbors had not waited for the two-piece suit donned in "Antwerp" to put two and two together: a young, attractive woman from the countryside, a dashing and generous philanderer from the city. Our cover was rock solid, more so than we knew; it had taken wing.

It was a while, after the war, before the villagers revealed to Adrienne the story they had woven about her. At first, they did not believe that Sylvain and I were Jewish boys with normal parents. (Many, after the liberation, claimed having sheltered Jews.)

Yet three people had pierced our cover: the *kantonnier* (roadman) whose main task it was to maintain the ditches along the roads, his wife, and the downed British pilot they were hiding. The pilot had been seen parachuting in the woods of Waasmunster. The roadman got to him first and hid him in a spot where the Germans could not find him. He returned at night, after the Germans had given up their search, and brought the pilot to his house.

Theirs was a heightened awareness of the situation. The BBC, a daily companion, had mentioned the disappearance of Jews in large numbers, never to be seen or heard of again. Leading a double life, they had developed that extra sense for others who shared similar, life-defining circumstances. It got them to pay attention to us. As the roadman told Gaston after the war:

"The little one, always there. No school. The big one, when he appeared — on Sundays, school vacations only, I noticed — always alone. No parents. Ever. Then I remembered that when they first came, they were both hanging around the house, for weeks, kind of lost. Gaston, with what was happening in Antwerp; and listening to the English radio... *allez.*"

The roadman, his wife and the pilot had debated whether to tell Gaston and Adrienne that they knew about Sylvain and me, in case we might need help, but decided to spare us the worry about uninvolved strangers in the know: the glass too many; the slip of the tongue.

✲ ✲ ✲

Ps 137, **"By the rivers of Babylon...** I recognize the words with a jolt. The famous poem! I didn't know it to be a psalm. Or did I forget? We read it in our Hebrew textbook of Jewish history, recited it in class. I still know it by heart.

"By the rivers of Babylon, there we sat, and we wept, as we remembered Zion.

I am reading thirstily, yet slowly, rocked by the Hebrew cadences, trying to inhale every word. The poem-turned-psalm is more haunting than ever. Riverbanks, willows, harps. Captors who ask their captives,

"Sing for us from the songs of Zion.
"How can we sing the Lord's song on foreign soil?
Those two lines, without the words "the Lord's song" had been set to music. The tune had made the words cling to the heart. The class also sang it as a canon; with four voices, it had sounded like the simultaneous rushing and ebbing of the surf, ending in a synchronized roar. I close my eyes and let the tune rise and resonate in my head. I sing it again. And I recall my solo rendition — a fleeting memory — at the end of an unusual episode in Silberstein's class.

He had caught me talking to my bench mate once too often. That called for a slap with his thin, square ruler across the palm of my hand. Sensing all eyes on me, I walked to the front of the classroom, trying to look stoic. One could salvage one's pride, even rise in stature, if one knew how to take the slap: without bending over fearfully, without that upward jerk of the knee as the ruler came swooshing down, and without uttering a sound. I was determined to pass the test. I stood on the podium in front of my classmates, with my arms at my sides and my head turned to the right to face Silberstein — he was sitting behind his desk. I waited for the order to present my hand palm up. Silberstein looked at me for a few tense moments, then, to my surprise, he offered me a choice — he had never done that before: a smack with the ruler or a "red 10," to wit, a 10 in red ink for bad behavior in my report book which had to be returned the following day with my father's signature.

I had been punished once with that dreaded red number, the highest on the scale. In that prior incident, I had waited to hand my father my report book until the following morning, just before I had to dash off to school. The shame I felt, asking him into my room, sitting on the bed and pointing sheepishly at the signature line. My father sat down, visibly annoyed. Without taking his eyes off the red 10, he took out his gold-tipped fountain pen, unscrewed the cap, slipped it over the opposite end of the pen, signed, closed the pen and slid it into his inner breast pocket. He left my room without uttering a word. It was scathing.

Silberstein had hardly finished saying "or a red 10" when I was holding my right hand palm up, at the ready — I had swung it with a flourish in a wide arc — and was looking away, over the heads of my classmates, trying my best to look unafraid and martyred. Was he testing my mettle? I had played up the drama, instinctively: Silberstein liked a good show. I expected a milder slap, not the whirring sound of the ruler that ended in a sudden, sharp sting. I was going to return to my seat, head high.

But nothing happened. I turned my head and saw Silberstein leaning forward in his chair, with one elbow on the desk, and smiling, with a glint of mischief, I thought, in his big brown eyes. Or was it admiration? Could I be getting off scot-free?

"Sing us a song," he said, "sing it well and you may return to your seat."

I was thrown off balance, for an instant. And I intoned:

"Sing for us from the songs of Zion.
"How can we sing on foreign soil?"

I sang it as a dirge, especially the second line. I had a good voice and I carried the tune well. Silberstein dismissed me with a broad smile.

I walked the aisle again, relieved, yet looking neither left nor right. I no longer felt like a hero, just a performer who had paid his way out of a fix. I could not have conceived of saying "I'd rather not sing."

The canon has simmered down. I'm letting go of the song. I savor a moment of silence before I open my eyes, before I return to the psalm, knowing and prepared, in a trance almost: **"If I forget Thee, O Jerusalem, let my right hand forget its cunning.... If I don't raise Jerusalem above my highest joy."** O glory! O hope! Something bright and warm is welling up in me, a feeling akin to liberation. To remember Jerusalem in my rejoicing. There *will be* rejoicing, I know. My heart is melting and expanding at the same time.

Our "poem" in history class had ended with the vibrant pledge to Jerusalem. To my surprise the psalm goes on: **"Hold, O Lord, against the children of Edom** — I am taken aback by the sudden turn; the tone is ominous — **the day of Jerusalem, when they said, destroy, destroy; down to Her very foundation.** *"Ahroo,"* Hebrew for "destroy," brings to mind *"AUS-RRa-die-ren"* ("wipe out"), Hitler's growl on the radio, referring to the towns of England, and *"AUS-RRotten"* ("exterminate"). I feel the blast of implacable hatred.

The pitch rises yet further, stunning:

"Daughter of Babylon the violated — that other deadly enemy; "*shdu-dah,*" Hebrew for "violated," evokes "*shah-dah-yim,*" breasts, and "*dah-dim,*" nipples; alliterations of the "sh" and "d" sounds. I see a full-breasted, flaxen-haired German maiden with steely-blue eyes in a taut face — **exalted shall be he who will repay you for what you have done to us.** My heart is racing, I am leaning on every word, **"Exalted shall be he who seizes and smashes your little ones against the rock."**

My mother, turning away and letting out, in a throttled fury, "*Of Dahtshe Mitter! NOR OF ZEYE gezoogt!*" ("On German mothers! Let it befall ONLY THEM!"). I see her face tilted upwards, pale and fierce in the dim blue light of the narrow hallway. She has just relinquished my brother and me to Govaerts, to be taken to strangers in a distant village, to fate.

There are no more verses in the psalm.

I am reading again, letting my passion, like smoldering lava, rise with each verse:

"Hold, O Lord, against the sons of Edom, the day of Jerusalem, when they said, destroy, destroy, down to Her very foundation.

"Daughter of Babylon the violated, exalted shall be he who repays you for what you have done to us;

"Exalted shall be he who seizes and smashes your little ones against the rock."

My heart is pounding. I didn't know that I could hate so fiercely.

✡ ✡ ✡

To be the only Jew left after the war, the silent witness to a vanished Jewish existence... I would flick this anguishing thought from my mind whenever it landed — rarely, only in moments of utter loneliness. This time the thought lingers on. Frightening, to see myself walking about Christian Europe with the Hebrew language, the memory of the Shabbat buried deep inside me. I, then, am responsible. For the survival. It is as frightening as the thought of going under.

I'll live and father good Jewish boys. She is as loyal as Ruth the Moabite, or as Zipporah the Midianite, Moses' wife. My sons will carry on in my footsteps, marry fine Gentile girls, and so on... No. Takes too long. Beside, a bunch of antisemites could cut it short. Or the pope; he wouldn't even need the Germans. He'd be frantic about nipping the new blossom in the bud. No, I can't depend on the line to continue. It hangs by a thread. Always did. Abraham and Sarah had Isaac, the only son to perpetuate the line, when they were one hundred years old. A joke, Sarah said when she became pregnant. And Isaac and Rebeccah had only Jacob to carry on. It is too precarious an enterprise nowadays, with God in hiding.

I will make converts. That's it. And they'll convert others. A big, spanking-new Jewish nation. In Africa. Europe has no soul; we gave them the Ten Commandments and they trampled them underfoot.

Sunny Africa. What an adventure! I had a vivid picture of Africa from the pre-war news reels about the Belgian Congo — eighty times the size of Belgium, we were told in class; and from the movie about the two explorers, Stanley and Livingston, Mr. Govaerts arranged for us to see. How exciting my mission will be. The Africans in their grass hut villages will give themselves over to their new belief, heart and soul; one could see that from their dancing and their music. And the women are so lively and beautiful. The Queen of Sheba was African, too. King Solomon was taken with her beauty and her wisdom. They had probed each other's minds with clever riddles. But he also wanted to see the shape of her legs, the only part of their encounter I remember, from a book of Hebrew legends by Bialik, a bar mitzvah gift from Menda. But the queen was covered from head to toe in gold-embroidered silks. The king tricked her into lifting her robe by releasing a sudden jet of water between a double glass floor built especially for that purpose; for one peek at her legs. They were shapely, but he noticed the hair and made a clever remark which I can't remember. She said something witty in return. And the beloved in the Song of Songs was black. An allegory, the Song of Songs is, of a higher love, the love between Israel the bride, black and beautiful, and God, the Bridegroom. That was the interpretation of one of the sages in the Great Assembly; it had moved the others, Silberstein had told us, into admitting the love song in the biblical canon. I remember my confusion: why hadn't the allegory been obvious to all of the participants in the deliberations? Had the Song of Songs slipped into the Bible through the crack of a clever pretext? I wonder whether there were precious texts that did not make it past the prosaic souls in the Assembly?

Well then, the Black Continent it is. But what will I teach the Africans? My knowledge is a drop in the ocean of Jewish learning. I only know how riveting it can be, and how special it has made me feel. Well... I will teach them Hebrew and the basics of our religion and of our way of life, get them started. I won't be too rigorous in my teaching — my family's brand of piety will be just fine. So then, I will go from village to village, sit in a circle with the men, in the sun. If Judaism is meant to survive, teachers and scholars will rise among them. The learning will grow and spread.

But how will I bring the Bible with all the commentaries, the *Shulkhan Arukh* (a compendium of laws), the tractates of the Talmud, the scrolls, the texts, into the heart of Africa? Just one copy of each would fill entire trucks. And will there be any left in the sacked houses of learning in Europe? An impossible task. Well then, I will take just one copy of the Pentateuch with Rashi's commentaries. They'll take it from there. As under king Yoshiyahu, when, after the brutal fifty-five-year-long reign of the apostate king Menashe, Judaism was resuscitated from the brink of extinction with the discovery of only one book of the forgotten Pentateuch, Deuteronomy. Strange, that Jewish king came closer to destroying Judaism than Hitler and the pope and all the anti-semites combined. It had all hung by a thread. If that scroll had not been found in the temple wall undergoing repair, or had it been willfully or accidentally destroyed, I would be a Pagan, no, an Arab. Nonsense, my parents would not have met... nonsense, they would not have been born. Simple, no Jews... No Christians. Things would have been totally different. The nose of Cleopatra, if the nose of Cleopatra had been shorter... Will we have once more a narrow escape? Will *I* see the day? But why have we been forced into a situation where we need a miracle of sorts? Our ancestors have been exiled because of their sins. Whose sins are we paying for two thousand years later, theirs, or ours? Am I holed up, are Jews punished, because I have torn paper on *Shabbas?* How petty! Well then, come Saturday I shall tear paper! On purpose! What if Zalcman was right? I would be making a fool of myself, on Saturday. Events, though, seem to unfold according to Deuteronomy.

Weary, I let my mind drift.

Ps 144, **"By David.**
"Blessed be the Lord my Rock,
"Who trains my hands for battle,
"my fingers for war."
Who will teach me?

I am down to the five last psalms. I knew them as prayers
— songs of praise and jubilation: they all start and end with
"Halleluyah." An easy read.

Ps 146, **"Put not your trust in rulers, in man who is**
helpless:

"Once his spirit departs, he returns to the earth; that very
day all his plans come to naught.

I pause briefly: these two verses had always slowed me down.
Then:

"Happy is he who depends for help on the God of Jacob...."
I depend for help on Gaston and Adrienne.

Ps 147, **"He counts the stars and names them all."** What an
awesome affirmation of power: to name them all, like creating
them anew, one by one, and charting their course. I had never
paid attention to that verse. I would recall it on many a night,
while gazing at the starry firmament. "He names them all" — the
myriads of stars that shine, bright; and the flickering ones I coax
out of the celestial dark, one after the other. And the stars I cannot see, that no one will ever see.

I have read the last "Halleluyah." The Catholic Mass also
has lots of halleluyahs. The priest squeezes the joy out of them
with his slow, lugubrious delivery. He makes the word sound so
alien. Does he know where it comes from? That it means "Praise
the Lord?" Probably not; another ritual utterance, that's all it is;
like "Amen." Händel — I once heard excerpts from his *Messiah*
on the radio, now *there* is someone who understood halleluyahs.
Exulting. Like rolling thunder. Leaves our *hazan* and choir in
the dust. Would Händel's *Messiah* be acceptable in *shul*? No. I
am quite sure of that. He was not a Jew. And which messiah did
he have in mind? Can they still sing all these halleluyahs on the

radio? The German radio? I guess so... Händel was not a Jew. And it is probably about their messiah.

I feel both giddy and sad. Unnerved. My hand rests in my lap with the closed miniature *Book of Psalms*.

✵ ✵ ✵

One day Gaston came upstairs and handed me a gray, soft-cover book, *AUTOMOBIELLEERGANG* (Automobile Course), by Ingenieur A. VAN LOY. I would find it interesting, he said. It was a rather thin folio with glossy pages, dated from 1924. Gaston told me that he had considered learning how to service automobiles: with motors and rubber tires there would be little need for shoeing horses and fitting steel rims on wooden wheels. The primer on the workings of an automobile had been his first step, and the only one: the forge in Belsele would not be displaced by a car repair shop. Indeed, with the outbreak of war, automobiles had almost disappeared from view. They had been requisitioned by the Germans or were garaged for lack of gasoline.

Intrigued, I started reading. The author began by noting that a mixture of gasoline vapor and oxygen is highly flammable. When compressed and ignited, such mixture will explode, releasing a great deal of energy. But how, I wondered, did one get from an explosion to a self-propelled vehicle?

Van Loy explained: when a compressed mix of air and gasoline vapor is ignited inside a cylinder with a sliding base — the piston, the expanding, burnt gases will thrust the piston toward the cylinder's open end. I was taken aback: the taming of an explosion, that's what it was: the piston gives, the cylinder remains intact. Not like a bomb... I had the sensation of entering a new realm.

Well then, how did the firing in a cylinder turn the wheels of a car?

A rod, Van Loy continued, acts like a forearm whose elbow is hinged to the piston and whose hand is gripping a crank on an axle — the crankshaft. The elbow moves outward with the piston, in a straight line while the hand goes around, turning the crankshaft half a revolution. The crankshaft completes its revolution by inertia, pushing the piston back to its initial position before the ignition.

I stared at the simple drawings of the cylinder-piston-rod-crankshaft assembly, the heart, I sensed, of the automobile. How bold, to conceive of harnessing an explosion. How clever to think of this simple assembly for converting a rectilinear thrust into the rotation of an axle. I felt a sense of elation similar to the one I had after opening the *Book of Psalms* for the first time.

I sat back, to absorb the revelation, to reflect on it: the horse pulling the wagon was replaced by a Van Loy cylinder-piston-rod assembly forcing an axle to turn, explosion after explosion. Simple. But a car...

I read on. A design emerged, providing solutions to one problem after another:

valves, for the intake of the fresh mix and for the expulsion of the burnt gasses;

cams, mounted eccentrically — how ingenious — to operate the valves. What drives the cam assembly? The rotating crankshaft;

a sparkplug delivers an electrical spark to ignite the compressed mix. What triggers the electrical discharge? The rotating crankshaft.

The crankshaft, the master clock, both driven and driving. Once it is set in motion, the system keeps going — a self-sustaining process, like the heart... until the spark is gone. So that's how... I was only a few pages into the book, yet it felt as if I had penetrated deep into a new world. There was still an entire manual of challenges in search of solutions which would raise further challenges. How is the gasoline vaporized? Where does the electrical spark come from? How is the first cycle kicked off? A car on wheels was still a long way off. But I had pierced the mystery. I was relishing the feast in store for me.

I pored again over the illustrations of the interlocking components and their operation: the motor... The word no longer connoted a mere object; it was pregnant with meaning, an idea made reality. A world of creation and contentment, light-years removed from the world of strife and fear around me, had sprung forth from the pages of *Automobielleergang*. It was a safe place. I felt an inner warmth. A moment of grace. I took a breather, to settle in, to let my mind wander.

———

Hearing Adrienne coming up the stairs with my plate of soup — I could tell by her step — pulled me out of my reveries. It had to be noon, meal time; Gaston would be there at any moment. He came and the three of them sat down to eat. As usual, I picked up my plate with the main dish from one of the lower steps of the staircase: I slunk down and went back up, quieter than Milou whose patter on the bare wood one could hear.

Gaston went back to the forge. Sylvain trotted over to Simoneke's — his little farm-girl friend must have stayed home from school with another one of her convenient headaches. Adrienne tidied up the kitchen, then scoured the black top of the potbelly stove and wet-mopped the floor. The sun was shining. The sounds rang softer, the air felt lighter, the bedroom looked cozier, intimating a world at peace. A gentler time of day. I felt its touch and savored the moment without drifting into an after-dinner torpor and sexual fantasies.

I reached for Van Loy's primer and geared up by revisiting the familiar figures; they amazed me anew. I moved on with the study of his work. I was reading with deliberate slowness, in the thrall of the author's narrative. He reminded me of Mr. Van Bijlen, our geometry teacher: concise, rigorous, and so clear; he instilled life into his theorems, made them seem inevitable. The name Van Loy imprinted itself on my mind as strongly as the book's title.

I closed *Automobielleergang* and waited for dusk, tranquilly. A curtain had parted, a new horizon had appeared. I was awestruck by the power of the mind. I imagined creative people out there in the world, engineers, inventors. I felt their presence, a gossamer network of kindred minds. I will be one of them, some day. I will become an inventor. I will go to Eretz Yisrael and invent important things. I sat, luxuriating in time's passing. I was going to read, to master the entire manual. No hurry though, time was on my side. It had worth, it counted, the pause as much as the music: *Automobielleergang*, like the *Book of Psalms*, had infused the pauses with meaning. I was no longer paddling on an endless expanse of water. I was rowing, slowly, silently, holding a steady course. The oars did not break the surface. The rowboat left no wake behind. I would reach land... I was bound to reach land.

I sat back and listened to the cows, the birds, a dog's barking, to the noises on the road. I did not feel alone.

Gaston did not ask me, that evening, about the book he had given me. I never mentioned it either. Van Loy's *Automobielleergang* had become part of my world of hiding, upstairs, none of which I ever brought downstairs. Nor would anyone inquire: politeness or even solicitousness could only have gotten mired in unhelpful, even awkward platitudes. Adrienne, however, kept watch, unbeknownst to me, following the vagaries of my appetite, trying to gauge my state of mind.

For days the invention of the automobile unfolded before my eyes, with sketches, descriptions and explanations, form the carburetor, the steering mechanism, the flywheel, the suspension, the cooling system, down to the lubrication grooves in the piston rings, to the multi-cylinder engine — how inspired: four, six, even eight cylinders firing off at regular intervals over a two-revolution cycle of the crankshaft: one stroke of inventiveness yielding more, so many times more horsepower. There seemed to be no limit to man's ingenuity. And the attention given to extraneous agents and their effects, to the dust particles in the air, for example: they scratch the inner wall of the cylinder leading to a degraded performance. Van Loy went as far as to explain the need for an air filter by calculating the number of grams of dust contained in the air a piston sucks in from the atmosphere in a long spell of driving — a motor's appetite for air was staggering. The thought crossed my mind about the even greater volume of hot and dirty gases returned to the atmosphere. A blip, and it was gone.

I could not fathom the electrical system which Van Loy covered summarily, as if writing for the initiated in the fundamentals of electricity. Ohm's Law — the key to the electrical phenomena that generate the spark — was an abstruse three-letter formula. Its arcaneness heightened my respect for the inventors of the automobile and for Van Loy. An inventor must know a lot, I mused ruefully.

I absorbed *Automobielleergang* in measured doses, moving from concept to mechanism, and pausing for breaks, as I did in my reading of the *Book of Psalms*. I would relax with a game of solitaire, or by watching, unseen, the life of the road, like someone steeped in his own occupation contemplates with casual interest other people's activities, or with cozy daydreaming about a sunny life of noteworthy accomplishments, or with my *tillimel*: I would favor the more serene psalms that would take me for a short, magic spell to that other place where brothers dwell together in harmony, or I would roam with the Psalmist over God's Creation. O the freedom, to glide through space, to climb every peak and drink at every brook, my birthright, mine as the air I inhaled. I had great hopes. And I would resume my journey with Van Loy. The contentment I derived from *Automobielleergang* brightened all else.

Once, during a break in the study of *Automobielleergang*, as I was thumbing through my tillimel my eye caught the verse **"When Israel came out of Egypt, the House of Jacob from a people of alien tongue,"** — the festive *Hallel* prayer. I still glimpsed **"The mountains skipped like rams, the hills, like sheep,"** as I began leafing forward, in a sudden rush, to Psalm 118.

Reining in my haste, I read from the beginning, **"Praise the Lord for He is good.... From narrow straits I called upon the Lord; He answered me.... The nations surround me.... They surround me like bees.... I shall not die, I shall live.... He tormented me, but He did not deliver me to Death.... This is the day the Lord has made, let us be glad and rejoice in it...** up to verse 25, the plea for salvation and success. I bent forward in my battle stance, heels on the front rung, head over knees, eyes closed. I had an expanded petition:

"Please, O Lord, RESCUE! Me... I MUST make it to Liberation.

"Please, O Lord, RESCUE! My people... in deportation... in hiding. Rescue my people!

"Please, O Lord, bring success; to me, AS AN ENGINEER. AS AN INVENTOR. To build... to create in Eretz Yisrael... Bring success to me.

"Please, O Lord, bring success." To our people... to the *halutzim* (the pioneers)... in the *kibbutzim*... in the swamps... in the valley... to the *shomrim* (the watchmen.) AN ARMY, A JEWISH ARMY... bring success to our nation.

✡ ✡ ✡

Spring 1943. Hiding is becoming harder as the days are getting longer. I am having all my meals upstairs. The six-hour stretch between dinner and supper grows more oppressive as the afternoon wears on. The air is heady, the light brighter. The sky and the clouds, the gently swaying foliage in the distance, dusk and the firmament are my only companions; the vibrant sounds, the vivifying scents of the outdoors, the cool breezes wafting into the bedroom and the garret, my tormentors. I have become restless. Coming downstairs after dark feels like dropping in on acquaintances. The evening, shorn of the intimacy of a shared meal, has shrunk to a hiatus between a long day and bedtime. The lingering light has unhinged winter's daily routine and eats into the hallowed night. I don't come down for days in a row.

And there is still daylight when the last train from Antwerp arrives on Saturday and the last Sunday train departs. In good weather, and especially on the weekend, people would while away the evening sitting in front of their houses to catch the late sun or the fragrant breeze, and chat. For me to appear on Sunday and be gone by Monday would get some neighbors wondering how they could have missed seeing me arrive or depart. A jarring note.

I was able, though, to put in a couple of Sunday visits. On Friday around midnight, I would walk the three kilometers to Gaston's parents' house. I kept to the sparsely built-up side of the road, under a canopy of large poplars, opposite the blacked-out *Warme Landen* cafés; occasionally a new or departing patron would open the door on a sultry or gaudy atmosphere. I felt safe. I forced the pace on the more stately, tree-lined Phillip and Cyriel Verschaevestraat. A tall, chateau-like villa stood at its entrance, on a large corner lot. The street's darkened, brick-and-stone houses looked lifeless yet menacing. Only minutes more to go, through the old village with its narrow streets and small, less inimical houses. The Kleemstraat, finally. The door opened before I had time to knock.

On Saturday I would board the late train from Antwerp at the Belsele Village train station, only minutes from Gaston's parents' house. I would get off at Sinaai, the next stop, walk up the Statiestraat, and cross the Lokeren Road, smiling and waving at Gaston, Adrienne and Sylvain and at the neighbors sitting in front of their houses. I drew big smiles.

On Sunday, after supper, when the weather was nice, I might bring out a stepping stool and join the others on the patio. Gaston would sit on the front step, providing a buffer between me and the neighbors. Conversation was sparse — casual remarks about bikers riding by, people out of work.

Gaston would be the first to get up: time for me to take leave. I was the center of attention. We would file into the house. From the face Sylvain made at Julia it was clear that for him my visit had lasted long enough. Minutes later I would emerge in jacket and tie, escorted by Gaston, Adrienne and Sylvain. I would cross the Lokeren Road, feeling all eyes on me; turn and wave to the well-wishing onlookers, feeling important, board the train, get off in Belsele, and walk briskly to Gaston's parents' house.

I would scurry home in the dark of night. Straight to bed.

In bad weather, with people staying indoors, we followed the easy winter plan: I would show up Sunday morning, and be gone by Monday.

I am counting the days to Easter vacation.

CHAPTER 8 — TO DRONGEN AND BACK

My first sight ever of the countryside in spring. The land, bare and brown when I had seen it last, was a patchwork of green and yellow — a tender cover of clover and rapeseed and sprouting wheat fluttering gently in the breeze. Patches of white and yellow daffodils opened up to the sun. Scattered dandelions brightened fresh meadows. In our vegetable garden the onions and carrots and radishes and peas had sprouted tender shoots; Gaston had pointed out the various beds to me. Soon he would erect a trellis for the peas to start their climb, and poles for the beanstalks. The poplars along the road were filling out with young leaves. The forsythia bushes threw off splashes of vivid yellow. The magnolia trees were a dazzling white and mauve, the tightly-packed azaleas, a sensuous red. But most stunning were the orchards in bloom, dabs of bright colors on the land. Adrienne's parents had a hedged-in orchard, Gaston's parents had one behind the forge. I felt in an enchanted, safe realm under their low canopy of luminous white and pink blossoms. "Soon you'll see the fruit coming out," Gaston told me. "The apples and the pears, the cherries, the plums and the peaches." I was taking deep breaths, inhaling the renewed freshness that enveloped me. The anger had drained, and the longing: I was a regular city boy spending two weeks in the country, weeding the vegetable beds, walking on the back roads and the earthen paths, exchanging greetings, gaining confidence. My Easter vacation was on.

The Sunday after my arrival Adrienne decided that I should be seen going to church.

"I'll go with you," Gaston said. "They'll notice us and they will think that you are a good influence on me," he added with a chuckle. "We will have a beer afterwards at the *Oude Zwaan*."

I felt comfortable in the packed church, especially with Gaston. I had long since ceased to feel threatened at Mass, thanks partly to the congregants' constant coughing and snoozing during the sermon. Afterwards we waded into a noisy, jovial crowd at the *Oude Zwaan*. The loud, rumbling chatter, the bursts of laughter, surrounded me like a shield.

In the afternoon Gaston took me to an outdoor archery contest. The atmosphere was festive. The boisterous contestants, in shirtsleeves and suspenders, were milling around, sipping beer and waiting their turn. The arrows, sent swooshing from the solid, well-crafted bows, could have killed a goat. The archer would look intently at the target, as if to exorcise it, slowly raise his weapon, aim, tense up as he pulled the string, adjust his aim, and, after a moment of coiled immobility, release the arrow. I got caught up in the suspense. The more impressive the shot and the deeper the chorus of gasps, the more serious his mien, in a silent, noblesse-oblige display of modesty.

I took part, a few days later, in a rat hunt. Gaston had recruited his father and me to catch "the beast" that was eating the rabbits' food and decimating their young. Gaston had spotted the rodent inside the rabbit cages.

"It is living there. In the back. Out of sight. That big," — he was holding his hands thirty centimeters apart — "that's without the tail.... Milou!? Would be terrified of it," he said in answer to my question.

I was terrified, too, but didn't let on.

Gaston closed off the pump house from the backyard and from the kitchen. He then opened the door from the pump house to the stable. His father, armed with a stick, took up his assigned post by the rabbit cages. Gaston hoisted me on top of a shelf about five feet above the ground, to sit in the hay used as litter for the rabbits. He handed me my stick. I was looking down at the cages lining the opposite wall. I could see the rabbits below through the wire mesh. Gaston stood in ambush in the pump house, at the open doorway to my left. His father was to scare the rat out of its hideout. I was to deny it refuge on my shelf and force it to the ground.

The rat was hunkering down in the back of a cage, hugging the wall: I had seen its dark mass through the wire mesh when I entered the shed. Gaston gave the signal and his father began to knock furiously at the base of the cages. The panicked rat climbed on top of the cage and shot forth like a projectile across the shed toward my shelf in a straight, upward sloping line, as if aiming for me — I saw all of it, a furry gray beast with a long tail and, most electrifying, the muzzle and two glistening eyes. I was sitting cross-legged in the hay, petrified, holding up my stick with both hands. The rat changed course in midair, just as Gaston had predicted, bounced off Adrienne's hand-operated wash wringer, and landed on the floor, ready to streak through the doorway, its only escape route. Gaston pounced and nabbed the rat by the neck and pressed down on it, choking it to death.

"It's over," he said with a resounding curse. "This goddamn beast!"

His father also let out a juicy curse.

I lowered myself to the ground. Gaston was standing in the backyard, by the kitchen window, holding up the rat by its tail, like an important catch. There was blood at the tip of the animal's mouth. Adrienne knocked angrily on the glass pane and yelled at him to get rid of the damn thing instead of sticking his nose in it. He took it to the outhouse. The old blacksmith took a pinch of snuff. I brushed the hay off my pants.

At the dinner table, Adrienne stopped Gaston short:

"Not another word about that repulsive thing!"

"Gaston, you'll tell me later how you trapped it," my brother said. He had been playing with Simoneke.

"Didn't you hear? 'Not another word.' Do you want me to get into trouble? Ask Henri, when the two of you are alone."

"Oh, that wouldn't be fun."

✦ ✦ ✦

That Easter vacation, our "absentee" father came visiting. At long last. It was Adrienne's idea, prompted by conversations with Irène: the Don Juan from Antwerp had fired the young woman's imagination. She would not pass up an opportunity to refer to him, obliquely or even directly. Adrienne would relate those conversations with amused laughter:

" 'Poor boy,' Irène said to me, and with such compassion, 'having to travel to see his own father.' "

"And what did you say?" Gaston asked.

" 'Yes, it is sad, in a way. People can be strange. But the boy likes it, you know.' "

" 'But Adrienne! Doesn't he want to see where his little son lives, how he lives, the surroundings?' "

"And what did you say?"

"I told her that I had mentioned it to him, so had Henri. 'You know, Irène,' " I said to her, " 'in those lofty circles, they don't think like you and me.' "

" 'But Adrienne! Antwerp is so close!' Is she ever curious. And lusting."

"And what did you say?" Gaston's face was taut, his eyes had narrowed: he didn't like what he was hearing.

"I told her that I'll try to have him over. Come to think of it," — Adrienne was no longer smiling — "a father, however indifferent, would have been here, if only to keep up appearances. It is not altogether normal. Irène is coming out with it, but others may be having the same thoughts. Chasing women, working hard, that's all well and good. But with the Easter vacation even a woman-crazed school inspector can find the time for a short visit."

Gaston kept silent.

"I think," Adrienne continued after a pause, "that the papa has to show up *op den Hoek* (at the Corner, as the area around the Lokeren Road intersection was called)."

"How will you manage that?"

"Oh, the coming and going is simple. Sylvain will meet him at the station. He'll cross the Road holding his little boy by the hand. Same thing taking the train back to St-Niklaas."

"And how will you arrange for the women *op den Hoek* to sit, at that precise moment, by their windows and lust?"

Adrienne sat thinking for a short while, her hand at her chin.

"I'll call in Irène. She is better than the radio for spreading news."

"But Adrienne! The papa has a foreign accent as thick as my fist!"

"The papa will not open his mouth. Irène will be here for just a few minutes before he must leave. I'll do much of the talking. All about the children, of course. She'll chime in, excitedly, as I know her. The papa will nod, smile, laugh, he has a good laugh. He'll constantly stare at her with his big, smiling eyes. She won't know what to do with herself. Sylvain will have things to say to his father, you can rely on the little chum. It will only last a few minutes. She'll get up to take leave, 'I don't want to disturb any longer,' the usual thing, and I'll say 'but you haven't disturbed, not at all,' the usual thing. He'll get up, keep staring in her eyes and shake her hand, she'll melt, I'll scrape her off the floor and take her to the door. What else do you want to know?"

Gaston turned his head, speechless, in disbelief.

"*Ah godverdomme!*" ("goddamn!"), he rumbled with grudging admiration. He repeated the curse under his breath. "Have you ever!... Do as you please. I'll be at work."

"Gaston, I was just going to say, you should come." He looked dumbstruck. "Please do," she continued in the same breath, "so that I can later tell Irène — she surely will notice — that you have been here; it will seem odd if you don't put in an appearance."

Gaston turned slowly to Sylvain and me with his air of mock helplessness-in-the-face-of-stark-raving-madness   that   always made us laugh.

My father arrived. Gaston came calling. It was like a reunion of comrades-in-arms; my father's face lit up. When it was time for the big event, Adrienne turned to my father: "I'll do the talking, you work the charm." She then went to get Irène. Gaston was on his bike, at the gate, when the two women were crossing the road. He gave them a big hello.

Irène walked in, all worked up. My father motioned her with a smile and a wave of the hand to the nearest chair. In his prosperous-looking wide-striped, gray-blue suit, with his big smiling eyes behind black-rimmed eyeglasses, his large forehead, bushy eyebrows and thinning black hair flattened backwards he struck an impressive pose. Adrienne remained standing, which left Irène feeling even more exposed. Sylvain was standing by his papa. For an uncaring father and an abandoned child they looked rather chummy and at ease. My father had his arm around my brother's waist and was looking at him with smiling eyes that reflected the afternoon light streaming in from the kitchen window. A tender tableau. Sylvain was picking up the occasional slack in the conversation, telling his father in a tone of privacy about the farm, about Simoneke, about animals. Neither cared the least bit about animals. Sylvain never played with Milou. The only time he mentioned cats was when rumors made the rounds that cats were disappearing to turn up at the dinner table as rabbit: "We know where *our* rabbit comes from." Not a word about playing behind haystacks. Adrienne and Irène would chime in:

"Tell your father about the milking of the cows, how you won't drink the milk fresh out of the cow's udder." Or "You two are not rolling in the hay, are you?" That was Irène.

I was leaning with my elbows on the kitchen table.

My father fumbled once — to have kept silent at that moment would have been awkward: he let "*Ja, een deugniet*" ("yes, a rascal") slip out, pronouncing it "DOIKH-neet," with the "g" like the guttural in the German "*Macht.*" The "eu" sound, like in the French "*heureux,*" he missed altogether.

Irène got up, saying she didn't want to take up any more of our time. Adrienne protested mildly, "Okh, Irène, on the contrary, the boys talk about us in Antwerp."

She kept up the small talk, making it possible for my father to look smilingly into Irène's eyes and shake her hand without saying a word. Adrienne walked Irène to the front door. She came back grinning triumphantly.

"First class. She did say, though, 'A slight German accent, no?' "

"Yes?" my father asked, with raised eyebrows, serious all of a sudden, "and what did you say?"

" 'Seems only,' " I said. " 'He speaks mostly French, though. Wish I could speak Flemish like that.' "

"Will that start her thinking?" my father asked.

"Nooo, not Irène. She thanked me effusively for inviting her. She was going on and on over you. No, she got to see her man. Now she can fantasize."

They laughed.

☼ ☼ ☼

I needed a new suit: I had grown. My jacket was pulling at the waist and the sleeves showed too much wrist. I should be arriving in a well-fitting suit, as was becoming a boy from a well-to-do family.

Getting the material was the easy part: my father gave Adrienne the suit he had worn the day he and my mother arrived in Duizend Appels. (He was left with one, his finest, the one he had donned to impress Irène and which he hoped to wear on liberation day.) But where did one find a tailor? Adrienne turned to Maurice, Alice's husband, during one of the couple's frequent Sunday visits to Belsele. Maurice De Viaene was the man-about-town in the family; Drongen, where they lived, was a short tram ride from the city of Ghent.

Indeed, Maurice knew a tailor in Ghent, "Someone on the good side. He even knows English," he told Adrienne.

"You know him that well?" Adrienne asked.

"No. But he was in Canada around the time I was there. Bring me the suit. Send the boy to us after the Easter vacation and I'll take care of it."

"What could he have been up to, during his wild years, in those far away places?" Adrienne mumbled to me. She took the suit to Belsele.

Maurice's quest in North America remained an enigma to us. Once, commenting about manners and propriety, he told me that in the great plains of Canada the men would squat and relieve themselves wherever they happened to be, without interrupting their conversation.

"Right in front of you — nothing unusual," he said with a hearty laugh.

I was struck by that tableau on the Canadian prairie. It did not occur to me to ask any questions about the land. Canada was two men in a squatting tête-à-tête, in the middle of the flat, endless plain. That's all I ever heard about Maurice's sojourn in the New World.

Adrienne arranged with Alice for me to stay with her and Maurice for the entire two months until the summer vacation. "I will give her half of the support money I get from your father," she told me. "You will pass for Maurice's orphaned nephew. Drongen is a town; people are less nosy. That will give you a stretch of four months in the open."

The train compartment was empty. I nestled in the shady corner by the narrow window. The random slamming of the heavy oak doors was exciting, like an orchestra's tuning up before the concert. A last, lone slam, then silence. I waited for the sound of the stationmaster's whistle: it soared, imperious, through the scintillating, tranquil air. Silence again, for an instant, then the rush of the engine's first steam-letting. Another few seconds of intense anticipation and the train began to move. I suddenly felt lighter: I was going away, a regular passenger, to the reassuring sound of the engine's ever faster chugging. I was traveling to a distant, new destination, ensconced in an impregnable fortress, free: no raiding party could board the train, not before the next station. It had to stop before all laws and decrees could take effect, the laws by which the weak are governed by the mighty, and the decrees that seal their fate. I savored the movement, the puffing of the engine, the rumble of the wheels.

Within minutes the train pulled into 't Heike, a tiny hamlet on the way to Lokeren. A kerchiefed woman opened the door to my compartment and, grabbing hold of the iron side-bar, climbed in, one high, shallow step at a time. She then picked up a plump toddler held aloft by another woman who in turn climbed in. Both women had bags of produce. They sat down facing me, with the little boy to one side, by his mother, I concluded. The two women sized me up — the prelude to a dismissal — while striking up a conversation, and took no further notice of me. I had felt at ease from my first glimpse of them.

The little boy got restless. His mother gave him a crusty piece of bread which he fumbled voraciously into his mouth. His nose and cheeks disappeared behind the bread and his fat little wrists.

"Hearty eater," remarked her traveling companion.

"Oh yes, a pleasure," the mother said. "You should see how he finishes a big, plump tomato. Crazy about tomatoes. When he gets one in those little paws of his, *nothing*, but *nothing in the world* will make him let go of it. You try."

I looked at the invincible little paws. *Yes, nothing in their world.* There were no Germans in their peaceful village, on their horizon. Nothing, for those women, had changed. I could see them in a distant field at harvest time, wide-skirted, kerchiefed figures tying stalks of grain into shining bundles; I could see them milking the cows. I could see the tomato fiend chasing a hen on the farmyard. *You try.*

They got off in Lokeren. I was sorry to see them go; the next passenger might be curious about me, even engage me in a conversation. But no one took their place. A man in city clothes climbed in from the other side of the compartment and took a seat by the window on his side. *Country or city? Which city?* I looked at some desolate platforms on my side of the train, just so I could turn the back of my head to him. A couple came in and seated themselves opposite him. *Good. They'll be talking to each other.*

Silence. The train pulled out of Lokeren. The conductor entered
our compartment. He seemed to know the man: they had a brief,
friendly exchange and I noticed his country dialect: *not from
Antwerp*. I felt reassured: Antwerpians have an eye for Jews. The
other man chimed in, the woman made an approving, chuckling
sound, and a lively conversation ensued and continued long after
the conductor had left.

I could give myself over to the contemplation of the landscape in spring colors: patches of bright yellow; of tender green
shoots; of dense clover; of neatly streaked brown earth; stands
of trees; run-off ditches; meandering earthen paths; a stretch of
woods; thinly fenced-in meadows; free-roaming horses, placid
cows; lone, dark-red, brick structures, aglow in the sun; rows of
sleek, wind-breaker trees whose young foliage fluttered in the
breeze; white apple and pear orchards, pink cherry orchards —
some, abutting the right of way, blotted out the landscape for a
few entrancing moments with a burst of sun-dappled white and
pink blossoms. The train lumbered across the flat, sun-drenched
countryside, with a few short stops at rural stations. In turn lulling and exciting, stirring: I wished the land to be mine, to be of
it, be free.

I was feeling comfortable and safe, almost legitimate, well before the train entered, in short order, the stations of Dampoort
and Gentbrugge, in Ghent. Mine was the following stop, St-
Pieters, Ghent's main station.

I got off. I moved with the flow — I relished being in the midst
of the anonymous crowd. *Gent, O Gent...* A city, like Antwerp, but
whose inhabitants, like the villagers of Belsele, were not practiced in spotting an Antwerpian Jew.

I emerged from St-Pieters station onto a square with a cir-
cular, tree-lined little park. Electric streetcars were circling it,
coming from or riding off into the avenues that converged on
the square. I cut across the pocket park, bearing left, as instructed, toward the traffic island where I was to wait for the tram
with end destination Nevelen. Suddenly I caught sight, with a
jolt, of a bareheaded German officer on the terrace of a café.
He was reading a book. In a true reader's pose. Like my father.
His head — dark hair with an intimation of gray, civilian trim —
was slightly bent, his neck, curving. He was looking down on the

page, elbow resting on the table, hand by his chin, two fingers lining his cheek. On the bare, whitish round table, an officer's cap, a white cup and saucer, and his book, a real book, I knew it right away, an oeuvre, not a military manual. I took it all in in one glance. A German, absorbed and peaceful; civilized. I was shaken: *Would he also kill me? Could there be a reason? A legitimate reason?* Moments later I was standing at the tram stop, looking straight ahead, casual, like an habitué; and feeling wretched, for having doubted, for that one moment of doubt.

To remain unnoticed on the tram I leaned back in my seat and looked out the window, avoiding eye contact with the passengers facing me on both sides of the aisle. *Would he?...* I closed my eyes but opened them almost right away and stole glances at the passengers opposite me: no lingering looks in my direction. Back to staring through the window.

The trees lining the road came into view one by one, and, as we picked up speed, flitted by in a rhythmic, numbing whir. Buying my ticket from the friendly, avuncular conductor got me focused again on my destination. Drongen. A township by the Leie river, with row houses and sidewalks, and a big Catholic seminary. "You'll see it across the Leie," Maurice had told me. "A castle on a large property stretching down to the water. The Catholic Church," he had continued with an edge to his voice, "the biggest land and property owner around." I would pass for an orphaned relative of his, past school-age, up from Wallonia for a two-month stint; my schooled Flemish and fluent French would fit right in. People knew little about Maurice: he was not an old-timer and not given to personal confidences, and he knew how to handle busybodies, Alice had assured me with a grin. His custom-made shoes were prized for their fineness and elegance. "Real works of art," Alice's mother had told me. "Fetching a lot of money." It had aroused my fancy. I had pictured myself helping Maurice and learning how to make shoes, taking breaks in the kitchen with a cup of coffee. A working man.

The tram was rolling along, leaving behind the lone houses by the road, the flowering gardens, the farms scattered on the land, the orchards in bloom. Occasional bicycle riders plied the earthen bicycle path on the far side of the road. A bright afternoon, and all was well. I felt like a traveler again. My excitement mounted as we approached Drongen. Finally, the main street, row houses, buildings, paved sidewalks. My stop came up, the café *Aan den Groenen Boomgaard* (At the Green Orchard). Alice was waiting. Her face lit up in a big smile. I had arrived.

✿ ✿ ✿

I took to Drongen from the first day. A small town hugging the river Leie, it offered the anonymity of a city neighborhood. I roamed freely, to the shady town square, in the countryside, on the grassy river bank. I ran errands for Alice. My presence did not raise eyebrows. A stranger's friendly nod, in a store, or even a neighbor's, on the street, were not freighted with question marks. No one seemed particularly interested in me, not even the baker or the grocer — on my occasional visits in Duizend Appels I had always felt the villagers' eyes on me, the polite boy of privilege from a troubled family. I loosened up.

I watched Maurice craft the fine shoes he was known for. He worked by the window of his top-floor workshop. He would pause occasionally to cast a lingering look at the sky, the roofs and the yards of Drongen. No, he could not teach me shoemaking, leather was too scarce and expensive to waste. But he showed me how to use a lighter sewing machine and gave me a heap of soft top shoe leather scraps to do with as I pleased. I patched together a huge shopping bag that got much use.

I liked walking by myself on the narrow field paths — the wheat was coming up, green and tender, sprinkled with red poppies — and along the railroad right-of-way. I'd be absorbed in thoughts, or wondering about the life in the houses and on the farms dotting the flat Flemish land. Once, I lost my way. Tense moments: to be late for dinner was a disturbing thought, like a breach of trust; yet asking, in schooled Flemish, in the middle of farm country, for directions to Drongen would have seemed odd. I sweated it out, hurrying the pace, and made it on time. I took, henceforth, straight, easy-to-retrace itineraries.

I liked strolling by the Leie despite the occasional barking that came from the villas under the shade trees, on top of the embankment. *These damn dogs. Is someone watching me from behind the curtains?* On a sunny afternoon I might go down to the river, lie in the warm grass, and peruse the "Complete Works of Hendrik Conscience" that Maurice had handed me; or stare, both awed and thrilled, at the vastness above. The sky was mine again. Mine also the earth under me, the grass, the dandelions. I delighted in catching grasshoppers, just as I had as a nine-year old in Heide, before the war. Forgotten was the capsule suspended between sky and earth with the garret window as porthole. I had regained my place in Creation.

Once, I spied, on the opposite bank, the seminarians — a column of black cassocks with thick, white-and-pink necks and heads of close-cropped hair — taking, two abreast, a regimented, subdued walk through the landscaped gardens of the seminary. Farm boys, most of them, it was obvious to me; well-fed and protected. *Studying Latin... I'll bet anything my Latin is better than theirs... And Hebrew...* I could not imagine them tackling Hebrew. The Old Testament without Hebrew! Maimed. And without the commentaries of Rashi and Rashbam, and the Midrash. How ignorant they would remain... Learning our Scriptures, and training to be our enemies. *Jewish boys should be hiding under these cassocks.* The seminarians filed back into the seminary.

We were four in our household: Alice's older sister Maria had come to help out with the heavy chores. She had begun to date a young man from Drongen, Louis Steyaert, and was in no hurry to return to Belsele. Alice did the cooking only, and some shopping. She was nursing an intestinal ailment that required rest and regular visits to the doctor in Ghent, but was of good cheer despite her setback. Maurice baked bread for her: the baker's did not agree with her. He worshipped his wife. An agnostic, he had only scorn for the wealthy Catholic Church and the pope who "had blessed the Italian arms." He was good at telling stories and jokes and was the first to burst out laughing at the punch line. Alice also liked a good laugh. I dried the dishes, in addition to running simple errands. I would stand behind Maria, tease her, stack the dishes in a whimsical way on the porcelain counter, or keep an overturned, dripping pan rocking on its round ears and grinding away, rhythmically. I might even eke a reluctant smile out of her: she could be a bit morose and snappy. She was nicknamed *Muis* (Mouse) for her habit of picking up bread crumbs with her index finger, at the table, and taking them to her mouth. The two women had taken to calling me Rik, short for Hendrik, the Flemish equivalent of Henri. Once, waiting impatiently by the outhouse for Maria to come out, I made up a poem, on the spot:

Lieve Juffrouw Muis / Kom vlug uit het kakhuis,
Ik moet scheiten gaan / En kan nie' meer staan.
In free translation:
Dear Miss Mouse / Come quick out of the shit-house,
Shit I must / Lest I bust.

The door flung open, narrowly missing me, and Maria shot out, laughing. Running to tell them, I knew. Indeed, my poetic prowess had preceded me in the kitchen: I got a grinning reception and the sobriquet "Rik... *de Scheiter*" ("the Shitter").

One Sunday afternoon the five of us — Maria's beau was of the party — took the tram to Ghent. Emerging from the narrow Veldstraat, I glimpsed the Korenmarkt, the old Grain Market: the wide-open square was flooded with sunlight and lined with imposing, age-darkened edifices and old houses. We were in the heart of Old Ghent, a vibrant, lived-in place. People everywhere; I was taken with their casual deportment.

Maurice led us onto the St Michaels bridge, off the lower end of the Korenmarkt, to the left, "the best place to see the city," he told me. Downstream, on an island in the Leie, stood a medieval fortress.

"The Gravensteen, the castle of the Counts of Flanders," Maurice explained. He waited. Following my gaze, he swung his arm to the right, in line with the bridge, and ticked off:

"St Nicholas Church on the other side of the Korenmarkt. The belfry further down, and last, St Bavo's Cathedral. This one" — to the right, by the bridge — "is St Michael's Church."

Clad in elaborate stonework and standing in close proximity to each other, the four structures looked like a city unto themselves rising from the deep past and towering in the sky. I finally lowered my gaze to a row of step-gabled houses by the bridge along the Leie.

"The guild houses," Maurice said. "Do you know about the guilds?" he asked.

"Yes," I said. "We learned about the guilds in school."

We had dwelled on Ghent, the mythic city-state, in Govaerts' class at Tachkemoni. Its prosperous traders, bold architects and fearless warriors had seemed to me like a lost tribe.

"You know," Maurice said. "We taught the French a lesson."

"I know," I said. "Jan Breydel, *de Guldensporenslag* [the Battle of the Golden Spurs]" — Maurice smiled, "*Goedendag*," and I waved an imaginary spiked bludgeon, the weapon, suggestively called "goodday," with which Jan Breydel's citizen-soldiers welcomed the French horsemen after luring them into a swamp. Among the fallen were more than 500 noblemen recognizable by their golden spurs which the Flemish gleefully retrieved.

"We," Maurice had said: the line was unbroken.

We walked across the Korenmarkt, past St Nicholas Church, to the Belfry, on to City Hall, looping back on a narrow, curving street, up the Korte Munt in the direction of the Gravensteen. Streets and squares, old and new, were brimming with life. I refrained from gawking, trying to look as casual as the locals, but took it all in, thirstily: the strollers in their Sunday clothes — couples, families, some with children in tow; the bustling public establishments — the waiters, loaded trays aloft, would glide between tables, serve, hover over patrons, dart back to the counter; the yellow trams; the gleaming steel tracks; the glistening cobblestones; the venerable buildings; the houses with the secure life behind unrevealing windows. Ghent, old and new, was basking in the sun, contented. The only German soldier I saw — he walked briefly in front of us — had a female at his side. His pants were tucked, somewhat untidily, into coarse black boots. Her bare, thick legs were covered with sores. Well paired, I thought. Motley, but unthreatening.

We went to the Veneziana, a fancy ice cream parlor near the Gravensteen, the Counts' Castle. Maurice treated. Alice and Maria ordered, each, a *dame blanche*. I had never heard of such sophisticated ice cream; clearly a discriminating woman's choice. I had vanilla. The two men got beer. Louis treated next. I sensed from his casualness and smug smile that he was observing a protocol between men. After a short while I signaled the waiter: "Five Spa-citron." The two women begged off, No, not for me, please. "Three Spa-citron," I told the waiter. Maurice and Louis took a sip. I forced myself to drink most of my beverage, and felt foolish. The next time we went to Ghent, Maurice told me in his avuncular tone that I should not spend my money. I wasn't going to, I said.

✵ ✵ ✵

About two weeks into my stay in Drongen, Maurice told me
that we were going to see the tailor in Ghent. Mr. Kiem was his
name. Maurice wrapped my father's suit in a cloth and tied it to
the baggage rack of his bicycle. I took Alice's bike. And off we rode
to Ghent along the tree-lined, sun-dappled Drongen Road, onto
Einde Were and Ekkergemstraat to the tailor's house. "Remember
the route," Maurice told me, "you'll go by yourself for the fittings."

We walked up the stoop. Maurice rang the bell. The tailor
opened the door and let us into the front hallway. A stairway
hugging the wall to the left led straight upstairs. We entered the
living room off the front hallway, at the right.

Maurice was brief: I needed a suit; it was to be cut out of a suit
that had belonged to my late father. The tailor took the jacket,
held it up by the shoulders, examined it, front and back.

"Well made," he said to himself as much as to Maurice.

He then held it up by the collar with his left hand, opened up
one side, glanced at the lining, opened up the other side... something had caught his attention, I could tell.

"The lining is also in excellent condition," he said. "A real
fine suit."

He folded the jacket and put it over his left arm. He had a
brief look at the trousers.

"You want long pants," he said to me.

"Yes." My first, like a man's.

He slung them on top of the jacket, looked at Maurice and
quoted an amount. Maurice agreed. The tailor then put his right
hand on my shoulder, looked at me with big, dark eyes, and said,
intently, "My boy, you are going to have one fine suit. You'll feel
proud in it." His gaze lingered on me a little bit longer. His tone
had the solemnity of an oath. He turned around, parted a curtain separating the living room from his atelier, and proceeded
to take my measurements. I was to come back for two fittings.
Maurice and I left.

As we biked back to Drongen, I asked, "Maurice, is he wondering about me?"

The tailor had not asked one single question. Relieved as
I was about his discretion — all questions, in those days, even
the polite ones that animated small talk, held the threat of a
challenge, of a stumble — his silence with an impassive face had
struck me as deliberate.

"Maybe," Maurice answered, "but not about what you think. Anyway, he's on the good side."

I was not worried. I had felt safe from the moment the two men faced each other, the tailor with his big, searching eyes, Maurice with his self-assured matter-of-factness. And the tailor's laying his hand on my shoulder had made it a full moment, given entirely to the pleasure of getting "one fine" new suit. I lived intensely in those moments, unburdened by thoughts about the past and the future, about holding on. It raised only further my trust in Maurice, in his judgment. We hadn't even rehearsed our visit to the tailor as I would have for any departure from routine. "No need to," Maurice had said when I had brought it up. I stopped wondering about the tailor's unformulated questions and enjoyed thoroughly the ride in the sun.

When I went that same week for the first fitting, the tailor was not there.

"He should be here any minute," his wife told me, and she asked me to wait in the living room.

I sat down on the couch by the window. Two armchairs, one on each side of the couch, faced each other. To the left I could see the hallway through the open living room door. The staircase further down the hallway was not visible from the couch. The tailor's wife moved to the left armchair, between me and the living room door. It was obvious from the way she sat down and the stiff posture she assumed that she intended to uphold the protocol for important callers and keep me company until her husband's return. She tried small talk. She was stiff and polite; I was stiff and uncomfortable. The wait dragged on. The conversation was awkward, alternating with deep, palpable silences.

It was during one of those silences that I heard a muffled, almost inaudible noise on the carpeted staircase. The tailor's wife began talking at once, at a higher pitch. I acknowledged her words with dutiful nods, but my attention was riveted to the carpeted staircase behind the living room wall. I heard, in the middle of one of her labored sentences, the same muffled noise again. A step. No doubt. The tailor's wife kept talking. But the feather-light steps on the staircase, separated by the same long intervals, were getting through. She tried to talk some more, but all she uttered were dwindling fragments of sentences. I cast an involuntary glance at the hallway. She stopped talking altogether.

The silence deepened with each deliberate, muffled step. A frail old woman? Her mother, perhaps? Certainly not a Jew; that would have given him away. The sound of steps was followed by a faint shuffle, upstairs. A pause, then the distinct sound of a door pulled shut, gently. Moments later a cat walked through the living room door, arching its back, tail curling upward.

The tailor's wife picked up the cat with both hands and pressed it against her chest. "You devil of a cat!" she exclaimed, "you were upstairs again! You know that you can't go upstairs!... What were you up to this time!?... Hey!?... You mischievous cat!" She kept up the scolding for a while, in the same loud voice, before letting the cat off her lap.

There was more small talk — about the cat. More silence. The tailor walked in. We stood up. We exchanged greetings while his wife stood there, looking straight at him for a short while before she said with a bit of mock exaggeration: "Guess what... our cat did it again..." He looked at her, questioning, tense. "Went upstairs" — he lowered his gaze; he understood, I knew it — "while we were waiting for you... you were quite late!" A moment later she was gone.

The tailor parted the drape and preceded me into his workshop. There was only a piece of a jacket with one sleeve and the front side showing the coarse inner lining of one lapel, all held together with long stitches of crisscrossing white thread. With a thin wafer of white chalk, the tailor drew long lines and little crosses and marked the padding of the shoulder. He tore and pinned. The first fitting was over.

Back at the house in Drongen, I found Maurice and Alice in the kitchen. Maurice was standing by the stove with a cup of coffee in his hand.

"The fitting went well..." I let the sentence hang, making sure that I had their attention. "There's a Jew in that house."

"Yes?... What makes you say that?" They looked surprised, but not one bit incredulous.

I told the story of the strange noises and the effusiveness over the cat, and of the tailor's silent, knowing stare. "He must have sneaked out of the kitchen at the end of the hallway and left the door open, to avoid all noise. The cat got out and came into the living room. I distinctly heard footsteps going up the staircase. Nothing came down."

"It wouldn't surprise me of him," Maurice said. "Now you see, he can be trusted all right. Anyhow, he still knows nothing about us. If anything, we know about them." Indeed, Maurice had never mentioned my name or an address; neither had I. We were never asked, either.

I got a lift from having been in that other safe house, from having seen more caring Gentiles; and from knowing of another Jew in hiding, free. A kindred, unseen stranger. A shared experience. A common history, that old, unbroken link. I had never heard of Jews in Ghent. Well of course! That would be the place to hide! There might be more Jews in Ghent. And in other places where Jews had never lived before. And in Wallonia.

The second fitting was even shorter than the first. More tracing with white chalk, more tearing and pinning. I didn't see much change; but then, I believed in progress even when I could not see it. There were no strange noises.

I returned on the appointed day to pick up my suit. It fit well; it made me feel good, as the tailor had promised.

One day after the war, I was sitting with Maurice and Alice at the terrace of a café in Drongen, having pastry and coffee, enjoying a tango, small talk and the balmy air of a Sunday summer afternoon, when Maurice suddenly turned to me, "Guess whom I met in Ghent." He was grinning, and Alice had the smile of an accomplice.

"The tailor," I said in a stroke of inspiration.

"Yes."

"So?" I prodded, "what happened?"

"Well... we greeted each other, this and that, you know..."

"... Yes. And then?"

"He asked me if my little Jew had gotten through all right?" Maurice leaned forward, laughing; his big, green eyes reflected his past surprise and were gauging mine.

"How did he know!?" I blurted out.

"I didn't ask."

"Why not?"

"I wouldn't give him the satisfaction!" Maurice and Alice were grinning.

"So what *did* you say?"

"Well," Maurice said, "I just answered his question. All I said was, 'My little Jew got through just fine.' "

"...Then?..."

"Then I asked him, 'And did *your* Jew make it through all right?' You should have seen his face!" Maurice burst out laughing. "Was he flustered! Right away he asked me how I knew."

"And did you tell him?" The wrong question to ask, but he had me squirming like a fish on the hook.

"No! Of course not!"

"Then what *did* you say?"

"I just said, 'suppose You tell me first how you knew.' "

"So..."

"So he told me," Maurice continued, with a somewhat sobered grin, "that your father's suit still had the original label on the lining of the inner breast pocket: 'MOSCOVICZ TAILLEUR ANVERS'. 'I knew right away, on your first visit,' he told me, 'the moment I looked at the lining.' Then he asked me again how I knew." Maurice's grin widened. "So I told him about the noises you heard and his wife's comedy with the cat. I told him that you knew right away. You should have seen his face. 'I *told* her that she didn't handle it right with the damn cat!' he burst out. 'I gave her an argument about it!... The smart lad.' "

They were both laughing. I could see in their eyes the approval for the 'smart lad' I had been. Flattered, I must have smiled. But I was taken aback: we had been exposed without even suspecting it.

"Then he asked me," Maurice was talking now without further prodding, "whether you had given us any trouble? I said 'No, not at all, he was fun to have around. He comes to visit now and then. And how about your Jew?' "

" 'Lord,' he said, 'what an awful experience! He was in his twenties. Could not sit still. Took risks. Would leave the house. Go to the movies, or God knows where. We couldn't control him. We would sometimes wait for hours, not knowing whether he would return, whether we were still safe. He left the day the English showed up. We never heard from him again.' "

We were silent for a while.

✡ ✡ ✡

The summer in Belsele saw my graduation as a working man. Gaston had started a sideline business, the processing of oats into a table cereal. To this end he had built several pieces of equipment from parts and scraps: a thrasher — a stationary horizontal cylinder whose rotating axle had radial bars soldered to it, for separating the husk from the grain; a whirlpool sort of washtub — the floating husk would be skimmed off the top; a dryer blowing hot air through a large, fine-meshed sieve holding the grain — on warm days Gaston might spread the wet grain on a canvas, in the sun; and a laundry-wringer kind of contraption to flatten the grains into flakes. The equipment, activated by the main assembly of electrically driven pulleys and belts, was housed in the rear, in a secluded part of the forge accessible directly from the kitchen. The space had good daylight, with a view of the orchard. Gaston's mother sold the oat flakes in Belsele village.

I would leave the house dressed in khaki pants and shirt — no one was to know that I worked solid days at the forge making oatmeal cereal — and change at Gaston's parents' house into work overalls that Adrienne had sewn for me.

Gaston gave me a brief initiation. I soon got the feel of the operation and kept the oats moving and the machines humming; no hitches, no dead periods. I was in control, master of my private realm. Gaston came by occasionally to see how I was doing and to pick up the finished product. He approved of my work — the handling, the tempo; I could see it in the narrowing of his eyes. His repressed smile, though, and his silence, were the real compliment: I was too old for praise; I was expected to perform well.

As sales tapered off, I would take days off from work, to walk in the countryside and to putter in the vegetable garden.

On my way to and from the forge I would sometimes spy groups of vacationing Blackshirt youth, boys my height and smaller. Their abode was the castle-like villa on the shaded estate wedged between the Phillip and Cyriel Verschaevestraat and the New Road. They would run around on the lawn or engage in marching drills at the sounds of a whistle. Glimpsing them, at day's end, as they stood in black formations and gazed upward at their fluttering flag, hearing the clear-voiced, rousing call, "*Vliegt the blauwvoet*" ("When the merlin flies"), and the single-voiced response of the assembled, like a battle cry, "*STORM op zee!*" ("STORM at sea!"), felt like watching a scene from an alien world. (The line from a poem by Albrecht Rodenbach was the slogan, and the merlin, the symbol of the Flemish struggle against frenchification in the nineteenth century. Both slogan and symbol had been appropriated by the Flemish Blackshirt Youth.) I would hurry past. *Ignorant rabble. Blood enemies.* I had nothing in common with them, I felt, not even the Flemish tongue. I spoke a different language.

✡ ✡ ✡

I paid a Sunday visit to my parents in St-Niklaas. They looked gaunt. We had, as usual, the little dining room to ourselves. Their hosts kept busy behind the closed, glass-paneled kitchen door. We spoke softly.

"Your suit is well made," my father said.

"Looks good on you," my mother concurred. "Wear it in good health," she said intently. "In freedom, soon, soon."

"*Oomeye'n*," my father echoed.

"How was your stay with Alice and Maurice?" he asked.

"Wonderful."

"Fine people," my mother said.

"All the Van Dammes are fine people," my father said. "Exceptional."

"Did you have enough to eat?" My mother's unfailing question. They were hungering.

"Of course. Even ice cream, in Ghent."

"Ice cream..."

I felt privileged, had felt so the moment I walked in the door.

"How is Alice doing?" my father asked.

"She is of delicate health," I said. "Something with the digestive system. She sees regularly the specialist in Ghent."

"Does it affect the household?" my mother asked.

"Not at all. Maurice dotes on her, bakes the most delicious bread just for her. And Maria is there for weeks on end to do the heavy work."

"Maria does not feel put upon?"

"On the contrary. She likes it there. She has a suitor. They go often to Ghent, just a tram ride away. Everybody is as happy as can be."

"So you had a great time."

"The best so far. Complete freedom. I walked a lot. We laughed all the time."

"No nosy neighbors?" my father asked.

"No. They didn't bother us. It's a street like ours in Antwerp but busier, with a few shops. And the tram runs through it. In Antwerp the neighbors might have had a hunch. Not in Drongen where Jews are the last thing on people's minds."

It felt good having things to tell.

"Are there relatives?" my father asked.

"Yes. A mason and his family. We stopped by, once, on a visit."

"They don't know..."

"Nooo! I don't know exactly what Maurice told them. But he is very smart. They never asked any questions."

In fact, they all knew that I was a Jew in hiding. It came out after the war; the mason's son told me. I was dumbfounded, and a little peeved, that my secret had not been airtight. An entire household, knowing without the need to know. Then also, it warmed my heart to find out that I had had silent supporters, people rooting for me.

"I understand that Maurice is much older than Alice," my mother said.

"Yes, but he is a great guy. Lively. And so funny. How he speaks about the Church! Its wealth! Its land holdings! He despises the pope for blessing the Italian arms. Holy water or the sign of a cross, I don't remember, over a tank."

"Did you make any comment?" my mother asked.

"No. I listened and enjoyed."

"Good. Remember, it's their pope and their religion. They can say anything they want. Hearing it from an outsider might rub them the wrong way."

"I know that."

"Does Maurice have a lot of work?" my father asked.

"Oh yes. Repairs. And he makes new shoes, fine, luxury shoes. Expensive. For men and women. You should see that, the craftsmanship. How clever, real artistry. He caresses the shoes as he fashions them."

My father smiled, a gleam of recognition in his eyes. He prized a well-made shoe. He had run his mother's leather and shoe business in Kolbuszowa before emigrating to Belgium. He always took a good look at his shoes at bedtime as at noteworthy artifacts, turning each one over before putting it down. Back in Antwerp he would shine or buff our shoes as part of his early morning routine.

"I asked him to teach me shoemaking," I continued. "He said that it would take too long and that he could not afford to waste good leather."

"Nu," my mother mumbled. "Shoemaking..."

"Well," my father said, laughing, "you want to sweep streets and he wants to repair shoes."

My mother cracked a reluctant smile. We fell silent.

"How do you like the Italians?" I asked, to reanimate the conversation. Ten days earlier, on the second day of September, King Victor-Emmanuel and General Badoglio had taken Italy out of the Axis in the wake of the allied successes in North Africa and the landings in Sicily and the Boot of Italy.

My mother was looking away. Her face had turned grim.

"Such good news, mama, the end is in sight, and you get worried all of a sudden?"

"When am I not worried, child? You know that they rounded up the Belgian Jews? The exempt, so-called. Adrienne must have told you."

"She did." I had put it out of my mind.

Gaston's mother, Léontine, had learned it from Van Kerckvoorde, the Judiciary Police official for whom she had become an Underground courier.

"One day they lose the Italians," my father said. "The next, they swoop down on the few remaining Jews. They are getting desperate in the face of defeat."

"I am sure they planned it regardless," my mother said. "They are after the very last Jew they can get, win or lose. It's a hatred that knows no bounds."

"The Kahans..." I ventured. My parents' friends, the booksellers. Belgian nationals, old-timers — Mr. Kahan was born in Antwerp.

"They went into hiding from the beginning," my mother said. "In Wallonia. They did not believe in German promises. They wanted us to join them. They even found a place for us. Govaerts would have taken us there had we not been able to come to Belsele to be near the two of you." Then, after a pause: "We have to be very careful."

"We are very careful, mama."

We grew silent again.

That summer of 1943, the military governor had yielded to mounting pressure from Berlin to liquidate Belgian Jewry — Himmler himself, the head of the SS and the German secret services, had gotten involved. On an early-September night the German police and military, with the assist of the Flemish and Walloon SS, struck simultaneously in Antwerp and Brussels: they captured about one thousand people — hitherto "exempt" Belgian nationals — in violation of their pledge to the Belgian authorities. They also hauled in committee members and employees of the Antwerp *Judenrat* and their families. (Weeks earlier they had released a number of Belgian Jews detained at the Dossin barracks in Mechelen to bolster the general feeling of immunity; it lured some out of hiding.) The "Belgian" *Transport*, XXII B, left three weeks later for Auschwitz.

It took another three weeks for the dismayed secretaries-general to send a letter to the military governor, wishing to "draw his attention to the painful impression made on the Belgian population by measures that target some of their fellow citizens," and beseeching him to "intervene to put an end to a situation which offends the most vital rules of law and the most basic feelings of humanity." By then more than 22,000 people, including more than 8,000 children, had been deported, foreigners all.

The Military Authority placated the officials by pledging to halt all further arrests of Jews holding Belgian citizenship. Once again the Germans scored without making a dent in their working relationship with the country's administrators.

It was time, I felt, to take leave of my parents when my father broke the silence:

"Rosh Hashanah is coming up," he said.

"On what day?" I asked.

He told me. Ten days after that will be Yom Kippur, it went through my mind.

"I'll fast on Yom Kippur." Faux pas. I knew it as I was speaking.

"You are a committed Jew," my mother weighed in. "Piety is something else — it goes with a normal life. In our circumstances one must eat to preserve one's strength."

"I understand." But I had already resolved to fast.

"The main thing," my father said, "is that you are both safe, and you both have the essentials." ("Don't fast on Yom Kippur. Eat what you will be given. You are exempt," he had told me a year earlier — it was Rosh Hashanah night — when my brother and I left the hideout above the Flemish butcher shop in Antwerp for Belsele.)

After another short silence my father took my hand in his, and said in a solicitous tone: "We are happy to see you. Go now, go. There is no sense for you to be locked in with us."

"Yes, my dear one," my mother said. "Enjoy the outdoors, the sun. And take care. Take good care."

We got up. My father kissed me avidly on both cheeks. My mother pressed me against her, eyes closed.

In September I was back in Drongen for another two months. Adrienne had arranged it with Alice in trying to provide me with as much of a reprieve from hiding as was deemed safe: there was a limit to the time a youngster could be seen idling about, in Drongen or anywhere else, without arousing suspicion.

I resumed my activities of the previous spring, most of all, the walks along the Leie and in the fields. The wheat, graced with bluebottles, stood tall now, ears bending under their own weight.

A couple of days before Yom Kippur I asked Alice for a beef-steak to fortify myself for the fast. Meat was scarce and expensive. She prepared a rich, delicious meal and kept me company as I sat eating before dusk. I later took my place at the supper table but did not partake of the meal.

"Are you allowed to relieve yourself?" Maurice asked me. He was serious.

"Of course," I answered, laughing. How strange our customs and rituals must seem to others, I thought.

I spent Yom Kippur day walking on country roads, sitting by the river, napping, feeling both reconnected to my past and severed from it. Maurice gave me a slice of Alice's special bread to break the fast. I then partook of supper.

CHAPTER 9 — BELSELE

The sky was gray. The bare treetops in distant Sinaai looked desolate. The gable of the *Chalet* was a dull off-white, the roof of the butcher's house, a lifeless black. The *tillimel* lay on the glass-topped night table next to the packs of cards. By the chair, the latest issue of *Het Vrije Waasland.* (It had not occurred to me to ask Adrienne, before leaving for my second stint in Drongen, to save the September and October issues: I had not been able to see beyond the two more months of carefree days in the open.) I was standing in the bedroom doorway. From the open garret window came a chest-expanding, lonesome freshness. Time, again, was trickling by.

It had taken me several days to get readjusted. I had arrived "from Antwerp," on a Saturday, still flush with Drongen, with the smooth, pleasant train ride — I had *my* seat, *my* compartment; even the countryside had felt mine: the bond I had forged with it gave me title.

Walking up the staircase in Adrienne's and Gaston's house, that night, and entering the garret had signaled the end of six months of freedom. Still a free day left. It was over on Sunday night when I took off my shoes shortly before the last train for Antwerp was to leave. Adrienne pumped water in my pail and took it upstairs; she was the first to retire for the night. Gaston would be last, as usual. I calmed down in the garret: there was the buffer of a night's sleep. The shock came on Monday morn-ing, the shock of facing familiar, sterile surroundings, of having to relive the past: another fall in hiding, another winter? I could not concentrate, at first, on the printed page or on a card game. I did not resume praying: the *Book of Psalms* was to be my sole link to my people. I would still read them. But the fervor was gone. I was doing time again, without a set term; it felt like life.

Once more, a routine set in; it felt drabber than the one be-fore the six-month hiatus. My imagination did not roam as far afield as it had the previous year. I fell back on a few staple fanta-sies, entertained fewer and less trenchant arguments. I relegated God to the dark cosmic recesses.

I was into my second fall-and-winter stretch of hiding. It was harder than the first.

———

That winter we ate a lot of succulent fish: an exceptional, season-long haul of North Sea herring — no one could remember such abundance — turned into a bonanza for Belsele. Trucks weighed down with heaping loads of fish would rumble by at night on their way to Antwerp. They would slow down to a crawl as they climbed the New Road overpass above the railroad tracks one mile east of us. Herring would slide off and spill onto the roadway. It was not long before young men and youngsters equipped with rakes and buckets waited in ambush at the foot of the overpass. It became an organized nightly expedition. One young man endowed with feline agility — his big, deep-set, gray eyes in a strong face glared like those of a predator — would hoist himself onto the back of the truck as it was shifting into low gear, sink into the herring, shovel frenetically with arms and body, and jump off at the crest of the overpass. His helpers would collect the fish into buckets and cart it away. Plump, fresh herring was plentiful and cheap all winter.

Those predations did not go unnoticed, but there was little the truckers could or would do about it. Tightly fastened tarpaulins were snapped off in seconds. I found it all exciting, especially the Tarzan-like exploits of the Big Cat. I asked Gaston, who was as agile and strong as anyone, whether he would consider a nightly catch. The long and hard look he gave me stripped the glamor off the enterprise and revealed it for what it was: thievery by a bunch of low-life characters. Shamed, I regretted the question, even the thought.

✿ ✿ ✿

News about the deportations reached Belsele. I overheard Adrienne mentioning it to Gaston: "People were talking about it. At the baker's, in the village. They heard it from some men working in Antwerp, it seems." After a pause: "*Zuh mawkuh dee kapot*" ("They are killing them").

Silence filled the house. I kept hearing "*Zuh mawkuh dee kapot.*" Them. The deported. The ones they catch. Like so many chickens. Not me. Still, that frightening ghost... It had never felt that close. So there, no more mystery. But then, it never was a real mystery. Not to us. Would the villagers be more prone to wonder about us? My mind went blank.

Sounds of life roused me out of my numbness: the click of a door handle, the clanging of the pump, the splash of water falling. I moved the queen of hearts over the king of hearts; the following half dozen moves led to gridlock. I put the cards away. I felt diminished.

That evening, after supper, we sat at our usual spots around the stove. The potbelly was cooling down to a bluish black. Gaston had put out the fire with ashes from the trap in the base of the stove, to save the remainder of unburnt coal. He was leaning, with his chair tilted backwards, against the wall.

"*De Moffen*," Gaston hissed. "They are at it again. Killed hundreds of saboteurs in Russia. Saboteurs don't come in packs of hundreds."

"Civilians of course," Adrienne chimed in. "Hostages, maybe, for an act of sabotage. Like they do here."

"Invading. Killing. Crowing. That's what they do best," I sneered.

"Well, they are getting it back, with interest," Adrienne said. "The bombardments. They must be dying like flies."

"Not at all," I replied. "After the massive bombing of Wuppertal, Goebbels went there, and vowed revenge, in front of a row of 144 open caskets. One-hundred-forty-four. That's *nothing*."

"You are one bloodthirsty chap."

"I don't drink blood," I said, chastened. " But I agree with Clémenceau."

"Clémenceau?" Adrienne asked.

"Yes, the French president, or prime minister, in the previous war. When he was told how many Germans there are, he said, 'That's thirty million too many.' "

"You would do away with thirty million men, women and children?"

"I wouldn't kill a dog. But I hope the Russians do it."

"Women? Children?"

"...No," I said, a bit shamed, yet spiteful, recalling in a flash the psalm's imprecation: *Wicked daughter of Babylon... Happy who will smash your newborn against the rock.* "But the men? Yes," I said emphatically. "Bloodthirsty murderers is what they are. As long as they are around there will be wars."

"Not after this one," Gaston said. "We won't be as tender with them as we were after the last war. They won't rise up again."

"They will rearm for another rematch, another grab at Europe. That's how they are. A German alone is a philosopher. Two Germans drink beer. Three Germans plan for war." I was pleased with myself.

"Where the hell did you get that?"

"Oh, just a quip I heard in Antwerp. There are quips for other nationalities. But this one is true."

"So what will you do if they come back?"

"We will all be in Palestine."

"Palestine?"

"Well, the Holy Land, Gaston," Adrienne said. "Where our Lord preached."

"Yes, our homeland," I said. "From where the Romans banished us. The land the Crusaders conquered from the Arabs."

"Who lives there now?" Gaston asked.

"Arabs and Jews."

"Jews? If the Romans banished you..."

"Some remained. And many of us returned there in the last fifty years."

"And who rules?"

"The English. But they will leave."

"And the Arabs?"

"They stay."

"And who will be the boss?"

"We will."

"How will they like that?"

"What we do there benefits everyone. Besides, we were there long before the Arabs. Long before the Romans invaded us. A thousand years and more before the Romans."

"That's history. Old stuff. For the books."

"Old stuff. Yes. And they are all gone, the Romans, the ancient Greeks, the ancient Egyptians, the Gauls, the Phoenicians, the... the Babylonians. It's a long list. All disappeared, their languages — nobody speaks them anymore. Their religions, gone. Everything. Forgotten, if it weren't for the books. But here we are, with nowhere to go but our homeland. With the old religion, the old language, the alphabet. Original. Unchanged. Authentic. Even the names, straight out of the bible."

Gaston swung forward, feet and chair coming down on the floor. He and Adrienne looked at each other with a half-smile of incredulity.

"*Potverdekke!*" Gaston let out. "Some speech. Have I ever..." After a pause:

"Even the names, you said? What kind of names?"

"Abraham, Isaac, Jacob, David. Biblical names."

"But you have Belgian names."

"War names."

"So what are your names?"

"My brother's name is Salomon."

"What kind of a name is *that?*"

"Gaston," Adrienne called out, "King Salomon, the wisest man on earth. We also name our boys after our beloved king Albert."

Gaston grumbled, then said, "All I know is that if I were an Arab, I wouldn't give a hoot about all that nonsense about being there first — like quarreling children; about not changing. What's wrong with changing? Growing up? Do we remember what it was like to be small children?"

"Gaston, I don't agree," Adrienne countered. "If we were banished to, say, well, pick a country."

"Turkey," I said.

"Why did you pick Turkey?"

"They are Muslims and they speak Turkish."

"Fine. Wouldn't you want us to remain Christians and teach our children Flemish and try to come back to our land?"

"Well, yes," he conceded. "But the people who would be living on our land would sneer at our pretensions of *authentic*" — he gave a nod in my direction — "and give us a good fight. Henri, all I know is that the English will have to protect you."

"They are on the side of the Arabs," I said ruefully. "They are not letting any more Jews into Palestine, even though the Arabs are siding with the Germans. Iraq invited them in. And the Mufti of Jerusalem — their pope, sort of — fled to Germany. Saw Hitler."

"Okh God! Both Arabs *and* English against you? You got yourselves into one pile of shit." He was rolling his eyes. I did not find it funny. "Henri, they don't stand a chance."

"There will be a Jewish army. There already is one; they call themselves the Watchmen."

"That's not an army. And you need weapons."

"They have weapons."

"I mean cannons…"

"We'll buy cannons."

"And tanks."

"We'll buy tanks." My voice was rising.

"Airplanes."

"We'll buy airplanes."

"Gaston," Adrienne broke in. "Stop that military parade."

"And we'll buy ships too."

"It's not a game, you know," Gaston said matter-of-factly. "Raising and training an army is serious business."

"Gaston, stop teasing the boy. The Jewish Bible, our Old Testament, says that the Jews were promised the Holy Land. And they have to be back there for the Second Coming of Christ."

Good Lord, I thought, that's all we need. For once, though, Christ was a help of sorts.

"I don't think the Arabs care about the Second Coming any more than they care about the Jewish bible," Gaston said.

"And I don't think that we should argue now about what the Jews, the Arabs, the English, the Germans will do after the war," Adrienne retorted. Turning to Sylvain and me: "Tell you what, after the war, you will go back to Antwerp, back to school, you'll have a nice apartment, and the hard times will be forgotten."

"And we'll smoke big cigars, hey Gaston?" That was Sylvain.

"Yes. But not mine, comrade."

✡ ✡ ✡

In the black-and-white photograph in the Flemish Underground paper her skirt was black, her blouse, white, her hair, black, her eyes, two big shadows. She lay, sprawled on her back, in the open, on an incline, head downward. I knew right away. A Jewish girl, the caption confirmed. On the railroad embankment. Shot dead as she jumped from the train. Prim, in her death: long sleeves; the skirt covered her knees.

I put the paper aside, in a reflex. To see no more. To numb myself. (Adrienne had given it to me. Van Kerckvoorde, from the Belgian judiciary police, had involved the Van Dammes in Underground activities. Gaston's mother, Léontine, and his sister Alice had become couriers.)

Years later I saw in Ephraim Schmidt's "History of the Jews in Antwerp" a tabulation, by gender and age brackets, of how many people jumped from the deportation trains, how many escaped, how many were caught. There were six children, 15 years and younger, among them. The figures were obtained from the archives of the Belgian Ministry of Public Health. Schmidt mentions just one name: Eva Resler, the only girl. She was thirteen, he adds; shot dead. I recalled, for the first time, the scene in the bedroom, the Underground paper on the floor mat, the black-and-white picture jumping out at me.

I looked her up in *Mémorial de la Déportation des Juifs de Belgique* by Serge Klarsfeld and Maxime Steinberg; it contains a copy of the captured German records of the deportations from Mechelen:

Resler   Eva   2.10.29   XX/329   (born 2 Oct, '29; 20th *Transport*, Nr 329.)

Her parents, one brother and two sisters were with her on the train, numbers 324 through 328. Eva was the youngest.

In a prefatory overview to the "Mémorial," Klarsfeld and Steinberg relate that *Transport* XX left Mechelen on the night of April 19-20, 1943. The youngest deportee was Suzanne Kaminsky, number 215, thirty-nine days old; the oldest, Jacob Blom, number 584, a few days shy of his ninety-first birthday. 231 of the 1631 deportees jumped from the moving train, on Belgian soil. All but a few had broken their way out of the cattle cars with tools that inmates employed in the workshops of the Dossin barracks had slipped to them. The remaining few, 17 at most, jumped when their car was opened from the outside. A young Jewish physician, Georges Livschitz, armed with a small caliber revolver and a torch, and two former co-students, Jean Franklemon and Robert Maistriau, Gentiles, took it upon themselves to "liberate" the convoy after the Underground had shied away from such an audacious undertaking. Livschitz got the train to stop. Under the ensuing fire from the train's guard turrets — 23 "jumpers" were shot dead — only Maistriau managed to open a car in the middle of the long convoy. It was the sole such attempt in Final Solution Europe.

Livschitz was wounded and caught in a later action and executed.

✧ ✧ ✧

Gaston came down with the flu. Bedridden, with a burning fever, he had kept Adrienne up at night. From early on the next morning she made countless trips up and down the stairs to bring him water and soup; to wash him, give him fresh long underwear, change the bed linens; to empty the chamber pot; to tidy up. Gaston, the shaper of metal by fire, the manhandler of awesome Belgian workhorses, was like a felled warrior. Sylvain went to stay with Adrienne's parents. I was confined to the garret, with occasional reprieves in the kitchen. It was unsettling to think of him languishing, prone and dependent, in the adjoining room. An atmosphere of controlled crisis reigned. Life's chores that ordered the days, cooking and tidying up, shopping and mending and running washes, became incidental or were deferred. I washed up without the ritual flourish. I prayed without moving my lips. Ate absent-mindedly. Even confinement in the garret felt different, free of the bouts of anguish. The sky did not inspire flights of fancy. It didn't feel like hiding; just waiting for Gaston to return to the forge, waiting to resume hiding as usual.

At noon Gaston told Adrienne that he was determined to get out of bed the next day. He would break the fever by sweating it out until morning, with lots of water and the highest allowable dose of aspirin. Adrienne related this to me that evening in the kitchen.

"That means another agitated, wet night," she concluded. Her voice was flat. "I might even come and sleep in your bed."

I looked down, speechless, incredulous, panic-stricken, insulted, *She thinks I'm twelve, a boy.* My thoughts were in a whirl.

"Any objection?"

"No... I don't know," I finally mumbled, without looking up.

"Hmm..."

She busied herself with the last chores of the day. She added coal to the fire to keep the chill out of the bedroom — the door to the landing would be left open.

It was time for me to go upstairs. I bade her good night and went up, fast, and closed my door shut: that panic again. To uphold my dignity as a man, I told myself. And waited in the faint glow of the night.

Minutes later I heard her turn off the light. A slight pause to find the bottom step in the dark while holding on to the hand-rail — I could visualize her in that stance, and she was coming up the stairs. I knew every creaking sound. She reached the top. Another slight pause. Then two steps in short order: she had walked past my door into her bedroom. I stood up, slowly, torn, heart pounding. Silently, I opened my door a crack. To undo the snub. Hoping that she would see it, push the door open, and walk in in her night gown.

I got into my pyjamas, climbed into bed and curled up, by the wall.

The next morning my door was still ajar. I heard Gaston's and Adrienne's voices in the kitchen. They were having break-fast. When I went down to fetch my plate — Adrienne had put it on one of the lower steps and had given the tapping signal — I pulled the drape up a bit to show my face.

"Good morning," I said, trying to sound casual.

"Well good MOR-ning," Adrienne replied as she turned around to face me. "And how did *you* sleep?" she asked. "Closing the door on me," she continued reproachfully. "Now I know who my pals are."

I was embarrassed but kept mum: *I am not a little boy.* Gaston made a face, disapproving, but not harsh, and dug into his food.

"I... I didn't mean to..." I finally stuttered, and drew a blank. "I..."

I let go of the drape and was about to pick up my plate.

"Come, eat with us," Gaston said. "The doors are locked."

✿ ✿ ✿

Days have gone by. Then weeks. Months.

I am sitting still, and restless. The house is quiet. The sky is radiant. Spring is near.

A distant "*djurr*" rings out. A moo rises and fades; another moo. A cock crows. The sounds are pure. They come from afar, carried by silence. They linger and fade, rise and course again, gorged with life.

An inner throbbing draws me to the garret window. I sit down on the bed and stare, wistful and transfixed, at the blinding patch of sky. The air above quivers with light and the twitter of birds.

O 't ruischen van het ranke riet (O, the rustling of the slender reed). The title line, that is all I remember of Guido Gezelle's poem. It lodged itself in my mind, like a seed carried by the wind. Its rhythm is soothing, then also, exhilarating; it exacerbates the desire to walk toward the horizon. I don't know a single poem by Gezelle; only this one verse.

O 't ruischen van het ranke riet. The Flemish sounds have silenced the tongue of the Psalms; the Flemish soil has eclipsed the Promised Land. To work as a farmhand... To *be* a farmhand... I hold a horse's reins and lean on the plow. I chop wood. Walk in soiled overalls. Eat with unwashed hands thick slices of dark farmer's bread with smoked ham; gulp coffee from a canteen. I dig my hands in the thick Flemish earth. Work without stopping. I am lying in the tall grass, hands cupped under my head. Dozing off. I am one with sun-drenched Creation.

The thudding sound of wooden shoes on the earthen path: they are moving away at an unhurried pace. To walk on this earth, to cast a shadow and be unafraid... like the barefoot village boy, I see him, suddenly, in his loose-hanging shirt and torn pants running his rusty bicycle rim on the gravel-encrusted bicycle path, the day my brother and I, with Govaerts towering between us, arrived in Duizend Appels. He had cut in front of us, absorbed in his game. He had made me conscious of my neat city attire, of Rosh Hashanah and Shabbat, of the diamonds in the hollow heels of my shoes — too small on me, now, they are tucked away at the bottom of the big armoire in the bedroom. My father had stopped Adrienne just in time from bartering them for food. How distant, how gossamer Shabbat and the Holiday are, under that same iridescent sky. No place for it on this earth. Vanished, with my people.

I fix my gaze on the irradiated dust particles swirling in the shaft of sunlight under the garret window. They seem animated as if answering a mysterious call. Some burst into a sudden glow, as if set on fire, only to fade the next instant. They are the Jews caught by the Germans. The invisible particles that hover in the shadow — I can even spot some — are the Jews in hiding. I close my eyes.

I push myself off the bed and return to the bedroom. I remain standing in the doorframe. My eyes adjust to the softer light.

The sun touches the treetops on the horizon, comes down on the tiled roofs, lights up the gables. Little white clouds are drifting by and thinning out. Slight tremors seize distant branches in random fits.

The right window is open on a crack down the middle. The sheer white half-curtains flutter in the playful breeze; they swell and go limp, or hug the glass panes. I sniff as I inhale, trying to capture the cool scent, the way I caught, on the chic avenues of Antwerp, the elusive whiffs of perfume given off by the elegant women with rouged lips and pale, powdered faces, the mysterious women who looked past me through the sheer black veil under their modish hats.

I take heaving lungfuls of air. I have come back.

It was a slow spring afternoon at the forge. Quiet also reigned in the adjoining Van Damme house. Gaston's father, Emile, was napping upstairs. Gaston's sister Maria was busying herself in her room. An old Jewish couple was hiding in an adjacent room. Gaston, taking a break from work, stepped into the kitchen, followed by little Johnny and Marcel — they had been playing outside. Rays of sunlight slanted through the window. A half loaf of dark bread lay on the bare table next to a jar of home made cherry preserves. In the air hung the faint, stale smell of a tidied up country kitchen well past its cooking and meal time, and the smell of the forge given off by Gaston.

Standing by the stove, Gaston was about to pour himself a bottom of cold chicory coffee when two Flemish SS, one in black uniform, the other in *Feldgrau*, stormed in, guns drawn. The SS in black shouted at Gaston to stand, hands up against the wall opposite the kitchen entrance. He whacked him in the neck for turning his head sideways.

The commotion in the kitchen roused Gaston's father, Emile, from his nap. It also brought the old Jewish couple onto the landing. Gaston's sister Maria who was on her way down when the fracas broke loose, signaled frantically to the pair to disappear. Up. Up. They scampered up into the attic where they hid in an armoire. The SS in *Feldgrau* bounded up the stairs, past Maria, to search the house. Emile came down the one flight of steps from his bedroom and remained standing, dumbstruck, in the kitchen doorway. The children had moved away, towards the rear of the kitchen. Johnny's head — big brown eyes shining with terror — hovered just above the table. Maria joined them. Her entrance and the rampage from room to room upstairs, drew the SS's attention away from Gaston. Gaston, who was watching the SS from the corner of his eye, turned his head, and signaled his father — he rolled his eyes from left to right, from left to right — to clear the doorway. The old blacksmith inched sideways to lean against the wall between the doorway and the window.

Gaston had vowed not to be taken alive. No sooner did the SS relax his hawk-like watch — he was no longer holding his gun at the ready — than Gaston bolted: out the kitchen door, a sharp right through the yard into the forge and out into the orchard. The first bullet fired by the pursuing SS missed its target. Gaston now anticipated the shots — his military training stood him in good stead. He leapt with uncanny timing, as he ran, to the left, to the right, to the left, to the right, anticipating the shots and eluding the bullets.

The gunshots caused the SS in *Feldgrau* to break off his search — he had not gotten to the attic — and rush back downstairs. He joined in the manhunt. But Gaston, a former soccer player, raced on and disappeared. The two SS rushed back to the house, ordered the old blacksmith into the car, and instructed him to direct them to his son's house, leaving a young woman who had accompanied them in charge of the children — she had been sitting in the car until now.

In his flight Gaston ran into our neighbor, Simoneke's father. The farmer was working in his field. Gaston pleaded with him to hurry back and warn Adrienne: "Tell her the Germans are at the forge. Tell her to get everybody out of the house." The farmer could take the main road, the shortest way, which Gaston wanted to avoid for fear of being spotted by the SS. The farmer listened, stunned, then asked whether Gaston was with the Underground. "No. Just tell her to get the children out of the house." The farmer was afraid to get involved, but he could not ignore Gaston's plea. Head bowed, he trudged, in his wooden shoes, back to his farm.

Adrienne had just finished the early afternoon chores. The wet-mopped kitchen and pump house floors were drying up in patches, looking new again. The sun shone bright and warm. In the house it was cool and shady. Sylvain was on the road, playing with a group of village boys. As Adrienne stepped out into the backyard with pail, rag and mop, she noticed our neighbor standing in the farmyard in front of the cowshed, motioning her over without uttering a sound. (He had still made it in time: the old blacksmith was leading his captors along a winding detour.) Puzzled by the farmer's silent summons and unusual demeanor, Adrienne took off her apron, closed the backdoor to the pump house and left for the neighboring farm.

I was weeding the onion patch. The much-awaited, two-week long Easter vacation — my second in Belsele — was drawing to an end. "We must be out of butter, or eggs," I thought when I saw Adrienne step briskly across the garden. I had not noticed our neighbor.

I was squatting on the dry, crunchy, warm earth, right by the gravel path which ran behind me from the front gate to the backyard, alongside the blind wall of the house. I was facing the large garden with its many beds of sprouting vegetables. The air was astir with the sounds of distant voices, of birds chirping, of leaves rustling, of a cow's insistent moo. The fickle breeze caressed my brow and sent cool, playful puffs down the open collar of my shirt. The life of hiding had dissolved, like an unpleasant dream.

Suddenly the mounting roar of a car ripped the stillness. "Only doctors and police have cars. Such hurry," I reflected, when the vehicle braked in a coarse, short-tempered pitch. "Not the doctor. A neighbor got into trouble," I told myself. But my world was collapsing. The stiff, earth-gripping front wheels veered abruptly onto the bicycle path. *For us.* It shot through my mind even before I saw, over my left shoulder, a chrome radiator and a black hood stop at the open gate between the house and the hedgerow.

What followed seemed to happen all at once. A man in black emerged from the far side of the car and disappeared in front of the house and a tall officer, bareheaded, in boots and *Feldgrau*, gun drawn, stormed onto the gravel path. His trance-like gaze crossed with mine and disengaged just as I turned my face down, back to the onion patch. *Will he stop behind me with his knees at my neck?* I shrank. The thudding boots raced past me to the rear of the house. *That frenzy, the gun, can't be for Jewish boys... But he saw me.* I heard the officer grapple with the door latch of the pump house.

I stood up. My heart was bouncing in my ribcage. With my hands in my pockets, to act casual, and head bent, to hide my face — my self, my fear, I moved toward the bicycle path: it was just a few steps away. To disappear from view behind the hedge. To disappear. I reached the open gate and the thought flashed through my mind that a glimpse of the car might give me a unique, perhaps saving clue about my chances. But I dared not look; I kept staring down and away for fear of confronting an inquisitive eye and eliciting that motion of the hand or the commandeering nod of the chin that would make me stop. I didn't even notice the onlookers across the road, my brother among them. I was going to play it dumb, as if it didn't concern me, as if I were just passing by.

I felt another jolt when I turned my back to car and house. I willed myself into walking on the bicycle path along the road, with the glistening black monster at my back. *Is someone staring at me? I am just another village boy. I have no reason to run. I must not run.* But I was incapable of running: the silence fraught with uncertainty, at my back, weighed me down, like in a nightmare. It took what seemed a very long time to cover a few meters, to reach the next tree, and the next. I was walking with my hands in my pockets, my gaze riveted to the tips of my shoes. Trying to act casual, I kicked a stone off the bicycle path and felt some relief.

I got halfway to the neighbor's farmhouse. *Whoever is in the car does not suspect anything. It's working.* I stole a glance at the distance. I saw the luminous opening under the canopy of the poplars, where the new by-pass road around St-Niklaas joined the Old Road. As in a nightmare, I saw myself stepping toward the incandescence at the far end, and, looming in the back, unseen yet present, the German in *Feldgrau*, gun in hand: I had feared, as I was walking, that he might reappear at any moment in front of the house. *He saw me. He won't shoot if I don't run. No looking back either.* To appear casual, unconcerned; I could think of nothing else.

The earthen path! I remembered the earthen path. It was just twenty meters or so away, right past the farmhouse. It led into the fields, behind a high, untrimmed hedge. My heartbeat again quickened. Then a voice rang at my back, like a shot. *"Halll-te!"*

I twitched but continued to walk. The summons grew louder. It was seething with rage. I could no longer ignore it; it would be like running. I turned halfway around and saw the officer in *Feldgrau* standing at the black car. He was motioning me to return. I feigned surprise and, with my hand on my chest gestured an innocent "who, me?" then turned my back to him and resumed my walk. This time, the sound of his voice carried rage only and when I turned around I saw a hand on a holster. Slowly, I started back. Two more attempts at stopping and acting surprised, showing even a trace of indignation drew the same lunge of the hand toward the holster. The second time the SS unsnapped it.

I was now walking, slowly, steadily. *"Schneller!"* ("faster!"), he snapped. I continued at the same unhurried pace: I was not going to be shot on my way to surrender, no matter how exasperated the SS might get. I watched him fixedly. I did not see the children on the other side of the road, or the villagers on their doorsteps. I didn't even see the houses. Yet I knew that I was being watched. They would see how I was being drained of all will by this arrogant SS who wouldn't even take one step forward.

The gravel-encrusted bicycle path was incandescent, the shiny black car looked ominous; and the officer, in his gray-green uniform, black boots, black belt and holster, was waiting, hands on his hips, elbows sticking out. I had a moment of intense fright just before he grabbed me by the shoulder and stepped me through the narrow hallway into the kitchen.

I found myself facing the SS in black uniform. He towered over me.

"Your name," he said in German, in a bullying tone of voice.

"What?" I asked in Flemish, feigning to grope for the meaning of the words.

"Your name." In Flemish.

"Henri, Henri Govaerts."

"How old are you?" That also had to be translated into Flemish.

"Fourteen." At fifteen every citizen and resident was required by Belgian law to carry an identification card. I was a month shy of sixteen, but small of build, even for a fourteen-year old. And I wanted to appear small, instinctively.

There was a short pause while the SS in black looked at the officer in *Feldgrau*. *Are they confused? Did they run into me by chance? A search with drawn revolver, for two Jewish boys?* Hope seeped into my fright.

"*Du bist Jude!*" ("You are a Jew!")

It's over. He was looking down at me, enormous, menacing. But he didn't touch me.

I stiffened: "What?"

"*Du bist Jude!*" Still, no move to grab me, to order me along. "*Jood! Jood!*" In Flemish, as if he wanted me to understand; to confirm?

"A Jew!?... Me!?... With what right are you calling me a Jew!?" I was yelling, out of control, interjecting local dialect in my Flemish. "You have no right!"

Another pause, another exchange of glances between the two SS. *They are not sure.* The thought flickered in my mind that I might have played it right.

"*Hose ab!*" ("Pants down!"). The words struck like a blow.

It's over. "What?" I still managed to ask.

"*Hose ab! Hose ab!*" The SS punctuated his order with a gesture of the hand. I backed away.

"No dirty stuff! I am not a swine!" I shouted, still trying to act unknowing and indignant.

The SS reached for the buckle of my belt. I seized it first with both hands, forearms tight around my waist, and held on desperately while repeating under my breath, "I am not a swine. I am not a swine, *godverdomme!* (goddam!)." He had to use both hands to pry one of my hands loose. In frustration he tugged at my pants. I grabbed my belt at the hips. He went for the buckle again, but I got there first. He tried to loosen my grip again, but I was holding firm. He let up. He straightened out his big frame but held on to me by my belt, as onto a package, and looked at the officer in *Feldgrau*. I had glanced at him a few times, afraid that he might come to the aid of his acolyte. Standing in the door frame to the hallway, he had been staring at the floor tiles, or looking out the front door. Was he embarrassed? Disapproving perhaps? Would he stop it? By his stance and with his leaner frame, his neat head of hair and regular features, he no longer struck me as inhuman. *They are not sure. It's as if they feel they are wasting their time.* I looked at him with bated breath as he was looking at my SS. He broke off eye contact. At that instant two big hands came from behind and gripped mine with heightened fury while two massive arms pressed mine against my body.

I was holding on to my buckle. The SS tried to immobilize me using his knees as pincers. He was breathing down my neck. I felt my blood rushing to my face. I wasn't afraid of blows anymore, gaining confidence as my resistance lasted. I cursed under my breath, clinging to the thought that he could not do anything to me as long as he was not sure that I was a Jew. *He doesn't really know yet. He doesn't know.* I threw glances from under the big head jutting out over mine at the officer who was now watching the bout. I wanted to impress upon him that it was all a tragic mistake. Our eyes met once but he averted his gaze. The tug of war continued. The big hands clawed at mine, in vain, dropped to my knees for a tug at my pants, then lunged back up. My hands moved in sync with his, but faster, from the buckle, to the hips, then back to the buckle. He tried a feint, going for the knees then back up, fast, only to meet the same small unyielding hands over the buckle. His hands were moving erratically now; I could sense his frustration.

The struggle was at its peak when Adrienne walked into the kitchen from the pump house. It brought the scuffle to a dead stop. I held on to my buckle and the SS kept my hands in his clutches. She saw me looking at her from under the black mass. Her face did not register shock, she didn't even show surprise; only the gloom of defeat. She leaned against the wall with her right hand to her chest. She looked at me. I saw tenderness in her eyes, and concern that I might come to harm. She nodded in my direction, once, slowly, then closed her eyes, helpless and hurting, as if to say, It's over. *She knew. No accident. No use.* And I let go.

Frantic fingers fumbled with the buckle. I felt several tugs at my trousers; they came down on my feet. My briefs got pulled down to my knees. I saw the profile of his big head, face down, at the height of my chest. I watched him lift the front tails of my shirt, with a feeling akin to detachment, as if my nakedness were no longer mine.

"*Beschnitten. Mitkommen*" ("Circumcised. Come along"), the SS snapped matter-of-factly as he dropped the shirttails. He straightened himself up and muttered something about the Jews having spread all over the place.

Head bent, I pulled up my briefs; then my pants. I tucked my shirt in and tightened my belt. *It's over.* The fear was gone. I felt defeated and ashamed. And calm. Calm?... I felt lame.

The two SS had a brief aside, then ordered Adrienne to appear at their offices in Antwerp the next day. They turned to leave. The SS in black positioned himself at the front door. The SS in *Feldgrau* led me from behind, through the narrow hallway. Adrienne caught up with us and handed me my jacket. I put it on. At the sight of the black car I stiffened. There it was, with gaping front door and shady interior, and I was expected to step into it, just as I had been expected to walk all the way back on the bicycle path. And the surrender in the kitchen. In a flash I saw how every one of my steps was leading to the next one; unto the end. Terror and humiliation flowed into one and welled up like a tidal wave, ripping through my numbness. I planted myself in the doorway and asked in ragged sentences that I be shot. I opened my jacket, "Here... Here," and I pointed at my chest. "You have a gun," and I pointed at the holster, "it's easy, you can shoot me here. I am not going." Adrienne let out a moan. I knew that the SS, who had not struck at me even when I had resisted him, would not shoot. I knew how ridiculous my posturing was, how ridiculous anything would be. But it gave me another few moments, precious and unpredictable. And I wanted to show him, and the onlookers who had seen my humiliation on the bicycle path — I was acutely aware of their presence — that I was not afraid of the gun, of death. And had he pulled his gun, I would not have budged, so deep was my commotion, so carried away was I by my acting, and so terrified by the open black car.

The SS grabbed me by the shoulders and pushed me, almost hurled me into the front seat. I did not notice Gaston's father, Emile, sitting in the back seat. I did not see the silent onlookers across the road. The SS in black took the wheel, the other climbed in the back. The car took off. By the time it pulled up in front of the forge I had regained my composure.

We filed into the kitchen. Gaston's father, hunched-over, trudged in first. I walked in second. "Another one," muttered the SS in black uniform to the young woman who had stayed with Johnny and Marcel. She looked at me with big gray-blue, glossy eyes, a faint smile on her face. I was an unexpected catch. Standing aside, with her hands in the pockets of her open, loose-hanging raincoat, she gave the impression of someone who had been taken along for the ride. They had come for the children, and had extended their search to Gaston's house. Had someone informed on Gaston's parents? Or did the Germans get hold of an Underground list? Gaston's mother, Léontine, had accepted financial aid for the children in her care. Gaston and Adrienne had turned down any suggestion of help from clandestine quarters. My parents had been opposed to it: as long as they had money for their children's upkeep, no list would carry their names.

The cowed little boys were standing by the stove, near *Vaderke* (little father). The old blacksmith had eased himself into his armchair near the stove; he was leaning forward with his elbows on his knees, head low. His face was ashen. In contrast, his unkempt, dust-filled crown of gray hair looked white under his shapeless worker's cap. His eyes moved slowly under his bushy eyebrows and met mine. He stared at me as if in a daze.

The two SS had a short, low-voiced colloquy. "You will come along," the man in black enjoined Gaston's sister Maria. "Time to go," he snapped, sending a shudder through the kitchen. The old man sank on his right knee and took off his cap. He took Johnny's little hands in his left hand, then crossed himself; his hand moved deliberately, from crown to guts and from side to side, as though rending his whole being. The sign of the cross... moving. He then took Johnny's head with his right hand and kissed him on the forehead. Tears rolled down his cheeks. He let go. Johnny threw himself against him. He was sobbing hysterically, "*Vaderke*, I want to stay with you." The blacksmith was choking on his tears and shaking. The SS in black uniform began moving toward them but Maria preceded him. The old blacksmith had to nudge the little clenched fists from his crumpled shirt. The little boy, arms still outstretched, feeling no support, turned his head away from *Vaderke*, gasping silently, with slight, rapid convulsions, his eyes closed, his face crimson, and broke into loud, resigned crying. Maria took him in her arms. Marcel, the oldest, was standing nearby, stiff, with tears rolling down his cheeks, his mouth distorted by a desperate effort to repress sobbing. *Vaderke* opened his arms and Marcel moved to him. The old man took the boy's hands into his and crossed himself again, and kissed him. Marcel moved to Maria. She took his hand and he stopped crying. I took his other hand. The SS in black held the door open. The officer in *Feldgrau* stood aside, impassive. Maria was dropping tears now. I was standing, dry-eyed. The blacksmith remained kneeling, wiping his face. And watching it all was the young woman with the big gray-blue glossy eyes, her hands in the pockets of her loose-hanging raincoat, and that constant, faint smile on her fleshy face.

✧ ✧ ✧

The officer in *Feldgrau* made himself comfortable in the back behind the driver's seat. Maria sat next to him, with Johnny nestled on her lap. Marcel leaned against her shoulder. Squeezed to the right, I was leaning forward, clutching the back rest behind the "guest" rider. The SS in black uniform slammed my door, then took the wheel. I settled down, preparing for a long ride: a journey to the unknown could not be short.

The bright and tranquil Flemish countryside was moving by and slipping away. The orchards were in bloom. Some came up fast, like a sudden cheer, patches of dazzling white and pink, just one bright instant along the road. Others would dwell a while on the horizon, then vanish. I saw farmers in distant fields; I perceived them as mere silhouettes moving with unconcerned slowness, inseparable from their land, secure. Never had I sensed so keenly the life-preserving power of their rootedness. My roots were in a community that no longer existed. I, and Johnny and Marcel, were being removed like foreign bodies. "They'll be surprised in Duizend Appels to find out that I have been there all this time," I thought. Now they know the big lie I lived, how we deceived them. "How few of us are left?" I wondered. It was inevitable, I knew. I had always suppressed the thought. "We'll ferret them out, down to the last one," the Gestapo chief of Antwerp had boasted, "even out of rabbit cages." Adrienne had overheard it somewhere. It shook me when I overheard it from the landing by the bedroom, like hearing my own death sentence. And I had seen a Jew crouching in a rabbit cage with his beard between his knees and his eyes shining with fear. Following that day I was visited, more often than before, by the vision of a dwindling number of isolated Jews shipwrecked in the sea of Christendom and waiting to be picked off. I was finally freed of my two greatest fears: to be caught, and remaining a lone Jew.

The car was moving in a steady drone, master of the road. The oncoming trees and houses grew, faster as they were getting closer, to whir by and be left behind. Every house with its brightly colored shutters looked like another haven. I found myself wishing to be here, or there, to start hiding all over again. I latched on to every villager in sight; the clearer the face that streaked by, the sharper the momentary loss. It took several rushing trees and fresh imprints to banish the figure of the sturdy farmer in wooden shoes with a hoe on his shoulder whose face I had glimpsed in full: deep set eyes under the low worker's cap, a bushy moustache and deep grooves running down the cheeks, offsetting a strong chin. To join him in the fields... a thought, a fantasy. A delusion.

We drove past two boys standing on the bicycle path, waiting to cross over. They had sized up the car and its occupants with sudden curiosity. I wondered what might have crossed their minds, struck, as so often before, by the lack of concern of boys my age about their freedom, their past, their future. I tired of trying to discern faces, to glimpse profiles. I watched, numb, the unending stream of tightly meshing cobblestones zoom up into the windshield and disappear, swallowed up by the voracious car.

The driver brought the car to a stop. Leaving the motor on, he got out and climbed up the side of the road onto a large, well kept lawn where neatly dressed children of different ages were playing. It made me think of a boarding school. The SS had a short, casual exchange with a young, well groomed woman. I was stunned. He got back into the car and drove off. I was straining to see through the side window, then from the rear, the big house, the woman, the children. Another haven.

"What's the matter?" asked the SS at the wheel, eyeing me in the rear-view mirror, "do you know of any Jews there?"

How stupid of me to show interest. What if there were? "No," I snapped, "never seen the place before." And, after a slight pause, "Wished *I* were there," I said, to allay all suspicions about my looking back.

The SS did not react.

I slumped a little forward, leaning with my forearms on the back of the front seat. It relaxed the tension in my body. My mind eased off. The dulling drone of the car enveloped its silent occupants.

It wasn't until we had wound our way through Beveren and its large marketplace that I realized, with a shock, that we were heading toward Antwerp... Antwerp, where it all began. The Gomorrah I had fled in a bygone age. The city got dredged up from the past and stripped of its distance. It was only minutes away now; it had always been there, I realized, right at the end of the road, less than a half-hour ride from Duizend Appels, an hour, barely, on the crawling local train. I was trying to pierce the distance. The Left Bank. The toll booth. The tunnel. It got darker, then the light turned yellow on the glistening tiles.

A strange awareness was gradually getting hold of me as we moved deeper and deeper into the tunnel: we were all trapped in that car, and, all alike, safe from death. The tunnel was nowhere: no place to dwell, no place to die. My heartbeat jumped once again. I wished the tunnel to last forever. I would outlast the brutes. How wary they would grow; frightened, worn out with terror. But no, it was an idle wish. We were approaching a bend; the tunnel would surely end there. And I called in my heart for a cave-in. I would survive. I glanced to my left and made myself think that Marcel and Johnny and Maria would also survive. That tunnel could withstand ten Scheldt rivers. I knew that it was designed to last forever. But I entertained the thought, wishing the stones to come tumbling down. It would confound them, not me, *let the boulders crash in front of the driver, I won't fear.* I would know that a superior design on my life had voided the Germans'. That little latter-day variant of the Red Sea crossing, to me, was the only way out. I was smarting to renew the confrontation I had backed down from earlier, about the buckle, on the bicycle path when I was too scared to glance at the car and run away.

The car drove around the bend. Still no end to the tunnel in sight. I was leaning forward, looking intently into the tiny dark spot where yellow tiles and yellow lights were converging. The "guest" rider turned her head. I looked her defiantly in the eyes, then resumed my staring in the distance, ignoring her. She glanced at the back seat passengers before turning her face away. I looked to my left, over my shoulder. Maria was watching me; my inner turmoil must have shown on my face, in my posture. The concern in her eyes — was she worried about me? — made her appear searching and distant. It occurred to me that she might have been ordered to come along for the trip only, to handle the children. I looked at her, trying to convey that she should not be concerned. She turned her face without changing her expression. Marcel was looking up at me, quiet and anguished. Little Johnny was resting on Maria's lap, quiet and solemn. The officer in *Feldgrau* was staring ahead, impassive. I resumed my intense watch for the tunnel's mouth. The tunnel would not cave in, of course, and it was not endless. Perched on the end of the back seat, my body was taut. My heart was beating fast.

Daylight showed, gray and sparse for a while in the fading glare of the yellow lamps and tiles, then piercing, then bright.

The car alighted from the tunnel's mouth. It was just as well that all had proceeded as the laws of nature manipulated by human intent had willed it in the first place. A spike of resentment against God was shamed into flight by disbelief in divine intervention in modern days: *There will always be daylight at the end of a tunnel; and a cave-in would have meant drowning.* The car was climbing the ramp. The shimmering hood turned fiery... How drunk with sunlight, the big, bustling city. People by the thousands, and carefree! Bikes and cars and trams and trucks. Everything was so bright and lively.

They were walking on the sidewalks, the same sidewalks I had walked on all my life. Nothing had changed: the Italiëlei, the trees, the buildings, the signs. To my right, beer drinking patrons were enjoying the afternoon sun on the sidewalk terraces of the cafés. It was all so much the same; yet without a Jewish face, without the Jewish presence that had been my lifelong anchor in the sea of mankind, it all seemed almost unreal. *Judenrein.* And we were not missed.

We were approaching one of the busiest intersections in Antwerp, where the De Keyserlei and the Italiëlei meet. A traffic agent with white gloves and white helmet, standing in a traffic turret, ordered the Italiëlei flow to a halt. Our car stopped by the curb. I looked at the faces of the oncoming passers-by. I wondered if they would take notice of us. Some threw unseeing glances in the direction of the car, some didn't even look our way. Some took a furtive, impenetrable look at the occupants of the car and averted their eyes. A man moved into sight. I followed his eyes: they noticed the black uniform at the wheel, then moved to the officer in the rear and, in a puzzled sweep embraced all the other passengers in the car. The man broke his pace, he even flexed his right knee, thrusting his face forward and down, with eyebrows raised. I put my face in the window. His eyes — clear, brown eyes — peered into mine, longer than that fleeting, conventional instant; open, searching eyes. "Does he understand?" I was not letting go. The face moved on and out of sight, and the man was on his way.

From his turret the traffic agent reopened the Italiëlei to traffic. We crossed the wide De Keyserlei, the chic, tree-lined avenue that I had crossed every day on my way to and from high school during the first two years of the Occupation. My high school, though close by, did not come to mind. Only things that moved into sight called forth memories. I had walked those streets with my dreams. They seemed strange, and the people seemed remote, like strangers in an eerie dream who are not really strangers.

There was in the mansion occupied by the Gestapo on the Koningin Elisabethlei an office-like atmosphere. A young woman in a spring dress carrying what looked like an important folder sauntered by in the ornate entrance hall. She smiled and exchanged a pleasantry with a man in civilian clothes. I saw only one man in uniform, the boyish-looking Flemish guard — he was my height — who had locked us up and was standing at the door with his rifle, peeping at times through the small opening. He had seemed impressed with the little band of captives and had shown considerateness in the way he had led us to our cell — eyes cast downward. He had ushered us in, as though we were important and delicate guests.

Our cell, a five-by-five-foot closet, was well lit, with smooth yellow walls. Maria sat down on the only stool, with Johnny on her lap. Marcel stood next to her, leaning occasionally against her. They were huddled together. Quick-tempered Maria had a look of boundless solicitude and patience in her eyes, the look one has in the presence of one's gravely ill child. She, her sister Alice, and the old Van Dammes were attached to the little boys. When, in early September of the previous year, Johnny had to have his tonsils and polyps removed, Alice, on the advice of Professor Regniers, her treating physician, and with Maurice's full backing, registered the little boy as her illegitimate child at the hospital *Toevlucht van Maria* (Refuge of Mary) in Ghent. Alice's mother, Léontine, came to stay with the child. They were given the surgeon, Dr. Eeman's, room. She alone took care of the circumcised little boy, day and night. After a two-week stay with Alice and Maurice, *Moederke* (little mother, as the children called her) and Johnny were back in Belsele.

Time passed, minutes upon minutes of silence. My mind was blank, after the buffeting of the last hour; no thoughts, no fears. Just an awareness that I would be reunited with my people. I could not see beyond the present moment, the yellow walls, the tips of my shoes, Maria's busying herself with Johnny's hair, the children pressing in on her. I smiled at her. She gave me a wan smile in return. I shrugged my shoulders and heaved a sigh, as if to say, "Well yes, here we are...," as if to say... nothing; just to communicate. Her smile broadened, her eyes started to glisten.

More time passed. Maria got up to stretch and to relieve the tension in her back. Johnny stood next to her, his head nestled in her hand. She told me to sit down, but I refused: I was not going to sit while a woman and two children were standing. Marcel sat on the stool at my suggestion and after a nod from Maria.

She sat down again and the three regrouped as before. I stopped shifting my weight and sat down on the floor. More time passed. I drew myself up from the wall I was leaning against, turned idly around, and noticed inscriptions. I gasped: there were dozens of signs and inscriptions crisscrossing the pale yellow wall in all directions, in lettering of all sorts and sizes. How many prisoners had spent time in this cell? There was even a poem, in French, a quatrain about spring and hope, gentle and beautiful. I was feeling again, empathizing with an unknown comrade. Did he have hope, real hope? His poem sounded like a soft cry. I wondered where he was now. I felt calmer, as if that perceived hint of weakness in somebody else had set off my own strength. I was in the middle of an inscription when I caught sight of "IK BEN NIET BANG" ("I am not scared") in large block letters. I felt a thud at the heart and stared at it for a few seconds. "J'ACCUSE" jumped at me from amidst another patch of signs and inscriptions. "J'accuse," I repeated to myself. Strong language; could even be dangerous. Couldn't the Germans find out who wrote what by checking off the new inscriptions? "Had to be a Gentile," I thought. " 'J'accuse' would never have crossed my mind." Accusing Germans. Of what? Of being German? Might as well accuse a tiger of being an animal of prey. I moved on and had a sudden chuckle: The famous line "If the nose of Cleopatra had been longer, I would not be here." In French. My admiration bordered on envy: that's what I would have liked to write. That man hit it just right. I showed it to Maria and translated it to her. It fell flat. "She must think that I'm going nuts," I thought. It dampened my inner hilarity. I read more inscriptions and decided to leave my own mark. I had no pen or pencil, just a comb in my outer breast pocket. And with the back of the comb I carved the first stanza of the hit song:

Het gaat alles ten einde,	All things come to an end,
Het gaat alles voorbij,	It all goes by,
Na ied're December,	After each December,
Komt weder een Mei.	Comes again a May.

It gave me a sense of accomplishment. I showed it to Maria. Squinting — she was a bit nearsighted — she moved her head from left to right, line by line. She nodded, blandly.

I sat down on the floor. Stood up. Sat down. Marcel and Johnny fidgeted. Once only did I wonder, fleetingly, about my brother, *He must still be free. They did not expect to catch me. I was a bonus.* I also wondered about my parents' fate: *They'll be told about me. Lucien will order them to leave; the fear that I will give them away, or out of meanness.* Then I quickly dismissed everybody from my mind, as if to remember them was to incur the risk of compromising them and of getting myself into trouble. Maria did not speak of Gaston's escape, or of the Jewish couple's rush into the attic. We kept quiet. The two little boys were not making a sound; just staring, and looking up to Maria. She adjusted their clothes, tied a shoelace. Ever so mildly.

The door to our cell opened and the young guard stepped in bringing, as if it were contraband, two thick cheese sandwiches of dark bread. He was out in a second. "Not a bad guy," I thought, "he may even be embarrassed at having to lock up and guard a young woman and two small children." I was heartened by his gesture that bordered on complicity. I took a few bites: I was not hungry. Marcel ate heartily. Johnny nibbled, and Maria took, out of habit, the crumbs to her lips.

In my idleness I reached, semi-consciously, into every one of my pockets, and from the inner breast pocket of my jacket I pulled out the picture of Adrienne with me and Sylvain taken by the street photographer at the December fair in St Niklaas a couple of months after our arrival in Duizend Appels. Maria saw it. She threw me an anguished look. I was scared and embarrassed. "I'll go to the toilet," I whispered. I knocked for the guard. He accompanied me, with his rifle slung over his shoulder. To my distress he held the door to the small lavatory open and planted himself in the doorway. He must have read my surge of anguish as intense shock at his indiscretion, for he retreated, mumbling "I thought you only..." I closed the door, tore the print into tiny

shreds, dropped them in the toilet bowl, urinated, waited a little
bit, and pulled the cord to the overhead tank. The water gushed,
then settled, covered with bits of photographic paper: every little
piece was there, floating. I was flustered. I pulled again, but the
tank was empty and only a trickle of water leaked down. I waited,
but not long enough, pulled again, with no better result, pulled
again, desperate. The guard was standing beside me now, leaning forward, peering with me into the bowl. We looked at each
other. "What is it?" he asked. I shrugged my shoulders: "Nothing
really. I was just cleaning out my pockets." He looked again, then
tried to flush the bowl himself; the bits of paper remained floating. He shrugged his shoulders, closed the door and led me back
to the cell. I nodded reassuringly to Maria. A few minutes later
the memory of the incident had dissolved in the mild stupor of
our imprisonment.

More standing, shifting, sitting on the floor, standing.

The door to the cell opened. The guard came for me. He
looked around for my personal belongings, but there was nothing for him to carry. His demeanor was almost apologetic. That
was the farewell call and all sensed it. Being separated from the
children shocked me into realizing that mine would be the fate
reserved for men, for Jewish men. My heart jumped. I turned to
Maria to say good-bye. I tried to smile and show no fear, like a
good soldier going off to war. She remained sitting on the stool,
with Johnny on her lap, unable to hide her anguish. I bent down
toward her, with my hand on her shoulder, for the customary tri-
ple kiss: left cheek, right, left. She pulled my head down, gently,
by the neck, and kissed me warmly on the cheek. I put my arm
around her shoulders and kissed her. We looked at each other,
dry-eyed, both. I was still trying to play my part of the stoic fellow.
She looked at me, wide-eyed, intently, as if for the very last time. I
felt her warmth. She had been in Drongen during both my stays
there. We had eaten all our meals together, we had enjoyed, the
four of us and her paramour, Sunday afternoons in Ghent. She
and I had shared chores. I had made her laugh in spite of herself.
I kissed Johnny and Marcel. They looked bewildered. The guard
locked the door on Maria and the children.

I found myself again in the spacious hall. My anxiety grew
with every step. I looked at the guard for a clue; the uniformed
peasant boy was walking alongside me, with bent head, without

pressing the pace. He wasn't leading a prisoner as much as he was showing the way to a lost boy. I asked him what was going to happen. There was no immediate answer, but, from his pensiveness and his mien I could tell that he knew. "Don't get agitated," he said finally, "and you'll make out fine."

"Make out fine..." Would it depend on me? We stopped at a large double door. The guard opened it and closed it behind me.

I recognized the SS in black uniform, and once again I was looking up, this time at a pale face atop a big black shadow in the blaze of a sunlit, ceiling-high window. *Interrogation!* In German that was synonymous with torture. I froze. I had never let the thought get a foothold in my mind. I had lulled myself into thinking that my ordeal was over, that I was merely waiting to meet my destiny.

"Don't be afraid," I heard him say, "we do no harm." His tone of voice was reassuring. The man was not a stranger, he had not beaten me despite his frustration, and he was speaking a pure Flemish. I found his words soothing.

"What's your name?"

"Henri... Henri Grunstein." Once my Jewish identity had been established I could not have conceived of being anyone but Grunstein.

"How old are you?"

"Fourteen."

"Do you have your parents?"

"No. I am alone."

"You don't have to hide anything from us. We have no intention of harming anyone. Believe me." The man wasn't menacing at all and I wanted to believe him.

"Where are they?... You can tell me." It sounded like a plea for a good cause, a desire to be helpful. I was almost tempted to believe him. Was it possible that that long ordeal of hiding like moles had been of our own making? That we had been trying to escape from some imaginary...

"I don't know... They were caught," I said, deeply disturbed by the drift of my thoughts. "Maybe now I'll find out," I added, to lock my story in tight. "Perhaps I may even get to be with them."

"When was that?"

"Shortly after the beginning... the deportations, I mean."

"How did you get to that village?"

"I just went there. They did not turn me away. I had money. I bought a train ticket."

"How did you know about these people?"

"I didn't. I got off at a small train station, a village. I saw a woman scrubbing the patio, in front of the house..." He kept silent. "I went to her... She took me in."

"Any brothers?"

"No."

"Sisters?"

"No. I am an only son."

"Any relatives? We don't mean harm. You know." As unctuous as a prelate he was.

"I know. There is no reason to harm anyone." I was relieved that the questions were veering away from my immediate family.

"Uncles? Aunts?"

"No... Well, yes, uncles," there was a flicker in my mind, " and... their families."

"You can tell me. You know that we won't do them any harm."

"I know you won't," I said incisively. I wanted to sound trusting, but I had the definite impression that I had sounded cocky. I could no longer help it.

"What's their name?"

"Gross. Avrum Gross. Itshe Gross." I wanted to get the Yiddish-sounding first names in.

"Where are they? You can tell me."

"In America."

I was ready. But the blow didn't come. The interrogation stopped there. He waved me out of the room. There was a bright spot in my mind; from that sunlit high window, I thought. It spread throughout my brain. Bright spots were flashing in my eyes. I had gotten through, without damage to myself or to anyone else. I had even gotten back at him. There was a sudden blot of darkness: "What if they checked city hall records? They would find out about my brother. I should have given a false Jewish name... No, that might have led to worse complications. He didn't take any notes! If he still remembered my name, the way I mumbled it, he would spell it wrong." They had never spelled my name right the

first time; even in school. And when they had my name in front
of them, black on white, they would pronounce it wrong:

"GROON-steyn."

"No. GRUN-steyn," I would correct, stressing the "u" (as in
the French *plume*).

"Then with an umlaut."

"No. Without an umlaut."

I felt that the matter was over. "Besides, on the books my first
name is Hersch, not Henri," I remembered. I could not get over
my surprise about the short interrogation. My "America" had no
effect on him. As if it were just any faraway little place. I was
both relieved and disappointed. Didn't he get the meaning of
"America"? Does he still believe in a German victory? "He must
be an idiot," I concluded.

The Flemish guard took me to a room and left. Marcel and
Johnny were standing there in the company of two women. There
was no Maria.

"You are coming with us," said the shorter of the two. She
was rather petite, young, with dark hair and dark, vivacious eyes.
The other one, also young, was taller than I. Light brown hair
framed her full face. Her blue-green, somewhat protruding eyes
peered from behind thick lenses. Both wore dark, loose coats.
They looked like kindergarten mistresses.

We left the building. On foot. No one else was around. The
threat of violence had evaporated from one minute to the next,
as if the entire German nation had taken a step backwards. I was
walking in the middle, with a boy on either side. I was holding
their soft, trusting little hands in a firm grip, like a big brother.
The two women were walking on the outside, each also holding
a boy by the hand. The five of us spanned the entire width of
the sidewalk. I was looking down at the familiar concrete flagstones. The change in protagonists was reassuring. I immediately
checked my reaction: *Handguns in their handbags.*

"Do you speak French?" asked the dark petite. She used "*vous*,"
the formal plural. There was not a trace of a foreign accent in
her French.

"Yes." I looked at her. She kept looking down at the sidewalk.

"And the children?"

"No."

"I'd rather speak French," she said, turning her face to me, briefly.

I didn't answer.

"How was it for you, where you were?" she asked.

Her question took me by surprise.

"Fine. How else?" "Just look at me," the tone of my voice and the slight movement of my shoulders and arms implied.

I saw her gaze drop to Marcel's dirty knees and take in the smudgy pants and shirts he was wearing. The two boys had been playing in the yard in front of the forge before the irruption of the SS.

"Were you together, the three of you?" she asked.

"No."

"Were these people nice to the two little boys?"

"Yes, of course, they were nice," I snapped. "They are human beings, if you know what I mean."

"I know what you mean," she retorted.

I was surprised at the turn of the conversation. We walked in silence for a short while.

"We are Jewish," she said, quietly. She was looking at me from the corner of her eye.

I was stunned. I turned my face squarely at her. Her head was bent. I turned to the blond one. She was looking ahead. Neither one looked particularly Jewish. My shock turned into revulsion: those agents for the Germans, trying to convince me that they were Jewish, trying another twist in the cat and mouse game. But why? I wondered. Were they trying to win me over? To get information? Were they afraid that I might bolt? Perhaps no guns, after all. Why women? It was all so un-German. What if they were Jewish after all? I was at a loss. Still indignant, I played up my disbelief. It was also the only tactic I could think of to draw them out. I wanted to know, desperately, whether they had guns. I looked at the petite with mock curiosity and insolence. She was looking down.

"Who do you think we are?" she asked.

"Gestapo women. Nothing to be ashamed of... if one is German, that is."

"We are Jewish," she stressed. "We are social workers of the AJB [*Association des Juifs en Belgique*, the *Judenrat*]."

"Does that still exist?"

"Yes."

"What for?"

"To provide for children caught without parents, like you. You have been turned over to the AJB. From now on you won't see any more Germans."

"Where are we going?"

"To a children's home. You'll remain in Belgium."

"All this to end up in a *pensionnat*?"

"In a children's home," she corrected me. "Certain people in high places have interceded with the German authorities," she explained.

My thoughts were a tangle. I was groping. I looked around me, for the first time since we had left the Gestapo building. The houses appeared like so many inviolate sanctuaries; their doors were closed, their windows opaque. But I became aware of trees and space. And I wanted to run. I saw Johnny and Marcel from the corner of my eyes, and the image, gone in a flash, of two little hands reaching up for my hands but remaining empty.

"Can you prove to me that you are Jewish?" I asked.

"How?"

"Show me your handbag. Just open it."

The two women exchanged a glance, then stared ahead mutely. A chilly silence set in. I sensed my gaffe. I had to be sure. About the guns.

We boarded a tram and clustered around the center pole on the rear platform. More passengers climbed in behind us. As the tram was reaching its cruising speed, the desire to jump off rose in me. I had done it often; it was a sport, a boy's way to get off a tram in motion, shortly before or after a stop. One would stand on the intermediate step, knees slightly flexed while holding on with the left hand to the side bar, and let go with an outward swing of the right arm and shoulder, right foot reaching down and forward. I knew how to hit the ground running while leaning back at just the right angle to break the forward thrust.

My face must have shown my inner turmoil, my intent even, for no sooner had I taken my left hand off the center pole than our dark-haired chaperon grabbed me by the wrist. I thrust my right shoulder into the standing crowd while trying to wrest my left wrist free of her grip. She held on tight. The tram came to a stop. The silent, dogged wrangle at waist level inconvenienced a passenger:

"This boy is big enough to stand by himself, don't you think!?" he burst out.

"I have my reasons to hold on to him," came the reply, curt and firm.

The dark-haired petite stared the stocky man down. Cordoned off by the two outstretched arms, he shouldered his way around me to the exit, simmering with anger. Passengers climbed slowly down the narrow, high step, blocking the exits on either side of the middle hand bar. I had muffed it again. I felt shame for having failed. The two little boys were looking up at me. Marcel's wide mouth was parted. I looked away but felt the anguished glare of the upward looking eyes in the tilted faces. And I felt shame for having tried. I reached for their hands. They gave them to me, hesitantly. I held each hand in a loose grip, incapable of pressing them reassuringly. Their faces were still turned upwards. And I knew that I would stay with them, that I would never run, never try.

We got off in the residential quarter of Gitschotel. The late afternoon sun was still lighting up the sky, but it had surrendered the street and the sidewalks to the shade cast by the silent houses awaiting dusk. After a short walk we stopped in front of a house. The dark petite rang the bell. It took a while before the door opened, quietly, as if of its own accord, and I knew that we had been observed. A blond, blue-eyed woman let us in and led the way to a brightly furnished living room. Our two chaperons had an aside with her during which she threw us a wary glance. Their chat went on for a short while. The lady of the house was mostly listening.

They broke up. The dark petite turned to me: "You are in Madame Steinhauer's home, a Jewish home. You will stay here for the night. You will be very comfortable here."

She extended her hand as if to intimate, Let bygones be bygones. I hesitated slightly before shaking her hand. I bore no grudge. True, she had bested me. But I had been indecisive. She had only been firm. The look in her eyes, though, was still probing. What did she want to know? Or was she still concerned about me, about what I might do? Couldn't she tell that I would be reasonable? Her companion shook my hand. She had a faint smile. They bade Madame Steinhauer goodbye, waved to Marcel and Johnny, and left.

Madame Steinhauer asked me in a heavily accented Flemish if I would like to wash up. "And the children?" she asked, as if fearing that she might have to do it.

"I'll take care of them," I said.

The two boys were covered with the dirt of a day's romping around the forge and in the orchard. Rubbing their hands clean took a long time. I washed their faces into white masks through which their eyes shone even bigger.

She showed us into the dining room. Like her living room, it was quite different from the rather darkly furnished East European Jewish homes I was used to, where only the silver, the glass and the crystal, and the white tablecloth gave off light. Mellow colors flowed through Madame Steinhauer's dining room. The dining table, though large, did not dominate. It was covered with a light cloth. Inviting scatter rugs led to the spacious living room. Everything suggested a freer flow. I sensed that in this home lived people with a different inner life.

While we were washing up, our hostess had put food and four settings on the table — mine and the children's on one side, hers on the other side, facing us. Sitting between the boys, I buttered their bread and peeled the skin off their slices of cheese.

"Help yourself to some fried fish," she said. She sounded apologetic. "It's cold."

Using my plate, I made sure to remove every bone before I put some fish on the children's plates. I could tell from Madame Steinhauer's look that she was impressed with the way I had taken over with the children as if they were solely my responsibility.

"Do you understand German?" she asked.

"Yes."

She switched to German.

"May I know your name?" She used "*Ihren*," the formal plural for "your."

"Henri Grunstein." Was she checking up?

"...That name is not familiar... Is your family from Antwerp?"

"Yes."

"Did you have relatives in Antwerp?"

"Yes."

"What was their name?"

"Gross." I was waiting, ready to dish up America again.

"No... I don't think I ever heard of them either," was all she said.

My suspiciousness took a back seat. I was vexed that she had not heard of my family, not even of my uncle Itshe Gross, one of the richest Jews in town.

"Was your family of strong religious persuasion?"

"Very traditional," I answered, using my mother's class code: it was a familiar social balancing act, stressing, somewhat pointedly to Madame Steinhauer, my family's commitment to Jewish law and life; yet I was not going to let her lump us with the *frimme*, the truly religious East European crowd that lacked the worldly, Western finish — *unkultiviert*, without *Kultur*, as the German Jews would say of them.

"I am sorry this could not be a *Shabbas* meal for you," she said. Her somber mien gave her young face a matronly look.

I was touched. And the word *Shabbas* shocked me into remembering that I was in a Jewish home on a Friday night.

"Oh..." I said, searching for words, "in times like these..." for she had to be alluding to the absence of the *khallah* (Sabbath bread), the wine, the sweet carp, the meat. But then, wouldn't it have devolved on me, as the only man present, to recite the *Kiddush* over the wine and the blessing over the bread? "In times like these," I repeated, "who would ever think... 'of *Shabbas*,' " I almost said but didn't, for she, Madame Steinhauer, had thought of *Shabbas*, "think of... peacetime."

Shabbas. Incongruous. So unreal...

Madame Steinhauer broke the silence:

"In hiding, were you really hiding? I mean, could you go out?"

"No. Really hiding. I stayed inside."

"How was it?"

"Oh, fine."

Hiding, familiar, yet strange all of a sudden, seemed as unreal as *Shabbas* in Antwerp. The screeching car had ripped it like a veil.

"Better times are not too far off," she said blandly.

I brought myself to ask, "Do you work for the *Judenrat?*"

"No, I just help out on occasion, when they need some room." She knew that my curiosity ran deeper, for she said, "My husband is in Vittel."

It sounded like a resort. I was perplexed. I looked at her, expecting to hear more.

"In the Vittel internment camp, in France. He is an English subject."

"Safe," flashed through my mind.

"He is protected," I said. It was all crystal clear now. I could relax.

"Yes," she said, "they can't touch him. Or at least, that's the way it is supposed to be." She looked preoccupied.

"There is the Red Cross," I said, trying to allay her preoccupation, and learn more.

"Yes. He gets food packages and other necessities. From England too."

I thought of oranges and chocolate. I knew about the power of a British passport: it could cover a Jew's stigma and enable him to claim the right to life and dignity. And the Red Cross and all the nice institutions would be there, to sustain and to pamper.

"They don't intern women?" I asked.

"It depends. I have to report regularly to the *Kommandantur.*"

There was a silence. I saw a clean, enviable situation: a British passport shielding two people. After the war — it could not last forever — they would be reunited. He would have so much to tell her. She would also have things to recount. Her face was clouded, like a winter sky. Her manner was distant and circumspect, as if to stay clear... of us? of our fate?

She said: "You don't have to worry about anything now, you know."

I looked at her.

"Didn't the two ladies tell you?" she asked.

"Yes, that we would not leave Belgium."

"That's right."

"Where will we stay?"

"In one of the homes for children administered by the *Judenrat.* You will be there tomorrow."

Silence enveloped us again. Her perpetual frown of concern deepened. Finally she said: "Madame Ringer will drop in any

time. A neighbor and a good acquaintance." And, taking a moment before answering my unspoken question, "She is in the
same situation as I."

We finished eating, but remained seated, without talking. To
ease the silence I busied myself wiping Johnny's mouth and his
and Marcel's hands. No conversation ensued. The silence stifled
thinking.

Shortly thereafter Madame Ringer walked in, still holding
the key to Madame Steinhauer's home in her hand. She turned
cheerfully to us. "So these are the boys," she said in Antwerpian
dialect, "I am Madame Ringer. I am so glad to see you." I stood
up and nudged the two boys along. She came forward with outstretched hand and I moved towards her. She took my hand with
both her hands. She ran her hands through the boys' hair. A
husky-voiced young matron in a black coat and dress, and a *shaytl*
(wig worn by ultra-orthodox women), she lavished on us her
warmth and her smile as on newly discovered relatives. With her
animated demeanor, her voice, her words, she had irrupted in
our midst like a bearer of good tidings: the House of Israel was
a shambles, but it was still standing. All was not lost yet, so it
seemed.

She got into a chummy, low-key chat with Madame Steinhauer.
"Sit down, oh please, sit down," she enjoined us. Johnny, Marcel
and I returned to our seats. The two women pulled up chairs
at a slight distance from the table and continued their talk. I
was left to my thoughts, lazy, unfocused thoughts induced by the
soothing sight of two Jewish women humming along across a
nicely decked table in a softly-lit dining room on a Friday night.
I did not understand what was happening. I had understood it
in Duizend Appels, under the garret window: there, the Sons of
Light had sustained a relentless siege by the Sons of Darkness.
Here, there was a truce. A little truce. For Jews holding a British
passport. And for children, it seemed: people in high places had
interceded... I counted as a child, just like Marcel and Johnny.
The two boys were not making a sound, or moving a muscle.
Savoring the lull, I let go and leaned back in the high, uphol-
stered chair.

Madame Ringer looked at her wrist watch and got up abruptly,
invoking the lateness of the hour. She had been with us a very

short time. Madame Steinhauer got up too, without uttering the customary, polite, "But do stay a while longer," or "Why the hurry?" Yet the unnaturalness of their deportment struck me as familiar... The Jew-curfew! Of course! The classic parting scene. It was unmistakable. I had witnessed it too often. So it was still in force, in a city without Jews, so to speak, for the kin of some British subjects, the Jewish Council and their charges. Or did the few who were allowed to exist toe the line out of sheer habit? I felt as though I was moving in an invisible cage staffed by Jewish women and tethered to the Belgian soil. People in high places... I knew that I would go on, from moment to moment, as I had in the preceding hours, straining to understand, trying to divine the right way to act, waiting for the next thing to happen. In the silence surrounding the protected bubble of Madame Steinhauer's dining room I suddenly felt, like a void, the disappearance of my world: the Jews.

As she was heading to the hallway, Madame Ringer turned to me: "Is there anything you need?"

"*Tefillin*" ("Phylacteries"). The word jumped off my lips.

She looked at me for an instant. "I'll get you that," she said.

She left with a smiling, full-throated *à demain, tot morgen* (see you tomorrow).

Madame Steinhauer suggested, before even clearing the table, that we retire for the night, saying that we all needed a good night's rest. She showed us to our room.

"This bed is big enough for the three of you," she said to me, "you'll be very comfortable."

The bedroom, big, had its private bathroom. With that constant frown clouding her face she fetched, in her slow, tentative way, two towels and wash gloves, and asked if I needed anything else? No. She inquired whether I could manage with the children; yes. She showed me the light switch; bade us good night; walked out and closed the door behind her. I felt that we had been disposed of for the night, in another bubble along an unreal, preplotted journey. I countered that feeling with the thought that I was being treated with deference and style: I had never seen such an elegant bedroom with such a plush bed.

The next instant I was totally involved in washing the boys' faces, necks, hands, wrists and feet, and in rubbing the encrusted dirt off their knees. I washed up and urinated last. I put the two boys to bed in their underwear, with Johnny, the little one, in the middle. It was a large and luxurious bed. The cover, a silky, stuffed blanket with diamond stitching, showed through the oval opening in the middle of the embroidered white duvet; quite different from the pink, feather-filled puffy bed covers in their buttoned white linen cases that my parents had brought from Poland. Once again I thought of the Steinhauers as different: not altogether our kind of Jews. Yet it didn't raise a thought about my parents: they, my brother, the Van Dammes had dropped off my horizon. There was only the here and now. I looked around the room with my hand on the light switch. The dark window curtains were drawn shut. The overhead lamp gave off a dim light. It did not occur to me that I was in Antwerp. I had no sense of place. It felt I was on a boat in the middle of the ocean on a moon-less night.

The two boys, immobile, with their faces up and their chins on the cover, had their eyes on me, as on a familiar stranger, the same eyes that had looked at me, on the crowded platform of the streetcar, when I tried to break away. Two little children, silent and impassive, with their pent-up fright and repressed cries. I said, Good night, Marcel, good night, Johnny. Marcel mumbled "Good night." Johnny remained mum. I flipped the light switch, crawled into bed and adjusted the cover over them, more as a pro-pitiatory gesture than out of necessity. Curling up in my under-wear, I felt snug in Madame Steinhauer's luxurious bed. A long night lay ahead, with the promise of a new morning. Promises in the air had been my main fare for almost two years, allowing me to close my eyes and, night after night, coast into a sleep popu-lated with dreams lost beyond recall. I had often tried to fathom death, the self coming to a halt, the End: it was a dark void closed off to thought and dream. I would have faced death by the bullet, that afternoon, without fright. I had invited it, in a way, in a mo-ment of utter dreamlessness. In Madame Steinhauer's pitch dark bedroom I could dream: there seemed to be a future, a near future at least. I fell asleep.

✽ ✽ ✽

Water, its foaming edge spreading towards me, flooded the schoolyard of the Tachkemoni school, or the courtyard of the

Moriah *shul*, I wasn't sure which. I wanted to back away but couldn't. "They flushed us off," I snapped, half-awake. "They" were the housewives of Antwerp, rushing, with their wet-scrubbing brooms, wavelets of soapy water across the sidewalk and down the curb, in front of their houses. It was a Saturday morning chore. On our way to *shul* my father, my brother and I would step down the curb and circle a flooded patch of sidewalk. Fully awake, I ran my hand to my groin and thighs: I was dry, my bladder wasn't even pressing. *That's all I need, to wet this bed.*

I remained immobile, to stay awake and to revisit my dream, to capture it. The sun-bleached courtyard of the dream, still fresh in my mind, felt real: it stretched to the horizon; no walls in sight. Yet there was no mistaking it for anything other than the small schoolyard, or the tiny *shul* yard. And I could see myself, as in a replay, standing in the foreground, anguished, and lonely but not alone, for I had sensed the presence of Jews all over the yard; and of Gentiles, close by, visiting, like tourists on Sunday. And I had known about the Germans, spread out on the horizon, standing guard. I had not seen them, but then I had known that they were there. And, standing a step ahead of me: Marcel, to my left, and Johnny, to my right. Marcel had his head turned towards me, his wide mouth agape, like a large tear. He was smiling though. Johnny, a sullen profile, was looking into the distance. Marcel had reached out with his hand as if to take mine.

"We are going to the sun," he had said, as if they were ready to hop playfully, all the way. "Come with us."

"No. This is not the sun, it's the column of fire. And the fire burns."

"We are going into the day," he had insisted.

"This is not day," I had remonstrated. "*Zondag is niet voor ons*" ("Sunday is not for us").

How easily I had pierced, in my dream, the mysteries of life and death and day and night and Gentile and Jew. Only moments ago I had held the whole world, all of history, in the palm of my hand, past and present, the reason for all things. Even the wandering in the desert, the dark cloud and the column of fire, Sunday and Jew-day, had become clear: no wonder the Jews had been scared and obstreperous.

I was losing my dream. The more I tried to decrypt it the more obscure it became. I was left with anguish, vague, insidious.

Next I remembered hearing *"Gehe!"* ("Go!") I had stood, immobile. Then, *"Aber Mensch doch."* "He said 'Mensch!' " I had exclaimed, reassured, in my dream. *"Um Gotteswillen* [for God's sake], *gehe!"* And I had attempted to walk. All walked. They had been walking all along, in silence, invisible. Except the Gentiles: they were drinking their foamy beer in the rays of the sun. Their profiles were relaxed yet inscrutable. And Marcel was no longer smiling: the big tear across his face, that was pain.

That was when they flushed us off. But I had stayed dry.

Wide awake, I surveyed the shadows in the room, then turned on my side and closed my eyes.

✿ ✿ ✿

The knocks on the door woke me up. "Yah," I responded in my first breath of consciousness, eyes closed, as I had always done when my father woke me up. The next instant I knew where I was.

"Time to get up," I heard Madame Steinhauer say on the other side of the door.

"Yah."

The curtains glowed darkly. Daylight filtered into the bedroom. I thought: "Another beautiful day," and my heart started beating with sudden expectation. Marcel was awake, too. I asked him if he had slept well. He nodded. Johnny opened his eyes and glanced at me, then at his brother, without moving his head, or a muscle, without making a sound. *The little one, he knows. And he'll be stubbornly quiet, to the end.*

I helped the children get dressed, tied their shoelaces. Breakfast was waiting.

"You were sound asleep," Madame Steinhauer said with a faint smile, the first I had seen on her face. "It wasn't easy to wake you up." She seemed more relaxed.

The door bell rang soon after breakfast. Madame Ringer came in first. Then I saw, crowding into the hall, a large group of children. Friday's catch. I was astounded: were the SS spending all that brutal energy of theirs only to turn each one of us over to caring Jewish hands? Yet it had to be so — one only had to watch Madame Ringer bustling about.

A young girl came into the hallway. She was the tallest of the group, and pretty: an open face with a generous mouth, dark hair, sparkling dark eyes, dimpled smile, straight nose. The two *Judenrat* women closed the little procession, whereupon Madame Steinhauer closed the front door. None of the children were as small as Johnny and none seemed to be over ten years of age, except for the girl. She moved through the stirring little crowd straight towards me. A smile was shining in her eyes and spread across her face even before she said:

"Bonjour. You are Henri." She had used straightaway "*tu*" (the familiar "you").

"Oui... Bonjour..." I was surprised.

"My name is Sylvie."

"Bonjour, Sylvie."

"Madame Ringer told me about you. I am thirteen, one year younger than you."

So she knew all about me. I felt trapped in my false age. I knew how impressed girls were with older boys. I would now have to prove my maturity, I concluded, since it could not be taken for granted.

"You spent the night at Madame Ringer's?" I asked.

"Yes." Then, with a knowing smile, "You tried to run away."

I was taken aback: she knew that too. But she seemed impressed. I was flattered.

"She told you?"

"Yes. And Madame Steinhauer was afraid. She locked the door of your room for the night."

I was stung by her disclosure while noting, mentally, that she had been taken into the babbling confidence of the powers-that-be. Locked in... It had not occurred to me to try the door. I understood why Madame Steinhauer had given us that big, isolated room with its private bathroom; and her cheerful morning greeting: "You were sound asleep." I felt that the boys and I had been handled like packages. "Anyhow," I debated with myself, "running away," which, I now felt, I should have wanted to do, "was not a consideration." And I did not find any consolation at the thought that Madame Steinhauer had felt threatened. Just good for my image with Sylvie.

"*Et bien...*" ("Oh well"), I said.

I took to contemplating the tips of my shoes.

"What are you thinking about?" she asked.

"*Oh, rien. Comme ça...*"

"Aren't you glad it's all over? We'll be with everybody now. It will be great."

"What do you mean, great?"

"We are going to a children's home, don't you know?"

"Well... kind of..."

So, she was sold on it. But then, maybe it *was* a children's home. A stopover, like Mechelen, but better. Or something permanent. Maybe the Jews had some power after all. I didn't really care. To be among my people, surrounded, was the important thing; a homecoming, a liberation of sorts.

"And I'll see Edmond again," she said. "These two ladies know him." Her face was radiant.

"Edmond?"

"Oh, I thought you might know him. Everybody knew him. He is *some*body. We were neighbors on Kievitstraat."

The Jewish quarter. How unself-conscious. I kept silent. It was nice to know that we were going to join other Jewish boys and girls, but I could have done without Edmond.

"And this is for the young man." That was Madame Ringer handing me, almost as in a relay race, a small package. I hardly managed to thank her. It occurred to me that I had no head cover or skullcap. *I'll get one.*

"I know what this is," Sylvie said.

"Yes?"

"*C'est ces machins trucs*" ("It's these whatshumucallit thingies"), and she touched her forehead. "Madame Ringer showed them to me last night."

"*Ces machins trucs*," I repeated, touching my left arm. We laughed. The thought of a mature woman showing an eager young girl the *tefillin* that I had requested had titillating implications for my ego. I liked her, despite her age, and despite her ignorance of things Jewish, no, because of it, a light-hearted free spirit she was, and this was wartime. "Never in peacetime," went through my mind, never would our paths have crossed. Not that I could ever have fallen in love with her; I had decided that from the moment she said "bonjour." The way she had stepped forward, with an open smile, without holding back, revealed the whole person. Nice. Impressionable. Simple. *Ces machins trucs.* Nothing compelling about her. No mystery. Then also, Edmond...

The *Judenrat* women drew our attention. They were moving from child to child, pinning yellow stars of David on their clothes. They had theirs pinned up. The worn, rumpled stars, made of flimsy fabric, dangled like small rags over the children's hearts. I got mine.

"To keep uninformed Germans and collaborators from arresting us all over again," the taller one explained to me.

The Jew-star was to be our safe-conduct. I wasn't really surprised; it just had not occurred to me.

"The little innocent ones, with the yellow star," Madame Ringer said to Madame Steinhauer, and, taking Sylvie and me into her confidence, "Most of them don't know who they are. They only know the first names of the Flemish people who kept them. Some don't even remember their parents."

"They'll soon learn that they are Jews," Madame Steinhauer muttered.

"Some already learned," Madame Ringer replied.

"We'll be taking the train at the Berchem station," the dark petite said to Sylvie and me. A local stop, the first after the bustling Central Station.

It was time to go. The small children, about ten of them, were assembled, two by two, in a column. Each pair was made to hold hands. The short, dark-haired *Judenrat* lady walked out the front door with the first two. All followed. Sylvie and I held the middle on either side of the column. I took Johnny by the hand. Sylvie was one row ahead of me. The other *Judenrat* lady brought up the rear.

Our small band was marching in the sun. We turned the corner; it was quiet there too, but for the soft trudging of the little feet. A housewife on her doorstep: she gasped, hands moving to her cheeks. A man on the opposite sidewalk: he froze, shock turning to pain. He watched us, then pivoted slowly on his feet, not letting us out of his sight. I looked at the group and saw the solemn faces, the sloppy, dangling yellow patches, the odd assortment of clothes and headgear, some worn, some not fitting. Most of the children were moving under too many layers of clothes, the last act of love, I knew, of their Flemish guardians — Adrienne had rushed to hand me my jacket, on my way out. With them, my kin, my lot was cast, and with them, I knew, I would stay, until the end.

I was looking straight ahead; there was nothing for me to see. The only thing for anyone to see, I felt, was on my chest. We turned a corner. A woman was scrubbing her flooded patch of sidewalk. She turned her head from one side to the other, as if looking for help, or for something to do. She put the pail aside and ran her broom over the flagstones, in a frenzy, to get rid of the water before we reached it. Her stretch of sidewalk was ready for us. But our star-bearing leader led her flock to the opposite sidewalk. I felt sorry for the woman with the broom. In our shul-going days, Flemish housewives had, occasionally, cleared the sidewalk for my father, my brother and me. They would stand with their brooms at the curb, or by the house, waiting for us to pass by. My father would tip his hat, my brother and I would nod or say "*goeden dag*" and I would catch the whiffs of fresh female sweat.

We were nearing a church. I tightened, by reflex, my grip on my bag with the *tefillin*, as though feeling them for reassurance. The church doors were wide open. A glimpse in passing: the dimly lit nave was empty; not a living soul. Another step and the sun was in my face again. I felt freed of the awesome un-Jewishness of the world.

I looked again at the small band of children walking quietly along. I was keeping an eye on them; I felt I should. Sylvie had also cast an inspecting look at the children. Our eyes met. She smiled her dimpled smile. Open face. Shining eyes. She made it feel like papa and maman taking their brood for an outing. I smiled back.

CHAPTER 11 — TO WEZEMBEEK AND AISCHE

The home, a large, three-story house with a small garden in the township of Wezembeek-Ophem, on the outskirts of Brussels, was a crowded, closed-off place. It sheltered about one hundred pre-teen children. A Jewish staff of nine women and one man lived on the premises. I recognized my kin in their faces, their French, their gestures. The *directrice*, with her big blue eyes, light hair and wide cheekbones, her accent-free French, her serious, determined demeanor, looked and sounded Gentile, down to her name: Marie Albert. Her warm welcome soon erased my first impression.

Our little band was quarantined an entire week to tease out whatever infectious disease one of us might have been incubating. We had a view of the backyard and we would watch the roll calls after dinner: the children were arrayed in troops bearing Hebrew names; each troop was headed by a member of the staff. Standing back was Mlle. Albert.

We came out of quarantine on a Friday. That evening I took part in an *oneg Shabbat* (a Sabbath get-together). A small group of older children — the young ones had gone to bed — sat in a circle on the floor of the playroom. Mademoiselle Albert sat on a chair, leaning forward. A dim light shone on us. The children sang, with the melancholy that surrounds a campfire, songs Mlle. Albert had taught them; they sang in French; and in a hackneyed Hebrew — it was obvious that they did not understand what they were mouthing.

"Your turn," Mlle. Albert said to me. "Sing us something."

In keeping with the general mood I gave a low-pitched, dirge-like rendition of *sheer ha'aymek*, the Song of the Valley [of Yizre'el].

"Do you know *Ivrit?*" — the Hebrew term for modern, spoken Hebrew — she asked. A code word, I sensed. *She must know Ivrit.*

"Yes," I answered.

The atmosphere lightened when she led the children in more spirited, hand-clapping songs.

After that Shabbat night Mlle. Albert took to confiding in me as a teacher would in a more mature student. One day, I noticed a twelve-or-so-year-old girl who looked forlorn. "From Germany," Mlle. Albert told me. "Hers was an assimilated family. They had a Christmas tree for *Weihnachten*. German is her primary language. She feels lost."

I felt sorry for her. Not like the rest of us, I thought. We know who we are. "Christmas, in a Jewish home," I said. "I don't understand."

"Well no, not with your background," Mlle. Albert retorted. "The poor girl is confused. First, her Germany no longer exists. Then her parents disappear. At least *she* realizes that it is some evil beyond her, something to do with Hitler. You don't know how hard it is to explain to some — younger ones — that their parents who have been arrested have done nothing wrong. That the Germans are the bad ones. Or that they, the children, have done nothing wrong, that their parents did *not* abandon them. And there are children who lost their home twice, like the ones you came with." She paused. "They may seem vivacious, at times. But they are sad. And they know fear. We have to keep them supervised and busy all the time to prevent them from slipping into a funk; some, even, from bolting."

I felt chastened. The sadness alluded to by Mlle. Albert was brought home to me when I watched, a few days later, a group of closely chaperoned children about to go on a walk in the home's vicinity. Covered in their army-green capes with the yellow stars showing bright, they were pressing against each other in a tight column on the sidewalk, two abreast, quiet and solemn-looking.

I did not leave the premises during my stay in Wezembeek-Ophem.

The Sunday after coming out of quarantine I went to the home's little synagogue, next to the refectory, to put on my phylacteries and recite the morning prayer. A boy around eleven stood there by himself, absorbed in his prayer book. He was delighted with the newcomer, a big boy who was obviously versed in the ritual.

"Will you come every day at this time?" he asked expectantly.

"Yes. After breakfast."

"For *minkha* and *ma'ariv* too?" — the afternoon and evening prayers.

"No."

His expression changed, fleetingly. He turned to me with questions:

"When must you keep your feet joined?"

"Only during the *Ameedah*," I said.

"When do you genuflect and bow?"

"Do you understand what you are reading?" I asked.

"No."

"It's important." I was getting impatient with his uninformed ardor.

"Can you teach me?" he asked.

"Hebrew takes a long time to learn. It would not be possible here."

We kept coming to the chapel, without much to say to each other. I understand now that to him, the God of Israel was real and near; to acknowledge and worship Him with devotion was the imperative. And I realize, with a twinge of shame, that beyond mere instruction he wanted contact. I never knew his name.

I wrote a letter to Gaston's parents in Belsele telling them that we were in a children's home in Belgium and well taken care of, and that I was more concerned about them, the people I had left behind, than they should be about me. I was hoping that word would get to my parents in St-Niklaas. I waited for some reply but none came.

✡ ✡ ✡

The Brussels *Judenrat* had opened the home of Wezembeek-Ophem during the first wave of roundups and deportations, in September of 1942, to shelter children whose parents had been caught. Gentile neighbors, even total strangers, would bring them, sometimes off the street, to the *Judenrat* offices of Antwerp and Brussels.

The following month Gestapo men rounded up the home's children, fifty eight in all, and the Jewish staff, to make the quota for a *Transport* due to leave that day. Before clambering onto one of the trucks, Mademoiselle Albert slipped a piece of paper to a gentile charwoman with the telephone number of Mademoiselle Yvonne Névejean, head of the *Oeuvre Nationale de l'Enfance,* (O.N.E.), a child welfare organization that administered hundreds of homes for poor, needy or orphaned children. Yvonne Névejean contacted Queen Elisabeth, the O.N.E.'s honorary president. The Queen Mother interceded with the military governor. The Germans, trapped in their own lie that only the need for manpower was driving the deportations, agreed to retain in Belgium children under sixteen (the working age) who were caught without their parents, the *"Alleinstehende,"* the "left alone," in Gestapo parlance. That night — only hours before the departure of convoys XVI and XVII — the Dossin *Kommandant* released the Wezembeek-Ophem contingent, with seven more children who had been found huddling in a corner. Mlle. Albert then argued for, and obtained, the release of the entire staff. Ever since, the Germans had been turning over the "left alone" to the *Judenrat,* instructing it to open new homes.

Less than a year later, in September of 1943, when the Germans, in violation of their pledge, rounded up the Jews holding Belgian citizenship, they placated the officials of the land by pledging to halt all further arrests of Belgian Jews and of the elderly — there were three Jewish old age homes in Brussels administered by the *Judenrat;* and by promising anew to exempt from deportation the "left alone" under sixteen. (In Antwerp, when a family was not taken to Mechelen the day they were caught, the underage children were brought to the Jewish orphanage while their parents were held overnight, or longer, in the city jail — Belgian law forbids the incarceration of minors. The Germans would collect the children the day the family was to be trucked to Mechelen, thus upholding their other pledge to the Queen mother, "to keep the families intact.") To declare Antwerp *Judenrein* (cleansed of Jews), they ordered the Jewish orphanage to leave the city. It relocated in the Brussels vicinity.

The *Judenrat*-entrusted population, all duly indexed at the Gestapo, kept growing as the Germans and their collaborators hauled in more of the "left alone." They showed a fierce determination to find them in their hiding places; the "war against the children," the historian Maxime Steinberg calls it in *L'étoile et le fusil.* To accommodate the constant trickle of new arrivals, from infants to teenagers, the Brussels *Judenrat* opened more homes and staffed them with Jewish personnel. In the spring of 1944 there were seven institutions — all but one in or around Brussels — with scores of staff caring for about 600 children, secure, some believed, under the Queen's protection and in the glare of public opinion, a token Jewry attesting to the humane side the Germans sought to project in the West. Others were convinced that the homes were mere holding pens — antechambers of Auschwitz was what they were called after the war. They advocated enlisting the help of the Resistance to vacate the premises and disperse the children. The Jewish notables would not consider it.

Each home was peopled mainly by children of one age group, toddlers in one, big boys and girls in another, with some age overlap depending on space and other requirements. Johnny, three years old, was transferred to the home of Linkebeek where most children were his age or younger. Marcel, seven years old, remained in Wezembeek. I stayed there a couple of weeks only: I had been slated, from the start, to move on to a home in Wallonia, in the village of Aische-en-Refail. It had been opened only months earlier to handle the overflow of children and most of the big kids. I forgot my *tefillin* in the chapel.

The home of Aische-en-Refail impressed me as a grand *colonie de vacances* (summer camp), with a vibrant Jewish presence. It was located on a large estate hidden from view by trees and bushes. A private driveway led to a wide, turreted brick-and-stone castle overlooking a vast lawn which was bordered, on the far side, by shrubs and a stand of birches. Children, from grade-schoolers to adolescents, would run, unconstrained, shout, laugh, play ball. I was also buoyed up to see vigorous young men among the Jewish staff, from the director to counselors and tradespeople. (In Wezembeek, the concierge was the only man.) *Ahm Yisrael kheye!* (The nation of Israel lives!); the old battle cry — it had even been set to a horah dance — welled up in me. I quoted it in a letter to Mlle. Albert. It struck me, though, that the personnel of Aische were a kind of Jews I had never known before. I had heard, back in Antwerp, of someone or other labeled a *freye*, one who had freed himself from the yoke of the commandments, or even a heretic, like the watchmaker of Kolbuszowa. But the men and women on the staff did not seem to have even an inkling of the Law, like the gardener, old Mr. Horowitz, and his son the director. Viennese both. The father spoke only German. He had served in the Austrian army. The son spoke French with an Austrian accent. The old man, gruff and scowling, looked like a brick tower; the director, tall, athletic, with a dark mustache, like Errol Flynn. They would work on Shabbat as if they had never heard of the day. A different kind of Jews; but Jews to the core: I was sure that those men and women could readily have found themselves hiding places. Yet they were there for us. It made a deep impression.

The children were organized, scout-fashion, in ten troops with names such as *les éclaireurs* (the pathfinders), *les semeurs* (the sowers), *les laboureurs* (the tillers), each headed by a big boy or girl.

I became a *semeur* the day I arrived: I joined my troop at the evening roll call on the lawn. We stood at ease, hands clasped behind our backs. The line-up formed an arc. And in the center stood *le grand chef.* Edmond. *The* Edmond of whom Sylvie had spoken so admiringly in Mrs. Steinhauer's hallway. Two assistants stood at his sides and back one step.

He was short — my height — and stocky, with a round face and deep-set, brown eyes. Pushing back his shoulders he commanded, "*Tout le monde, au gaaardà-VOUS!*" as he, also, snapped to attention. He took a few moments to inspect the troops — an unhurried sweep from left to right, from the youngest to the oldest, from the pathfinders to the tillers.

"*Place repos*" ("at ease"), he ordered. Then, "*Chefs de patrouilles.*"

The chiefs, in turn, repeated the exercise with their troops and ticked off, while standing at attention, a brief report of the day's activities and accomplishments.

Edmond was seventeen. He had the steady gaze of someone who does not blink first. He rolled his shoulders when he walked, with a forward thrust of the head, as if getting ready for a fight. He *was* a fighter. He told me later that the Gestapo who had arrested him and his mother on a Brussels street was taking them away by tram. "I jumped off and ran, approached a policeman and asked him for directions to the AJB (*Judenrat*). He offered to walk me. 'The Jewish Council' I told him, 'not the Germans.' 'Fine,' he said." Being in command, a leader, came naturally to him. He had come to the attention of Mlle. Albert and the directors of other children homes for his skills as a youth organizer and his deftness in relating to others.

Mr. Horowitz, the director, favored a tight, army-like discipline to frame the day's events. Edmond fashioned it; he set the tone in Aische. Trumpet calls — we had a capable trumpeter among the big boys — would rouse us in the morning, announce meals, assembly, call-ups, curfew. We would stand by the long row of refectory tables until Edmond would say, "Sit down." The round backs of the slouchers straightened up at his command, "*Tout le mooonde...DROIT!*" ("EV'ryone, STRAIGHT!") A few seconds of silence. Then, "*Bon appétit,*" and we would dig into our food.

Edmond was keen on upholding his rank's privileges: he had his own room; ate with the staff, on occasion with Mr. Horowitz, and sometimes with us, to grace our table with his presence. Yet we liked him: He had a winsome manner. He was good at organizing games and played hard. He taught us songs while strumming the strings of a guitar, beginner-fashion — to be a guitar-toting crooner was high on his list of aspirations. He could, by turns, be avuncular, suave even; or stern and snappy; or smiling and seductive; dosing it just right. He oozed confidence. The big girls had a crush on him.

Morale was high, due in large part to the director's approach: Mr. Horowitz charged the older children with whatever responsibilities they could shoulder and gave them great latitude in their assignments. He would stress in his pep talks the virtues of duty and responsibility, of initiative and self-reliance; of discipline. The chiefs — he had chosen them himself, with an assist from the head counselor, Mr. Gouzu — were to shepherd their troops through the day's routine, keep them busy and entertained, maintain order and promote tidiness. They rose to the task and earned the friendship and good will, even the love, of their troops. The older girls would get the youngest children ready in the morning, tuck them in for the night; they took turns helping out in the kitchen, with the laundry. I taught an arithmetic class once: school was sporadic; teachers were not always available.

A close camaraderie had developed among the older set, as well as affection and respect for Mr. Horowitz. About fifteen of them had volunteered to come with him in January when he was charged by the *Judenrat* with managing the conversion of the dilapidated, abandoned castle into an establishment with modern conveniences. The pioneers, as the volunteers called themselves, worked alongside the tradesmen and contractor crews. They roughed it, without heat and warm water in the cold winter months. Mr. Horowitz was appointed director in the spring when the castle was ready to take in children.

We were also encouraged to apprentice ourselves with the tradespeople among the staff: a shoemaker, a tailor, a seamstress, a barber, a carpenter, and the gardener, Horowitz père. One boy was in apprenticeship with the village baker; two boys worked on the neighboring farm while others helped out when the need arose, in exchange for potatoes and vegetables; a coveted job given the reward at day's end: a ride on horseback.

I chose gardening, to be out in the open, in the sun — it was ideal spring weather; also, to be at what seemed a safe distance from the castle — in a secluded place at the far end of the property, past the wooded area — just in case the Germans broke their pledge not to arrest us. I felt in a protected enclave; still... But to bolt, no. I would have felt like a deserter. And whereto, with no money? It never crossed my mind.

Gardening was hard work, under a tough taskmaster. I was his only apprentice; the other one had quit. I showed up on time and worked at a steady pace, drawing praise — once — from old Mr. Horowitz. I worked even while observing, one day in August, the fast of *Tishe bov* commemorating the destruction of the temple. One of the big girls who intended to fast told me the date — she knew from a letter. I decided on it to make up for the Yom Kippur I had not observed in Belsele shortly after I arrived there in September of 1942. I got two thick slices of bread with cheese from the kitchen to break the fast after sundown. I never worked on Shabbat — Horowitz père did. But I no longer prayed. Nor did I open the Hebrew grammar and reader Mlle. Albert had given me.

To warn the home of an intrusion and to harden us big boys, Mr. Horowitz had instituted an around-the-clock watch at the iron gate: with three of us spelling each other off, one would stand solitary guard for two hours and rest or sleep the next four; there were two sleeping cots in the gatehouse. A boy who was too scared to patrol alone the darkened paths by the gate would be assigned a mate, but got to sleep less. A hunting horn served to signal the approach of stranger or foe. (I never knew what the staff's instructions were, if any, in case the Germans came in their cars and trucks in the middle of the night, or even during the day.)

I stood watch only once. To be awakened from a short, deep sleep was jarring. But soon I felt enveloped by the night's mystery; the starry sky lent it majesty, the silence deepened it, the rustle of leaves softened it, the crackling of a twig punctured it. Everything was clearly drawn in shades of dark: lawn, castle, foliage, trunks, bushes — forbidding, even the asperities of the road. The nervous mouse taking a sudden, timid leap was just a leaf caught in a soft, intermittent breeze.

I was awakened to an ever-so-faint paling of the darkness. Dawn heralded, slowly, life returning. The early morning light brought relief. The first ray of sun set the dew a-sparkling. A lazy day lay ahead; of waiting; for the relief crew.

One day a call went out for soccer players: we had been challenged to play the local team that coming Sunday. A real match. Official.

I volunteered. I had played soccer before the war, in the park, on the hard-sand beaches at low tide of the Belgian Coast, or kicking the ball, solo, against a wall. I had even mastered a couple of dribbles. And I could run.

Mr. Gouzu accompanied us. The rain had stopped. Everything was glistening, dripping wet, the leaves, the stones, the grass. Billowing, dark clouds moved slowly overhead. We had no preparation save for Mr. Gouzu's few pointers. We just ran as fast as we could after the ball, kicked it as hard as we could in the general direction of their goal. And won. To our surprise.

We returned in single file, in our capes, triumphant, with the rain running down our faces. I marched in the lead, being the shortest, holding a tin cup — we had won the cup! A few children came running up to us, delighted. We presented the cup to Mr. Horowitz.

The days went by, punctuated by trumpet calls. We had a
rest period after the noon meal, a private time for reading and
writing, or to stretch out on our beds; nap time for the smaller
children. We slept in two- and three-tiered bunks, spread out,
according to age, over several dormitories in both wings of the
castle, the boys on the second floor, the girls on the third. The
meals were good and copious. But the long stretch from supper
to bedtime in spring and summer got some stomachs rumbling.
The less bashful or more hungry amongst us would sneak by the
kitchen before it closed and cadge a slice of bread or a piece of
cheese. I was used to those lean stretches. Beside, that was the
way it was: I took everything at face value, even the disciplinarian Horowitz' reminder, *"plier ou casser"* ("bend or break"), that
the children, big and small, knew to shrug off with a smirk. I
was kept outside an informal boys-in-the-know loop, especially
about matters on the bawdy side, such as boys trying to sneak
upstairs to the girls' floor, or to peer upwards at the shadows
moving across the translucent, distorting glass floor of the girls'
showers to pierce the mystery between their legs. I was shocked
when I heard about it months later; from a ten-year old. Some of
the staff reacted to me with a touch of formality. Their smiles,
though, were genuine and warm. And I had earned the esteem
of Horowitz père, a hard, unyielding worker.

One sunny afternoon Mr. Horowitz convened us in the refectory — a long, glass-enclosed porch hugging the rear of the
castle. He looked grim. And he told us in a tone dripping with
anger and contempt that a boy on guard duty — it turned out
to be a chief — had "deserted"; with help from outside; that the
deserter had brought shame on us all; that the ill-considered,
selfish act of one harmed us all; that we were in it together, "one
for all and all for one". On he went, in angry and convoluted remarks whose logic escaped me — the words "deserved collective
punishment" stood out: we were to sit, arms folded, in silence,
and reflect on our responsibility towards each other, on loyalty
and solidarity. He left.

I had no reflecting to do: I had determined to stay with my
people. I felt at peace; smug, even. And more so after hearing
Mr. Horowitz's strong words. Anyway, we were "covered" by the

Germans' pledge to Queen Elisabeth. The proof: they were leaving us alone.

I did not feel angry, though, at the boy who bolted in the dark of night: he had wanted out. A coward, perhaps. But gutsy, in a way.

We sat motionless. After a while, the fidgeting began. It spread. Glances darted left and right. Furtive smiles. Whispers broke out. The hum grew.

Mr. Gouzu dismissed us.

Mr. Horowitz was in a tight spot: we were all indexed at Gestapo headquarters in Brussels. If they ever made a head count, the discrepancy would raise their hackles. Fortunately, the Jewish Council had a contact at the Gestapo, someone on the take. Index cards would disappear, occasionally, or get changed. Children from *Judenrat* homes would be whisked off to gentile institutions, or convents. Once, children were ransomed out of the Dossin barracks in Mechelen and brought to the *Judenrat* homes.

A few weeks later another boy ran away. There was no collective punishment.

✼ ✼ ✼

Then, one night, they came for us.

Gouzu was standing in the dark dormitory, yelling:

"WAKE UP!! WAKE UP!! Follow me! The Germans are here. Don't push."

We followed him past the third floor, up a dark and narrow winding stairway, into a turret. We huddled in silence.

Suddenly, the thumping of boots was coming our way. It grew louder. The beam of a flashlight swept over our faces. "*Verdammte Glockenläuter!*" ("Damned bell ringers!") washed over us like a crashing wave. The German soldier kept shouting it as he motioned us down with the light beam. "*Zurück! Zurück!*" ("Back!")

"Go back to your dormitory," Gouzu enjoined us calmly. "Come." And he led the way. "Don't rush. Watch your step."

The German, hunched over in the low-vaulted space, kept up a loud *Glockenläuter* growl while we filed past, heads bowed, under his nose.

———————

The Gestapo of Charleroi had come for us, with trucks and a retinue of Military Police. Our boy on guard duty saw them coming. He sounded the alarm, then he and his two comrades ran. The soldiers surrounded the castle. Inside, panic erupted. Horowitz was having a late-night meeting with his staff. Most of them hid or fled to the neighboring farm. Freddy Horowitz, Ben Gouzu, his wife Jeanne, and Edmond Mel stayed put. Two boys got on the roof and clung to a chimney. A group of small children in their nightgowns, led by Herbert Kessler, one of the big boys, made it to the other turret. A soldier, waving a pistol and shouting at the top of his voice, flushed them out.

"Are you not ashamed to frighten small children?" Herbert, a refugee from Germany, confronted him in flawless German. The soldier lowered his gun.

Horowitz invited the Gestapo chief to his office where he cleared up the misunderstanding: we were authorized Jews duly covered by Gestapo headquarters in Brussels. Having gotten wind of our "hideaway" and unaware of our special status, the German had set out for a big haul. To salvage his expedition, he resolved to take the youngsters of working age. There were none that old, Horowitz contended. The German wanted to see for himself. Some of the big boys and girls were brought to the office; Gouzu accompanied them. Most of them looked their age, sixteen and older. (I had turned sixteen, but was listed as a fourteen-year old, the age I had declared when I was caught, and could pass for a twelve-year old.) They were coming along, the German declared. They were staying, Horowitz retorted, they were authorized by Brussels. Moreover, he (the German) had no right to come on the premises.

Going by the version of events I picked up a few days later, the confrontation in the director's office escalated into a shouting and desk-pounding match. Horowitz did not budge. Well then — and the German pointed at a sturdy boy and at Ruth, a tall, buxom girl with black hair and large, dark eyes — those two were coming along; they were at least sixteen years old if a day. (They were seventeen.) Horowitz stood his ground. All stayed. The Gestapo chief of Namur had blundered onto Brussels turf, and one of his soldiers had killed an authorized Jew: the tailor; felled while helping others escape. The German told Horowitz that no one was to find out about the dead man;

and that he'd advise him what to do about the body. He left with his cohort.

The members of the staff returned one by one.

The tailor's body was removed two days later. The Germans came in a civilian car, followed by a truck with a coffin. We were taken for a walk in the woods to shield us from an unsettling spectacle. The personnel stayed indoors; the Germans did not want anyone around. The seamstress, her tall and slim frame convulsed in sobs, broke through: she wanted to bid the tailor a last farewell. They had been lovers. For weeks she would be seen moving about, staring with red-rimmed eyes in the distance.

Horowitz accompanied the coffin to Namur. He was not allowed to attend the interment; he was not told where it took place.

One morning a few days later — we were sitting down for breakfast — the Gestapo of Charleroi showed up again, with a truck. The boy on guard duty sounded the alarm. The big boys and girls managed to hide. The Germans had come for the adolescents of working age. There were none, Horowitz maintained. Once again his command of the German language and his firm demeanor made their impact. But it became clear that distant Aische was no longer safe for overage children.

Shortly thereafter Freddy Blum, the head of the Children's Section at the *Judenrat*, took the overage boys and girls in a tarpaulin-covered pickup truck on a scary night trip to Brussels where they were dispersed, some, made younger or hired as staff, in the children homes, others, in surrounding villages. Edmond and Ruth spent weeks in hospital beds, with the connivance of the head doctor and the head nurse, before they were safely placed.

☆ ☆ ☆

To fill the void left by the departures, new — younger — chiefs were chosen to head the troops. I was picked to be the big chief; Gouzu broke the news to me. I was stunned. He had talked with Mlle. Albert, he said; she had endorsed me without reservations. I was flattered, speechless. I looked down at the tips of my shoes as we walked side by side, on the grass. No, I should not worry, he said, reading my silence. I would be doing just fine; he, Gouzu, would help me. Gouzu was everyone's favorite, though quick to yell. Short and handsome, of solid build, he had a swarthy complexion, black hair and velvety, brown eyes.

I inherited Edmond's bright little room.

Slogging through the days, in the beginning, was torture; the night, a refuge. I would get up in the morning, anxious at the prospect of facing an entire colony. I did not feel impelled to control their movements or capable of directing their activities. I lacked Edmond's zest for being in the lead, his savvy and self-confidence. I had noticed, in his day, the grammatical errors in his Flemish-accented French. I realized now how pithy his instructions were, how smooth his delivery. Problems left him unruffled. He was on top of things. I was out of my depth.

Back in the privacy of my room, in the evening, I was relieved to be alone.

I began my tenure by copying Edmond, at roll calls, at the meals, down to the *Tout le mooonde... DROIT!* routine. But I took my meals with the children, more as their equal — no need to pretend while eating potatoes and vegetables. I would have felt awkward, stressed even, eating with the staff: mine was a make-believe authority. Edmond's structure was sustaining me as much as I was upholding it. The afternoon rest hour also gave me some respite.

On the surface, things looked the same as before. I relied on the chiefs, and on the children themselves. Their goodwill reflected their grasp of the situation: they knew how unusual it was, and that it would last only till war's end; their parents would then return, their families would be whole again. They were disposed to cooperate. All, but one boy. He would drag his feet, stay at rest a bit too long — his chief, facing me, did not notice; he would arrive last at roll call, when all were standing in place. He was my height; a bit heftier. He looked fourteen. Did he feel overlooked for a chieftainship? Or for the top job, perhaps? Edmond would have known how to handle him. I did not know how to react. Talk to him one-on-one? And if he were to laugh in my face, what then? Referring him to a higher authority, to Gouzu, for example, would be admitting defeat to the troops and failure to Gouzu; it did not occur to me. Discipline was my responsibility, upholding it, my job.

His acting up had gone on for a day. Everyone was noticing it; I caught some darting glances in my direction. I had to do something.

At the morning roll call the next day he was missing altogether. And his chief, standing at attention, reported it for all to hear.

"Did he report sick?" I asked.

"Not that I know."

At that moment the gaze of many children shifted upwards, toward the castle. I looked back. And there he was, standing on the balcony in front of his dormitory, one hand on the wide stone balustrade.

I tore away, into the castle, up the stairs, through the dormitory, onto the balcony. I positioned myself at the balustrade, in full view, facing him. The children arrayed on the lawn could see us in profile. And they could hear me. I ordered him to join the roll call. He refused. I knew he would. I ordered him again, expecting him to be even more defiant. He was. And I slapped him once across the face, hard, for all to see; it could be heard as well. I had taken a big gamble, in cold rage.

He went. We emerged from the castle, my authority reaffirmed. I had acted out my fears and fury. I did not reflect that my desperate yet calculated move could have gotten me in a mess: hitting was unknown in Aische. I did not dwell on the egregiousness of my action. It worked. I put the unsettling episode behind me.

Days went by. I gained confidence. I could get involved with troops and their chiefs without being self-conscious. Gouzu told me that I was doing fine. His smile seemed to imply, "I told you so."

✻ ✻ ✻

June 6, 1944: the Allies landed in Normandy. The atmosphere became both hopeful and tense: Would the Allies liberate us? Would the Germans keep their word and let us be?

Then, on August 15th, an advance party of a retreating German antiaircraft unit requisitioned our castle; we had a couple of hours to clear out. The villagers of Aische came to our help with carts and horses to pull our belongings and the little ones. We trudged out, unafraid, giddy: the castle was what the Germans wanted, not us. They did not know that we were Jews. Let the Gestapo from Namur come, with their trucks. I felt liberated, almost.

We piled up in the village school for the rest of the day and the night. From there we were dispersed in the surrounding villages: an appeal had gone out to the local mayors. Some farmers and tradespeople welcomed an extra hand during the busy season. They chose their kids based on looks and sturdiness. We had the perfect cover, I thought: needy children from all parts of the country displaced by the Germans.

I ended up with about fifteen of the bigger children in the village of Orbais, in the neighboring province of Brabant. The mayor, Monsieur Brichard, a wealthy landowner, took me in, at Gouzu's recommendation. I was treated like an important guest. I had my own room in the master house; close to the roof, by the skylight, I noticed approvingly. Just in case. I ate with the Brichard family — they had an eight-year old girl. I had breakfast alone: with no one to wake me, I slept in. A maid would wait on me. The foreman and one of his farmhands gave me a tour of the stables.

I did not go to church the following Sunday — it was not necessary, the Brichards assured me in response to my half-hearted suggestion. No wonder, I thought: tall, elegantly dressed, aristocratic-looking, they were not eager to be seen with a strange boy in a thrift-shop loud-green, ill-fitting jacket. I did not know then that Horowitz and staff had divulged our identity to the mayors and priests of the sheltering villages.

Several of the children went to church with their hosts. I met some after Mass. They were elated: "The priest said that we are Jewish children, the children of Jesus-Christ." My heart sank: he blew our cover, that well-meaning idiot of a priest! When the Allies were so close. How reckless. I told the children to stay out of their houses as much as possible. They were puzzled. I took to roaming in the countryside, in the fields.

From that Sunday on, a Jewish child could do no wrong. Chocolates and nice clothes materialized, cakes were baked.

✼ ✼ ✼

One sunny afternoon, about a week later, there was through the streets of the village a sudden rush of people carrying baskets with fruit and tomatoes; one man held a bottle of wine in one hand and a long-stemmed glass in the other. "The Americans! The Americans are here!" I followed them out of the village, into a meadow. I stopped under a tree, about fifty meters from the road: there, a column of rather small tanks had come to a halt. A soldier was leaning against the side of each tank. Tired-looking, almost crumbling, their faces smudged, they looked with a wan smile at the exuberant villagers running up the grassy slope. The soldiers tried to decline the offerings with slow, almost begging gestures. To no avail. They would end up handing the fruit — the tomatoes first — down the turrets — there had to be mounds of it inside the tanks. But they would gently, yet firmly, push back the hand holding up the glass shimmering with dark red wine.

The Americans had been for days on the heels of the Germans. Maintain contact, give them no respite, was the order of the day. Rest, later.

I stared, transfixed: so those were the demi-gods for whose coming we had yearned all these years: smiling, unassuming, grimy and worn out men unable to fend off villagers bearing fruit and hugging and kissing them unabashedly.

Suddenly, as if on cue, the men turned around, in unison, climbed like cats up the tanks and disappeared down the turrets. The column pulled away at a snail's pace. To stop almost immediately. The men came out. The villagers rushed back.

I wanted to go up there. Touch a soldier. But how could I just touch someone, like an object? Especially an American? Sacrilege. I would shake hands. But they were mobbed, every one of them. And the bombs: tanks, under the open sky, might attract enemy fire. To die now, of all times...

I tore myself away — I wanted to come close to an American, badly, to see his eyes, to see and be seen — when the soldiers climbed back in. The tanks rolled on, faster that time. For good. In hot pursuit. I was liberated, but not yet free.

✵ ✵ ✵

In Brussels, events unfolded differently.

One day in late August, ten days after the German anti-aircraft unit had ordered us out of the Aische castle, Adolf Eichmann's deputy and roving emissary, Anton Burger, an Austrian, (also known as the butcher from Vienna for his role in the liquidation of Jewish communities), showed up at the *Judenrat* — Paris was free, the Allies were rushing toward Belgium. Burger was the man who, back in July of 1942, had launched the deportations from

Mechelen with Berlin's order of ten thousand workers for the
German Reich. He demanded now that the notables draw up a
list of authorized Jews by name and address, including apartment
number or floor. (The children and the elderly in the *Judenrat*-
administered institutions were all indexed at the Gestapo.)

The Jewish notables met off-premises. They moved to abandon the old age homes to the Ministry of Public Health, got word
out to the directors of the children's homes to flee with their
charges, and went into hiding.

The personnel of the six homes in and around Brussels got
their charges out in a matter of hours. With the help of the
Underground and other concerned individuals they were placed
in Catholic convents and other institutions, and with private citizens. The director of the Brussels orphanage found shelters for
his children among the neighborhood shopkeepers. The children and staff of the Linkebeek home for toddlers spent the
night in the nearby Soignes forest.

The British liberated Brussels on September 3rd, 1944. They
entered Antwerp, twenty miles to the north, the following day.

It is not clear whether the *Judenrat* had alerted the Resistance.
In any case, the Brussels Underground got word of the dire situation from one of its agents, a beer merchant who made the
beer deliveries to the Dossin barracks. The beer merchant dealt
with an inmate, Albert Van Koevoorden, who had been put in
charge of the beer supply for the camp's staff. Van Koevoorden
was the lover of the *Kommandant*'s secretary, Liselotte. She was
the first to read the dispatch from Berlin instructing her boss to
prepare for the arrival and deportation of Belgium's remaining
Jews. She promptly told her lover, who told the beer merchant.
(This episode was recounted, with names left out, at the first
international gathering of the Hidden Child Conference in New
York, in 1991, by Andrée Geulen, a member of the wartime *Comité
de Défense des Juifs*, an organization that had placed about 2500
Jewish children in Belgian families and institutions and provided
for them.)

The rescue of the more than six hundred children, and staff,
was a rare — probably unique — episode in the annals of the

Shoah. The children of the Warsaw ghetto orphanage marched behind their director to the loading platform. (The Polish Underground offered to whisk him to safety but he declined.) In his life story, Aharon Appelfeld writes that the director of the Czernovitz orphanage had his charges march, singing, to the train station.

In France, shortly before the German retreat, two hundred children were taken from the homes run by the *Judenrat* of Paris and deported with the last *Transport* to Auschwitz. Others were deported via Belgium: Father Bruno Reynders, a Benedictine monk who was instrumental in the rescue of hundreds of Jews, mainly children, recounted that the day before Brussels was liberated, four trucks with 140 Jewish children from a home near Arras in north-western France were seen stationed briefly on the Place Rouppe. They left for Germany.

☆ ☆ ☆

After a couple of days, freedom felt as permanent as the occupation had. Irreversible. We stayed put in Orbais. Days of anticipation. Days of joy. A detachment of exhausted Americans settled in the village. They were feted. They slept in the school; on the grass; they had nice green blankets. They handed out chocolate and cigarettes, corned beef in trapezoidal, easy to open cans. People, especially our children, were gravitating to them. An adventurous village lad wanted to join them.

A few days later a tall, dignified-looking man stopped me on the street. He wanted to talk to me, the chief, the responsible one, he said. Two big girls from the children's home — he named them; his family had given shelter to one of them — were hanging out around the soldiers. And there was the upcoming Saturday night dance. He and his wife, and the other family as well, had tried to warn the girls and hold them back. They would not listen. "Well... You and I know what soldiers want." I nodded. "Here today. Gone tomorrow. And the consequences, who bears them? Don't get me wrong; they liberated us. But soldiers are soldiers." Would I speak to the girls? They might listen to me. I said I would.

I sought them out the same day. They were together. I felt on shaky ground: slightly taller than I, they were young, very young... women, it dawned on me.

"Listen," I said, trying to sound authoritative. "I have to talk to you." I paused. "Stay away from the soldiers." They grinned. "You know what soldiers want." They giggled. Were they making fun of me? Mustering my courage, I soldiered on: "And you know who bears the consequences." They stopped giggling. "Well, that's all." They gave me a hard look, turned around and walked away.

We missed the Rosh Hashanah celebration organized by a few Jewish officers and soldiers at the home in Aische: we, in Orbais, had moved back to the home later than most. The place was buzzing with stories from the villages, of Liberation, about the Americans, about black soldiers: they would drive their trucks at breakneck speed on the narrow, winding roads — the juggernauts would sway, the earth would shake. One of the boys saw his uncle emerge from a tank. The family had fled Germany. The uncle had moved on to the States. "He will bring me to America," the boy said.

We had a reception for the villagers who had sheltered us. They were welcomed with snacks and songs. Gouzu asked me to say a few words on behalf of the children; I still retained some of the big chief status, though discipline was much relaxed. I ascended the podium without any preparation, smug in the belief that the right words would roll off my tongue, propelled by memories and emotion. I uttered, haltingly inane sentences of gratitude.

Public transportation was chaotic. Still, we had visitors. And some of us left, mainly for children's institutions in Brussels. A sturdy nineteen-year old dropped in: he had found refuge on a farm, had learned farming, and was trekking solo to Palestine, his guitar strapped to his shoulder. He sang and played for us one evening, on the grass. He camped out on the lawn.

The past, a closed book, opened up for the first time: "Where did you live before the war?" "In Brussels!? What street?" "Do you have brothers and sisters?" "Two older brothers, but I don't know where they are." Anxiety seeped into hope. Children had begun wondering about the whereabouts of fathers and mothers, of siblings. I took it for granted that my parents and brother were safe: I was the only one caught on that day in April; a fortuitous catch: they had come only for Johnny and Marcel.

Edmond came back. I was glad to see him. He took over and I returned to the dorm, relieved, feeling quite happy. I marveled at his touch in the new atmosphere of controlled turmoil. He would coax, persuade, admonish: "You don't want me to be disappointed in you, do you?" Like a caring but firm shepherd. He had retained his sway of old.

Then one late afternoon — I was standing with others on the lawn — I saw, emerging from behind the bushes by the entrance gate, my parents walking up the path to the castle. They were a striking couple, trim and elegant, both bareheaded, my mother in a summer dress, her black hair in stark contrast to her pale face, my father in a gray-blue, wide-striped suit. I had known, ever since Liberation, that we would be reunited; I had not expected it to happen in Aische. I ran towards them. We embraced. My mother cried. "Finally," she mumbled. "Thank God," they both repeated. "Let's go inside," I said. I was conscious, every step of the way, of the stares that accompanied us. We sat down in the refectory.

They had learned of my whereabouts at an ad hoc Jewish information office in Brussels. They came to Aische as soon as they could. They left my brother in St-Niklaas with a couple who took them in when I was caught. They were happy now, the family was intact, thank God; they would send for me as soon as they found an apartment in Antwerp. They were happy to see me in good shape — I had a nice tan. I told them that being caught had ushered in a new life, among Jews, in the open; that I had breathed freely; that the food was good; the personnel were all Jews. I could not think of much else. And then I asked them without ado to leave as soon as possible, that this was a place of children without parents.

They understood. It was too late to travel back, so they would check with the director as to where they could stay for the night; they would leave early the next morning. Anyway, they wanted to greet him.

Mr. Horowitz offered them a room. He invited them to have supper with him.

I saw them once more, in passing, at table with Herr Horowitz, in the refectory. They were having a quiet conversation. In civilized German. They left at dawn.

A day later I made my way to a group of about eight boys of different ages standing on the lawn. They fell silent as I drew near, then one of them continued:

"He'll send for me as soon as he is settled."

"How old is he?"

"Five years older. Eighteen."

"I have a big sister," said another.

"Where is she?"

"I don't know."

"I have an aunt. She is in Switzerland right now."

"Léopold has an uncle in America."

I turned around, slowly, and peeled off. A pause. Then I heard, "He has his parents."

The following day I recognized in the hand of a ten-year old a silver knife from my family's dairy set: he was showing it to a couple of boys. He had found it, he said. (My parents had left it behind — a useful implement, to cut bread, or cheese, during the snail-paced train rides of those days. Mr. Govaerts had brought it to Belsele along with their clothes and other belongings.) I wanted to reclaim it, but could not: I would have had to say the words "My parents."

EPILOGUE

After my capture in April 1944, my brother spent the rest of the day in the woods of Waasmunster, and the night in the barn of Adrienne's parents.

That afternoon in St-Niklaas — the news from Belsele had traveled fast — Lucien, my parents' host, ordered them out of his house: he was convinced that I would give them all away. My father countered that, should he and my mother fall into German hands, *he* would give him away; he demanded that they be taken to a certain barber, who, from stories heard, could be trusted. (The barber had been beaten up in his shop by Flemish Blackshirts for his pro-English outspokenness.) My mother refused to go on hiding: Lucien had told them point-blank that both Sylvain and I had been caught. "Enough," she wanted to surrender to the Germans. My father asked her for time — "just one night, to put our heads down, to think it over"; he would surrender with her the following day if she was still of the same mind. My mother gave in.

The barber took my parents to acquaintances, Joseph and Josephine Van Poecke, a childless couple in whose house his mother had rented a room she was no longer occupying. The Van Poeckes offered them shelter for the night. They invited them to dinner — my parents' first good meal in a long spell. At one point in the conversation, Josephine asked:

"Are you Jews?"

"Yes," my father answered.

"Do you have a place to go to?"

"No."

She looked at her husband. "Would you excuse us," she said. They went into the kitchen. Minutes later they returned and Josephine said:

"You can stay here until the end of the war."

"Do you know what would happen to you if they were to find us here?" my father asked.

"Yes," Josephine answered. "What will happen to you will happen to us."

My parents were moved. And my father told them everything that had happened. Still, he and my mother needed that night to talk it over and decide.

The Underground in St-Niklaas, it turned out, was fully informed about the events in Belsele — through Gaston's mother, Léontine? — for Lucien was dispatched the following day to fetch Sylvain; he was sheltered by the chief of the local Underground. It restored my mother's will to live. Josephine reiterated her and her husband's invitation to my parents. She flatly refused my father's offer to pay rent: "You take these bank notes off the table or you leave." A few days later they took in my brother as well. He called them Uncle Jef (Flemish abbreviation for Joseph) and Tante (Aunt) Jos. Sylvain, unlike my parents, was not housebound.

Jef was in the coal business. He started before the war. A photograph of that time shows him bent under a load, arms arched overhead, holding the sack; his blackened face with the shining eyes is that of a coal miner. He had a wallpapering sideline to supplement his income.

Jos had been a textile worker before the war. She never went to school. She could not write, but taught herself to read, and became an avid reader.

My parents' life improved markedly. They were free from the constant, gnawing hunger, the immobility, the stifling silence — they regained their voices which had weakened to a whisper. The convivial meals, a card game, a liqueur, a smoke, stories and reminiscences, the news on the BBC of the Allied advances (glasses were raised for each significant Allied success), made for pleasant evenings around the dinner table, a distraction from the pain caused by my capture and assumed deportation. (Lucien had been notified of the reassuring letter I had written to the elder Van Dammes from the children's home in Wezembeek. He did not tell my parents, even though he knew where they were.) Once, as my brother fussed over a bedtime treat, my mother let her anguish slip out: "Who knows where Henri is, whether he has enough to eat," she mumbled. My brother, who was ten years old at the time, broke down crying: "He has enough to eat, Mama, I know it. He'll be back in good health. I know it." It gave her a jolt. She took him in her arms. It got her hoping again.

✻ ✻ ✻

Gaston, having dodged the bullets of the SS, found refuge on a farm in Duizend Appels. He ventured home that night. He and Adrienne decided that she should appear the next day in Antwerp, as ordered: they assumed that the SS would let her go, since they had not taken her along with me. But it was a trap: the SS wanted to know the whereabouts of her husband. She pleaded ignorance. Nor did she confide in a "priest" who came to "comfort" her in her cell and offered "to convey messages to her loved ones." When she failed to return, Gaston made his way to Drongen, where his sister Alice arranged for a hiding place.

On the night of his furtive encounter with Adrienne, Gaston disposed of my *tillimel* and my pocket prayer book in the out-house: incriminating evidence in case the SS came back.

Gaston's mother, Léontine Van Damme, was out on a co-vert mission when the SS took her daughter Maria and the children away. She enjoined her daughter Alice to take over her Underground duties, and surrendered the following day to the SS, claiming sole responsibility for the presence of Jewish children in the family, and hoping thereby to have Maria and Adrienne released. Maria was let go after a few days. Adrienne was deported. Léontine Van Damme was incarcerated in Antwerp's Begijnenstraat prison.

✻ ✻ ✻

In early September, a Polish unit attached to Montgomery's army entered St-Niklaas. My parents exulted. They welcomed their liberators in their mother tongue. The soldiers beamed. They sought each other out in the days that followed.

On the first night of Liberation, there was a knock on the door: friends of the Van Poeckes, the Verbeeks, were looking for a place to hide. They had turned pro-German and feared the vengefulness of resisters. "They have never collaborated, or done anything untoward," Jos explained to my parents while the new-comers waited in the hallway.

Now my parents were the ones walking confidently in the day-light — short distances only, they were weak-kneed from their long immobilization — and the Verbeeks were cooped up. The irony of the role reversal was lost on no one.

Within days, the Germans were back, sending my parents scurrying indoors and setting the Verbeeks free. The two couples took turns a few more times, as soldiers of one army or the other were sighted or were rumored to have returned. In the evening, all would gather around the dinner table. A convivial bunch.

St-Niklaas was secured a few days later. My parents were free. The Verbeeks ventured out, then, back home. They were not importuned.

The British liberated Antwerp. Belgium was free. Gaston's mother came home from prison. Gaston came to St.-Niklaas; Lucien directed him to my parents. It was a reunion under the cloud of Adrienne's absence, and mine. The news that I had written from a children's home in Belgium, which Gaston had learned from his father and his sister Maria, gave my parents a flicker of hope. Finding me was now uppermost on their minds. But they had run out of cash. My father asked Jef for a loan. Jef handed him his wallet: "Take what you need," he said. My father removed 25,000 francs, a sizable sum at the time. It took another week before they could reach Brussels. There, in a makeshift Jewish information center, they were told of my whereabouts. By the end of September our family was reunited in a small, furnished flat in Deurne, a municipality of Greater Antwerp. That was when I learned that Adrienne had been deported to Germany.

✵ ✵ ✵

Antwerp was struggling to get back to normal. There were shortages of food and other necessities. The prosecution of the war took precedence over all else.

Then, in the middle of October, the German unleashed the terror bombing of the city by the V-1 flying bombs and the V-2 rockets. They fell at random. In less than three months they killed close to 4,000 civilians and over 730 Allied servicemen. One flying bomb struck a packed movie theater on the De Keyserlei, killing more than 560 people, nearly 300 of them Allied soldiers, mostly GI's. (Antwerp's port — Europe's largest at the time — was of critical importance to the Allies. Having fled precipitously to escape encirclement by the British, the Germans had failed to leave behind, as planned, a "city without a port." In retaliation, they vowed to turn Antwerp into a "port without a city.")

The drone of the V-1 could be heard from a distance. The wail of the war-time sirens would rise in a macabre chorus. When flying overhead, the V-1 would rattle the glass. You were safe, as long as you heard it. The moment of terror came when the noise stopped. The silence, until the explosion, was terrifying, especially at night. The V-2, faster than sound, caused the glass to shatter and the stone to crumble before one would hear the shriek of the incoming rocket. Once again, someone's lateness, say, in returning from an errand, would stir anxiety at home.

When my mother was wounded in the ankle by a shard of flying glass from the suddenly imploded kitchen window, my parents accepted Jos and Jef's offer to return to St-Niklaas: the Van Poeckes had put an annex to their house at our disposal. Sylvain and I went to school for the first time since the summer of 1942.

In December of 1944 the Germans launched a lightning counter-offensive and breached the Allied front in the Ardennes. They were aiming for Antwerp, to cut off the Allies' strategic supply route to the western front. The people were apprehensive: the Germans' sudden thrust was deep, and they took 19,000 American officers and soldiers prisoner. There was long and arduous fighting in the snow and icy mud of the hilly and wooded Ardennes before the Germans' advance was halted, at Bastogne. Their offensive stalled, then collapsed.

The bombardment of Antwerp had stopped. The wounded city was hobbling back to normalcy. The diamond industry was slowly coming back to life. It was a cold winter.

The situation was much brighter in Brussels. The capital had sustained little damage. The municipal services were not lacking; the trams rolled. A mood of optimism, a zest for living, for getting back to normal, followed the euphoria of Liberation. The Belgian government in exile had returned from London. The city soon established itself as the governing center, the beating heart of the country. It attracted people uprooted by the war, people in search of missing relatives and friends. A sizable Jewish community had come out of hiding. (Close to three quarters of the capital's Jews had eluded the Germans and their Belgian collaborators, whereas only one quarter of Antwerp's Jews did.) The Great Synagogue, left standing, was packed on Saturdays. The train ride to Antwerp's Central Station — a stone's throw from the diamond district — was direct and swift (unlike the trek from St-Niklaas: first to Antwerp's Left Bank, then through the tunnel under the Scheldt). This was the Brussels to which we moved in March of 1945.

My brother and I went to French-language schools.

Two important visitors came calling:

A Jewish chaplain with the rank of colonel in the American army who, as a young man, had immigrated to the States from my parents' hometown, Kolbuszowa. He returned a couple of times, in his chauffeur-driven jeep, accompanied, once, by Jewish officers, and bearing precious gifts of American soap, cigarettes, and chocolate, before he moved on with the troops.

The other visitor, a soldier in the Jewish brigade from Palestine who volunteered with the British army, was a cousin of my father, also from Kolbuszowa. He had seen action in Italy. The blue-and-white insignia with the Star of David on his uniform made us proud.

✡ ✡ ✡

The news about the German camps, a trickle at first, would swell to a frightening flood. There were pictures in the newspapers. We would listen, in shock, to the evening broadcasts. Our co-tenants would join us. They felt safer in the company of others; each was missing a child, or a spouse. The ordeals of the recent past — hiding, running, hunger — did not come up in the spare conversations of our little group, only remarks and reminiscences about the missing loved ones. My parents kept mum. Then, camp survivors started showing up, like aliens from an unknowable place. They kept their unspeakable past to themselves. A thick silence separated us.

Once I heard my mother mumble the name of her sister, Surtshe. Neither one of my parents harbored any hope about their relatives in Poland. Both my mother's sisters perished, with their families. My father lost two brothers and two sisters, killed with their families; and his mother, a spry eighty-year old lady: she was taken in a convoy to Glogow where all were shot into a pit in the forest, he learned from a Kolbuszowa survivor. A local Pole was reported to have seen the earth the victims were buried under move for several days. Once, having mentioned his mother, my father added softly, looking down, "You know how she died." "Yes," I said, looking down.

A stone memorial stands on the site.

Menda showed up one day. And my mother's cousin Isaac; I had seen him last in 1941, in the Moriah *shul* in Antwerp, during the solemn *Nessaneh toikef* prayer on Rosh Hashanah, the day on which, according to the prayer, eveyone's fate is decreed from on high. He had been standing in the rear holding his two-year old girl on his arm. I had caught his eye, then, but could not sustain his hard stare.

Isaac had a similar look in his eyes when he came through the door, without knocking, in our apartment in Brussels. He stood with his hand on the door handle and looked for a few long and tense moments at my brother and me as if we were an anomaly. Yet he didn't seem surprised at our presence. He closed the door without averting his gaze. He sat down near the two of us. This time I could not turn away from his glare. His white face was like stone. The long, silent, and hard look in his dark eyes spoke of the loss of his children. He had survived, alone. He was bedridden at home, after a rushed appendectomy, "not transportable," and had watched the Flemish policemen take away his wife and two children. They had lived in the Jewish quarter. The police did not come back for him. He had recovered and had made it alone to Switzerland where he spent the remaining war years in an internment camp.

My mother was in the kitchen. She called out his name. He kept looking at me as if I wasn't supposed to be there. He looked at my brother. He looked at me again, then at my brother. It felt as if he would never take his eyes off us. Neither one of us moved. It was not the first time since the liberation that I felt uncomfortable existing, guilty, even. (When Menda walked in, later that spring, alone, expectant yet subdued, the embarrassment of having both my parents — worse: my entire family — had kept me riveted to the floor. I had looked down as we shook hands in silence.)

My mother called again: "Ee-zahk." Then, cupping her face with her hands, her voice falling: "Oy, EE-zahk... EE-zahk..." He moved to the kitchen and broke down sobbing. My mother wept silently. She closed the door.

✧ ✧ ✧

In May of 1945, Adrienne returned. She had spent a year in
the women's concentration camp of Ravensbrück, as a political
prisoner, doing forced labor in a munitions factory. She had also
overcome a bout of typhoid fever, and a death march before the
advancing Red Army. Her black hair had begun to grow back.

In the fall of that year Adrienne and her mother-in-law,
Léontine, were feted at official ceremonies with speeches, flowers and testimonials. She and Gaston had two children, Sylvain,
named after my brother, and Laurette, both grandparents today.

That summer — the Germans had surrendered on all fronts —
Brussels knew days that bordered on the delirious: Eisenhower,
Churchill and de Gaulle came on triumphal visits. Each time,
the crowds swarmed to the center where all traffic was stopped,
and thronged the avenues traveled by the victor's parade. It was
the first time that I felt genuine joy at being free. We had won.
Germany was crushed and in ruins.

In September, 1945, we moved back to Antwerp. Diamantaires
were returning, from London, New York, Rio de Janeiro. The
diamond business, both production and commerce, had taken
off. (As had happened after World War I, the rebirth of Antwerp
as the world's diamond center would significantly contribute to
Belgium's economic recovery.) The diamonds in my diamonds-
and-jewelry-bearing shoes had yielded needed cash and helped
my father get back on his feet when the diamond business resumed later that fall.

My brother returned to Tachkemoni. I went back to my high
school, the *Koninklijk Atheneum*. I was two years behind my former
classmates; they were in their last year. I would manage, eventually, to skip the last year by passing the qualifying entrance exams
to the engineering school of the University of Liège.

Uncle Avrum, my father's older brother, hid for two years in a
damp cellar. He emerged, physically broken; his faith intact. He
did not shave off his beard. He had lost his wife and both children: Shloimeh was turned in by the smuggler who was to take
him to Switzerland. He was twenty eight years old. Roochel, his

daughter, who had hired the smuggler, turned herself in, to share her brother's fate. She was nineteen. "Today Shloimeh would have turned thirty-two," Uncle Avrum mentioned one December day to my father in a barely audible voice. That was the only time he alluded to his loss. He died shortly thereafter. He was given the funeral of a *tsaddik* (a righteous), the kind Job must have gotten.

✳ ✳ ✳

Life rebounded. There was an influx of Jewish refugees from the Displaced Persons camps in Germany; of survivors from Eastern Europe; of Polish Jews who had returned from Siberia. The Jewish community was pulsating with energy. The focus was on the present and the future. Business was good. My father re-established himself as a broker. He resumed his functions as a board member of Tachkemoni. He kept up his commitment to the school for decades.

We followed with trepidation the developments in Palestine which culminated in the proclamation of the State of Israel. My father had become active in the Zionist movement. When a Jewish couple from Antwerp sought to travel to the new State, the Belgian authorities approached my father as a stand-in for an as yet inexistent Israeli diplomatic representative, to approve their travel applications — visas of sorts. It was a solemn moment: my father buttoned his jacket, covered his head with his yarmulke, recited the *she-hekheyanu* prayer, blessing the Lord "Who has restored us to life, sustained us, and brought us to the present time." He then sat down, and signed, with his gold-tipped fountain pen, one passport, then the other, while the would-be pilgrim — a friend of the family — stood at his side. (The couple's boy who they thought was lost to the Germans, had made it to Switzerland and Palestine. They returned without him, anguished: he had volunteered for the *Palmakh*, the shock troops of the Haganah, the Jewish underground army.)

✳ ✳ ✳

We never conversed about our hiding experience, as though it had been an illness.

Occasionally, a wartime memory would pop up. One Shabbat, as we were snacking on mother's delicious cake, she mentioned, with a delayed fright, the Sabbath cake she went to bake in our empty apartment at the height of the roundups — we were holed up in the Flemish butcher's house, across the street, "the recklessness, the foolishness of it."

Once, as she was serving her succulent *Braten* (roast), my mother told of a visit, when she was in her twenties, at her sister's home in Rzeszow, in Poland: "She served *Braten* and I didn't finish it." And breaking into a self-mocking laughter: "I berated myself, in the attic, 'Why didn't I eat Khahtshe's *Braten*? Why didn't I eat that *Braten*?' "

I would occasionally hop on a train to Duizend Appels, or to St-Niklaas to visit with the Van Poeckes. Chatting with my mother after one such visit, she reflected: "I would not have done for others what they did for us, total strangers." From the distant look in her eyes and her subdued tone of voice I knew that by "they" she meant all the Van Dammes, and the Van Poeckes.

Years only after the liberation did my mother tell me about the morning she woke up in the cold attic of Lucien and Palmyre's house in St-Niklaas, completely paralyzed, "From terror... the hopelessness... It took hours to unthaw... Nerves."

Exchanges about wartime experiences were sparse, even among friends. The glazed-over eyes and the hard-to-sustain, distant stare of camp survivors rendered our hiding ordeal trivial by comparison. "Flemish people hid us," was the answer to an occasional question. No other questions followed.

The nightmare I would have — a tall German in *Feldgrau* was closing in on me — stopped when, ten years after the war, I went to Israel, where I worked as an engineer.

Adrienne never talked about her year in Ravensbrück. We never mentioned my capture by the SS. During our get-togethers after the war, especially with my brother around, we reminisced only about happy times and incidents that had made us laugh. Shortly before her death in 1996, Adrienne recorded on audio cassette, at her daughter's insistence, a clip about her year in Germany; just twenty minutes. Gaston had died less than a year before.

✳ ✳ ✳

I did not open the *Book of Psalms* after the war. Reading it was incongruous with the new life, its dreams, its pace and exigencies.

It did not occur to me to mention the *tillimel* to my father even when he told me the story of his own treasured *tillimel*. It had belonged to my maternal grandfather. My father never knew him (both my parents had been toddlers when their fathers died). A pious Jew in Kolbuszowa, Moishe Kurtz, had the psalter. He lost it fleeing to Vienna before the advancing Russian army, during World War I, and found it miraculously three years later. When my parents got married, my father offered Moishe Kurtz the pick of any volume, any work at the bookstore in exchange for his father-in-law's *tillimel*. Moishe Kurtz turned down the offer, for a promise: that my father read from the *tillimel* every day. That psalter had been with my father ever since. I have today the thick little volume with the yellowed, worn pages where three different commentaries in tiny Rashi script and a translation in Aramaic crowd in, on each page, a few Hebrew verses. Scribbled in Hebrew lettering inside the cover are my grandfather's name, Zvi Yossef ben Yehudah, the year he passed away, 5662 (1902) and his *yahrzeit* date. Two Hebrew inscriptions in my father's handwriting on the title page read, one, "of my father-in-law Zvi Yossef z'l," and the other, "This Book of Psalms is the famous Book of Psalms that I received in the year 1928 from Reb Moishe Kurtz with the wondrous story of how he found it after the first World War after three years of wanderings."

The *Book of Psalms* is divided into seven daily portions. "I did not miss a day," my father told me. He knew the Psalms by heart. It did not occur to me to ask whether that fabled *tillimel* had been with him in hiding — I am sure it was: it must have been in my father's leather briefcase that Govaerts carried when they left Antwerp.

I took to reading the Psalms again after my father's death in 1988. It rekindled the memory of my psalms-driven inner journey.

My father died without knowing what the tiny Bezalel *tillimel* had meant to me. He never mentioned the *siddur* and the *tillimel* he had slipped into our overnight case before sending us off to Belsele the night of Rosh Hashanah in 1942. It occurred to me that he must have been worried, in hiding, about his sons getting estranged from Judaism. "Teach your brother," he had instructed me.

I never told my father that I had fasted on the second Yom Kippur in hiding. I was reminded of my fast in 2000, during a visit in Ghent with my son, to celebrate Alice's eightieth birthday. We reminisced about the good old times in Drongen, the pre-fast meal, among other things.

"Do you remember the beefsteak you asked for?" she asked.

"Yes. It was succulent."

We smiled. Of pleasures remembered.

I never told Gaston how much Van Loy's "Automobile Course" had lifted my spirits. It did not occur to me. It was too steeped in the ordeal of hiding.

✡ ✡ ✡

In 1958 I settled in the States. I married a Jewish American woman who was estranged from Judaism. Still, we had no pork or seafood in the house, nor did we mix meat and dairy. She adopted the seder (which each of us celebrated on separate nights, with the children, after we got divorced), Purim, and American-style, gift-intensive Hanukkah. My children learned Hebrew, my daughter for her bat mitzvah and my two sons for their bar mitzvahs.

Aside of copious note-taking and some scribbling about the war period, I wrote, in the 60's, just one wartime episode: the twenty hours starting with my capture by the SS and ending, the following morning, with our little band of *left alone* children traipsing to the Berchem train station — an overwrought narration that, toned down and revised, became, more than thirty years later, chapter ten of this memoir. I took up writing in earnest after my retirement in 1993.

✡ ✡ ✡

Almost fifty years after perusing the few *letters* in the Haeusser Method for the self-study of English, I opened, for the first time, the folder containing the entire opus: close to thirty *letters*. It was among my father's books that I had brought to New York, after his death. I noticed on one of the folder's flaps an inscription in my father's neat handwriting: "of two evils we must choose the less" (sic). I looked at it with the excitement of discovery: a glimpse into my father's life of the mind during hiding. It felt like I was hearing from him again. What had prompted him to write that? What was hiding like for him? We had never talked about our hushed-up lives. As if they had never been.

My father never picked up an English book or course again. He reverted to his old loves: the Bible; and Hebrew, Yiddish and German works. He sampled world literature in German or Hebrew translation. But he had mastered basic English using the Haeusser Method. In hiding. And he was able to communicate with my children. With his knack for languages and his deft use of the dictionary he could read their letters and write them little notes before they knew French. He even addressed my oldest son in English, at his bar-mitzvah; a memorable, carefully enunciated speech.

The brief exposure to English in hiding stood me in good stead: I went straight to reading English books, slowly at first, ever mindful of the proper diction, using the dictionary for pronunciation and emphasis as much as for meaning. My English, both spoken and written, was fluent and correct when I came to the States in 1958.

Leafing through the stack of Haeusser *letters*, I saw that the English texts, the translation assignments and the question-and-answer sessions became more substantive and stimulating as the course progressed. And I regretted my lack of perseverance, my failure to ask for more, for all the *letters*: what a boon it would have been to emerge from hiding in possession of another language, English, no less; what a sustaining endeavor throughout those interminable days. It would have changed my perception of time, the texture of those days. Hiding, I thought wistfully, might have been different. It became a recurring impulse, the desire to reshape the past, make my hiding days count — it did not leave me until this writing. In my latter-day fantasies I would be working on a farm, or plying a trade; I would lead an adventurous, or romantic, life; exact revenge; and, more often, reverse, through a retroactive infusion of daring and resolve, the humiliating outcome of the episode that brought hiding to an end.

Passing, fifty years later, through a town or village in Flanders or in Wallonia, I could look at a house and lapse into wondering what hiding would have been like behind those curtained windows. Would it have changed my life? Had a young, attractive

girl my age lived there? Or a mature, receptive woman? I would
scrutinize strangers on the street, trying to discern who among
them would have extended a helping hand. A disquieting question when turned on myself.

✻ ✻ ✻

Years went by. My brother became a diamantaire, just as
Adrienne had predicted. He was elected president of the Diamond
Club (one of the three diamond exchanges in Antwerp), the
youngest in its history. He reverted to his birth name, Salomon,
but remained Sylvain to the Van Poeckes, and to the Van Dammes
and their children. He has two daughters and four grandchildren; they live in Israel.

My children got to know Adrienne, Gaston and Alice at an
early age, each time we traveled to Belgium, to visit with my
parents and with my brother and his young family. We went to
Duizend Appels where they met, in a warm and welcoming atmosphere, the friendly people who had taken my brother and
me into their home during the war. It was clear to them that my
brother and I had been taken care of and protected. They are in
their forties today. One of my sons, the youngest, has an eight-
year old boy; they live in Paris. My daughter and oldest son live
in the States.

✻ ✻ ✻

For decades I had relegated the German nation to the mar-
gins of the human map. I did not set foot on German soil. I
would not consider buying a German car. Accounts of the fire-
bombing of their cities in World War II, of their suffering at the
hands of the avenging Russians, of parents killing their children,
then committing suicide, before the imminent arrival of the advancing Russians, still evoke the old vengefulness: "Not enough!
They deserved it, then. Not enough."

Adrienne had a bigger heart: when, in the late 60's, her son
got a job offer from a large German company that had used
slave labor during the war, she told him that the German people
should not be identified with criminals of the past.

In 2006 Germany hosted the World Cup. I watched some of
the events on television, and I would stare, almost incredulous, at

the delirious, mostly young, German fans in the stadiums and the night revelers in the streets and public places: they were shouting and jumping; they were waving toy flags and laughing and raising mugs of beer at the camera; they looked so refreshingly... American with their national colors stitched to their hats and caps, painted on their foreheads, on their cheeks. "Germans," I kept muttering mentally. How unlike the martial "*Sieg Heil*-ing," masses of my past! The images clinched what had been a gradual change in my perception of them. Feelings aroused by the past can no longer be transposed to the present. Today's generation cannot be saddled with the guilt for their elders' and great-elders' crimes.

I can face the Germans of today without rancor, without an accusing heart.

✿ ✿ ✿

My brother and I, Sylvain and Laurette (Gaston and Adrienne's children), all of us grandparents, are today's elder generation. Laurette and her family live in the Flemish region of Belgium. We keep in touch; we visit. Her brother Sylvain, a businessman, divides his time between Germany, India, and Portugal.

Dr. Menachem (Menda) Zangen, who retired from a long career as a scientist, is the father of four and the grandfather of sixteen. They all live in Israel.

Marcel and Johnny had lost their parents. An American aunt took them to the States. The elder Van Dammes got only one letter from New York with news about the boys. They never heard of them again, to their great sorrow. I tried to trace them; to no avail.

René Govaerts became principal of Tachkemoni. He died young.

The Van Damme family — the parents Emile and Léontine, Gaston and Adrienne, Alice and Laura — as well as Joseph and Josephine Van Poecke were honored by the Yad Vashem Memorial Institute in Jerusalem as Righteous Among The Nations.

9 781439 254660